A Crusader's Death and Life in Acre

A volume in the series

Medieval Societies, Religions, and Cultures

Edited by M. Cecilia Gaposchkin and Anne E. Lester

A list of titles in this series is available at cornellpress.cornell.edu.

A Crusader's Death and Life in Acre

The 1266 Account-Inventory of Eudes of Nevers

Anne E. Lester and Laura K. Morreale

Cornell University Press
Ithaca and London

First published 2025 by Cornell University Press

Printed in the United States of America

Library of Congress Cataloging-in-Publication Data
Names: Lester, Anne E., 1974– author. | Morreale, Laura K., author.
Title: A crusader's death and life in Acre : the 1266 account-inventory of Eudes of Nevers / Anne E. Lester and Laura K. Morreale.
Other titles: 1266 account-inventory of Eudes of Nevers
Description: Ithaca : Cornell University Press, 2025. | Series: Medieval societies, religions, and cultures | Includes bibliographical references and index.
Identifiers: LCCN 2024029631 (print) | LCCN 2024029632 (ebook) | ISBN 9781501779855 (paperback) | ISBN 9781501779862 (pdf) | ISBN 9781501779879 (epub)
Subjects: LCSH: Eudes, of Nevers, 1230–1266. | Civilization, Medieval. | Crusades—13th–15th centuries.
Classification: LCC CB355 .L47 2025 (print) | LCC CB355 (ebook) | DDC 909.07—dc23/eng/20241031
LC record available at https://lccn.loc.gov/2024029631
LC ebook record available at https://lccn.loc.gov/2024029632

Contents

List of Illustrations ix
Preface xiii
Acknowledgments xvii
Abbreviations xxi
Note on Names, Places, and Currencies xxiii
On the Text Editions xxvii

Part I. The Account-Inventory of Eudes of Nevers

1. Introduction 3
Material Outremer: Methods and Approaches 9
The Texts: Form and Function 13
The Chronology of the Rouleaux 16

2. Account-Inventory: Edition and Translation Rolls A–D 23
Statement on Transcription and Translation 23
Text Edition Account-Inventory of Eudes of Nevers 25

Part II. Commentary

3. Crusading in the Mid-Thirteenth Century 57
4. French Acre: The Language and Landscapes of the Rouleaux 63
5. Outremer Subjects: A Crusader's Retinue 74

6. Outremer Objects: A Documentary Archaeology of Crusader Possessions 91
7. The Threaded Heart: Converted Objects and Return Journeys 106

Part III. Contemporary Sources

8. Crusade Poems of Rutebeuf 113
Rutebeuf, Crusade Poet and Social Critic 113
Anne Latowsky
Poems 119
Translated by Anne Latowsky, Anne E. Lester, Laura K. Morreale, and Caroline Smith
The Lament for My Lord Geoffrey of Sergines *(La complainte de monseigneur Joffroi de Sergines)* 122
The Complaint of Constantinople *(La complainte de Coustantinoble)* 128
The Complaint of Outremer *(La complainte doutremeir)* 135
The Lament for Count Eudes of Nevers *(La complainte dou conte Hue de Nevers)* 141
The Poem of the Route to Tunis *(Li diz de la voie de Tunes)* 147
The Disputation between the Crusader and the Noncrusader *(La desputizons dou croisie et dou descroizie)* 156
The New Complaint of Outremer *(La nouvele complainte doutremeir)* 164

9. Two Wills from Acre, 1267–1272 175
The Will of Sir Hugh de Neville (1267) 177
Edited and translated by Caroline Smith

The Will of Prince Edward I of England (1272) 184
Edited and translated by Laura K. Morreale and Anne Latowsky

Part IV. Interpretations

10. The Landscapes of Acre 191
Andrew Jotischky

11. The Experience of Acre, ca. 1266 198
Jonathan Rubin

12. Textiles in Eudes of Nevers's Posthumous Inventory: A Meeting of East and West 206
Sharon Farmer

13. Of Gems and Drinking Cups 215
Richard A. Leson

14. The Material Culture of Devotion and Vestiture: Eudes of Nevers at Prayer 223
Maureen C. Miller

15. The Crusading Households of John of Joinville and Eudes of Nevers 229
Caroline Smith

16. Shared Things: Inventories of the Islamic World 237
Uri Zvi Shachar

Appendix: Genealogy of Eudes of Nevers 245
Glossary 247
Bibliography 253
Index 275

Illustrations

Maps

1. The crusading Mediterranean 4
2. Religious institutions in Acre listed in Eudes's inventory, after Pringle. L. Morreale 65

Figures

1. Paris, AN, series J 821, no. 1, Rolls A–D in order of size.
2. Detail, Paris, AN, series J 821, no. 1 Roll C (verso/dorsal).
3. Paris, AN, series J 821, no. 1, Rolls A–D as stored together.
4. Paris, AN, series J 821, no. 1, Roll A, held in the hand for scale.
5. Paris, AN, series J 821, no. 1, Roll A, held in the hand.
6. Paris, AN, series J 821, no. 1, Roll A with stitching visible.
7. Paris, AN, series J 821, no. 1, Roll B (recto) unrolled showing full text.

8.1 and 8.2. France, *gros tournois*, silver coin equivalent to roughly 12 *deniers tournois*, or 1 *sous tournois*, reign of Louis IX, (1226–1270), issued after 1265. Linked visually with the coinage of the East. See below, 11, which also shows concentric circles of text. Princeton University Numismatic Collection, France 321, Laf. 198c. Obverse and reverse.

9.1 and 9.2. Coin, France, *denier tournois*, silver penny of Tours, later reign of Louis IX, 1266–70. Princeton University Numismatic Collection, France 846, Laf. 201. Obverse and reverse.

10.1 and 10.2. Jerusalem, silver *denier* of Damietta, John of Brienne, 1210–25. Princeton University Numismatic Collection MPS.43.748.5. Obverse and reverse.

11.1 and 11.2. Alexandria, gold *dinar*. Princeton University Numismatic Collection, Fl Fatimid 9195, al-Mustansi 1085, ACFC 1685. Obverse and reverse.

12.1 and 12.2. Crusader Acre, Kingdom of Jerusalem, imitation gold *dinar*, ca. 1148/59–1187. An imitation of Egyptian dinars in the name of Caliph Al-Amir. Princeton University Numismatic Collection. Obverse and reverse.

13.1 and 13.2. Seals of Eudes of Nevers (Eudes de Bourgogne), Paris, AN, J 256, no. 56 (1255), and Dijon, AD CdO Ad 21. B 304—ps 428 (1265).

14. Seal of Érard of Vallery, Paris, AN, J 208, no. 13 (1276).

15. Illumination of King Arthur and his retinue. Robert de Boron, *Romans arthuriens*, France (possibly St.-Omer or region of Thérouanne), ca. 1270–90. Paris, BnF, MS fr. 95, fol. 345v.

16. From Genesis 42–48, showing Joseph's reception of his brothers with a feast and baggage train on the move. New York, Pierpont Morgan Library, MS M.638, fol. 6v. Old Testament miniatures, Paris, France, ca. 1244–54. The Morgan Library & Museum. Purchased by J. P. Morgan (1867–1943) in 1916.

17. Ring with small sapphire, England, 14th century. Gilded silver, sapphire; diameter: 2.9 cm (1 1/8 in.). The Cleveland Museum of Art, Purchase from the J. H. Wade Fund 1950.383.

18. Ring Brooch, German, ca. 1340–49, Middle Rhineland, Germany. Gold, spinels, and sapphires and rubies (2.2 x 0.5 cm). New York, Metropolitan Museum of Art, The Cloisters Collection, 2006.257.

19.1, 19.2, and 19.3. Silk Robe made of "Tartar cloth of gold," 13th century, Central Asia. Silk, woven; 142 cm. Aga Khan Museum, Toronto, ON, Canada. AKM816.

20. Cloth of gold with winged lions and griffins, ca. 1225–75, Central Asia. Silk and gold thread: lampas; 124 x 48.8 cm. The Cleveland Museum of Art, Purchase from the J. H. Wade Fund 1989.50.

21. Illumination of Saint Martin. From *Images de la vie du Christ et des saints*. France, ca. 1250–1300. Paris, BnF, MS NAF 16251, fol. 89r.

22. A hunter and a beaver, from a bestiary. Unknown illuminator, possibly made in Thérouanne, northern France, ca. 1270. Tempera colors, gold leaf, ink on parchment; 7 ½ x 5 5/8 in. Los Angeles, J. Paul Getty Museum, MS Lugwig XV 3 83.MR.173, fol. 83r.

23. Coral Tree with serpent's tongues hanging. Germany before 1562. Gold, silver-gilt, coral, fossilized shark teeth. Vienna, Treasury and Museum of the Teutonic Order, inv. no. K-037.

24. Illumination of Abraham and Melchisedek (Genesis 14:18–20). From *Psautier dit de Saint Louis*, France, ca. 1270–74. Paris, BnF, MS lat. 10525, fol. 106r.

25. Coffret of the Blessed John of Montmirail or the Longpont Coffret, Limoges, ca. 1270 (or 1242?). Copper, engraved, stippled, and gilt champlevé enamel; 15 x 78.7 x 17.5 cm. Treasury of the Abbey of Longpont (Aisne), France.

26. Illumination of knights setting up tents outside of Camelot. Robert de Boron, *Romans arthuriens*, France (possibly St.-Omer or region of Thérouanne), ca. 1270–90. Paris, BnF, MS fr. 95, fol. 324v.

27.1 and 27.2. Silver-gilt drinking cup, possibly northern France, near Amiens/Coucy, ca. 1190–1219, profile and interior. Syria National Museum, Damascus (Inv. Nr. 29313/14).

28. Reliquary Cross, ca. 1180, Limoges France, possibly from the Abbey of Grandmont. Silver gilt, rock crystal, glass cabochons, wood core. New York, Metropolitan Museum of Art, The Cloisters Collection, 2002.18.

29. Pyx, ca. 1250. France, Limousin, Limoges. Gilded copper, champlevé enamel. The Cleveland Museum of Art, Purchase from the J. H. Wade Fund 1952.328.

30. Illumination bottom margin, *Mon Seigneur Jehan de Lens* playing chess with his friend. *Psalter*, Amiens, France, ca. 1280–90. Paris, BnF, MS lat. 10435, fol. 61r.

31. Rutebeuf, "La complainte dou conte Hue de Nevers," Paris, BnF, MS fr. 1635, fol. 42r. France, possibly Champagne or Burgundy, ca. 1201–1300.

32. Illumination of the Siege of Acre from Rutebeuf, "Li complainte daccre" ("La nouvele complainte doutremeir"). Brussels, KBR, MS 9411–9426, fol. 34r.

Preface

The Account-Inventory that sits at the heart of this study is a source that was put together over time and represents the work of many different individuals who listened, accounted, compiled, copied, and assembled information. In a similar fashion, this book is, and has been from the start, a work of collaborative scholarship. Collaboration guides its methodology and structures its contents. Our goal is to make accessible and legible an outstandingly complex and detailed Account and Inventory that has long been overlooked. In part this is because some scholars deem such texts to be rather dull. They offer at first glance only lists of things, one item following another, with monetary values assigned. There is no narrative momentum; no story. But as this book shows, this is not at all what we have found. Rather, it is very clear that there are many narratives and histories contained within and behind Eudes of Nevers's Account-Inventory. Moreover, the extraordinary convergences that link the archival rolls to the poems of Rutebeuf, Eudes's contemporary, and in turn to the wills and other extant sources produced in Outremer, allow us, and any reader, to breathe new life into this list of things. It is through working with others—our own contemporary colleagues and collaborators—and across the genres of writing, and in thinking with those who knew Eudes of Nevers and who wrote about him, that a history of his things and of the material Outremer takes shape. One of our goals is to model what such a material history and methodology looks like in practice.

This book was begun in the midst of the COVID pandemic lockdown, in the spring of 2020, when universities, schools, libraries, and offices were closed, and when no one could go to an archive and look at original documents. It was under those conditions—with an eye to creating a text for teaching medieval objects and materiality—and as an outgrowth of our work on the DALME Project, that this book first took shape. With access to the high-quality images of the Account-Inventory rolls we (Lester and Morreale) undertook a new edition of the text and the first English translation. As we worked, we soon realized that to weave a history from the detailed texts we were deciphering we would do well to ask colleagues and experts in a series of subfields and specializations to read and comment on the texts. Once we had a working draft of our source, in the spring of 2021, we convened an online symposium, and the speakers at that virtual gathering contributed the rich and insightful short essays that make up the final section of this book, essays that present, each with their own voice and emphasis, a facet of Eudes's world.

The experience of living and dying in Outremer sits at the heart of the Account-Inventory. But Eudes died, as far as we know, without a formal testament. Nevertheless, the final moments of Eudes's life, as he may have moved to dictate his intentions for the dispersal of his things, are paralleled in two still-extant wills also drawn up in Acre in the 1260s and 1270s: those of Hugh de Neville (dated to 1267) and Prince Edward, future king of England (1272). These are included in this book—in new editions and translations—to give further context to the composition of the Account-Inventory and to set it in conversation with the intentions of contemporaries facing the prospect of dying in Outremer. Imagining the streets and spaces through which Eudes once moved and his material world in Acre—the ways he dressed, what he ate, how he traveled, and how he prayed and formed close bonds with those around him—comes into sharper focus still through the poetic corpus of Rutebeuf. Indeed, the third collaborative venture that sits at the center of this book is the translation into English, for the first time, of seven crusade poems or "Complaintes" by Eudes's contemporary, the mid-thirteenth-century vernacular poet simply known as Rutebeuf (fl. ca. 1250–85). He wrote a series of crusade poems in Old French that illuminate the political, cultural, and religious world around Eudes. Rutebeuf's poems reveal a mental outlook of great devotion and practicality, both of which had come to characterize the crusade movement in the second half of the thirteenth century. The poems we have gathered and translated here resonate with and enrich our understanding of Eudes and of the world of Outremer. Rutebeuf evokes the complexity of this moment through metaphors, allusions, elaborate and evocative wordplay, and by intertwining biting satire and spiritual critique. Together, the poems exemplify the rhetorical and vernacular literate culture that was a key part of Eudes's cultural orientation and experience in Outremer.

Finally, the volume closes with seven short essays authored by different scholars each focused on a particular set of objects, places, and experiences that emerge from Eudes's Account-Inventory. These short essays—intellectual deep-dives as we think of them—enrich our interpretations and model the exchanges that propel research and scholarship. We hope that students and readers will turn to the essays to see how the practice of medieval history unfolds as an ongoing interdisciplinary intellectual conversation.

We hope that this book will offer a model for a new sort of book, one that is professedly collaborative and benefits from being digitally born (during the pandemic, from digital scholarship) and understood from the beginning to be used in part as a digital tool accessible through online library catalogues, especially for teaching. In this way, we envision that this book could be taken in as a whole, which asks the reader to take part in the interplay between primary text and historical reconstruction and interpretation, or it could be assigned and read in its separate parts. For example, the Account-Inventory or the poems of Rutebeuf could be extracted and read on their own, by or with students in the English translation, or coupled with a few essays. Likewise, the longer commentary in part II could stand on its own in a teaching or research context. The volume is intended to invite further collaboration with and for the reader, and to build on the conversation begun here.

Acknowledgments

It is always a pleasure to recognize those who help build a scholarly project and bring it to fruition. This volume, from the start, was begun in collaboration, first between Anne Lester and Laura Morreale, when we began preparing the Account-Inventory for inclusion in the online digital humanities project on the Documentary Archaeology of Late Medieval Europe (DALME). The book then expanded to encompass a wider translation circle, with Anne E. Lester, Laura K. Morreale, Caroline Smith, and Anne Latowsky, as we turned to include the poems of Rutebeuf. This elaborate collaboration started in the darker and lonelier days of the pandemic when we sought consolation and a shared intellectual space with colleagues and friends. Dedicated weekly and biweekly meetings to transcribe, edit, and translate became the core of the collaboration and brought all of us great inspiration, escape from the doldrums of everyday life at home, and renewed intellectual vigor—a spark kindled by coming together to do the work medievalists do with manuscript and archival source material. In those difficult times, our work together was and remains a source of joy, filled with rabbit holes and research tangents that led us across our academic disciplines and that greatly enriched the whole.

In March 2021, Lester and Morreale convened an online symposium dedicated to reading and understanding Eudes of Nevers's Account-Inventory. We thank the History Department, the Alexander Grass Humanities Institute, and the Medieval World Seminar at Johns Hopkins University for sponsoring that event, which was attended by over 150 participants. We thank Sharon Farmer, Andrew Jotischky, Richard Leson, Maureen Miller, Jonathan Rubin, and Caroline Smith for taking part in that event and for contributing short essays to this volume, and Uri Shachar for adding his contribution thereafter. We thank Daniel Lord Smail for moderating the event and are grateful to the audience in attendance, many of whom offered extremely useful questions and feedback in the chat and in email correspondence afterward. We wish to thank in particular Jaroslav Folda and Elizabeth A. R. Brown for their insights about the creation, copying, and survival of the rolls.

The staff of the Archives nationales, especially Jean-François Moufflet and Dimitri Douillot, were extremely helpful in securing high-quality digital photos of the rolls during the COVID lockdown, and in allowing us to see and photograph the rolls in the archives in Paris the following March 2022. And we are grateful for permission to reproduce images of the rolls here and online. We would also like to acknowledge the National Endowment for the Humanities, which supported Lester with a Faculty Fellowship during the 2020–21 year that facilitated time away from teaching and supported the research and writing of this book.

Many other colleagues have helped along the way. We thank in particular William Chester Jordan, Nicholas Paul, Daniel Lord Smail, and Tamer el-Leithy, who kindly fielded questions over email and in conversation that clarified specific points and difficult issues that dogged us as we worked. Winston Black taught us about the exact uses of certain medicinal remedies, Mark Cruse shared his knowledge of foreign relations between French forces and those they encountered in the east, and Stephanie J. Lahey and Lisa Fagin Davis helped us decipher difficult paleographical questions. Jochen Burgtorf served as a crucial reference for personnel from the military orders and expertly smoothed the way for otherwise hard-to-obtain images and rights acquisitions. Barbara Boehm and Élisabeth Delahaye answered pointed questions about enamels and metalwork at just the right moment, and we thank Richard Leson for facilitating that. Randall Pippenger, Mark Gregory Pegg, Hussein Fancy, and Theodore Evergates graciously answered queries about specific crusaders mentioned here, and we are grateful for their expertise. We also thank S. C. Kaplan, who was on the spot for a last minute reference. Alan Stahl, likewise, took time to meet for a lovely lunch and to educate us on the specifics of the multiple currency forms mentioned in the text. He also allowed us to photograph examples of these coins from the Princeton University Numismatic Collection, which are reproduced in this volume, and for which we are extremely grateful. That experience further reinforced the importance of holding the material in hand to understand concepts like weight, dimensions, and wear over time, which are rarely well captured or described in print. Along the way we have presented parts of this book and the Account-Inventory to many different audiences, and we are grateful for their comments, questions, and enthusiasm. Finally, Xavier Hélary made this book better in countless ways both precise and general. His comments came at the perfect moment, saved us from errors, and made the commentary immeasurably richer. Likewise, William Chester Jordan read the manuscript and offered characteristic and invaluable feedback, making the book and especially the commentary section much stronger. Thank you. Needless to say, any errors that persist are ours alone.

Finally, we are extremely grateful to the three outside readers for the press, both for their vision in imaging with us what such a collaborative volume could be and for their extremely valuable comments, questions, and insights that have made the editions and commentaries far better. Cecilia Gaposchkin had faith in this book and was a consummate advocate of the project. Both Cecilia Gaposchkin and Maureen Miller pioneered the use of the text with their students, and we are grateful for their feedback. Likewise, Mahinder Kingra has been, as always, wonderful to work with in every way. We also thank Karen Hwa for overseeing production of the book and Enid Zafran for preparing the index.

Our families have lived with our interest in Eudes over these years. Eudes has become a household name, and his many and varied things—silk overcoats, linen underwear, personal chapel, beaver testicles, and chessboard, to list a few—have been a touchstone of conversation and the center of not a few inside jokes. We are grateful to Scott, Mirabelle, and Vivienne Bruce for helping us remember what is really compelling about life and its fine and wonderful details; and to Pete and Leo Morreale for tolerating the many hours we spent pouring over an errant *point* or mysterious minim. And we are thankful for friendship, which is at the heart of so much of this work, both now and during Eudes's own time. All we can say is *l'amour, toujours, l'amour*.

Abbreviations

AD	Archives départementales
AN	Archives nationales (Paris)
Bastin and Faral, *Onze poèmes*	*Onze poèmes de Rutebeuf concernant la croisade*, ed. Julia Bastin and Edmond Faral (Paris: Libraire Orientaliste Paul Geuthner, 1946).
Bastin and Faral, *Oeuvres complètes*	*Oeuvres complètes de Rutebeuf*, ed. Julia Bastin and Edmond Faral, 4th ed., vol. 1 (Paris: Picard, 1977).
BnF	Bibliothèque nationale de France (Paris)
Chazaud, "Inventaire"	A.-M. Chazaud, "Inventaire et comptes de la succession d'Eudes, comte de Nevers (Acre 1266)," *Mémoires de la Société nationale des Antiquaires de France*, 4th series, 2 (1871): 164–206.
DALME	Documentary Archaeology of Late Medieval Europe, https://dalme.org
DMF	*Dictionnaire du Moyen Français*, http://zeus.atilf.fr/dmf/
Joinville, *VSL*	Jean de Joinville, *Vie de Saint Louis*, ed. J. Monfrin (Paris: Garnier, 1995).
KBR	Royal Library of Belgium (Brussels)
Lespinasse, *Le Nivernais*	René de Lespinasse, *Le Nivernais et les comtes de Nevers*, 3 vols. (Paris: Honoré Champion, 1911).
RHC	*Recueil des historiens des croisades: Historiens occidentaux* (Paris: Imprimerie nationale, 1841–1906).
RHGF	*Recueil des historiens des Gaules et de la France* (Paris: Académie des inscriptions et belles-lettres, 1738–1904).
TdT	*Cronaca del Templare di Tiro (1243–1314): La caduta degli Stati Croniati nel racconto di un testimone oculare*, ed. and trans. Laura Minervini (Naples: Liguroi, 2000).
Zink, *Rutebeuf*	*Rutebeuf: Oeuvres complètes*, ed. and trans. Michel Zink (Paris: Classiques Garnier, 2001).

Note on Names, Places, and Currencies

The many types of sources collected, edited, and translated in this volume employ a wide variety of naming styles in multiple different vernacular languages as was common in the linguistically diverse world of the medieval Mediterranean. In the case of well-known individuals, such as Louis IX, Thibaut V, count of Champagne and king of Navarre, as well as Eudes of Nevers and John of Joinville, we use an English version of their names. For knights of middling rank, without baronial titles, men like Geoffrey of Sergines and Érard of Vallery, we have retained the French forms of their first names. Likewise, for lesser-known individuals with names that derive from toponyms or occupations we have retained the original (typically French) spelling of their names as is the case with Étienne de Sissy, Gaucher de Merry, Étienne le Clerc, Guillaume le Chapelain, and Rutebeuf, the French poet whose name has no equivalent in English.

Similarly, the people and things described in Eudes's Account-Inventory reflect the wide geographical span of the crusade movement, which connected crusaders like Eudes of Nevers and those from France, England, and Flanders to objects, merchants, mercenaries, and aristocrats from the Islamic world—stretching from Baghdad to Cairo to Granada. The diverse array of objects listed in our texts use a similarly wide range of place-names that reference production, manufacture, and sale. In many cases these were well-known locales with modern names such as Troyes, Burgundy, Liège, Damascus, Acre, and Constantinople. In other instances, when specific names of local regions or towns are mentioned, we have chosen to leave those in their vernacular or original language and to italicize those place-names. Wherever possible, in our translations, we have endeavored to use place-names that are familiar to an English-speaking audience. In most cases the original French and Latin names have been retained in the text editions, although we have capitalized places and proper names that would not have been capitalized in the original manuscript as such practices were not standardized in the thirteenth century.

The business of living and dying in Outremer was conducted in multiple different currencies simultaneously. Eudes's account reflects this clearly. Those living with Eudes in Acre could move with seeming ease among the currencies of France, England, Germany, the Kingdom of Jerusalem, and the Muslim world. Not surprisingly the most common currency referenced and used in Eudes's circle was the French *tournois*, that is, the coin of account produced in Tours. One French *livre tournois* (*l. t.*) was equivalent to 20 *sous tournois* (*s. t.*); and one *sous* equaled 12 *deniers tournois* (*d. t.*) (see figures 9–10). The English pound, however, was of slightly better quality and thus slightly higher value than the French pound and was known as the mark, for it set the standard for good currency. When large sums were sent across international credit networks, aristocrats often used marks of silver rather than French pounds. One English mark (*m.*), for example, was equivalent to two-thirds of a pound, or 13 *s.* and 4 *d.*, or 160 pennies. Versions of the mark and its equivalent were used in the southern Low Countries and in parts of northern Germany and, as is the case here, in Burgundy as well. The Account-Inventory also references the currency denomination *de reaus*, or "of the realm." In the context of Acre, this is most likely the gold coin, or imitation gold dinar, that was the common crusader currency of the Kingdom of Jerusalem, or the silver *dinar* similarly minted in the crusader territories of Outremer (see figure 10). Jerusalem dinar (both silver and gold) had been minted over the course of the twelfth century, from the founding of the crusader kingdom in 1101 until the fall of Jerusalem to Saladin in 1187. Although no new Latin currency, with minor exceptions, was minted after 1187, the Jerusalem dinar continued to circulate as the coinage "of the realm" (see figure 11). It followed the similar valuation in which one pound, *libra* = 20 *solidi*; 1 *solidus* = 12 *denarii*. References to Italian coinages are surprisingly absent from Eudes's Account. All of these coins were silver coins. Although the denominations of coins included pounds, *sous*, and *deniers*, until the late 1250s only the *deniers* or penny coin was ever minted in England, France, and the Holy Land. Thus, even if records of account list payments in pounds, when payment was rendered, it would have been in deniers, or penny coins, with 1 pound = 240 *deniers*. When payment of, for example, 12 pounds, 8 shillings was rendered in coins, it would have amounted—materially—to 2,976 silver pennies in coin. That would be several bags or chests of coins. When 500 marks were sent in aid to the Holy Land, that was the equivalent of 120,000 pennies, or *deniers* silver coins, possibly more given the strength of the English mark. Transport of such sums required significant logistics or sophisticated credit mechanisms, like those established by the Templars and the Italian banking families.

By far the currency with the greatest international reach mentioned in the sources was the bezant coin, which was a heavier and more valuable gold coin. The bezant or *besant* was equivalent to the Islamic *dinar* but took the name *bezant* from the Byzantine gold coin issued on the same model. By the thirteenth century, one *bezant* was equivalent to 24 *quarrobles*, which was equal to roughly 6 *solidi* and 8 *denarii tournois*. Bezants were minted under the Fatimids, then (after 1258) under the Mamluks in Egypt, and in various mints along the Levant Coast (figure 11). The Latin rulers of the Kingdom of Jerusalem also issued an imitation gold *bezant*, which was made from an equivalent quantity of gold and had inscriptions in Arabic running in concentric circles around the coin (figure 12). While the qualities of the Latin mints were, in most cases, not as good as those of the Islamic state, the two currencies were used interchangeably. The king of France, Louis IX, briefly minted a Christian gold coin with Latin inscriptions in Acre and again in France, after his return in 1254. Neither were successful or used extensively, and they appear to have been more of an ideological statement about Christian sovereignty than a true attempt at reforming the coinage of either realm.[1]

1. For values of coins and equivalences, see Peter Spufford, *Handbook of Medieval Exchange* (London: Royal Historical Society/Boydell and Brewer, 1986), for the *bezant* of Acre, 297–98. See also the equivalences gathered in the Medieval and Early Modern Data Bank hosted through Rutgers University Libraries: https://memdb.libraries.rutgers.edu/spufford-currency. For the values in Eudes's Account-Inventory, see Chazaud, "Inventaire," 173–75. For crusader coinage and circulation more specifically during the later thirteenth century, see David Michael Metcalf, "Burgundian Money in the Latin East," *Israel Numismatic Journal* 5 (1981): 73–82; and Metcalf, *Coinage of the Crusades and the Latin East in the Ashmolean Museum, Oxford*, 2nd ed. (London: Royal Numismatics Society and Society for the Study of the Crusades and the Latin East, 1995); and David Michael Metcalf, Robert Kool, and Ariel Berman, "Coins from the Excavations of 'Atlit' (Pilgrims' Castle and Its Faubourg)," *'Atiqot* 37 (1999): 89–164. On the use of gold *bezants* as a money of account in the West, see B. J. Cook, "The Bezant in Angevin England," *Numismatic Chronicle* 159 (1999): 255–75; also Yorio Otaka, "La valeur monétaire exprimée dans les oeuvres épiques," in *L'épopée romane: Actes du XVe Congrès international Rencesvals tenu à Poitiers du 21 au 27 août 2000*, 2 vols. (Poitiers: Centre d'études supérieures de civilization médiévale, 2002), 969–78. More work is needed to understand how the multiplicity of coinage influenced the circulation of materials and cultural perceptions. On Louis IX's use of gold coins, see William Chester Jordan, *Louis IX and the Challenge of the Crusade* (Princeton, NJ: Princeton University Press, 1979), 206–13; and Jordan, "*Etiam Reges*, Even Kings," *Speculum* 99 (2015): 619–21.

On the Text Editions

We present two longer text editions in this volume. Both are single text editions, in other words, they are editions created from one manuscript. In the case of the Account-Inventory, the edition and translation below are based on the one surviving text made of five rolls of parchment now in the Archives nationales de France (Paris, AN, series J 821, no. 1, Rolls A–D). In the case of the seven poems attributed to the poet Rutebeuf, we have generated our edition and translation using one manuscript in the Bibliothèque nationale de France (Paris, BnF, MS fr. 1635). Michel Zink's edition and modern French translation of the complete works of Rutebeuf follows that of Bastin and Faral's edition and was generated from twenty known manuscripts that contained Rutebeuf's poems.[2] It should be noted that there is no single "complete" medieval manuscript containing all of the poems attributed to Rutebeuf, and that both Zink's and Bastin and Faral's "complete editions" are in effect modern gatherings of the poet's works. In 1946, Bastin and Faral produced a shorter collection of Rutebeuf's eleven crusade poems. For that edition they drew from four extant manuscripts.[3] For this and other reasons we have chosen to base the present edition and translation on one manuscript, BnF, MS fr. 1635, which was produced in the late thirteenth century and is the most complete gathering of the poems.[4] It contains fifty-one of the fifty-six poems attributed to Rutebeuf, and contains all eleven of the poems on the crusades. BnF, MS fr. 1635 was most likely created in eastern Champagne, Burgundy, or southern Lorraine, therefore in the region that shares a dialect of French similar to the French that Eudes and those in his retinue would have known and used. In

2. Zink, *Rutebeuf*, 37–45.

3. Bastin and Faral, *Onze poèmes*, 3–4.

4. The manuscript has been digitized and is available on Gallica, https://gallica.bnf.fr/ark:/12148/btv1b9058335d.

choosing to produce a single-text edition, we have given priority to this collection and its use as one recension of these poems, rather than attempt to generate a new version of the text by comparing and amalgamating multiple manuscript variants. Our edition is therefore somewhat distinct from those of Bastin and Faral and of Zink. In all cases, however, we have consulted both modern editions as we worked.

A Crusader's Death and Life in Acre

Part I

THE ACCOUNT-INVENTORY OF EUDES OF NEVERS

1

Introduction

On the seventh of August 1266, the crusading count Eudes of Nevers lay dying in Acre. In the days leading up to this moment and in the months that followed his closest knights and companions created a series of documents that accounted and inventoried his goods and assets. They assembled a text comprised of five long parchment rolls written in Old French. Together, the rolls, or *rouleaux* in French, are a remarkable survival of Eudes's little-known crusade expedition that opens a window onto the practicalities and ideologies of crusading in the mid-thirteenth century. The text itself and the various actions of those who assembled it make clear the crusade movement's material complexity. For the historian, it is a sophisticated record of things in motion. Unlike more traditional sources that prioritize person-centered narratives, this is a historical record of things, and it is from these things that we have excavated the lives and actions of those who collected, used, sold, gifted, and described these objects.

The Account-Inventory offers a particularly vivid picture of aristocratic life in crusader Outremer. Initially carved out between 1098 and 1109, in the years following the First Crusade, the latticework of territories and principalities that stretched along the eastern Mediterranean coast came to be known to French-speaking crusaders as *Outremer*. Never a defined unified state, Outremer was as much a cultural designation as it was a territorial unit. Its boundaries and influence expanded and contracted throughout the period of the crusades (roughly from 1095 to 1291, but ideologically extending far beyond the thirteenth century). After the Fourth Crusade (1202–4) Outremer came to include parts of mainland Greece, the Latin Empire of Constantinople,

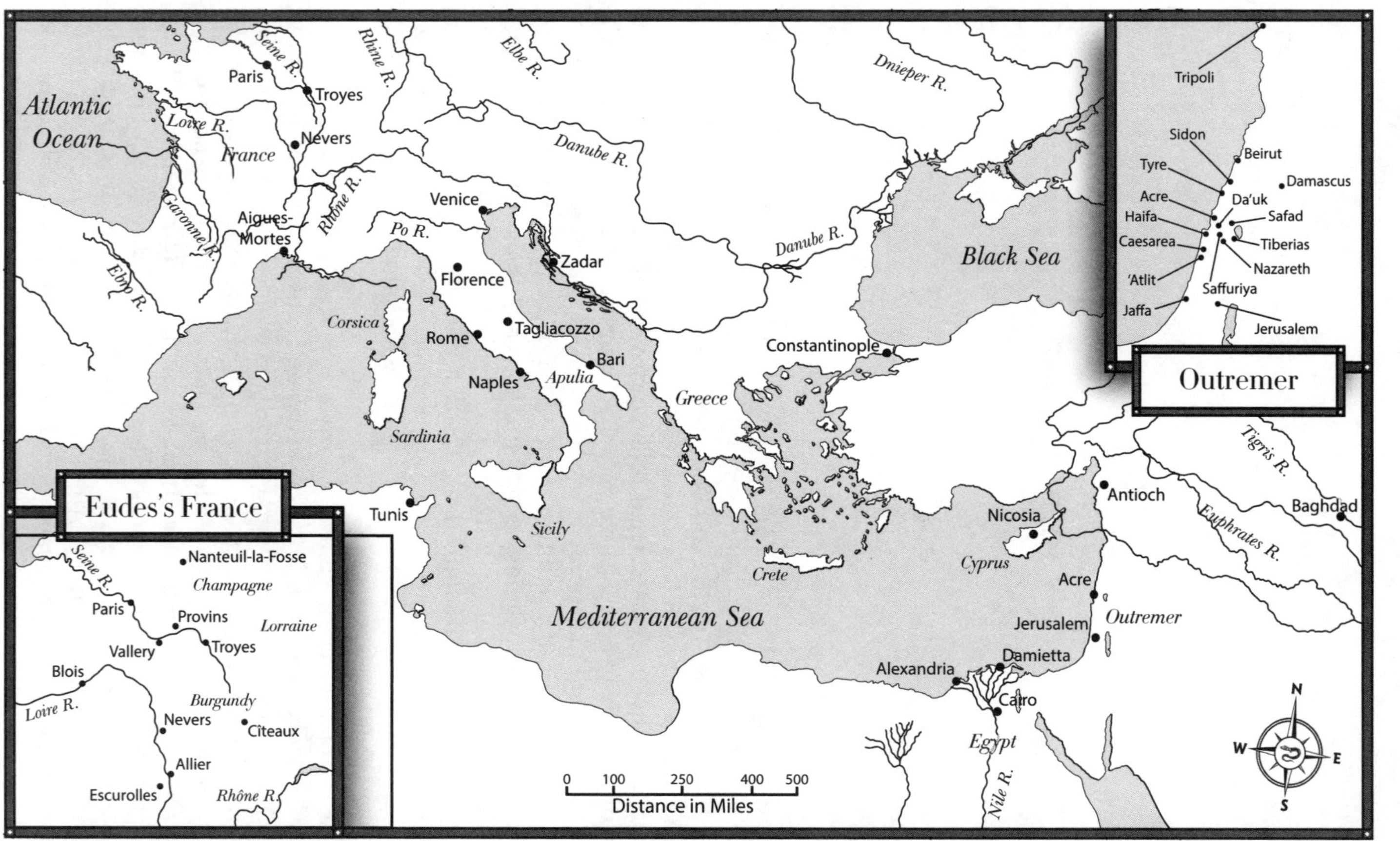

Map 1. The crusading Mediterranean

and Cyprus—all regions where French was the language of law and administration and where French culture intertwined with the cultural worlds of the eastern Mediterranean. By 1266, however, after repeated losses in the East and following a series of failed crusade campaigns, Outremer constituted only a slim corridor of castles, towns, and cities along the shoreline of Syria and Palestine, and the island of Cyprus. Franco-Flemish and Italian pilgrims, visitors, crusaders, and settlers lived in Outremer side by side with local Jewish, Muslim, and Eastern Christian communities especially in the two larger port cities of Acre and Tyre.[1]

Outremer, as used within this book, refers simultaneously to this shifting coastal territory with a physical capital in Acre, and to a cultural understanding of one's location as away from and beyond the sea, outside of the kingdom of France itself (see map 1). Outremer encompassed an identity in reference to: an identity that simultaneously framed itself by looking to the West, to France and Christendom, while also being rooted in the Holy Land as both a lived reality and a spiritual ideal. French crusader Outremer ceased to exist as a territory in 1291 when the last stronghold of Acre fell to Muslim Mamluk forces and the remaining Latin inhabitants were forced into captivity or exile, or fled to Cyprus and the West. Nevertheless, the idea of Outremer as an Other France, another France, persisted in varied forms with layered associations and ambitions for generations.[2] By the nineteenth century, as France built up a colonial empire, medieval Outremer was renewed as an imaginary through which its overseas dominions were defined and historicized. For many reasons, then, Eudes's Outremer is significant because it conveys what medieval men and women saw as appropriate to sacrifice oneself for, to die for. That model had an enduring complex cultural and colonial resonance long after Eudes's death.[3]

Although comparable to some crusader testaments drawn up in the east, the Account-Inventory, as it has come to be known, is far richer and much less self-consciously stylized. Rather, it offers remarkable insights into what it meant to live and to die in Outremer in all of its material complexity.[4] Now

1. See Joshua Prawer, *Histoire du royaume latin de Jérusalem*, trans. Gérard Nahon (Paris: CNRS, 1970; repr. 2007); and Uri Zvi Shachar, *A Pious Belligerence: Dialogical Warfare and the Rhetoric of Righteousness in the Crusading Near East* (Philadelphia: University of Pennsylvania Press, 2021).

2. See Laura K. Morreale and Nicholas L. Paul, introduction to *The French of Outremer: Communities and Communications in the Crusading Mediterranean*, ed. Laura K. Morreale and Nicholas L. Paul (New York: Fordham University Press, 2018), esp. 1–2.

3. See Michelle R. Warren, *Creole Medievalism: Colonial France and Joesph Bédier's Middle Ages* (Minneapolis: University of Minnesota Press, 2011).

4. See, for example, "The Last Will and Testament of Barzella Merxadrux, 9 December 1219," and "The Codicil of Count Henry of Rodez, Acre 16–31 October 1222," both translated in *Crusade and Christendom: Annotated Documents in Translation from Innocent III to the Fall of Acre, 1187–1291*, ed. Jessalynn Bird, Edward Peters, and James M. Powell (Philadelphia: University of

kept in Paris in the Archives nationales, series J 821, no. 1 (Rolls A–D), the Account-Inventory has remained surprisingly understudied.[5] This may be, in part, because Reinhold Röhricht (1842–1905), the great crusade historian of the late nineteenth century, uncharacteristically missed it when he calendared the known documents relating to the Latin East.[6] Although several scholars have used Eudes's Account-Inventory to highlight the prized objects a major baron carried with him to the East, the text itself has not received sustained scholarly attention since it was first edited in 1871.[7] This may also be the consequence of the text's nonnarrative form. It does not recount Eudes's deeds done in the East, nor does it offer an explanation for why he chose to travel to Acre in 1265, or even how he died. It is a list of all of his things and remained, for many scholars, a rather laconic and challenging text to write about and to contextualize.

In recent years, however, scholars working on the crusades have begun to question long-standing chronologies and narratives generated from chronicle texts. Turning to a diverse array of sources, they have begun to reframe the practice and significance of crusading as an ongoing project with meaningful implications for habits of thought and dominion.[8] This work has generated

---

Pennsylvania Press, 2013), 439–45. See also the final testaments for Hugh of Neville and Edward I of England included in this volume.

5. The texts were edited by A.-M. Chazaud, "Inventaire et comptes de la succession d'Eudes, comte de Nevers (Acre 1266)," *Mémoires de la Société nationale des Antiquaires de France*, 4th series, 2 (1871): 164–206. Hereafter we refer to the texts as the Account-Inventory. Below we include several images of the rolls themselves. The full parchment rolls are now viewable on the Documentary Archaeology of Late Medieval Europe (hereafter: DALME) website: https://dalme.org/collections/ecclesiastical-inventories/ with permission from the Archives nationales.

6. Reinhold Röhricht, *Regesta Regni Hierosolymitani (MXCVII–MCCXCI)* (Oeniponti: Libraria Academica Wageriana, 1893). See Jonathan Riley-Smith, "The Crown of France and Acre, 1254–1291," in *France and the Holy Land: Frankish Culture at the End of the Crusades*, ed. Daniel H. Weiss and Lisa Mahoney (Baltimore: Johns Hopkins University Press, 2004), 45–62, who makes this point at 59n69. Riley-Smith's final project was to oversee the digitization of the *Regesta*: see Reinhold Röhricht, ed., *Regesta*, http://crusades-regesta.com/about.

7. Réne de Lespinasse, *Le Nivernais et les comtes de Nevers*, 3 vols. (Paris: Honoré Champion, 1909–14), 2: *Maisons de Donzy, de Bourbon, de Flandres (1200–1384)*, 270–86, offers an overview of the contents of the Account-Inventory. The rolls have been discussed more recently by Riley-Smith, "The Crown of France and Acre"; and Jaroslav Folda, *Crusader Art in the Holy Land, from the Third Crusade to the Fall of Acre, 1187–1291* (Cambridge: Cambridge University Press, 2005), 356–58.

8. See, for example, William Purkis's work in his Arts and Humanities Research Council–funded project "Bearers of the Cross: Material Religion in the Crusading World, 1095–c.1300," and the special issue of the journal *Material Religion* 14 (2018), titled "Material Religion in the Crusading World." See also Nicholas L. Paul, *To Follow in Their Footsteps: The Crusades and Family Memory in the High Middle Ages* (Ithaca, NY: Cornell University Press, 2012); Anne E. Lester, "Remembrance of Things Past: Memory and Material Objects in the Time of the Crusades, 1095–1291," in *Remembering Crusades and Crusading*, ed. Megan Cassidy-Welch (London: Routledge, 2017), 73–94; Lester, "What Remains: Women, Relics and Remembrance in the Aftermath of the Fourth Crusade," *Journal of Medieval History* 40 (2014): 311–28; Linda

new perspectives on the histories of the medieval Mediterranean, the emergence of nation-states and ideologies in western Europe, the genesis of imperial ambitions, and the construction of difference, whether based on religion, geography, language, or race. The ways crusaders styled themselves, how they lived, what it meant to inhabit a multilingual, eastern Mediterranean milieu, and what cultural habits and ideas emerged from this require further research. Eudes's texts offer remarkable insights into these aspects of living together. Imbricated in the complex linguistic, cultural, religious, and social world of Outremer, the texts shed light on how Eudes and those in his retinue lived—for a brief time at least—in Acre between 1265 and 1266.

When characterizing those who took part in the First Crusade as they traveled together from Francia and the heart of Europe to Jerusalem in the years between 1095 and 1099, the crusade historian Jonathan Riley-Smith suggested that they must have appeared to their contemporaries "like a military monastery on the move."[9] This image has shaped crusade scholarship profoundly, transforming it from a study of serial military campaigns to one defined by its devotional tenor and ambiguities. For the last three decades scholars have been far more interested in identifying the spiritual motivations of crusaders and interpreting the sermons, vows, prayers, and religious objects that transformed them into pilgrims, rather than to envision more mundane and material aspects of their pursuits.[10] Yet, as Riley-Smith would later note, by the thirteenth century, the practice of crusading more closely resembled a baronial household on the move than a monastery.[11] Such households were equipped not only with chapels and chaplains, books and liturgical objects, but also with knightly retainers, sergeants and servants, food stuffs, objects for

---

Paterson, *Singing the Crusades: French and Occitan Lyric Responses to the Crusading Movements, 1137–1336* (Woodbridge: D. S. Brewer, 2018); Megan Cassidy-Welch, *War and Memory at the Time of the Fifth Crusade* (University Park: Pennsylvania State University Press, 2019); and Marissa Galvez, *The Subject of Crusade: Lyric, Romance, and Materials, 1150 to 1500* (Chicago: University of Chicago Press, 2020).

9. Jonathan Riley-Smith, *The First Crusade and the Idea of Crusading* (Philadelphia: University of Pennsylvania Press, 1986), 2.

10. There is a vast bibliography that could be cited, but recent exemplary work focused on these questions includes William J. Purkis, *Crusading Spirituality in the Holy Land and Iberia, c.1095–c.1187* (Woodbridge: Boydell, 2008); M. Cecilia Gaposchkin, *Invisible Weapons: Liturgy and the Making of Crusade Ideology* (Ithaca, NY: Cornell University Press, 2017); and Danielle E. A. Park, *Papal Protection and the Crusader: Flanders, Champagne, and the Kingdom of France, 1095–1222* (Woodbridge: Boydell, 2018). To be sure, this religious or spiritual inclination was in reaction to previous interpretations that cast crusading in colonialist terms. For these longer-term trends in the historiography, see Giles Constable, "The Historiography of the Crusades," in *The Crusades from the Perspective of Byzantium and the Muslim World*, ed. Angeliki E. Laiou and Roy Parviz Mottahedeh (Washington, DC: Dumbarton Oaks, 2001), 1–22.

11. Riley-Smith, "The Crown of France and Acre," and Riley-Smith, "Towards an Understanding of the Fourth Crusade as an Institution," in *Urbs Capta: The Fourth Crusade and Its Consequences / La IVe Croisade et ses consequences*, ed. Angeliki Laiou (Paris: Lethielleux, 2005), 71–87.

use in kitchens and bedrooms, in stables and butcheries, as well as cloth and clothing, jewelry and plate for livery and diplomacy, among much else. The Account-Inventory of Eudes of Nevers exposes the workings of just such a household. It conjures the material world of a noble crusader in Outremer and shows all that was required—wealth and labor, especially—to accommodate such a lifestyle.[12]

The text is unique as an inventory of objects in the possession of a crusader in Acre and unparalleled in its details. The text was also a living document whose composition, editing, readjusting, and final tallies were worked out over the months that followed Eudes's death. It reflects the lived decisions and movements of objects and the changing meaning and valuation of things in the East. The inventory is also an invaluable complement to surviving narrative and poetic texts, like John of Joinville's *Vie de Saint Louis* and Rutebeuf's poetic crusader laments, treated below. Moreover, as a text composed in Acre, in the heart of Outremer, it reflects the ideas and practices at work in that shared world of coastal Syria and Palestine rather than in a remembered and reconstructed account written after a crusader's return to the West. As such, we can see before us how and when French crusader habits, tastes, and routines came into contact with or were altered to accommodate life in Acre, among communities of Jews, Christians, and Muslims, carrying an imprint of Outremer back to the West in turn. This experience was not only performed through obligations and interlocking relationships of trust, debt, reliance, and dependance, but also used to reinscribe recursive, self-fashioned ideas of crusading and courtly culture. Courtly and "chivalrous" practices associated with such qualities as *prudhommerie* and *gentillesse* proved more enduring than their end goals, much as the performance of chivalric ideals in a Romance text was more important than the successful completion of a quest.[13] Within

12. For an example of how to read household possessions as frames for identity, see Deborah Cohen, *Household Gods: The British and Their Possessions* (New Haven, CT: Yale University Press, 2006); Malcolm Vale, *The Princely Court: Medieval Courts and Culture in North-West Europe* (Oxford: Oxford University Press, 2001); and Katherine L. French, *Household Goods and Good Households in Late Medieval London: Consumption and Domesticity after the Plague* (Philadelphia: University of Pennsylvania Press, 2021).

13. For a discussion of these terms, see the introduction to the poems of Rutebeuf below and the glossary. Crusading as an imagined practice made its way into a vast corpus of romance texts, but much more work is needed before those textual refractions can be related in a sustained and analytical way to the lived practices of crusading. We believe Eudes's Account-Inventory will enrich this discussion. Literary scholars who have worked on related texts include Sharon Kinoshita, *Medieval Boundaries: Rethinking Difference in Old French Literature* (Philadelphia: University of Pennsylvania Press, 2006); Shirin A. Khanmohamadi, *In Light of Another's Word: European Ethnography in the Middle Ages* (Philadelphia: University of Pennsylvania Press, 2013); Galvez, *The Subject of Crusade*. For an important resonance of these ideas regarding crusading differences as it was deployed in the construction of race, see Cord J. Whitaker, *Black Metaphors: How Modern Racism Emerged from Medieval Race-Thinking* (Philadelphia: University of Pennsylvania Press, 2019). For a sense of this sort of cross-pollination among vernacular texts and

this context, the inventory also demonstrates the care and attention it took to wind down a life, to give away one's possessions, to think about a family legacy, and to manage the longer-term care of one's body and soul.

Material Outremer: Methods and Approaches

The Account-Inventory is first and foremost a list of things. In some cases, they are described in great detail, and in others only laconically recorded and itemized. This makes the text a marvelous case-study for thinking about the material Outremer and crusader materiality. Recent interdisciplinary work on material culture and materiality has yielded an ever more sophisticated set of methodologies for working with objects and material remains. Scholars have become extremely adept at interpreting both tangible things, accessible in museums and private collections, and textual things, that is, objects in texts like wills, inventories, and charters, as well as hagiography, romance, and lyric, together in light of one another.[14] The methodologies integral to the study of materiality depend on several layered interpretative strategies that move between the textual and the tangible, drawing together knowledge gleaned from both. Methodologically, materiality is committed to and reliant on the fact that things in the past are and were relational, that is, parts of networks and imbrications, assemblages and entanglements.[15] A materiality approach follows the connections that draw together access to materials (linen

---

lived experience, see Nicholas L. Paul, "In Search of the Marshal's Lost Crusade: The Persistence of Memory, the Problems of History and the Painful Birth of Crusading Romance," *Journal of Medieval History* 40 (2014): 292–310; and Paul, "Possession: Sacred Crusading Treasure in the Material Vernacular," in "Material Religion in the Crusading World," ed. William Purkis, special issue, *Material Religion* 14 (2018): 520–32. Relatedly, Anne E. Lester, "Crusading as a Religious Movement: Families, Community, and Lordship in a Vernacular Frame," in *Between Orders and Heresy: Rethinking Medieval Religious Movements*, ed. Jennifer Kolpacoff Deane and Anne E. Lester (Toronto: University of Toronto Pres, 2021), 127–69.

14. There is a large and growing literature on materiality and its methods. As pertains to this project and the distinction between "tangible" and "textual" things, see Daniel Lord Smail, *Legal Plunder: Households and Debt Collection in Late Medieval Europe* (Cambridge, MA: Harvard University Press, 2016), esp. 1–30, at 10. Also Laurel Thatcher Ulrich et al., *Tangible Things: Making History through Objects* (Oxford: Oxford University Press, 2015). A useful case for studying the movement and meaning of things from inventories is made by Robert S. DuPlessis, *The Material Atlantic: Clothing, Commerce, and Colonization in the Atlantic World, 1650–1800* (Cambridge: Cambridge University Press, 2016).

15. As should be clear, the methods of materiality rely on fundamental insights from anthropology and social theory. Concerning myriad different approaches to materiality, see the comments on the "material field" in Anne E. Lester, "Possession, Production and Power: Reading Objects in the Material Field," *Medieval Feminist Forum* 56 (2020): 204–20. On the major theories alluded to here, see Arjun Appadurai, ed., *The Social Life of Things: Commodities in Cultural Perspective* (Cambridge: Cambridge University Press, 1986); Bruno Latour, *Reassembling the Social: An Introduction to Actor-Network Theory* (Oxford: Oxford University Press, 2005); Ian

and wool, gold and parchment, for example) with the knowledge practices to transform those materials into objects of use or esteem, and through the networks of people and things that deployed, traded, sold, recycled, or gave them away and thus set things into circulation anew. Following objects and their use as things opens new relationships and affordances for scholarly interpretation. An object made for one purpose may be deployed, repurposed, described, or returned as something quite different, but its persistence through time and space is indicative of its changing meaning, value, and relationality. Finally, materiality always presses the point of the silent and silenced story. Objects cannot talk (with rare and enchanted exceptions), and their experiences are not reflected in subject-driven narratives.[16] Moreover, the labor of their making, partial use, and emotional or intellectual value is often occluded or kept deliberately silent. That objects held other histories—of symbolic, commemorative, associative, and affective value and resonance—should haunt us as we read and write, for this was yet another dimension of their role in the past.[17]

Two more precise articulations of materiality's methodology have been integral to this project. One is the use of material philology and the attendant codicological analysis of the parchment rolls themselves, their layout, scribal practices, use of language and abbreviation, and the placement of words on the page.[18] As a method, material philology seeks to discover "how surviving documents of all kinds insert themselves into their context, culture, and language practices."[19] In this sense, as Stephen G. Nichols defined some years ago, material philology is an "ensemble of practices and methods for the study of medieval culture broadly conceived," not simply the concern of those producing or consuming a manuscript edition. It is "a means of reading contextually and against a broad horizon of cultural" circumstances.[20] Elaborated further to the space and "dynamics of the parchment page"—or what Nichols has called the "manuscript matrix"—we can see the page "not [as] an inert place of inscription, but rather an interactive space inviting continual

Hodder, *Entangled: An Archaeology of the Relationships between Humans and Things* (Malden, MA: Wiley-Blackwell, 2012); and Daniel Miller, *Stuff* (Cambridge, MA: Polity, 2010).

16. For examples of such exceptions, see Bettina Bildhauer, *Medieval Things: Agency, Materiality, and Narratives of Objects in Medieval German Literature and Beyond* (Columbus: The Ohio State University Press, 2020).

17. See Lester, "What Remains," and Lester, "Remembrance of Things Past." Outside the crusade context, see Tiya Miles, *All That She Carried: The Journey of Ashley's Sack, a Black Family Keepsake* (New York: Random House, 2021).

18. See Stephen G. Nichols, "Why Material Philology," *Zeitschrift für deutsche Philologie* 116 (1997): 10–30; for further elaboration of these ideas, see also Nichols, "What Is a Manuscript Culture? Technologies of the Manuscript Matrix," in *The Medieval Manuscript Book: Cultural Approaches*, ed. Michael Johnston and Michael Van Dussen (Cambridge: Cambridge University Press, 2017), 34–59.

19. Nichols, "Why Material Philology," 13.

20. Nichols, "Why Material Philology," 13.

representational and interpretative activity."[21] Eudes's texts were spaces where the multifaceted, multicultural, religious, and linguistically diverse world of Outremer came together, a world that was always constructed relationally as away or other (*outre*) to a place across the sea. Outremer continually presented another French space of cultural production, and another religious and cultural sphere of living and dying.[22]

A second and equally important methodological approach is that of documentary archaeology, that is, recovering or excavating objects from the imprint they leave in the textual record.[23] As a practice and method that consciously "relies on descriptions of things generated by contemporaries in the act of reflecting on their own material world," documentary archaeology is critical for seeing and re-creating relationships of objects through the textual record.[24] Rather than jettisoning language in favor of purely tangible objects, documentary archaeology uses the relational ideas and concepts suggested by language and its grammar on the page to address what Daniel Lord Smail, Gabe Pizorrno, and Laura Morreale refer to as "folk taxonomies," that is, the ways in which individuals described and characterized objects in their worlds, as known through their experiences. These local and specific descriptive terms offer yet another layer of information for interpreting relations between objects and people. Indeed, "the ultimate goal of documentary archaeology, is to provide a framework that translates between the modern domain ontologies used by scholars to characterize museum objects and archaeological artefacts and the historical folk taxonomies" used by people in the past to describe objects.[25]

In the case of Eudes's things, no known tangible objects survive, but we can use the linguistic assemblages of nouns and adjectives that give shape to each textual thing to excavate objects from the page as they were once made, used, and set in motion, and to frame them in relation and reference to other comparable objects in tangible collections. The archeological process is critical here, for many objects in Eudes's inventory come into clearest view when read in relation to other things on the parchment page, or as assemblages of textual

21. Nichols, "What Is a Manuscript Culture?," 39; see also Nichols, "Introduction: Philology in a Manuscript Culture," *Speculum* 65 (1990): 1–10.

22. For thoughts about this process of dynamic definition, see Anthony Cutler, "Everywhere and Nowhere: The Invisible Muslim and Christian Self-Fashioning in the Culture of Outremer," in Weiss and Mahoney, *France and the Holy Land*, 253–81.

23. See the presentation of this idea in Smail, *Legal Plunder*, 9–12. The pioneering work on this concept is Françoise Piponnier, "Archéologie et histoire," in *Le Moyen Âge aujourd'hui: Actes de la Rencontre de Cerisy-la-Salle, juillet 1991*, ed. Guy Lobrichon and Jacques Le Goff (Paris: Le Léopard d'Or, 1998), 83–100; and Mary Carolyn Beaudry, ed., *Documentary Archaeology in the New World* (Cambridge: Cambridge University Press, 1988).

24. See the comments by Daniel Lord Smail et al. on "Methodology" at DALME, https://dalme.org/project/methodology/.

25. Smail et al., "Methodology."

objects. Accounting for textual stratigraphy aids in disentangling one object from another and in relating it or finding its echo—its second imprint—in other parchment rolls, when it was sold off, given away, or left as a remainder to be carried back into the West. In short, the methods archaeologists and anthropologists have long used to make sense of things unhinged from texts can be redeployed here for the parchment rolls and within the textual configuration of the page itself.

Finally, as a long-form text that traveled out of Outremer, the Account-Inventory shared a trajectory and set of linguistic practices and terms with other contemporary literary texts both prose and poetry. Indeed, physically, the Account-Inventory rolls traveled alongside or along the same networks as the parchment codex counterparts that were listed among Eudes's baggage. It has been helpful to adapt methodological insights from literary theory and literary studies that address the role of objects in texts that call attention to character development, emotional registers, memorial devices, and plotted action.[26] Theoretically inflected readings of the role of things in texts point to the poetic echoes in Eudes's inventory. The words on parchment we now read would have first been formed as a spoken text set onto parchment after they were delivered or performed. Indeed, accounting and inventorying were almost always an active, embodied, and often collaborative endeavor in the medieval world. Each entry, description, and summation most likely originated first as spoken words, recollections, or negotiations before finding a more permanent form on the page.[27] Likewise, the choice of words in many cases is revealing. Some descriptors are quite straightforward (numbers of objects), while others (old/new, best/worst, or color schemes) have valuative and affective valences that reveal even more about their meaning.[28] In the case of Eudes's Account-Inventory, such resonances are made all the more powerful in that they find echo, if not revealing correspondence, in the corpus of Rutebeuf's crusade poems translated in part III. Writing at the same moment, Rutebeuf and the inventory authors use very similar words and images that

26. The work of Bill Brown has defined the field in this regard. See Brown, "Thing Theory," *Critical Inquiry* 28 (2001): 1–23; and more recently, Brown, *Other Things* (Chicago: University of Chicago Press, 2015). Along these lines, see also Andrew Cole, "The Call of Things: A Critique of Object-Oriented Ontologies," *minnesota review* 80 (2013): 106–17; and the essays collected in the special issue on "Medieval Materiality," ed. Anne E. Lester and Katherine C. Little, *English Language Notes* 53 (2015). In the context of medieval literature and texts, see also Katherine C. Little, "The Politics of Lists," *Exemplaria* 31 (2019): 117–28; Galvez, *The Subject of Crusade*; and Bildhauer, *Medieval Things*.

27. On the memorial and emotive qualities of inventories and lists of objects, see Leora Auslander, "Beyond Words," *American Historical Association* 110 (2005): 1015–45.

28. For examples of such objects and readings, see Leora Auslander, "Deploying Material Culture to Write the History of Gender and Sexuality: The Example of Clothing and Textiles," in "Making Gender with Things," special issue, *Clio*, no. 40 (2014): 157–78; and Stephanie Downes, Sally Holloway, and Sarah Randles, eds., *Feeling Things: Objects and Emotions through History* (Oxford: Oxford University Press, 2018).

together conjoin and illuminate Eudes's world with poetic force and personal sentiment. We have thus taken into account the literary quality of Eudes's texts as we reconstructed both the textual composition of the rolls and the material world they sought to represent and contain.

The Texts: Form and Function

It is difficult to know if someone, or perhaps a team of scribes, created the parchment rolls originally as a fair-copy text set aside for posterity and archiving, or if they wrote them out as a living record, created for use at a particular moment. Most likely, as was often the case with documents of practice, scribes copied the rolls from notes taken on wax tablets or smaller, rougher, pieces of parchment. As they exist today, the rolls retain the flexible quality of a text in action as reflected in the repetition of the details and decisions the scribes recorded, in the summary totals reckoned, and in the omissions and lines crossed out that indicate changes after a scribe first wrote. Copied on both sides—the front (recto) and dorsal (verso)—of five unequal rolls of parchment (which the previous editor and archivists labeled A–D), the cleric-scribes created a text that is repetitive, complicated, overlapping, and highly detailed. The rolls reflect the work of Eudes's close companions and his clerics writing and rewriting, engaging in discussion and returning to procedures, and recalculating debts and sums owed. From the five separate pieces of parchment, someone sewed together the first two to render a record in four rolls, each about the length of two modern standard sheets of 8½ x 11–inch paper set end to end; two are quite a bit thinner and more delicate than this contemporary approximation (see figures 3–7). In all, the rolls measure as follows:

Roll A: The first roll is in two parts, originally sewn together:

Part 1 is 16 11/16 inches long and 7 9/16 inches wide (42.39 cm x 19.2 cm) at its maximum point; parchment is very thin.

Part 2 is 35 13/16 inches long and 7 13/16 inches wide (90.96 cm x 19.84 cm) at its maximum point; parchment is thick and shows signs of wear. In the archive today they are wrapped together, and Roll A is now and was then the outermost piece of parchment, which would have received the most wear and tear as a consequence. This is still clearly visible (see figures 1–4).

Roll B: The parchment is 19 1/4 inches long and 7 9/16 inches wide (48.90 cm x 19.2 cm) at its maximum point; parchment is softer and of a more standard thickness than in Roll A (see figure 7).

Roll C: The parchment is 16 7/16 inches long and 5 7/8 inches wide (41.75 cm x 14.92 cm) at its maximum point; parchment is slightly thinner and more finely prepared, and much whiter than Rolls A and B. This is the smallest and finest roll and would have been rolled inside the others preserving the quality of the parchment (see figure 2).

Roll D: The parchment is 23 11/16 inches long and 6 15/16 inches wide (60.17 cm x 17.62 cm) at its maximum point: parchment is also very stiff, as with Roll C.

Jaroslav Folda, an expert on manuscripts produced in Acre, notes that "overall, these different-sized pieces of parchment appear utilitarian and unexceptional in terms of their parchment, preparation, ink, lack of rulings, and the hands of the scribes. They look comparable to similar western European documents, and except for the content of the text there is nothing that would indicate they were done in Acre with regard to their codicological characteristics."[29] Indeed, it is very difficult to guess where they were created or copied. What is clear is that Eudes's scribes and executors were still working out the final totals and sums of the accounts. This suggests that the rolls were most likely produced and copied in Acre, in the weeks that followed Eudes's death, while those in his employ assembled and assessed the many and various items in his household for sale and for donation. It is harder to imagine a scenario in which this would have occurred in France. Had the rolls been fair copies it is unlikely they would have retained the ongoing calculations and uneven spacing that are still evident. It is also possible that there were more rolls than we now possess and that other objects—such as swords and weapons of war, missing from these parchments—could have appeared elsewhere, on rolls that are no longer extant.

The first editor of the rolls, A.-M. Chazaud, suggested that a rough draft of the accounts was to be found on the dorsal/verso of the rolls, and the fair copy or final version on the recto.[30] As we shall discuss below, this was certainly not the case. Rather, the documents are better understood as related pieces, interlocking and informing each other, some used for accounting, some for inventorying and appraising the values of objects, and others for a final reckoning. Most likely these were the final drafts or summary fair copies, as noted above, even if they continued to be augmented after scribes had copied them from wax or other working versions. Although the script is hasty, the hands are not unclear nor exceedingly abbreviated; rather this is the work of

29. Folda, *Crusader Art*, 356 and 643n925. In creating our edition and translation we worked from digital photos supplied by the Archives nationales. These are extremely useful for reading the text and resolving certain questions of orthography, layout, and use. In March 2022, when the archives opened after the COVID-19 pandemic closures and travel bans were resolved, Anne Lester consulted the parchments in Paris and confirmed the above measurements and made other observations in person.

30. As he notes, "Le verso de chacun de ces rôles est, en général, occupé par le brouillon ou une rédaction primitive d'un des états ou comptes dont la mise au net se lit au recto. Ces sortes de minutes nous ont parfois fourni quelques variantes." Chazaud, "Inventaire," 164.

well-trained administrative men in the service of the count writing in what could best be described as gothic cursive.[31]

Although most archival records in northern French collections take the form of folded or rolled charters or letters patent, the roll form of the Account-Inventory is not surprising for a fiscal administrative text, particularly one that was not subsequently copied into a formal register or cartulary.[32] Many of the French royal inquest and financial records dating to the 1260s and 1270s kept in the *Trésor des chartes* took the form of parchment rolls. The codicological and archival practice of using a series of parchment rolls for a working text like an expense account or inquest was not unusual, especially for account records kept from Burgundy and the Auvergne.[33] Beyond France, a comparable example is the royal inventory of gifts that Henry III of England (r. 1216–72) received and distributed between December 6, 1234, and July 16, 1236.[34]

More revealing is the fact that those who compiled the texts chose to write them in a northern dialect of Old French rather than in Latin, as was more common for the account records and inventories that royal and princely households and ecclesiastical institutions maintained.[35] The use of the vernacular communicates the preferences and abilities of the texts' primary users, the knights Hugh of Augerant, Geoffrey of Sergines the younger, and Érard of Vallery, as well as the graphic practices of their administrative partners, the Templars. Indeed, the correspondence kept between Geoffrey of Sergines the elder, Érard of Vallery, and the French crown shows that these men preferred to write and have their documents written in French.[36] Likewise, in his enrolled correspondence with the crown and in local agreements within

31. We thank Lisa Fagin Davis for her advice on the hand. For a discussion and example of similar forms, see Albert Derolez, *The Paleography of Gothic Manuscript Books from the Twelfth to the Early Sixteenth Century* (Cambridge: Cambridge University Press, 2003).

32. For comparisons, see Xavier Hélary, Jean-François Nieus, Alain Provost, and Marc Suttor, eds., *Les archives princières, XIIe–XVe siècles* (Arras: Artois Presses Université, 2016).

33. See Alexandre Teulet et al., eds., *Layettes du Trésor des chartes* (Paris: H. Plon, 1863–1909), 5:305–27, from the "Acta Omissa."

34. See Nicholas Vincent, "An Inventory of Gifts to King Henry III, 1234–5," in *The Growth of Royal Government under Henry III*, ed. David Crook and Louise J. Wilkinson (Woodbridge: Boydell and Brewer, 2015), 121–48; and Benjamin Linley Wild, "A Gift Inventory from the Reign of Henry III," *English Historical Review* 125 (2010): 529–69. For a discussion of the objects listed and the larger royal networks, see Amanda R. Luyster, "Reassembling Textile Networks: Treasuries and Re-collecting Practices in Thirteenth-Century England," *Speculum* 96 (2021): 1039–78.

35. Chazaud suggests that this is French "en roman du Nord" ("Inventaire," 168). As will be elaborated below, we suggest it reflects more clearly the vernacular used in Champagne and Burgundy, much like what Rutebeuf likely employed rather than a dialect like Picard, for example. Indeed, BnF, MS fr. 1635, the manuscript containing Rutebeuf's crusade poems that we have used as the basis of our transcription and translation, shares many linguistic commonalities with Eudes's *rouleaux*.

36. Teulet et al., *Layettes*, 4:228–29, no. 5293 and 4:230, no. 5295.

Burgundy, Eudes of Nevers communicated primarily in French.[37] Moreover, by the 1260s, French was the predominant language of the eastern Mediterranean; a true lingua franca.[38]

The Chronology of the Rouleaux

The parchments that encompass Eudes's Account-Inventory are not straightforward texts. Despite being archived together, they were compiled at various moments between Eudes's death on August 7, 1266, and a final reckoning of accounts on October 7, 1266 (as reflected at the end of Roll A), in Acre when all three executors—Érard of Vallery, Hugh of Augerant, and Geoffrey of Sergines the younger—were present. A consideration of the material qualities of the rolls, of their codicology, the nature of parchment use and reuse, as well as the paleography and graphic placement of the text on the page, suggests a clear chronology for the writing and use of the *rouleaux*.[39] In making this chronological reconstruction we have set aside the modern archival numbering (which often does not reflect recto-dorsal parchment use). Moreover, the original editor, Chazaud, chose to subsume and suppress parts of the texts that were repetitive or did not fit his idea of a modern French edition. In some cases, although Chazaud was overall an extremely competent editor, the organization of his text privileged nineteenth-century conventions of presentation

37. Teulet et al., *Layettes*, 3:374, no. 4329 (September 10, 1257, in which Eudes pays homage to Count Thibaut V of Champagne for the county of Nevers); 3:415–16, no. 4421 (June 8, 1258; agreement between Eudes of Nevers and Louis IX for the marriage of Yolande and Jean Tristan). This contract would be recopied and selected for inclusion among numerous volumes by Duprey and other *érudites* throughout the seventeenth century as the beginning of a form for such contracts. See Paris, BnF, MSS fr. 4508, fr. 4329, Dupuy 98, and Collection de Picardie 331. See also Maximilien Quantin, *Recueil de pièces pour faire suite au cartulaire général de l'Yonne* (Paris: Durand et Pédone-Lauriel, 1878), 292–93, no. 601 (June 1261) in French concerning the rights to justice shared with the monks of Reigny; 304, no. 621 (July 1265), written in the months before he departed.

38. The French (or langue d'oïl) used in the lands outside of France has been studied along two axes: the southern axis, extending from the Kingdom of France, southward through the Italian and into the Iberian peninsulas, and then eastward to the Holy Land, Cyprus, and the Morea; and the northern axis, which includes the British Isles, the Low Countries, and the German lands, though significant crossover occurred between these geographic regions. See Morreale and Paul, *The French of Outremer*; and Nicola Morato and Dirk Schoenaers, eds., *Medieval Francophone Literary Culture Outside France* (Turnhout: Brepols, 2019). For the case of Acre, see Jane Gilbert, Simon Gaunt, and William Burgwinkle, "History, Time, and Empire: The *Histoire ancienne* in the Latin Kingdom of Jerusalem," in *Medieval French Literary Culture Abroad*, Oxford Scholarship Online, 2020, doi: 10.1093/oso/9780198832454.003.0005. For various genres in French, see Shachar, *A Pious Belligerence*.

39. Nichols, "Why Material Philology."

and information over and above the ways Eudes's knights, companions, and kin wrote, copied, and used the rolls.[40]

Chronologically, Roll B appears to be the first text written among the five rolls. The contents of this roll take up most of one long side of moderately well-prepared parchment. Given the size, the parchment itself was probably made from sheep or cowhide that was cured, cut, and prepared in the West, or from sheep or goat skin prepared in and around Acre. There is a slight curvature to all of the rolls, reflecting the size and shape of the animal.[41] Roll B is one of the finer pieces of parchment but carries some discoloration at the top and bottom margins, probably from storage rather than use. The ink is light brown and has seemingly faded somewhat. Compared to the other roles, especially Roll D, the stylus seems to have been a less fine-pointed instrument, creating broader strokes as the scribe wrote. The text is written in a clear, fast-moving, administrative or bureaucratic hand not unlike that used in northern France for administrative documents and royal *enquêtes*.[42]

Roll B begins with a short offset title: "These are the things of the Count of Nevers that he had the day he went from life to death [*Ce sont les chose lou conte de Neverz quil avoit au jor quil ala de vie amort*]" (see figure 7).[43] This appears to be the earliest roll to have been created, written on the day Eudes died—August 7, 1266—and drafted from within his lodgings. The inventory first lists things in the hand (*la main*) of different men in the count's retinue, namely, *sergeants*. These appear to be from among the count's personal possessions. They included items with specific provenance, associations,

40. An analogy to play scripts or song scripts is perhaps apt here as we develop below. On this process generally, see Carol Symes, "The Medieval Archive and the History of Theater: Assessing the Written and Unwritten Evidence for Premodern Performance," *Theater Survey* 52 (2011): 29–58; and Symes, "Knowledge and Transmission: Media and Memory," in *A Cultural History of Theater in the Middle Ages*, ed. Jody Enders, A Cultural History of Theater 2 (London: Bloomsbury, 2017), 199–211. For the case of inventories as scripts, see Katherine Anne Wilson, "The Household Inventory as Urban 'Theatre' in Late Medieval Burgundy," *Social History* 40 (2015): 335–59. Below we address our editorial conventions and how our choices differ from those of Chazaud. For example, we have chosen not to impose modern accents in French where no accents were used and to retain the thirteenth-century spelling and orthography. See the text edition here.

41. To take a materiality approach to the text reminds us that in dealing with parchment records we are also setting ourselves within the network of animal-human relationships that structured much of the medieval world. At this point it is impossible to know where the animals came from, whether France or the Levant. See Bruce Holsinger, *On Parchment: Animals, Archives and the Making of Culture from Herodotus to the Digital Age* (New Haven, CT: Yale University Press, 2022); and Sarah Kay, *Animal Skins and the Reading Self in Medieval Latin and French Bestiaries* (Chicago: University of Chicago Press, 2017).

42. For comparable graphic practices, see the essays in Xavier Hermand, Jean-François Nieus, and Étienne Renard, eds., *Décrire, inventorier, enregistrer entre Seine et Rhin au Moyen Âge*, Mémoires et documents de l'école des chartes 92 (Paris: École des chartes, 2012).

43. For quotations from the text itself, see below in the edition and the corresponding images online as noted above in note 1. Hereafter we refer to the "Edition," followed by roll letter and section: Edition, Roll B Front.

and descriptions that only a user/owner might know. From there, Roll B lists objects in each of the rooms in the count's residence including the longest entry for his wardrobe (*robe*), ending with a note that "everything that is in the old wardrobe mentioned above was given to the poor hospitals of Acre and to the poor religious houses."[44] On the verso/dorsal of Roll B is a list of the jewels and rings that the count gave to his closest knights and retainers, one presumes on his deathbed, that is, on "the day he went from life to death." The text is otherwise undated. We believe this parchment roll is as close as we come to a deathbed testament or inventory and reflects Eudes's most intimate objects and spaces.

Roll C was drawn up between the time of the count's death (August 7) and September 15, 1266, when his executors paid off his remaining debts at the Temple. The recto, or front-side, of this roll offers both a list of the appraised value of each item in Eudes's wardrobe, reflecting the opulent clothing and whole cloth he carried with him or purchased while in Acre, and a list of those institutions or individuals who received each item as a charitable donation. Although an appraisal was done for many of these objects, the clothing was donated in kind, presumably intended for reuse or recycling and reappropriation as altar cloths or clerical vestments. Items like doublets, leggings, and head coverings given to the poor or to beguines were presumably either used as they were or sold for cash. On the dorsal, or back, of Roll C there is a second copy of the list of jewels and rings the count gave to his closest knights and retainers. This roll concludes by noting that the Hospital of St. John was to receive his two cooking pots from the kitchen and that all other kitchen wares were sold. This short dorsal list is a copy (although not exact) of the dorsal list on Roll B. Clearly it was useful to have two copies of the final list of gifts, one that corresponded to the spaces of Eudes's lodgings and that may have been generated as he lay dying, and a second copy his agents used to disburse the personal objects from his wardrobe. Indeed, scribes may have copied Roll C for use as a handlist or checklist when his garments and other objects were disbursed after his death. While the objects given away and circulating out in the world may have lost their connection to Eudes as they were reused or reappropriated, the inventory text itself anchored them to the deceased crusader. In this way the rolls are a historical record of connections between people (Eudes, the men in his retinue, and the poor men and women receiving his largess) and things.

Roll D was created on or before September 15, 1266, for on that date a final accounting was done as part of, or following, a series of estate sales, which generated "the record of the count's things that were sold." This account and its summary value were "made . . . before the master of the Temple, and my lord Érard of Vallery, and my lord Geoffrey of Sergines the younger."[45] The

44. Edition, Roll B Front.
45. Edition, Roll D Front.

dorsal of Roll D then goes on to list, in the same ink and hand, "things that were not yet sold."[46] At the bottom of the dorsal of Roll D, turned upside down, is a short list of "what the count had in deniers currency and bezants on the day he went from life to death."[47] This note is written in the same ink and hand as Roll B and is dated to the feast of Saint Laurence, August 9, 1266. Thus, Roll D appears to have been written on what had been a second, continued page of Roll B, and is here recycled to form part of a second final valuation and accounting of Eudes's goods taken six weeks after his death.

Temporally, Roll A was produced last. Formed from stitching together two parchment pieces of nearly identical width but varying lengths, Roll A is the most worked and utilitarian of the rolls and is the closest we have to a formal account (see figures 4–6). A scribe drew up the first section of Roll A shortly after the count died and listed the pay due to each of Eudes's retainers, including his knights, sergeants, and servants, for the two months that followed the count's death, thus through October. The second parts of Roll A were generated in mid- and then late September (the fifteenth and twenty-ninth respectively) when Eudes's debts to the Temple were concluded before the treasurer and master of the Temple. On October 7 final payments in cash and kind were made to his knights and retainers, several of whom were preparing to return to the West. With that, his estate in Acre was settled.

Beyond the considerations of compositional chronology, the Account-Inventory is a collection of several independent moments recorded over the course of a two-month period. The time taken to assess and record all of the objects in the inventory, to account for the outstanding pay owed to Eudes's knights and servants and to make those payments, and to account for the dates that successive additions were made is duly registered in the document, with the majority of the transactions appearing on Roll A, the longest of the rolls. Assessing what remained of Eudes's possessions and fulfilling the outstanding financial obligations was a lengthy process requiring coordination among those responsible for the count's administrative affairs and the institutions where he conducted business. Even if the rolls themselves were written at different moments and in response to immediate needs and circumstances rather than to a desire for narrative clarity, there is a clear chronology to how the accounts were settled, which is mapped throughout the parchments as a whole. We must then think like their creators and users and follow the flow of activity and the movement of people and things. The earliest recorded entry is the date of the count's death (August 7), the next comes on the "eve of the feast of Saint Lawrence" (August 9), and the last on "the Thursday after the feast of Saint Remy in the year 1266" (October 7). Table 1 below plots each dated entry, the roll where they were recorded, and at what point the dates appear in the inventory. As noted above, Rolls B and C are effectively undated

46. Edition, Roll D Back.
47. Edition, Roll D Back.

Table 1. Dates appearing in the Account-Inventory, 1266

Date as given	English translation	Modern date	Roll
Ce fu la veille de feste saint Lorant en lan m cc lxvi	This was done on the eve of the feast of Saint Lawrence, in the year 1266	August 9, 1266	A
le lundi devant la feste saint Leu	the Monday before the feast of Saint Leu	August 29, 1266	A
landemain de feste sainte croiz en septembre	the day after the feast of the Holy Cross in September	September 15, 1266	A
dela semeine de feste saint Michel jusques le diemanche	during the week of the feast of Saint Michael until Sunday	September 29, 1266	A
le jor de feste saint Michel en lan m cclxvi	the feast day of Saint Michael in the year 1266	September 29, 1266	A
la veille de feste saint Lorant en lan m cc lxvi	the eve of the feast of Saint Lawrence in the year 1266	August 9, 1266	A
lan demain de feste sainte croiz en septembre	the day after the feast of the Holy Cross in September.	September 15, 1266	A
le jueudi apres feste saint Remi en lan m cc lxvi	the Thursday after the feast of Saint Remy in the year 1266	October 7, 1266	A
landemain de feste sainte croix en Septembre	the day after the feast of the Holy Cross in September.	September 15, 1266	A
au jor quil ala de vie amort	on the day he went from life to death	August 7, 1266	A
au jor quil ala de vie amort	the day he went from life to death	August 7, 1266	B
lan demain de feste sainte croiz en septembre	the day after the feast of the Holy Cross in September	September 15, 1266	D
au jor quil ala de vie amort	on the day he went from life to death	August 7, 1266	D
laveille de feste saint Lorant a lan m cc lxvi	the eve of the feast of Saint Lawrence in the year 1266	August 9, 1266	D

for accounting purposes in that Roll C has no date at all, and Roll B notes only "the day the count went from life to death."

As an administrative tool, the graphic and functional quality of the material texts indicates how they were used as an account and an inventory. Scribes intended for the rolls to be separated, moved around, turned upside down, added to, even repurposed. Even in their current state they fold back onto themselves and use internal references to settle accounts. They engage a practice of listing and itemizing (*item* is the key term employed), use a numeric system (roman numerals of account), and employ a summarizing of totals that differs from modern or later medieval notarial double-entry bookkeeping. The executors' desire to appraise and to value objects, to create currency equivalences, and then to retain or reuse the valued object also suggests the ways that wealth was rendered portable. Eudes's wealth moved not as coins in wallets or chests—indeed, he possessed precious little currency (as noted on the recto of Roll D)—but in the form of opulent fabrics, jewelry, and plate, objects with multifold affordances that facilitated their reuse and deployment in many different ways: as diplomatic gifts, as payments, as personal tokens, as useful objects in their own right, as memorials, or as salaries. As such, we can glimpse an Outremer mentality at work in the need to have wealth ready at hand in the form of silver plate, opulent clothing, and small gold rings, but also to understand its relative value, its worth in *bezants* and pounds *tournois*, or marks sterling. Indeed, the Account-Inventory is fluent in these currency equivalents even if it is not fluid with coinage. Scribes worked out each of those operations in the rolls and actively calculated values and currency exchanges in the given moment that they were recorded. Likewise, the scribes and executors noted the reckoned values of things in denominations used in the local setting of Acre but also in the still more familiar currencies used in France. It was, furthermore, easier and cheaper to give over objects of value than to exchange currencies and make payments in turn. Portable wealth characterized the mindset of those who traveled and lived in and out of Outremer.

Finally, the many portable objects listed carried personal memories and associations that gave them value and meaning in and beyond the Outremer context.[48] The scribes used staccato descriptive identifiers to note that specific pieces of cloth came from Troyes or Provins, or were a gift from the countess of Burgundy, most likely Eudes's stepmother, Beatrice of Champagne (1242–95).[49] Described through associations, French cloth had a different meaning, manufacture, and value in the East than in its native West. Similarly, Tartar and Bukharan cloth of eastern provenance communicated something different still when taken into the West than it did in Acre. Eastern cloth carried its Outremer quality with it, its fibers, designs, and labors.[50] All of these

48. See Lester, "What Remains." I have developed these ideas further in my forthcoming book, *Fragments of Devotion: Relics and Remembrance in the Aftermath of the Fourth Crusade, 1204–1261*.

49. See the appendix for the genealogy of Eudes's family. His mother, Yolande of Dreux, died in 1248, and his father, Hugh IV of Burgundy, remarried in 1258 to Beatrice of Champagne, sister of Thibaut V, count of Champagne, and II, king of Navarre. The counts of Champagne oversaw the international trade fairs of Troyes and Provins, which were also major centers of cloth production.

50. On the many meanings of eastern cloth, see Anne E. Lester, "Intimacy and Abundance: Textile Relics, the Veronica, and Christian Devotion in the Aftermath of the Fourth Crusade," in "Material Religion in the Crusading World," edited by William Purkis, special issue, *Material Religion* 14 (2018): 533–44; and Luyster, "Reassembling Textile Networks."

attributes gave cloth its material value, rendering it—like the rings of Le Puy, the chapel and cross relic, and the vernacular books in Eudes's estate—something more than its appraised value. As the texts show, many of Eudes's things required functional descriptions to set them apart and to identify each piece, each object, as distinct, holding a copious carrying capacity that encompassed the economic, emotional, and historical, all anchored to places, people, and moments in time. In this way, the rolls contain so much more than an account and an inventory.

2

Account-Inventory

Edition and Translation Rolls A–D

Statement on Transcription and Translation

Because language norms were not yet fixed in thirteenth-century French-language documents, particularly those created in Outremer, we have opted to privilege original orthography and word spacing when possible. Moreover, this is an edition of one manuscript only, that is, a single copy written on five rolls of parchment, not a critical edition of multiple manuscripts. We have therefore adopted the following norms to make the Old French more accessible and to aid in reader comprehension.

For the Old French Transcription

- We have used the following currency symbols: *d.* (*denier*), *lb* or *l.* (*livre*/pound), *s.* (*sous*) *t.* (*tournois*), b' (*bezant*), and q (*quarroble*). When these denominations are spelled out or partly spelled out in the document, we have noted this in the transcription and done the same. In the translation we have used the above standard abbreviations for currencies. Marks and sterling are almost never abbreviated.
- We have retained the raised punctus [·] as and when it appears throughout the rolls and in the Rutebeuf poems. The punctus serves multiple purposes in the Account-Inventory and in the poems that might be addressed by a range of modern punctuation, including bullet points, commas, semicolons, and other sigla. In this text, the raised punctus is often used to designate and/or separate successive items in a list or grouping, or stanza and clauses in the poetic texts.

- The Account-Inventory contains pilcrows or paragraph markers (F. *pied de mouche*), which we have indicated with the ¶ symbol throughout.
- We have transcribed all proper names (people and places) as in the document. For all that are known, we have given the standard English version in the translations (for example, Tyre for *Sur*).
- We have silently expanded all standard abbreviations (e.g., 9 = moins, & = et, 7 = et, p = per).
- Accounting and valuation in Old French was done in Roman numerals and using multiples of Roman numerals. We have transcribed these as they appear throughout the text, putting the multiples in superscript as they are on the parchment page. In every case, it should be noted, the scribes' math is impeccable. We could find no errors in the accounts.

For the Translation

- We have standardized all proper names, and in the case of those individuals who appear throughout the book, we have given more standard anglicized versions of names (Érard of Vallery rather than *Erart de Valeri*, and Étienne le Clerc rather than *Estiene le clerc*). For those individuals who appear only once or very rarely in the Account-Inventory, we have retained the Old French spellings.
- Throughout, we have translated *item* as "likewise."
- In some instances, we have chosen to add punctuation in English at the end of object phrases or at the end of logical groupings of object phrases to reflect meaningful line-endings or the flow of a clause. In the rolls the frequent use of punctus marks served to delineate such breaks.
- In the translation we have calculated all Roman numeral groupings and multiples and expressed them in Arabic numerals, as is standard in English (e.g., vii^{xx} we translate as 140).

Our goal is to represent the text as clearly as possible and not to impose outdated editorial norms once practiced for print-only versions, conventions that were standard when readers of those hard-copy versions rarely had recourse to document images. Because we now have ready access to the online images, our aim is to facilitate ease of reading for users, understanding that our interpretations can be queried by looking at the high-resolution images placed alongside our transcription online through the link to the DALME database:

https://dalme.org/collections/records/6d042eaa-b4ac-451f-ab70-923c83f1048a/1a

Given the size and quality of the rolls, we would argue that it is possible to reorder them or that they would have been wrapped and therefore carried in a different order from how they were originally edited and numbered in the archival collection. This does not change the meaning or substance of the text, but rather how the rolls relate to each other. We believe they would have been "nested," that is, rolled one inside the other beginning in the center with the

Figure 1. Paris, AN, series J 821, no. 1, Rolls A–D in order of size. Photo: A. E. Lester.

small, delicate and still very clean Roll C; then Roll D—also of a smaller width and cleaner parchment; then Roll B; and finally Roll A (figure 1). Roll A is the largest and presents on the outside—that is, the exposed side or the dorsal of the parchment—two clear cut marks where the ties to close and bind the rolls would have been inserted to secure all the rolls together.

Text Edition Account-Inventory of Eudes of Nevers

Roll A Front, Part 1	
¶ Cest la paie des genz le conte de Neverz feite par mon segnor Hugue dAugerant · et par mon segnor Joffroi de Sergignes qui i estoit por mon segnor Erart de Valeri · ce fu la veille de feste saint Lorant en lan · m · cc · lxvi · dou lais[1] que li cuens lor fist ·	This is the payment made to the Count of Nevers's men by my lord Hugh of Augerant, and by my lord Geoffrey of Sergines who was there for my lord Érard of Vallery. This was done on the eve of the feast of Saint Lawrence, in the year 1266, according to the instructions the count made for them.
—Cest la paie des Chevaliers	—This is the knights' pay

1. The term *lais* could be rendered many ways, as something spoken or recounted aloud, as a set of bequests or gifts (*legs*) or arrangements made in favor of specific people or institutions.

¶ A mon segnor Gaucher de Merri[2]· vi^{xx} b/[3] por xl *l. t.*[4]	To my lord Gaucher de Merry, 120 b/ for 40 *l. t.*
¶ A mon segnor Gui de Chantenai[5]· vi^{xx} b/ por xl *l. t.*	To my lord Gui de Chantenai, 120 b/ for 40 *l. t.*
¶ A mon segnor Hugue dAugerant[6] vi^{xx} b/ por xl *l. t.*	To my lord Hugh of Augerant, 120 b/ for 40 *l. t.*
¶ A mon segnor Copin· vi^{xx} b/ por xl *l. t.*	To my lord Copin, 120 b/ for 40 *l. t.*
¶ Item a mon segnor Guillaume le Chapelain xlv b/ por xv *l. t.*	The same to my lord Guillaume le Chapelain, 45 b/ for 15 *l. t.*
¶ A Estiene le Clerc · xv *l* tornois pors qui valent xlv b/[7]	To Étienne le Clerc, 15 *l. t.*, which are valued at 45 b/
[Left column]	[Left column]
—La paie des Escuyers	—The squires' pay
¶ A Odet le decannat · xxx b/ por x *l. t.*	To Odet le decannat, 30 b/ for 10 *l. t.*
¶ A Huguenin de Givri · xxx b/ por x *l. t.*	To Huguenin de Givri, 30 b/ for 10 *l. t.*
¶ A Berthelot · xxx b/ por x *l. t.*	To Berthelot, 30 b/ for 10 *l. t.*
¶ A Jehan de Saint-Jorge xxx b/ por x *l. t.* ·	To Jehan de Saint-Jorge, 30 b/ for 10 *l. t.*

There is no known surviving testamentary document for Eudes. It is possible then that the term *lais* here refers to oral instructions he made just before he died. According to the *Dictionnaire du Moyen Français* (*DMF*), *Lais; laxare; legs*: "Fait de céder une chose à titre gratuit par disposition testamentaire, ce qu'on laisse par un acte de dernière volonté à une personne ou à une collectivité autre que l'héritier désigné, legs": http://www.atilf.fr/dmf/definition/lais. "Lais" is also the term Rutebeuf uses for making one's will at the time of death. See below, Rutebeuf, "La complainte dou conte Hue de Nevers," v. 163.

2. Gaucher de Merry (from Merry-sur-Yonne; arr. Avalon; border of Champagne and Burgundy). He or one of his relatives is listed among the "barons and great knight of the king" during the reign of Philip III in 1304. See *RHGF*, 23:803. Gaucher is grouped with the Champenois knights along with "Le seignor de Vallery." We thank Xavier Hélary for this insight.

3. For the most part we do not expand abbreviations for currency denominations, but rather render them in italics. In cases when the scribe writes them out in full, we follow the manuscript. We have employed standard abbreviations throughout the English translation.

4. In some cases, as retained in the transcription, the scribes have written the partially abbreviated form, *tornois*. We use the abbreviation *t.* in the English translations for consistency.

5. Gui de Chantenai, or Chanteneio, also took part on the crusade of Aragon (1285). See Elisabeth Lalou, ed., *Les Comptes sur tablettes de cire de la chambre aux deniers de Philippe III le Hardi et Philippe IV le Bel (1282–1309)* (Paris: Boccard, 1994), 60. It may be that Chantenai is Chantenay-Saint-Imbert (Nievre, arr. Nevers).

6. Hugh of Augerant or Angeran, was a knight from Burgundy close to Count Eudes. After Eudes's death he was given lands at Noain as a gift for service from Robert of Flanders, the second husband of Yolande of Nevers. By 1274, he also held the lordship of Granges (near Magny-Cours) and lands at Chantenay, Livry, and Riousse near Langeron. For the reconstruction of the Angeran lineage from extant sources, see "Maison d'Angerant," Terres et Seigneurs en Donziais, July 4, 2021, http://www.terres-et-seigneurs-en-donziais.fr/wp-content/uploads/2021/07/dAngerant.pdf.

7. This phrase was added in a slightly different ink and hand.

¶ A Thierriaut · xxx b/ por x *l. t.*	To Thierriaut, 30 b/ for 10 *l. t.*
¶ A Perriau de Sissy · xxx b/ por x *l. t.*	To Perriau de Sissy, 30 b/ for 10 *l. t.*
¶ A Guilleminde Premeaus · xxx b/ por x *l. t.*	To Guillemin de Premeaus, 30 b/ for 10 *l. t.*
¶ A Girart · xxx b/ por x *l. t.* ·	To Girart, 30 b/ for 10 *l. t.*
—La paie des Serjanz—	—The servants' pay—
¶ A Auberi le Barbu · xxx b/ por x *l. t.*	To Auberi le Barbu, 30 b/ for 10 *l. t.*
¶ A Huet de la Chambre· xxx b/ por x *l. t.*	To Huet de la Chambre, 30 b/ for 10 *l. t.*
¶ A Robet · xxx b/ por x *l. t.*	To Robet, 30 b/ for 10 *l. t.*
¶ Au Boen home[8] xxx b/ por x *l. t.* ·	To Bonhomme, 30 b/ for 10 *l. t.*
¶ A Jehan de Mussy · xxx b/ por x *l. t.* ·	To Jehan de Mussy, 30 b/ for 10 *l. t.*
¶ A Chauvin · xxx b/ por x *l. t.* ·	To Chauvin, 30 b/ for 10 *l. t.*
¶ A Henri de Brabant xxx b/ por x *l. t.*	To Henri de Brabant, 30 b/ for 10 *l. t.*
¶ A Jehan de Bese xxx b/ por x *l. t.*	To Jehan de Bese, 30 b/ for 10 *l. t.*
¶ A Travers · xxx b/ por x *l. t.*	To Travers, 30 b/ for 10 *l. t.*
[Right column]	[Right column]
¶ La paie des garçons[9]·	Pay for the boys
¶ A Perrinet de la Chambre · xxx b/ por x *l. t.*	To Perrinet de la Chambre, 30 b/ for 10 *l. t.*
¶ A Tastepeire · xxx b/ por x *l. t.*	To Tastepeire, 30 b/ for 10 *l. t.*
¶ A Afetie · xxx b/ por x *l. t.*	To Afetie, 30 b/ for 10 *l. t.*
¶ A Milet · xv b/ por c *s. t.*	To Milet, 15 b/ for 100 *s. t.*
¶ A Huguenin Barillet· xv b/ por c *s. t.*	To Huguenin Barillet, 15 b/ for 100 *s. t.*
¶ A Char de Beuf · xv b/ por c *s. t.*	To Char de Beuf, 15 b/ for 100 *s. t.*
¶ A Gilet· xv b/ por c *s. t.*	To Gilet, 15 b/ for 100 *s. t.*
¶ A Henri de Diepe · xv b/ por c *s. t.*	To Henri de Diepe, 15 b/ for 100 *s. t.*
¶ A Luile · xv b/ por c *s. t.*	To Luile, 15 b/ for 100 *s. t.*
¶ A Renaut de la Chambre· xv b/ por c *s. t.*	To Renaut de la Chambre, 15 b/ for 100 *s. t.*
¶ A Martin · xv b/ por c *s. t.*	To Martin, 15 b/ for 100 *s. t.*
¶ A Perrinet dou For · xv b/ por c *s. t.*	To Perrinet dou For, 15 b/ for 100 *s. t.*
¶ Au Vallet la vicomtesse de Limoiges[10]· xv b/ por c *s. t.*	To the valet of the Vicomtesse of Limoges, 15 b/ for 100 *s. t.*
¶ A Jehan de Pangi · ix b/ por lx *s. t.*	To Jehan de Pangi, 9 b/ for 60 *s. t.*
¶ A Brohe ix b/ por lx *s. t.*	To Brohe, 9 b/ for 60 *s. t.*
¶ A Renaut · ix b/ por lx *s. t.*	To Renaut, 9 b/ for 60 *s. t.*
¶ A Bricande vi b/ por xl *s. t.*	To Bricande, 6 b/ for 40 *s. t.*
¶ A Brunet vi b/ por xl *s. t.* ·	To Brunet, 6 b/ for 40 *s. t.*
¶ Au Bocu[11] vi b/ por xl *s. t.*	To Bossu, 6 b/ for 40 *s. t.*

8. *Boen home* and several of the names that follow in this section are unusual. It is possible here that *Bonhomme* refers to his status as a reformed heretic, a *bonhomme* of Languedoc. We thank the first reader of the text for this suggestion. We thank Mark Pegg for his expertise and advice about this possibility.

9. We take this to be younger or lesser boys, boys of lesser status, who most likely served as pages in Eudes's household and may have been called upon to run errands and charged with similar household duties.

10. The Viscountess of Limoges was Eudes's sister.

11. Again, an unusual name. This could be translated to "the hunchback man" as a nickname or colloquial name.

¶ A Perrinet de Biaune[12] vi b/ por xl *s. t.*
¶ A Jannet le Flament · vi b/ por xl *s. t.*
¶ A Pillaut · vi b/ por xl *s. t.*
¶ A Jannet de Nichiz · ix b/ por lx *s. t.*
¶ A Jannet de Talan · vi b/ por xl *s. t.*
¶ A Huquenet de Tornuz vi b/ por xl *s. t.*
¶ A Estevenaut dou For vi b/ por xl *s. t.*
¶ A Jehannin de la Ferrae · vi b/ por xl *s. t.*
¶ A Henri le Picart vi b/ por xl *s. t.*
¶ A Martain vi b/ por xl *s. t.*
¶ A Huguenant vi b/ por xl *s. t.*
¶ A Jehan le Loherant vi b/ por xl *s. t.*
¶ Au Vallet qui fu a larcevesque de Sur[13] vi b/ por xl *s. t.*

cette somme xiiii^{cccc} ~~b/ saz Estiene le Clere~~ xlvi b/[14]

[Left column]
cest la paie des ostex · et des trecoples ·
¶ por lostel mon segnor Gaucher de Merri et mon segnor Guion de Chantenai por II mois vi b/ xvi quarrobles[15]
¶ por lostel mon segnor Hugue dAugerant iiii b/ · par ii mois ·
¶ por lostel mon segnor Copin · i · b/ et xvi quarrobles
¶ por lostel Odet de Menant et Hermenin Le Veaul · ii b/ et xx quarrobles ·
¶ Por lostel Guillemin de Premuraus · i · b/ et iii quarrobles
¶ Por lostel au mulez · ii · b/ · et por lostel Uguenin de Givri et Tierriet · i · b/ et xx quarrobles

To Perrinet de Biaune, 6 b/ for 40 *s. t.*
To Jannet le Flament, 6 b/ for 40 *s. t.*
To Pillaut, 6 b/ for 40 *s. t.*
To Jannet de Nichiz, 9 b/ for 60 *s. t.*
To Jannet de Talan, 6 b/ for 40 *s. t.*
To Huquenet de Tornuz, 6 b/ for 40 *s. t.*
To Estevenaut dou For, 6 b/ for 40 *s. t.*
To Jehannin de la Ferrae, 6 b/ for 40 *s. t.*
To Henri le Picart, 6 b/ for 40 *s. t.*
To Martain, 6 b/ for 40 *s. t.*
To Huguenaut, 6 b/ for 40 *s. t.*
To Jehan le Loherant, 6 b/ for 40 *s. t.*
To the valet who served the archbishop of Tyre, 6 b/ for 40 *s. t.*

The total 1,400 ~~b/ excluding Étienne le Clere~~ 46 b/

[Left column]
This is the payment for lodgings and for the light cavalrymen
For the lodging of my lord Gaucher de Merry and my lord Gui de Chantenai for 2 months 6 b/ 16 q
For the lodging of my lord Hugh of Augerant
4 b/ for 2 months
For the lodging of my lord Copin 1 b/ and 16 q
For the lodging of Odet de Menant and Hermenin Le Veaul 2 b/ and 20 q
For the lodging of Guillemin de Premeaus 1 b/ and 3 q
For the lodging of the mules 2 b/ and for the lodging of Huguenin de Givri and Tierriet 1 b/ and 20 q

12. This is probably the city of Beaune, in Burgundy.

13. The archbishop of Tyre until April 1266 was Gilles de Saumur, who had been a close confidant of Louis IX and who was in the West serving as a papal legate until his death, only four months before Eudes. See Pierre-Vincent Claverie, "De l'entourage royal à l'entourage pontifical: L'éxample méconnu de l'archevêque Gilles de Tyr (d. 1266)," in *À l'ombre du pouvoir: Les entourages princiers au moyen âge*, ed. Alain Marchandisse and Jean-Louis Kupper (Geneva: Droz, 2003), 57–76. Whether this is a payment to Gilles de Samur's valet or to that of his successor, John of Saint-Maxentius (1266–72), is not clear.

14. This phrase was added in a slightly different ink and hand.

15. *Quarrobles* is a term that is typically partially abbreviated to *qrrobl*. For clarity, we have chosen to expand it in the French and use the abbreviation q in English.

¶ por lostel Huet et Jehan de Mussy · i · b ix quarrobles
¶ Por lostel au Boen home et Chauvin i · b/ et xvi quarrobles ·
¶ Item por lostel as autres mulez ii b/ et demi ·
¶ Por · v · aubeletriers · C · v b/ por la paie de · ii mois ·
¶ Por les iiii trecoples · c · xvii · b/
¶ Por Jehan de Dyjon · xvii b/ et quart xiiii · quarrobles que len li devoit por les armeures le conte ·
¶ Por mon segnor Guillaume de la Tor lx b/
¶ Por mon segnor Guillaume Arnaut xl b/ ·
————————Ceste somme iii^{ccc} lxvi b/ fecte par le changeour[16] le lundi devant la feste saint Leu

---

¶ Item apres ceste somme de sus dite por le loier de lostel mon segnor Hervic de Chantenai · ix b/
¶ Por la tonbe le conte lx b/ · por lamendement des vii verz[17] qui furent vendu por ii roiez · xii · b/
¶ Por la paie feite a frere Estiene de Sissy · m · b/
¶ Por la paie feite au Bocu xvi^{c} b/[18] ·

/\/\/\/\/\/\/\/\ stitching /\/\/\/\/\/\/\/\/\

[Roll break][19]
[first 4 lines repeated]
¶ Item apres ceste somme de sus dite por le loier de lostel mon segnor Hervic de Chantenai ix · b/ ·

For the lodging of Huet and Jehan de Mussy 1 b/ 9 q
For the lodging of Bonhomme and Chauvin, 1 b/ and 16 q
Likewise, for the lodging of the other mules 2 b/ and a half
For 5 crossbowmen 105 b/ for 2 months' pay
For the 4 light cavalrymen 117 b/
For Jehan de Dijon 17 b/ and a quarter, 14 q that was owed to him for the count's armor.
For my lord William de la Tor 60 b/
For my lord William Arnaut 40 b/
————————The total payment of 366 b/ was made out by the changer on the Monday before the feast of Saint Leu.

Likewise, after the total stated above for the payment of the lodging of my lord Hervé de Chantenai 9 b/
For the count's tomb 60 b/. For the remittance from 7 green [fabrics] that were sold, for 2 striped [fabrics] 12 b/
For the pay made to brother Étienne de Sissy, 1,000 b/
For the pay made to Bossu 1,600 b/

/\/\/\/\/\/\/\/\ stitching \/\/\/\/\/\/\/\

[Roll break]
[first 4 lines repeated]
Likewise, after the total stated above for the payment of the lodging of my lord Hervé de Chantenai 9 b/

16. This was most likely a money changer, someone paid for changing currencies at a specific rate of exchange. Here the payments are made in *bezants*, but could have come from monies in *tournois*. If it is a changer it is possible that the salaries were paid in *bezants* from the 500 marks silver that Hugh, duke of Burgundy, sent to Eudes that would need to be changed into local currency.

17. *Verz* is a very difficult term. It could mean here either green cloth or vair, that is, fur used for trimming garments. Both green cloth and vair were given (or here sold) to retainers within households like Eudes's. It is possible that Eudes had on hand both vair and green cloth for precisely this purpose. We have rendered *verz* here as "green [cloth]" as it is listed with another cloth type, that is, striped cloth, and it makes most sense in this context as part of an object phrase or grouping.

18. These seem to be extraordinary payments and included the costs for the count's tomb as well as the large sums paid to Brother Étienne and to Bossu, each over one thousand bezants. It may be that these payments included outstanding debts that the count owed Étienne and Bossu, similar to the outstanding pay that Eudes owned Érard of Vallery mentioned below.

19. This second roll is stitched to the first roll. Here, however, the ink and hand shift slightly. It is possible we have a different scribe or that the quill was different. It appears that this is also the dorsal (hair) side of the second parchment roll that forms Roll A, and thus the writing surface

¶ Por la tonbe le conte lx b/ · por lamendement des vii verz · et des · ii roiez qui furent vendu a marchaenz · xii · b/[20]	For the count's tomb, 60 b/. For the remittance from 7 green and from 2 striped [fabrics] that were sold by the merchants, 12 b/
¶ Por la paie feite a frere Estiene de Sissy[21] · m · b/ · que le quens li devoit	For the pay made to Brother Étienne de Sissy, 1,000 b/ that the count owed him.
¶ Por la paie feite au Bocu xvi^{c} b/ que le quens le devoit	For the pay made to Bossu, 1,600 b/ that the count owed to him.
¶ Por mon segnor Erart de Valeri · viii^{ccc} xxxi b/ et demi · de sa paie	For my lord Érard of Vallery, 831 b/ and a half, from his pay.
¶ Por le temple · vii^{cc} · xlii b/ · v quarrobles ·	For the Temple, 742 b/ 5 q
———Somme de tot cest escrit · vi^{m} lxvi b/ · xvii quarrobles	—The total of all that is written above: 6,066 b/ 17 q
———Somme de recepte[22] · viii^{m} · viii^{ccc} · iiii^{xx} · ix b/ demi et vii quarrobles	—Sum from what has been received: 8,889 b/ and a half and 7 q
—Ancel meniere demore · ii^{m}· viii^{ccc} xxiii b/ · ii · quarrobles · en la main mon segnor Erart de Valeri et en la main mon segnor hughes dAugerant –de recepte et dautre part · iiii^{xx} *lb* · et · c · vi *s*. tornois.[23]	—In this way, there remains 2,823 b/ 2 q, in the hands of my lord Érard of Vallery and in the hands of my lord Hugh of Augerant,—from what has been received. and from the other part, [there is] 80 *lb* and 106 *s*. *t*.
Cest compes fu feiz landemain de feste sainte croiz en septembre an lan · m · cc · lxvi · au temple par devant le grant maistre et le tresorier dou Temple[24] · et de lor ^{autres} compaignons.	These accounts were made the day after the feast of the Holy Cross in September, in the year 1266, at the Temple, before the grand master and the treasurer of the Temple and their other companions.
¶ Item celui jor meisme · apres le compe desus dit · messier · Hugues dAugerant bailla	Likewise, on this same day, after the abovementioned accounting, my lord Hugh of Augerant paid back to

is slightly different. The rolls are stitched together with green silk thread, and the stitched area has covered the final four lines of the outer or first roll.

20. This repetition and expansion of the information about the two cloths helps to clarify the confusion of meaning in the first instance. Here, we interpret this to mean that the cloth was ordered (*mendement*) and sold "by" (*vendu a*) merchants. We consider that the tomb and cloths were to be used together.

21. Étienne de Sissy, Cissey, or Sissey was from Burgundy, or possibly from Sissy in the department of Aisne. He was marshal of the Temple from 1261 to 1262 and then took charge of the Templar province of Sicily-Apulia from 1270 until his death in 1272/73. See Jochen Burgtorf, *The Central Convent of Hospitallers and Templars: History, Organization, and Personnel (1099/1230–1310)* (Leiden: Brill, 2008), 659.

22. This refers to monies coming in, literally "having been received," that is, paying into the estate, as opposed to expenses, monies going out.

23. See below, Roll D, for the "other part."

24. The grand master of the Temple at this time was Thomas Béraud (master from 1256 to 1273); the Templar treasurer is more challenging to identify. This may have been one Bienvenu

au tresorier dou temple · ii^{m} · cc · et lviii b/ por parfeire la paie avec ceu quil aveint eu
de · iii^{m} · besanz que li quens lor devoit[25]
an cel meniere ne demora en la main mon segnor Erart et mon segnor Hugue · que v^{c} · et lxv b/ ·

¶ Item. Ce est ceu que messire Hugues dAugerant a paie puis le compe devant dit
¶ Por · i · corretier[26] qui porchaca lemprunst des · iii^{m} *l* tornois que li Opitauz[27] presta le conte
xxii b/ et quart et por · ii · autres qui firent vendre les dras et largent ii b/ ·[28]
¶ Por · i · ostel ou li blez estoit et ou la mainiee dou for gisoit qui avoit este obliez a conter dou loier de · v · mois viii · b/ ·
¶ Por · i · escrin achete por porter a Cytiaus · iii b/ demi
¶ Por lestole ~~de li chapelle~~ et le fenoul de la chapelle neuve · vi b/ demi
¶ Por mon segnor Erart de Valeri xvi b/ quil doit por · i · pot dargent[29]
—Somme de tot cest escrit · viii^{m} · iiii^{cccc} · viii b/ de choses paiees
—Somme de recepte viii^{m} · viii^{ccc} · iiii^{xx} xi b/ et demi et vii quarrobles · sanz les tornois
ancel meniere demore iiii^{cccc} · iiii^{xx} iii b/ et demi vii quarrobles en la main mon segnor Hugue dAugerant
et dautrepart por xxxiiii · mars et demi

the treasurer of the Temple 2,258 b/ to settle up
the payment along with what they already have [from his assets] on the 3,000 b/ that the count owed them. In this way there remained in the hands of my lord Érard and my lord Hugh only 565 b/

Likewise. This is what my lord Hugh of Augerant paid toward the abovementioned account:
For the agent who negotiated the loan of 3,000 *l. t.* that the Hospital lent to the count,
22 and one quarter b/; and for 2 others, who
had the cloth and the silver sold, 2 b/
For 1 lodging where the grain was kept and where the retinue's animals were stabled, which had been overlooked in the accounting, for the rent of 5 months, 8 b/
For 1 box purchased to carry to Cîteaux, 3 and one half b/
For the stole ~~of the chapel~~ and maniple of the new chapel
6 and one half b/.
For my lord Érard of Vallery, 16 b/ that he owed for 1 silver pot.
—The total of everything written, 8,408 b/ from items paid out.
—The sum of the receipts, 8,891 and one half b/, and 7 q without the tournois.
In this way, there remains 483 b/ and one half, 7 q in the hands of my lord Hugh of Augerant and from the other part, 34 and one half marks sterling

who was active with Thomas Béraud in 1262; see Burgtorf, *The Central Convent*, 500. The companions, we presume, are other Templar brothers in attendance.

25. See Roll D for the 742 *bezants* worth of goods purchased by the Temple and applied toward the count's debt.

26. This term covers several individuals, both the broker of the loan between the count and the Hospitallers and the merchants or traders who sold the count's cloth and silver.

27. That is, the Hospitallers, although it was the Hospital as an institution that lent the sum to the count.

28. We understand these to be agents who liquidated the assets that appear in Roll C. In other words, Hugh and Érard were not selling off the count's materials assets themselves but paid local middlemen to do so.

29. See Roll D for the sale of one silver pot for 16 *bezants*.

destellins et xxx *d.* estellins · ii^{cc} · iiii^{xx} · ix b/. —Somme de touz les besanz de demorance sor mon segnor Hughes dAugerant · vii^{cc} · lxxii b/ demi et dautrepart · iiii^{xx} · vii · *l. t.* xii^{den} moins[30] ·	and 30 *d.* sterling, [which amounts to] 289 b/. —The total of all the bezants remaining with my lord Hugh of Augerant, 772 and one half b/ and from the other part, 87 *l. t.* less 12 *d.*
[on the right] ces vii^{cc} lxxii b/ et demi bailla messire Hugues a mon segnor Erart de Valeri por la main mon segnor Joffoi de Sergignes le juenne ·	[on the right] These 772 and one half b/ were handed to my lord Hugh [intended] for my lord Érard of Vallery by way of my lord Geoffrey of Sergines the younger.
¶ Cest li despens des tornois ¶ Por le chenge[31] de · xxxix · *lb* xii *d.* moins *t.* que Robet due de sa remenance de son compe quil paia en estellins et en autre monoie · et de xii *l.* *t.* que Estienes li clers bailla · c · *s. t.* · ¶ Por despens feit puis la mort le conte par monsegnor Hugue dAugerant et Robet et lor mainiee · et por autres menues chose paiees hors de despens xxviii *lb* xii *d.* moins tornois ·	These are the expenditures in tournois. For the fee for 39 *lb* less 12 *d. t.* that Robet owed on the remainder of his loan that he paid in sterling and in other coin, and from the 12 *l. t.* that Étienne le Clerc paid back, 100 *s. t.* For the expenditures made since the death of the count by my lord Hugh of Augerant and Robet, and their retinue, and for the other small things purchased outside of these expenses, 28 *lb* less 12 *d. t.*
et est contez li despens mon segnor Hugue et la mainiee dela semeine de feste saint Michel jusques le diemanche · antel meniere · demore sor mon segnor Hugue de la recepte des tornois · Liiii *l. t.* ·	And these are included in the expenditures of my lord Hugh and the retinue, during the week of the feast of Saint Michael until Sunday, and in this way, what remains to my lord Hugh from the payments in tournois currency, 54 *l. t.*
Et ces Liiii *l. t.* messire Hugue ot por son passaige · por lui et por Robet et la mainiee quil avoit retenue Cilz compes fu feiz le jor de feste saint Michel en lan · m · cclxvi et des tornois d[32] et des besanz desus diz	And these 54 *l. t.* my lord Hugh had for his passage, for himself and for Robet, and the retinue he had engaged. These accounts were made on the feast day of Saint Michael in the year 1266, and from the tournois and the bezants mentioned above.
¶ apres ce compe il fu paie por lespicier qui acira le cuer · le conte · por [un]guelient[33] et por choses quil [i] m[i]st et por sa peine vi b/	Following this account, it was paid, for the spicer who recuperated the heart of the count, for embalming, and for the things he put in there, and for his pains, 6 b/

30. On the rolls, the sign used here looks like a "9" and means "moins" in Old French, translated as "less" in English. We have silently expanded this in the Old French edition, but note it here for clarity.

31. This is a fee or charge for changing money. The loans were negotiated in several currencies, and this 100 *s. t.* was the fee for converting them.

32. We read this marking as a "d" and as a scribal error with no clear meaning.

33. Chazaud reads this as "[e]mgueliet," but the manuscript is unclear here and may read "oigneliet," from "oignement," or "unguelie[n]t" meaning "onction" or "onguent," that is, perfume or ointment, or to cover with spiced grease, *ongient*, and balsam, as per the *DMF*, http://www.atilf.fr/dmf/definition/oignement; see "unguere." With thanks to Stephanie J. Lahey (@SJLahey) for her

—Somme de touz les besanz de cest escrit paiez sans la paie dou temple · et dou Bocu · et de frere Estiene de Sissy · et de mon segnor Erart de Valeri · xix^{c} · xli b/ ~~vi^{e}~~ qui valent vi^{c} xlvii *l. t.* ·	—The total of all the bezants of this written receipt, not including the pay for the Temple, and for Bossu, and for Brother Étienne de Sissy, and my lord Érard of Vallery, 1,941 b/, ~~600~~ which is worth 647 *l. t.*
¶ Item. Cest la paie des chivalers · ¶ A mon segnor Renaut de Precegni · iii^{ccc} · lxxv *l* t[or]nois · et li est abatuz li quarz de lannee ¶ A mon segnor Robet de Juenesses[34] · ii^{cc} xxxv *lb* · ¶ A mon segnor Hugue daugerant de vii^{xx} · x *lb* que li cuens li devoit si comme il disoit et que la gent le conte le savoient bien · len li paia vi^{xx} · x *l. t.* · et le bailla len le henap a pierres que len cuidoit quil fust dor · por xxv *lb · t.*	Likewise, this is the pay of the knights. To my lord Reynaud of Précigné 375 *l. t.* and the quarter of the year has not been paid to him. To my lord Robert of Juennesses, 235 *lb* To my lord Hugh of Augerant, for 150 *lb* that the count owed him, just as he said, and that the count's people knew well. Of this he was paid 130 *l. t.* and the rest was paid to him with the goblet with stones that is believed to be made of gold valued at 25 *l. t.*

Roll A Front, Part 2 (rotated)

¶ Cest la recepte des choses le conte de Neverz quil avoit au jor quil ala de vie amort	This is the receipt for the things of the count of Nevers, that he had on the day he went from life to death.
¶ De la remenance dou compe Estiene le Clerc demora · xv *lb* · ii *s.* moins *t.* · quil bailla en la main mon segnor Hugue dAugerant · et a ce compe fu messire Joffroiz de Sergignes li juennes por monsegnor Erart de Valeri · et fu la veille de feste saint Lorant en lan · m · cc · lxvi · Item il demora · xii *lb* de tornois dautrepart de resus · que Estienes li clercs bailla · et xv *s.* iii *d.* de reaus[35] ·	From the remainder of the account of Étienne le Clerc there remained 15 *lb* less 2 *s. t.* that he gave into the hand of my lord Hugh of Augerant, and for this account it was my lord Geoffrey of Sergines the younger [who stood in] for my lord Érard of Vallery, and this was done on the eve of the feast of Saint Lawrence in the year 1266. Likewise, there remained 12 *l. t.* from elsewhere, from the receipts that Étienne le Clerc paid and 15 *s.* 3 *d.* of the realm.

reading: "? or maybe unguelie(n)t (= perfume, ointment), if the long, thin tittle from the /i/ is actually a suspension mark. 🤔," Twitter, October 28, 2021, 10:50 a.m., https://twitter.com/SJLahey/status/1453735981224366080.

34. The orthography here is difficult. This could be Robert de Juigentes. Riley-Smith reads this as "Juennesses." We have reproduced what we believe is on the parchment role.

35. We take "*de reaus*" here to mean "the money of the king, or the realm," therefore referring to the currencies minted by a succession of western rulers in Outremer throughout the thirteenth century. In 1266, this could be the king of France or the Latin king of Jerusalem. Here the idea is French or Latin "money of the realm," distinct from *bezants* and from currency *tournois*. A similar term, *réaux* (from the Latin *regales*), was used in fourteenth-century southern France; see Kathryn L. Reyerson and Debra A. Salata, eds, *Medieval Notaries and Their Acts: The 1327–1328*

¶ Item de la remenance dou compe Robet demora · iii^{m} · vii^{cc} ~~xviii~~ xvi b/ · et xxxviii *lb* xix *s.* tornois · et xiii *s.* de reaus —Somme de tornois · lxv · *lb* xvii *s.*· et xxviii · *s.* iii *d.* reaus qui valent · i b/ · et x quarrobles · —Somme de touz les besanz · iii^{m} · vii^{cc} · xviii b/ · x quarrobles ·	Likewise, from the remainder of the account of Robet there remained 3,7~~18~~16 b/ and 38 *lb.* 19 *s. t.* and 13 *s.* of the realm. —The total in tournois: 65 *lb*, 17 *s.*, and 28 *s.* 3 *d.* of the realm, which are valued at 1 b/ and 10 q. —The sum of all the bezants, 3,718 b/ [and] 10 q.
¶ Item La recepte des choses le conte vendues · v^{m} c · lxxi b/ ix quarrobles · et xix *lb* ix *s.* tornois. · dont li compes fu feiz lan demain de feste sainte croiz en septembre —Somme de touz les besanz · viii^{m} · viii^{ccc} · iiii^{xx} · ix b/ demi vii · quarrobles —Somme des tornois · iiii^{xx} · *lb* · c · vi *s.* tornois ·	Likewise, the receipt for the count's things [that were] sold 5,171 b/ 9 q. and 19 *lb* 9 *s. t.* for which the accounts were made the day after the feast of the Holy Cross in September. —The total of all the bezants, 8,889 b/ and one half, 7 q. —The total of the tournois 80 *lb* 106 *s. t.*
¶ Item puis ceste somme · por iiii · cuillers dargent vendues · ii b/ · et vi b/ por le drap de remenant des espervers et xxxiii *s. t.* por xi eniaus dou Pui · Ancel meniere est la somme · viii^{m} · viii^{ccc} · iiii^{xx} · xvii b/ demi · et vii · quarrobles · et de tornois · iiii^{xx} · vii *lb* xii *d.* moins.— —Somme que li viii^{m} · et · viii^{ccc} · et iiii^{xx} · xvii b/ demi valent a tornois · ii^{m} · ix^{c} · lxv · *lb* · xvi *s.* viii *d.* a vi *s.* · viii *d.* le besant prisie	Likewise, in addition to this total, for 4 silver spoons sold, 2 b/ and 6 b/ for the remnant of cloth for the coverlet, and 33 *s. t.* for 11 rings from Puy. In this way the total is 8,897 b/ and one half, and 7 q. and from the tournois 87 *lb* less 12 *d.* —The total, therefore, 8,897 and one half b/, is worth, in tournois currency, 2,965 *lb*, 16 *s.* 8 *d.* at a rate of 6 *s.* 8 *d.* per bezant.
[Right column] ¶ Item Il fu aporte de borgoingne · v^{c} · mars destellins que li dux de Borgoingne envoia · le conte par le temple au passaige daoust qui valoient au jour de lors en Acre · m · iii^{ccc} · iiii^{xx} · vii *lb* · x *s.* ~~. . . d~~ tornois.	[Right column] Likewise, 500 marks sterling were delivered from Burgundy, which the Duke of Burgundy sent to the count by way of the Temple, in the August passage, which were worth, on that day in Acre, 1,387 *lb* 10 *s.* ~~. . . d~~ *t.*

Register of Jean Holanie (Kalamazoo: Medieval Institute Publications, 2004), 104. For more information on Outremer coinage, see Alan M. Stahl, "The *Denier* Outremer," in *The French of Outremer: Communities and Communications in the Crusading Mediterranean*, ed. Laura K. Morreale and Nicholas L. Paul (New York: Fordham University Press, 2018), 30–43.

——Somme de totes ces choses desus dites a la vaillance de tornois mises est · iiii^{m} · iiii^{cccc} · xl · *lb* · et v *s.*· et viii *d. t.* · de recepte par la main mon segnor Erart de Valeri et mon segnor Hugue dAugerant

——The total receipts of all these things mentioned above, at the given rate of tournois, is 4,440 *lb* and 5 *s.* and 8 *d. t.*, received in the hands of my lord Érard of Vallery and my lord Hugh of Augerant.

—De ceu fu paié · au Temple · iii^{m} · b/ qui valent · m · *l. t.* ·

——From this, were paid to the Temple, 3,000 b/ that are worth 1,000 *l. t.*

¶ Au Bocu · et a frere Estienne de Sissy · ii^{m} · vi^{c} · b/ · qui valent · viii^{ccc} · lxvi *lb* · et xiii *s.* iiii *d. t.*

¶ Et por le lais que li quens fist a ses genz qui sen alerent por lor passaige et por sejanz et aubeletriers paiez · et por loier dostex · xix^{c} · b/ et xli b/ · qui valent · vi^{c} · xlvii *l. t.*

To Bossu, and to Brother Étienne de Sissy, 2,600 b/ that is worth 866 *lb* and 13 *s.* 4 *d. t.*

And for the bequests that the count made to his men who went along, for their passage [to the East], and pay for the servants and the crossbowmen, and the costs for their lodging, 1,900 b/ and 41 b/ that are worth 647 *l. t.*

¶ Et por le despens por mon segnor Hugues dAugerant et Robet et dont les parties sont en cest escrit lor mainiee tant com il furent en Acre · et por deniers que len paia de choses obliees et dautres choses · · xxviii · *lb* xii *d.* moins *t.* · et liiii · *l. t.* que messire Hugues prist por son passaige et por sa mainiee ·

And for the expenditures for my lord Hugh of Augerant and Robet (of which both parties are in this list) and the retinue, just as it was in Acre, and for the deniers that they paid for things that have been forgotten, and other things, 28 *lb* less 12 *d. t.* and 54 *l. t.*, that my lord Hugh took for his own passage and that of his retinue.

¶ Item por la paie mon segnor Renaut de Precegni · et mon segnor Robert de Juennesses · et por mon segnor Hugon dAugerant · vii^{cc} · xl · *l. t.*

——Somme de totes ces choses paiees · monte · iii^{m} · iii^{ccc} · xxxv *lb* · xii *s.* iiii *d.* · *t.*

Ancel meniere demore de la recepte desus dite · xl · iiii *lb* · xiii · *s.* iiii *d. t.* · les quelx messire Erarz de Valeri prist de sa paie de ceu que li quens li devoit cest asavoir · por les iii · parz de lannee[36] · xi^{c} · xxv *lb* et por iiii · chevax · que mortz que afolez · iiii^{cccc} · et l · *lb* · somme por tot · m · v^{c} · lxxv *l. t.* que len li devoit

Likewise, for the pay of my lord Reynaud of Précigné and my lord Robert of Juennesses, and for my lord Hugh of Augerant, 740 *l. t.*

——The total of all these things paid comes to 3,335 *lb* 12 *s.* 4 *d. t.*

In this way, there remains from the receipt mentioned above, 44 *lb* 13 *s.* 4 *d. t.* that my lord Érard of Vallery took for his pay from what the count owed him; it should be reckoned for the three quarters of the year 1,125 *lb*, and for 4 horses, which either died or were injured, 450 *lb*, for a total sum of 1,575 *l. t.* that he [the count] owed to him

36. The knights were paid for each quarter of the year. Thus, here Érard is paid for the first three quarters of 1266, January through the end of August.

et dautrepart il demora enla main mon segnor Erart choses qui ne porent estre vendues ainz que messire Hugues dAugerant sen alast · et furent prisiees · ii^{cc} · vi *lb* xiii *s.* iiii *d. t.*
Ancel meniere fu paiez mesire Erarz de sa deite jusqua la demorance de · ii^{cc} · et lxiii · *lb* · et xiii *s.* iiii *d.* · *t.* quil ot ancor a recevoir de sa paie
Cilz compes fu feiz le jueudi apres feste saint Remi en lan · m · cc · lxvi · en Acre · par mon segnor Erart de Valeri · et mon segnor Hugon dAugeran ·
et mon segnor Joffroi de Sergignes le juenne ·—

and additionally, there remained in the hand of my lord Érard, things that could not be sold before my lord Hugh of Augerant departed, and they were appraised at 206 *lb* 13 *s.* 4 *d. t.*
In this way, my lord Érard was paid from his due while he remained [until his departure] 263 *lb* and 13 *s.* 4 *d. t.* that he had yet to receive from his pay.
These accounts were made the Thursday after the feast of Saint Remy in the year 1266, in Acre, by my lord Érard of Vallery, and my lord Hugh of Augerant, and my lord Geoffrey of Sergines the younger.

Et ce sunt les choses qui demorerent mon segnor Erart de Valeri prisiees · por les · ii^{cc} · vi *lb* · et xiii *s.* iiii *d. t.* desus diz ·
¶ Premierement · i · chapel · dor a pierres et a perles · en pris de · iiii^{xx} · *l* tornois ·
¶ Apres li garnement de la chapelle nueve que li quens avoit feite por · vii^{xx} · x b/
¶ Li ~~du~~ dui esprevier · lx · b/ · Li dui tapi nuef · xx b/ · et · ix dras de tartais por xl · b/ · et · i · drap qui i estoit dor en fu percez sor le cuer le conte[37] ·
¶ Item Une tante · pro · xli b/ · li dui grant romanz et li chaunconniers pro · xxxi b/
ce fu li romanz des Loheranz[38] · et li romanz de la terre doutremer · et li chaunconns ·

And these are the things that will remain [with] my lord Érard of Vallery, appraised for the 206 *lb* and 13 *s.* 4 *d. t.* mentioned above:
First, 1 gold chapel made with stones and pearls valued at 80 *l. t.*
Next, the decoration for the new chapel that the count had made [appraised] for 150 b/
The ~~of~~ two coverlets, 40 b/. The two new cloth hangings, 20 b/; and the 9 Tartar cloths for 40 b/ and the cloth that was made of gold, and was threaded through/around the count's heart.
Likewise, one tent for 41 b/. The two large romances and the chansonnier for 31 b/
These were the romance of Lorrains and the romance of the Lands of Outremer, and the song book.

37. The precise meaning of the phrase "*drap qui i estoit dor en fu percez sor le cuer le conte*" is not clear. Because the nominal construction "*drap. . dor*" or cloth of gold is used, we take this to be a piece of gold cloth, perhaps one of the nine pieces of Tartar cloth (*dras de tartais*), which was often woven with gold thread (see the short essay by Sharon Farmer, below). This may refer to a piece of cloth that was either pierced or threaded through the count's heart or wrapped or threaded around (*sor*) his heart. For a similar reference, see Marie de France's *lai Laustic*, which ends with the *rossignol*, that is, the dead nightingale, wrapped in gold-embroidered cloth and placed in a *coffret*, much as Eudes's heart was wrapped in cloth, placed into a box or *escrin* (a term also used to describe a box or container for relics), and sent to the Cistercian abbey of Cîteaux in Burgundy. For an English translation of *Laustic*, see Judy Shoaf's, available from her University of Florida web site, https://people.clas.ufl.edu/jshoaf/files/laustic.pdf. We thank Anne Latowsky for this reference and for consulting on the translation and interpretation of this phrase.

38. This was a cycle of *chansons de geste* that included Hervis de Metz, Garin le Loherain, Gerbert de Metz, Anseïs de Gascogne (Anseïs de Metz), Yon ou la Vengeance Fromondin, and

—-Somme de cest choses prisiees a besanz · iii^{ccc} · iiii^{xx} · ii b/ · qui valent vi^{xx} · vi *lb* xiii *s.* iiii *d. t.*	—The total of these things, appraised in bezants: 382 b/, which is worth 126 *lb* 13 *s.* 4 *d. t.*
Ancel meniere est la somme avec le chapel conte · ii^{cc} · vi *lb* · xiii *s.* iiii *d. t.* ·	In this way, the total with the chapel comes to 206 *lb* 13 *s.* 4 *d. t.*

Roll A Back—would be the "cover" or outer side of the roll. This is the shelf mark.[39]

Ce sont li escrit des choses = [cut marks] **le conte de nevers apres son deces**[40] [Later hand (18c?): Etat de la Maison de Ed de Nevers et des Gages[41] d'icelle.]	These are the records of the things of the Count of Nevers after his death [Later hand: Estate of the House of Eudes of Nevers and the Wages of the Same]
~~Lueranz[42] areceu · iii^{ccc} xxx b/ · dont il a a conter ·~~ ~~¶ Len doit Jehan de Dyion~~ vi b/ et demi ~~xvii b/ et demi et ii quarrobles · por armeures ·~~[43]	~~Lueranz received 330~~ b/ ~~for which there is an account~~ ~~Jehan de Dijon is due~~ 6 b/ and one half ~~17 b/ and one half, and 2 q for armor.~~
[Later hand, marginal note, along the right side: 1~~3~~266 Compte des biens du Conte de Nevers apres son deceus]	[Later hand, marginal note, along the right side: 1~~3~~266 Account of the goods of the Count of Nevers after his death.]
¶ Len deit la paie de · iii mois a Salemon de Safforit et a Lionnet de Tabarie[44] de iii · et a Homede de · iii · et a Jehan le Porer de iii · ¶ Il devoit au temple C mars destellins et [*illegible:* vii mars moins quet]	3 months of pay was owed to Salemon de Safforit and 3 to Lionnet de Tabarie and 3 to Homede and 3 to Jehan le Porer. He owed 100 marks sterling to the Temple and [*illegible:* 7 marks less . . .]

Yonnet de Metz. See Laurent Brun, "Le cycle des Lorrains," ARLIMA: Archives de littérature du moyen âge, December 12, 2023, https://www.arlima.net/ad/cycle_des_lorrains.html. Several of these chansons were copied into Paris, BnF, MS fr. 1622.

39. It is also clear that this is the outer, dorsal, or hair-side of the parchment. This piece by far is the coarsest and thickest. In contrast Rolls B and C seem to be made of finer vellum.

40. It is this line or phrase that would have appeared on the outer side of the roll when tightly rolled together. This is where the two cut or slash marks appear where the roll would have been tied.

41. Refers to the wages the count paid his knights and servants.

42. Chazaud has "Renauz a receu lxii xxx besants."

43. The entries here include both cancelled debts that appear in overstrike and deleted amounts that are also struck through. The parchment also bears signs of being rubbed out, or erased, in some places and overwritten.

44. We believe these two names to be toponyms from local towns or regions in Syria. See the essay below by Jonathan Rubin.

¶ Item cest cue qui nest paie ancor de la daite le conte quil devoit en lan susdit au jor dou compe fait landemain de feste sainte croix en Septembre
[8 lines, cancelled and partly illegible]
~~¶ a mon segnor erart de valeri . . . l . . . l~~ tornois ~~est abatiz li quarz de lannee~~
~~¶ a mon segnor renault de precigni · iii^{ccc} lxxv *l* tornois · et est abatuz li quarz de lannee~~
~~¶ a mon segnor robet de jeneces · ii^{cc} xxxv *lb* · xiii *s.* viii *d.* moins~~
~~¶ a mon segnor hugue daugerant vii^{xx} · xv *lb* · dit lor xxv *lb* pour le henap a pierres a cel meniere . . . li deit . . . lens que vi^{xx} · x *lb*~~
~~¶ a mon segnor erart de valeri · xl · et xxv lb et est abatuz li quarz de lannee~~
~~et dautrepart iiii^{ccc} L *lb* por ses chevax morz · por mon segnor erart~~
~~m · v^{c} lxxv *lb lb*~~

Likewise, this is what was not yet paid by the said count that he owed in the abovementioned year,
from the account made on the day after the feast of the Holy Cross in September
[8 lines, cancelled and partly illegible]
~~To my lord Érard of Vallery . . . *l* . . . *l. t.* and not including the last quarter of the year~~
~~To my lord Reynaud of Précigné 375 *l. t.* and not including the last quarter of the year.~~
~~To my lord Robert of Juenesse, 235 *lb* 13 *s.* 8 *d.* less~~
~~To my lord Hugh of Augerant 155 *lb* said to be of gold 25 *lb* for the goblet set with stones in this way . . .. of the due there is only 130 *lb*~~
~~To my lord Érard of Vallery; 40 and 25 *lb* and not including the last quarter of the year and in addition, 450 *lb* for his dead horses for my Lord Érard 1,575 *lb lb*~~

/\/\/\/\/\/\/ stitching \/\/\/\/\/\/\/\/\

[Bottom section of dorsal side of the second parchment, below the stitching]
¶ Cest la paie des chevaliers le conte qui estoient de manaige feite des v^{c} · mars destellins que li dux envoia
¶ Por mon segnor Robet de Juenneces · cui len devoit ii^{cc} · xxxv *l. t.* · et xv *s.* ii *d.* · de sa paie jusquez aujor que le cuens ala de vie amort
· iiii^{xx} · iiii mars et xxii *d.* estellins

¶ Por la paie mon segnor Renaut de Precegni · cui len devoit ·iii^{ccc} · lxxv *l. t.* le quart de lannee abatu · C · xxxiiii · mars · et xii *s.* · ii *d.* estellins ·
¶ Por la paie mon segnor Hugon dAugerant cui len devoit · vii^{xx} xv *lb*
le quart de lannee ausit abatu xlvi mars xi *s.* ix *d.* estelllins qui valent vi^{xx} · x *l. t.*
et li fu baillie por xxv *lb* le henap dargent dore · a pierres et a esmaus que len couda quil fust dor

/\/\/\/\/\/\/ stitching \/\/\/\/\/\/\/\/\

[Bottom section of dorsal side of the second parchment, below the stitching]
This is the pay for the count's knights who were in the retinue, made from the 500 marks sterling that the duke sent.
For my lord Robert of Juennesses, to whom was owed 235 *l. t.* and 15 *s.* 2 *d.* for his pay until the day that the count went from life to death;
84 marks and 22 *d.* sterling.

For the pay of Reynaud of Précigné who is owed 375 *l. t.*, the last quarter of the year not being paid, 134 marks and 12 *s.* 22 *d.* sterling.
For the pay of my lord Hugh of Augerant, who is owed 155 *lb*,
the last quarter of the year also not being paid, 46 marks 11 *s.* 9 *d.* sterling, which is valued at 130 *l. t.*
and he was paid for the remaining 25 *lb* [with] the silver gilt goblet, set with stones and enamels, which was believed to have been made of gold.

¶ A mon segnor Erart de Valeri · ii^{cc} · mars · por · v^{c} · lv *l. t.* sor sa paie que len li devoit que montoit · m· v^{c} · lxxv *l. t.* ~~delanee~~ por les · iii · parz de lannee · et por ses chevax morz	To my lord Érard of Vallery, 200 marks for 555 *l. t.* on his pay that he is owed, which goes up to 1,575 *l. t.* ~~for the year~~ for the three parts of the year and for his dead horses.
——Somme de la paie feite des estellins · iiii^{cccc} · lxvi mars · ancel meniere demore · xxxiiii mars des v^{c} mars · et par dessus · demi-marc et xxx *d.* estellins qui fu trovee plus au pois dAcre—	——The total of the payments made in sterling, 466 marks. In this way there remains 34 marks from the 500 marks and from the above half mark and 30 *d.* sterling, which was found to be more in the measure of Acre—
[BLANK SPACE] ¶ Ce sont les choses q[45]	[BLANK SPACE] These are the things that

Roll B Front

¶ Ce sont les chose lou conte de Neverz quil avoit au jor quil ala de vie amort[46]	These are the things of the Count of Nevers that he had the day he went from life to death.
Ces choses estoient en lamain Robet et · cest a savoir premierement · viii boens eniaus · et · ii · saffirs et · i camahe · et xii · petiz eniaus dou Pui · ii · croisetes dor · une viez corroie dor a pelles[47] · et i chapel dor a pierres et a pelles · de rechief une corroie dor · ii bacins dargent a doner laigue · i henap dargent a pierres et a emaus · que len cuidoit quil fust dor · Une cope dargent ^{doree} cuvesclee · ii · poz dargent · ii · petis henas · dargent a doner daiguee · i · orfroi a perles · et · ii · sanz perles · et iiii · cuillers dargent ·	These things were in the hand of Robet; and let it be known: first, 8 good rings and 2 sapphires, and 1 cameo, and 12 small rings from Puy, 2 small crosses of gold, one old belt of gold with pearls, and 1 chapel of gold set with stones and pearls, and another belt of gold, 2 basins of silver to serve water, 1 goblet of silver set with stones and enamels, which was believed to be of gold. One cup of silver ^{gilded} with a covering, 2 pots of silver, 2 small goblets of silver to serve water, 1 gold-work plate with pearls, and 2 without pearls, and 4 silver spoons.
¶ Par la main Odet le decannat · i · aiguier dor · et une cope cuvesclee dor · ii · bacins dargent	By the hand of Odet le decannat 1 pitcher of gold and one cup with a cover of gold; 2 silver basins,

45. It appears that an inventory was begun on the back of Roll A toward the bottom of the parchment, but then broken off mid word, seemingly in favor of beginning on a new sheet of parchment.

46. In the rolls the phase *a mort* is often contracted as *amort*. This echoes Rutebeuf's use of the term *L'amors*, or *amors*, which is the word that begins his "Complainte" for Eudes.

47. We note the spelling changes in this section between "pelles" and "perles." We follow the *DMF*, which corrects "pelles" to "perles," with multiple attestations.

i · pot dargent · i · aiguier dargent · xvii · henas · dargent sanz pie	1 silver pot, 1 silver pitcher, 17 silver goblets without feet.
¶ Item par la main Afetie · xl · escuelles dargent · et xii cuilliers dargent · ¶ Item · i · texu dargent dore que Gararz livra qui estoit en larmeure[48] · ¶ Item par la main Robet · La toile[49] qui fu achetee a Troies que Simons Ysanbarz acheta, don il iot x pieces · x · pieces de toile de la toile la duchoise de Borgoingne · xxxvii · aunes de toile en i remenant et xxv aunes en · ii · autres remenanz · vii · paire de dras de lit nues · et · viii paire de dras linges avestir nues · xxxiiii · granz napes ovrees[50] a mangier nueves · et viii · xii^{nes}[51] de petites toailles amains ·	Likewise, by the hand of Afetie, 40 silver saucers and 12 silver spoons. Likewise, 1 gilded silver box that Gararz carries, which was in the armory. Likewise, by the hand of Robet. The linen cloth that was purchased in Troyes, which Simon Ysanbars bought, of which there are 10 pieces; 10 pieces of linen cloth, from the linen cloth of the duchesses of Burgundy, 37 ells of linen cloth, and 1 remaining piece and 25 ells and 2 other remaining pieces, 7 pairs of new bed linens, and 8 pairs of new dressing linens; 34 large, embroidered tablecloths for dining, new; and 8 dozen small hand towels.
¶ De rechief · xxxvi granz napes nueuves que Afetiez livra · et vi toailles amains nueves · et xxiiii napes viez Item · xxix · cuevrechies · x · paire de petiz ganz · et · iii paire de ganz de cerf sangles v · coutiaus · atrencher · vi paire de chauces · nueves · unes hueses nueves · et iiii · paire de sollers ·	In addition, 36 large new cloths that Afetie delivered, and 6 new hand towels, and 24 old cloths; Likewise, 29 head coverings; 10 pairs of small gloves, and 3 pairs of deerskin gloves, 5 short knives, 6 pairs of leg protectors, new; one set of leggings, new; and 4 pairs of shoes.
¶ Item · x · verz et une tireteinne cameline[52] · et ii raiez de Provins a maingniee · et ii remenanz dun autre raie · xv · aunes de saie noire · xiiii · pannes[53] de grosvair et une de menuvair ·	Likewise, 10 green, one camelin tiretaine and 2 hand-worked striped cloths from Provins and 2 remaining from another striped one, 15 ells of black serge, 14 furs of grosvair, and one of miniver,

48. Given the context, this could be a silver gilded box. The term *texu* is a bit unusual, but was not uncommon as a way of referring to boxes used to carry or store relics and other precious objects. The phrase "en larmeure" is a bit unclear. This could refer to the box coming from the armory or could characterize armorials or heraldic sigils depicted or adhered to the box, as was the case for example, with the coffret of John of Montmirail (fig. 26).

49. *Toile* is specifically linen cloth often made in Troyes. See the essay by Sharon Farmer.

50. In the cases of orthographic ambivalence between *u* and *v* we have employed the modern version with the *v* for clarity.

51. This is an abbreviation for the word *douzaine*, which translates into English as a dozen.

52. "Camelin tiretaine" is a very specific weave of cloth using a linen-wool blend. We believe in this case that "camelin" references the type of wool used. On both *camelin* and *tiretaine* cloth, see the essay below by Sharon Farmer.

53. We thank Barbara Boehm and Élisabeth Delahaye for their consultation and advice about this term. Here we take *panne* to mean either "textiles" or pieces of "fur." Probably these were pieces of *grosvair*, that is grey vair or fur (made from untrimmed squirrel) and *menuvair*, or miniver, that is, white fur (made from trimmed squirrel), which were often given as gifts of livery

· xiiii · dras de tartais · ii chameloz · iii boqueranz plains et i ovre · ii · tapiz nuef ovrez[54] ·
· ii · espreviers · a meitre sor lit · i · quarre et i · reont · et · i drap qui remest de lesprevier ·
· iiii paire desperons nueus · iiii quarriaus de soie · ii · sifles · i bacin arere · ii · coilles de bievre · une langue de serpent · une fiolete de baume · celle fu mise au euvre[55] ·
Item · une coute pointe de cendel[56] vermoill · et · i · ceurcot noir ·
¶ Item · cest de larmeure · ii · paires de cuiraces nueves · viii frains nues · et i mors de frain
viii · paire desperons nues · xi varengles nueuves · iiii cotes a armes et iii banneres ·
· ii · coutiaus · et iiii fers de glaive · ii · fracoires[57] nueves · ii · testieres a cheval et · i · piciere ·
et une paire de cuissiaus et de trumelieres de fer · i bacinnet a gorgiere de fer · i · ganbaison
unes couvertures blanches · i · petit ganbaison sanz manches · ii piaus blanches · une paire de coffres ·
une grant gorgiere de fer · une male de cur et ii · paire de bouges · i bahu et · i bast
et de la chambre · iiii paire de coffres · et ii · cofiniaus a chandoile · iiii males · et iiii bahuz
et iiii · baz · et de la peneterie · ii · males · i · bahu · et i bast ·

14 Tartar cloths, 2 camel-hair, 3 unadorned Boukhara fabrics, and 1 worked; 2 new quilted hanging cloths,
2 coverlets to put on a bed, 1 square and 1 round, and 1 sheet that goes on the coverlet,
4 pairs of new spurs, 4 silk cushions, 2 whistles, 1 shaving basin, 2 beaver's testicles, one serpent's tongue; a vial of balm that was encased.
Likewise, a quilted doublet of vermillion cendal, and 1 black surcoat.
Likewise, this is from the armory: 2 pairs of new cuirasses, 8 new reins, and 1 jaw brake,
8 pairs of new spurs, 11 new straps, 4 coats of armor, and 3 banners,
2 knives and 4 iron blades, 2 new axes, 2 horse bridle headpieces, and 1 girth strap,
and one pair of thigh and leg protectors of iron; 1 helmet with an iron neck protector, 1 gambeson,
a pair of white coverings [horse blankets], 1 small sleeveless gambeson, 2 coverings of white leather, a pair of chests,
one large iron neck protector, and a leather trunk, and 2 pairs of chests, 1 domed and the other flat.
And from the chamber, 4 pairs of chests, and 2 encased candleholders; 4 trunks, 4 domed chests
and 4 flat. And from the pantry, 2 trunks, 1 domed and 1 flat.

---

or used to embellish clothing. See also Malcolm Vale, *The Princely Court: Medieval Courts and Culture in North-West Europe* (Oxford: Oxford University Press, 2001), 93–135, esp. 118–19.

54. The three types of cloth or fabric listed here, *dras de tartais*, *chameloz*, and *boqueranz*, are most likely all expensive, luxury, cloth produced in the East and in Central Asia. On these three, see the essay below by Sharon Farmer.

55. This phrase is complicated. Typically, it is used to describe jewels or precious stones that were worked or encased in a frame, or mounted. Worked, *orfevres*, here as in what will become gold works, *orfavrerie*. We thank the reader for the press for this insight.

56. *Cendal* is a form of taffeta, but we are retaining the original French term because of differences in fabrication. See Sharon Farmer.

57. Chazaud suggests this term comes from *frangere*, that is, to break up or break into pieces. We take it to be an ax, from the L. *francisca*. See Kelly DeVries, *Medieval Military Technology*, 2nd ed. (Toronto: University of Toronto Press), 15.

¶ Item · une tante que li chastelains de Chastiaupelerin dona le conte ¶ Item de la botellerie[58] · xvii · barriz de fust · et · ii bouz de cur et ii · seillons ·	Likewise, one tent that the castellan of Château Pèlerin gave the count. Likewise, from the cellar. 17 wooden barrels and 2 leather flasks, and 2 casks.
¶ de la cuisine · iii · granz poz de cuivre, et i petit · iii granz chaudieres · et iii · petites ii · paelles · et · i · greill · iii · paelles de fer · et iii mortiers · une paellete perciee et ii · forchetes ·	From the kitchen, 3 large copper pots and 1 small, 3 large cauldrons and 3 small, 2 pans and 1 grill, 3 iron pans and 3 mortars, one small perforated pan and 2 small forks.
¶ de la marichaucie[59] · li granz chevax[60] grilles · et li chevax qui fu mon segnor Jaque Vidaut et li granz palefroiz noirs · iii · bestes mulaces et · i · mulet · et i asne qui aportoit laigue	From the stables, the charcoal great horse [war horse], and the horse that belonged to my lord Jaque Vidaut; and the large black palfrey; 3 pack animals and 1 mule, and 1 donkey who carried the water.
¶ La garnison de lostel · En celier · xxxvi botes de vin · En lardier · L · lez de char salee · et ix^{xx} xv gelines et · i · mouton · Es greniers · viii^{xx} · x muis de froment · et · cc · muis dorge	The supply for the lodgings. In the cellar, 36 barrels of wine. In the larder, 50 sides of salted meat, and 195 chickens, and 1 sheep. In the granary, 170 measures of wheat and 200 of barley.
¶ Les choses de la chapelle · premirement le calice · une croisete ou il a de la veraie croiz · le saintuaire que li patriarches[61] dona le conte · le messe et le brevieire · une chasuble viez et aube et roichet · et · ii sorpeliz · et i · amit · i · drap dautel · devant et darriere · estole et fenoul · v · toalles dautel dont lune tient au drap de lautel · devant · une boiste divoire ii toalles amains · ii · chainetes · dargent · le corporal et lestui · et ii · custodes parees · Item · une chasuble neuve de drap dor · et tunique et daumatique · et ii · chapes neuves · tot	The things for the chapel, first, the chalice, a small cross where there is part of the True Cross, the reliquary that the patriarch gave the count, the missal and the breviary, an old chasuble, and alb, and rochet, and 2 surplices, and 1 amice; 1 cloth for the front [the frontal] and the back of the altar, a stole and maniple, 5 linen cloths for the altar, one of which is attached to the cloth of the frontal, one ivory box; 2 linen hand cloths, 2 small silver chains, the corporal and the monstrance, and the 2 decorated pyxes. Likewise, a new chasuble of gold cloth, and tunic, and dalmatic, and 2 new liturgical cloaks

58. Here begins a more formal list of objects in each room or area of Eudes's lodgings. The verbal and graphic organization of the inventory page also changes slightly in that each section leaves ample space between rooms to add—if necessary—additional objects and amounts.

59. The text has this as an *i* not an *e*. The word is *marechaucie*, for *marechaussee*.

60. A "granz chevax" was a particular type of horse known as a "great horse," that is, the kind one would ride into battle. See R. H. C. Davis, *The Medieval Warhorse: Origin, Development and Redevelopment* (London: Thames & Hudson, 1989), 69 and 88. We thank Sharon Farmer for this reference.

61. The reference most likely refers to William II of Agen (Guillaume d'Agen), patriarch of Jerusalem, then resident in Acre. Another possibility is whomever was vicar for Opizzo Fieschi, the Latin Maronite patriarch of Antioch, who held his see in October 1254 but then was constrained to leave Antioch for Acre. He was back in Italy by August 5, 1265 (with Charles of Anjou): *Dizionario*

de drap dor · et le drap de lautel devant et darriere · iii aubes · iii amiz · iii · roichez · ii sorpeliz tot nuef · ii estoles · et iii fenouz nues ·	all made of cloth of gold, and the altar cloths, front and back, 3 albs, 3 amices, 3 rochets, 2 surplices all new, 2 stoles and 3 new maniples.
¶ Item · cest la robe viez · premierement · i · serecot de tireteinne cameline forre de grosvair ¶ Item · cote et corset desclarlate poonnace forre de menuvar[62] · Item · cote et serecot et corset de tiretenne brune forre de menuvair · i · mantel de saie noire de bievre[63] · forre de menuvair · une cote et ii · serecoz et mantel de saie de bievre roige forre de menuvair · i · corset de drap inde forre de menuvair · une garnaiche[64] de saie forre de gris · i · serecot de pers forre de locceviere · i · corset de tyreteinne forre de gris · i · petit corset de camelot[65] forre de grosvair · ii · serecoz de tireteinne et i · de vert[66] sangles · · i · corset de pers sangles · une garnaiche de pers sangle · cote et serecot et corset de tireteinne perse forre[67] de cendel vert · i · corset de camelot forre de cendel vert · cote et serecot et mantel de camelot noir forre de cendel vermeil · cote et serecot de camelot inde forre de cendel noir ·	Likewise, this is the old wardrobe: first, an overcoat of camelin tiretaine trimmed with grosvair. Likewise, a tunic and corset of iridescent scarlet cloth trimmed with miniver. Likewise, a tunic, overcoat, and corset of brown tiretaine, trimmed with miniver. 1 black serge mantel of beaver, trimmed with miniver · One tunic and 2 over coats and a mantel of serge of red beaver, trimmed with miniver · 1 corset of indigo fabric, trimmed with miniver · One large serge cape trimmed with grey [squirrel] · 1 aquamarine overcoat trimmed with lynx · 1 tiretaine corset trimmed with grey [squirrel] 1 small camlet corset trimmed with grosvair · 2 tiretaine overcoats and 1 of them green, belted. 1 aquamarine corset, belted · One aquamarine ganache [large cape], belted · A tunic and overcoat, and a corset of aquamarine tiretaine lined with green cendal · 1 camlet corset, lined with green cendal · a tunic and overcoat and a mantel of black camlet lined with vermillion cendal · A tunic and an overcoat of indigo camlet, lined with black cendal.

Biografico degli Italiani, vol. 47 (1997), entry by Giovanni Nuti. We thank Maureen Miller for these details.

62. This material is listed above the first line of the paragraph, but because of its placement and meaning, we have listed it afterward.

63. We take this to be serge or a type of wool blended with beaver fur, in this case black beaver, and in a following example, red beaver. We thank Sharon Farmer for this interpretation.

64. A *garnaiche* was similar to a houppelande, ganache, or garde-corps, that is, a large cape that covered the body.

65. *Camelot*, or camlet in English, is distinct from *camelin* (a wool fabric made in the West). Camlet was made typically from camel fur, often from Central Asia. See the discussion by Sharon Farmer below. See also David Jacoby, "Camlet Manufacture, Trade in Cyprus and the Economy of Famagusta from the Thirteenth to the Late Fifteenth Century," in *Medieval and Renaissance Famagusta: Studies in Architecture, Art and History*, ed. Michael J. K. Walsh, Peter W. Edbury, and Nicholas S. H. Coureas (Farnham: Ashgate, 2012), 45–72.

66. Here the word for *vert* is abbreviated using a form of *vt* with a sweeping macron above. This is very different from the word *verz* used elsewhere in the text. This is clearly "green" rather than "vair."

67. The scribe uses the word *forre* here, which we have taken to mean trimmed when mentioned above with fur (either *grosvair* or *menuvair*). Here when used with cendal, which was

~~une~~ iiii · doblez avestir · iiii · chaperons forrez de cendel · et v forrez de vair ·	~~one~~ 4 formal doublets · 4 capes lined with cendal and 5 trimmed with vair.
—tote ceste robe viez desus dites fu departie au pauvres hopitauz dacre et au povres maisons de religion[68] ·	——Everything that is in the old wardrobe mentioned above was given to the poor hospitals of Acre and to the poor religious houses.

Roll B Back

¶ Li boens saffirs le conte fu envoiez au segnor de Borbon ¶ Ce est ceu qui fu departi des choses le conte ¶ Messire Joffroiz de Sergignes li peres ot · i · saffir que li cuens pandoit a son col · ¶ Messire Renauz de Precegni · i · camahe ¶ Li Boichiers ses freres lesmeraude · que li cuens portoit en son doi · ¶ Messire Joffroiz de Sergignes li juennes une · esmeraude ¶ Messire Roberz de Juenneces · i · anel ¶ Messires Gauchies de Merri · i · anel · ¶ Messires Guiz de Chantenai · i · enel ¶ Messires Herves de Chantenai · i · enel ¶ Messire Copains · i · enel ¶ Messire Hugues dAugerant, i anel. ¶ Item messire Hugues dAugerant en porte[69] lenel que li dux avoit done le conte · et lenel qui doit estre as oirs de Neverz · ¶ Messire Erarz de Valeri a les · ii croisetes dor · et le petit vaisselet dargent ou il a reliques que li patriarches avoit donees le conte	The count's good sapphire was sent to the lord of Bourbon. These are the things that were given away from among the count's possessions. My lord Geoffrey of Sergines, the father, received 1 sapphire that the count wore around his neck. My lord Reynaud of Précigné 1 cameo. The Boichiers, his brother, the emerald that the count wore on his finger. My lord Geoffrey of Sergines the younger, one emerald. My lord Robert of Juennesses, 1 ring. My lord Gaucher de Merry, 1 ring. My lord Gui de Chantenai, 1 ring. My lord Hervé de Chantenai, 1 ring. My lord Copin, 1 ring. My lord Hugh of Augerant, 1 ring. Likewise, my lord Hugh of Augerant, carries [back to France] the ring that the duke had given the count and the ring that should be [given] to the heirs of Nevers. My lord Érard of Vallery has 2 small crosses of gold and a small silver case in which there are the relics that the patriarch had given to the count.
¶ Il i ot iii verz departis au chevaliers et · xii · pannes ·	There were 3 vair [pieces] given to the knights, and 12 furs.
¶ Li chapelains lou conte ot le breviaire de la chapelle · e i sorpeliz nuef et Estienes li clers ot i sorpeliz nuef · A lopital de Saint-Jehan furent done li dui grand pot de cuivre de la cuisine ·	The count's chaplain received the breviary of the chapel and 1 new surplice, and Étienne le Clerc received 1 new surplice. And the Hospital of St. John was given the two large copper pots from the kitchen.

a light silk-weave fabric, we take it to mean lined. It is possible that these garments were only trimmed with cendal.

68. We believe this line to be a later addition than the paragraph above because the ink and hand are slightly different.

69. It is Hugh who was the one carrying the rings back to the West and to the heirs of the count of Nevers. See the discussion in the essay by Richard Leson below.

Roll C Front

Ce sunt les chose prisiees ·	These are the things that were appraised.
Li corsez forrez de louceviere est prisiez · xii b/ · a saint Michel ·	The corset trimmed with lynx fur is appraised at 12 b/ [given] to Saint Michael ·
La garnaiche de saie forree de gris · est prisiee xvi b/ · donee au Jacobins	The ganache of serge trimmed with grey fur is appraised at 16 b/ given to the Jacobins
li corsetz de tireteinne forre de gris · iiii b/ ·	The tiretaine corset trimmed with grey fur 4 b/
La cote et · ii · serecoz et le mantel de saie de bievre roige forre de menuvair · xlvi b/	The tunic and 2 overcoats and the serge mantle of red beaver, trimmed with miniver 46 b/
~~Le mantel de saie de bievre~~ noire forre de menuvair · xiiii b/ ~~au Cordeliers~~	~~The serge mantle of~~ black ~~beaver~~ trimmed with miniver 14 b/ ~~to the Cordeliers~~
cote et serecot et corset de tireteinne brune forre de menuvair · xviii b/ ·	Tunic and overcoat and corset of brown tiretaine trimmed with miniver, 18 b/
le corset de drap inde forre de menuvair vi b/	the corset of indigo cloth trimmed with miniver, 6 b/
La cote et le corset descarlate poonnace forre de menuvair xx b/	The tunic and the corset of iridescent scarlet, trimmed with miniver, 20 b/
cote et serecot de tireteinne cameline forre de grosvair viii b/	Tunic and overcoat of tiretaine camelin, trimmed with grosvair, 8 b/
· ii · petiz corsez et le queuvrechief de menuvair · v b/	2 small corsets and the head covering [hat] of miniver, 5 b/
· i · corset de camelot forre de cendel vert · vi b/ ·	1 camlet corset, lined with green cendal 6 b/
cote et serecot, et corset de tireteinne perse forre de cendel vert · ~~x b/~~ xii b/	Tunic and overcoat and a corset of aquamarine tiretaine, lined with green cendal, ~~10 b/~~ 12 b/
cote serecot mantel de camelot noir forre de cendel vermeil · xii b/	Tunic, overcoat, mantel of black camlet lined with vermillion cendal, 12 b/
cote et serecot de cendel inde forre de cendel noir v b/	Tunic and overcoat of indigo cendal lined with black cendal, 5 b/
La garnaiche de pers et le corset sengle · v b/	The aquamarine ganache [large cape] and the corset, belted, 5 b/
· ii · serecot sengles de tireteinne · iiii b/ · et · i · serecot de vert sengle · iii b/	2 belted tiretaine overcoats 4 b/ and 1 green belted overcoat, 3 b/
v chaperons forre de menuvair · et iiii de cendel · x b/ ·	5 capes trimmed with miniver and 4 of cendal, 10 b/
—Somme dou pris de ces choses ii^{cc} · vi b/ ·	—The total value of all these things, 206 b/
Li prieux de Saint Michel le corset de loucevirere	The prior of Saint Michael, the lynx corset.
Li Jacobin la garnaiche neve forre de gris ·	The Jacobins the new ganache trimmed with grey squirrel.
Li Cordelier le mantel de saie roige forre de menuvair ·	The Cordeliers, the red serge mantel trimmed with miniver.
A Saint Antoine · le mantel noir forre de menuvair	To Saint Anthony the black mantel trimmed with miniver

A Nostre de Vamit · i · corset forre de gris · viez ·	To Notre Dame de Vamit, 1 corset trimmed with grey fur, old
A sainte Katerine le serecot corset descarlate poonnace forre de menuvair	To Saint Catherine, the scarlet iridescent overcoat corset trimmed with miniver.
A la Trinite le serecot de saie vermoille forre de menuvair a manches ·	To the Trinity, the serge vermillion overcoat, trimmed with miniver at the sleeves
A Saint Ladre des chevaliers[70] le serecot de saie roiges sanz manches forre de menuvair et le chaperon	To the Knights of Saint Lazarus, the overcoat of red serge, without sleeves, trimmed with miniver and the cape.
A Saint Thomas · la cote et le serecot de tireteinne perse· forre de cendel vert ·[71]	To Saint Thomas, the tunic and overcoat of aquamarine tiretaine lined with green cendal.
A ceus de Sas · le serecot vert sengle et i · chaperon ·	To those of the Sack, the green belted overcoat, and 1 cape.
A ceus dou Carme[72] la cote de saie roige · et i petit corset forre de menuvair	To those of the Carmes the red serge tunic, and 1 small corset trimmed with miniver.
A lopital dou Saint Esperit le corset de chamelot forre de vert	To the hospital of the Holy Spirit, the camlet corset lined with green.
A Saint Elide · le coreset de tireteinne perse forre de cendel vert et chaperon	To Saint Elide, the tiretaine aquamarine corset lined with green cendal, and [the] cape.
Au messelles de Bethleem · i · serecot de tireteinne sengle et chaperon de menuvair	To the female lepers of Bethlehem, 1 tiretaine belted overcoat, and a cape of miniver.
Au mesiaus de Saint Barthelemi de Bereithe le corset inde forre de menuvair.	To the male lepers of Saint Bartholomew of Beirut, the indigo corset trimmed with miniver.
a Saint Martin des Bretons · i · serecot de tireteinne sengle et i · chaperon	To Saint Martin of the Bretons, 1 tiretaine belted overcoat, and 1 cape.
a lopital de Saint Denis · cote et serecot de tireteinne · forre de grosvair	To the Hospital of Saint Denis, [a] tiretaine tunic and overcoat, trimmed with grosvair.
au nonnains de la magdelene · i serecot de tireteinne forre de menuvair	To the nuns of the Magdelene, 1 tiretaine overcoat, trimmed with miniver.
au nonnains Nostre Dame de Sur · cote et serecot de drap inde forre de cendel noir	To the nuns of Notre Dame of Tyre, [a] tunic and overcoat of indigo cloth, lined with black cendal.
a · ii · hermites a lun le queuvrechief de menuvair et a lautre · i petit corset de menuvair	To [the] 2 hermits, to one, the miniver hood, and to the other, 1 small corset of miniver.

70. The Order of Saint Lazarus of Jerusalem, or the Leper Brothers of Jerusalem, was a charitable military order founded ca. 1119 at the same time as the Hospitaller Order.

71. The phrase "forre de cendel vert" was added in a lighter ink, perhaps after the main text.

72. The Carmelite brothers, or the friars-hermits of the Blessed Virgin of Mount Carmel, was an order that came to follow the customs of the Dominicans but was dispersed from the mount following the campaigns of Baybars, though the house persisted inside Acre. See the essay here by Andrew Jotischky.

au nonnains de Saint Ladre de Betennie cote et serecot de camelot noir forre de cendel vermoil[73]	To the nuns of Saint Lazarus of Bethany, [the] tunic and overcoat of black camlet lined with vermillion cendal.
a ceus de Sainte Anne le mantel · de celle robe de camelot noir et la garnaiche de pers ·	To those of Saint Anne, the mantel of this robe of black camlet, and the aquamarine ganache [large cape].
a ceus de Saint Samuel · cote et serecot de tireteinne brune forre de menuvair	To those of Saint Samuel, a tunic and overcoat of brown tiretaine, trimmed with miniver.
a ceus de la Carpitre · i · corset sengle de pers · et le chaperon ·	To those of the Carpitanae 1 belted aquamarine corset and the cape.
au provoires de Saint Demitre la cote descarlate poonace.	To the provost of Saint Demetrius, the iridescent tunic of scarlet [cloth].
A lopital des Alemanz[74] · i cerecot blanc viez qui estoit dou lit le conte	To the hospital of the Germans, 1 old white coverlet that was on the count's bed.
~~A une beguine · i doblet avestir . . . Robez ot le bel over~~ · ~~et a une [unclear] beguine [unclear] et i [unclear]~~	~~To one beguine, 1 dress doublet . . . Robez has the beautifully worked [one].][and for another beguine. . . . .]~~
iiii doblez avestir feiz · furent done a iiii povres · et les hueses viez	4 dress doublets were given to 4 paupers, and the old leggings;
A lopital de Saint Jehan fu done les · ii · poz granz de cuivre de la cuisine · por de	To the Hospital of Saint John were given the 2 large copper cooking pots for the kitchen, for God.

Roll C Back

¶ Li Sires de borbon le boen saffir ·	The lord of Bourbon, the good sapphire
¶ Messire Joffroiz de Sergignes le peres a eu des choses leconte · i saffirs que le cuens pandoit a son col ·	My lord Geoffrey of Sergines, the father, had from the count's possessions 1 sapphire that the count wore around his neck.
¶ Messire Renauz de Precegni i · camahe	My lord Reynaud of Précigné, 1 cameo
¶ Li Boichiers · lesmeraude que li cuens portoit en son doi	The Boichiers, the emerald that the count wore on his finger
¶ Messire Joffroiz de Sergignes li juennes · une esmeraude ·	My lord Geoffrey of Sergines the younger, an emerald.
¶ Messire Roberz de Juenneces · i · anel	My lord Robert de Juennesses, 1 ring
¶ Messires Gauchies de Merri · i · anel	My lord Gaucher de Merry, 1 ring
¶ Messires Guiz de Chantenai · i · anel	My lord Gui de Chantenai, 1 ring
¶ Et Messires Herves de Chantenai · i · anel	And my lord Hervé de Chantenai, 1 ring
¶ Copains · i · anel ·	Copin, 1 ring
¶ Messire Huges dAugerant · i · anel.	My lord Hugh of Augerant, 1 ring
—Item messire Hugues dAugerant en porte au duc lenel que li dux avoit done ~~les~~ lou conte et lanel qui doit estre as oirs de Neverz ·	—Likewise, my lord Hugh of Augerant carries to the duke the ring that the duke had given to ~~these~~ the count and the ring that should be [given] to the heir of Nevers.

73. The phrase "forre de cendel vermoil" was added in a different ink, perhaps after the main text was written, to distinguish among objects.

74. That is, to the hospital of the Teutonic order.

¶ Messire Erarz de Valeri a · ii · croisetes	My lord Érard of Vallery has 2 small
dor · et · i · petit vaisselet	crosses of gold and a small phylactery
ou il avoit reliques que li patriarches aveit	in which there are the relics that the
donees le conte	patriarch had given to the count.
¶ Il i ot · iii · verz departis a chevaliers · et	There were 3 vair given to the knights, and
xii pannes · et vii verz a venduz et iii pannes	12 furs, and 7 vair were sold and 3 furs.
¶ Li chapelains le conte ot le breviaire de	The count's chaplain received the breviary
la chapelle · et · i · sorpeliz nuef	from the chapel and 1 new surplice,
et li clers · i · sorpeliz nuef ·	and the clerk [received] 1 new surplice.
¶ Alopital de Saint Jehan furent done · li	To the Hospital of Saint John were given
dui grant pot de cuivre	the two large copper pots and all the other
et totz li autres harnois de cuisine fu venduz ·	equipment from the kitchen was sold.

Roll D Front

Cest li escriz des choses le conte vendues ·	This is the record of the count's things that were sold.
¶; Ce sunt les choses que Messires Erarz	These are the things that my lord Érard of
de Valeri a achete des choses le conte ·	Vallery purchased from the things of the count.
¶ Premierement por lasne a tot le harnois	Firstly, for the donkey, for all of the
xvi b/ · et por xl gelines viii b/ et xiiii b/	equipment, 16 b/, and for 40 chickens 8 b/,
por busche ·	and 14 b/ for wood,
por · i · fer de glaive · et iii paire	for 1 iron blade, and 3 pairs of spurs, and
desperons et i · coutel · vi b/ demi ·	1 dagger, 6 and one half b/.
por · C · muis dorge C b/ · por · lxi ·	For 100 measures of barley 100 b/, for 61 cane-
quanne de napes · xxx b/ · et por · iii	lengths of table-covering 30 b/, and for 3 dozen
· xii^{nes} de toailles amains · vi b/ · por ·	hand towels 6 b/, for $^{10\ cane\text{-}lengths}$ of linen
toile $^{x\ quannes}$ vi b/ · por le for de fer et i	6 b/. For the covered iron pot, and 1
pot decuivre et une	copper pot, and one cauldron,
chaudiere et · i · paelle et · i · graill · et i	and 1 pan, and 1 grill, and 1 tripod, and
· trepie · et une forchete et une paellete	one fork and one perforated pan, 16 b/.
percie · xvi b/ ·	
por iiii quarriaus · ii b/ · por · v · paire de	For 4 quarrels 2 b/, for 5 pairs of new
dras nues · xxv b/ · por i siffle et por · x	fabric 25 b/, for 1 whistle and for 10
paire de petiz ganz · ii b/ · et por ii paire	pairs of small gloves, 2 b/, and for 2 pairs
de barriz · ii b/ ·	of barrels 2 b/,
por · iii · quannes de saie · xv b/ · por xv	for 3 cane-lengths of serge 15 b/, for 15
botes devin · ii^{cc} · xix b/ quart moins ·	butts of wine, 219 b/ less a quarter.
et por x lez de char salee x b/	And for 10 sides of salted meat 10 b/
—Somme · de ces choses · iiii^{ccc} · lxxvii b/ · vi quarrobles ·	—The total of all these things, 477 b/ 6 q
¶ Item · por · xviii · escuelles · dargent · et	Likewise, for 18 silver saucers and 12
xii enas et ii granz plateaus qui poisent ·	goblets and 2 large platters that weighed
xliii mars et demi · iii · estellins · moins ·	43 and half marks less 3 sterling that are
qui valent · iii^{ccc} liiii b/ et vi quarrobles ·	valued at 354 b/ and 6 q, the mark selling
le marc vendu viii b/ et iiii quarrobles au	at 8 b/ and 4 q to the mark of Acre.
marc dAcre	——The total of all, 831 and one half b/,
——Somme de tot · viii^{ccc} · et xxxi b/	for my lord Érard of Vallery.
demi sor mon segnor Erart de Valeri[75] ·	

75. This line appears to be written in a different hand with possibly different ink.

¶ Ce est ceu que messire Joffroiz de Sergignes li peres acheta · por · iii · chaudieres et ii paelles · ~~sol~~ xviii b/ · et iiii b/ por les · ii · botiaus de cur a vin · por xl lez de char salee · xli b/ · por · iiii paire de barriz vi b/ por · xvii · botes de vin · ii^{cc} · xxx b/ · x quarrobles ·	This is what my lord Geoffrey of Sergines the father bought. For 3 cauldrons and 2 pans ~~sol~~ 18 b/, and 4 b/ for the 2 bottles to age wine. For the 40 sides of salted meat 41 b/, for the 4 pairs of barrels 6 b/, for the 17 butts of wine 230 b/ and 10 q
——Somme · sor mon segnor Joffroi · iii^{ccc} · b/ ·xiiii · quarrobles moins ·	——The total charged on my lord Geoffrey is 300 b/ less 14 q
¶ Messire Hugues de la Baume · por · ii · fracoires · ii b/ · et por · i · coutel · iii b/ · por frains · et por trumelieres de fer x b/ · por · xx · pieces de toile · et por x pieces de napes et de toailles · v^{c} · lxxvi b/ demi et demi b/ · por testieres a cheval · por xii culliers · xvi b/ ·	My lord Hugh de la Baume, for 2 small axes 2 b/, and for 1 knife 3 b/, for brakes and for iron leg protectors 10 b/, for 20 pieces of linen and for 10 pieces of cloth and towels 576 and one half b/; and one half b/ for horse bridles. For 12 spoons 16 b/.
——Somme sor mon segnor Hugues · vi^{c} · viii b/ ·	——The total for my lord Hugh 608 b/.
¶ por C · muis dorge venduz · c b/ · por i· mulet · iiii^{xx} · x b/ · vendu a mon segnor Hue de Mont Cornet	For 100 measures of barley, sold, 100 b/, for one mule 90 b/, sold to my lord Hugh de Mont-Cornet.
¶ por ii · napes et · iiii petites toailles ii b/ · iii · quarrobles	For 2 cloths and 4 small hand towels 2 b/ 3 q.
¶ por une male et i · bahu xx s^{tornois} au chapelein · por · i^{m} · de busche · x b/ ·	For a case and a chest 20 *s. t.* to the chaplain, for 1 thousand [measures] of wood, 10 b/.
¶ por · c · et lv · gelines vendues · xxxi b/ · por vin et por froment vi b/ demi ·	For the sale of 155 chickens 31 b/, for wine and wheat 6 and one half b/
¶ Item por · viii^{xx} · et x · muis de froment · iii^{ccc} · lxxiiii b/ · et por une bote de vin · iiii b/ demi	Likewise, for 170 measures of wheat 374 b/ and for one bottle of wine 4 and one half b/
¶ por le mouton · x b/ · por les ii · coffres de larmeure vi b/ ·	For the sheep 10 b/, for the 2 cases for the armor 6 b/
¶ por le ganbaison le conte · et le bacinet · xxxvi b/ ·	For the count's gambeson and helmet 36 b/
¶ por · i covertor noir et · i · covertor blanc ovre x b/	For 1 black coverlet and 1 white worked coverlet 10 b/ and for 3 cane-lengths of striped [fabric] 21 b/
¶ et por · iii quannes de raie · xxi b/ ·	
¶ por · vii · verz et ii · raiez · iiii^{cccc} · li b/ [76] · et por iii quannes de saie · xv b/ ·	For 7 green and for 2 striped [cloths] 451 b/ and for 3 cane-lengths of serge 15 b/
¶ por · iiii · paire · desperons · et · i · coutel · vi b/ · et por une macete et · i · petit coutel · iiii b/	For 4 pairs of spurs and 1 knife 6 b/ and for one small mace and 1 small knife 4 b/
¶ por i · coutel de tartais · xxi *s.* i *d. t.* · por · ii · boqueranz · vii · b/ et demi	For 1 [cutting of] Tartar [cloth] 21 *s.* 1 *d. t.*, for 2 Boukhara [fabrics] 7 b/ and one half

76. Given the value listed here, we assume this would be measures of cloth, although no unit or measurement is given. If this is cloth from Provins, as the striped cloth listed in Roll A notes, it may have had a higher value in Acre.

¶ por uns cuissiaus · vi b/ · et iiii *s. t.* por · i · coutel atrencher · por · i · fer de glaive x *s. t.* ·
¶ Item · por · i · fer de glaive · et por · ii orfrois et por · i · eschaquier et les eschas vendu ensemble ix b/ ·
¶ Item · por · iii · paire desperons · ii b/ · por · i · coutel · i b/ · por · i · fer de glaive i · b/ ·
¶ por · i · petit ganbaison · et ii paire de chauces xxii *s. t.* ·
¶ Item · por iiii · paire de chauces · xxiiii *s. t.* ·
¶ Por unes covertures acheval blanches · xii b/ · por une gorgiere · et ii · barnieres viez · iii · b/
¶ por une barniere nueuve · ii b/ · por i · boquerant · iii b/ demi ·
¶ Por une corroie dargent · x b/ · et por ii · corroies dor lune viez
et lautre nueve · xxxvi b/ · et por · i · drap de tartais · xii b/ ·
¶ Item por ii · dras de tartais · xl b · por xvi quannes de toile · xii b/ ·
¶ Por · xl quannes de napes · et por une · xii^{ne} de toailles · xxviii b/ ·
¶ Por sorcengles · por · iiii · paire de braies et de chemises feites · et por iii · paire de ganz doblez · v b/ ·
¶ et por autres · iiii · paire de braies et de chemises feites · iii b/ ·
et por · iiii · paire de sollers nues · viii *s. t.* · et por unes hueuses · nueves · i b/ et demi ·
¶ Por une coute pointe vermoille · v b/ · por · ii · curs de dain · ii b/ ·
¶ Por · ii · pannes de grosvair · et
une autre panne roige et une forreure achaperon
de vair · viii · *lb* · tornois · por les coffres de cur boli · ou la chapelle estoit xvi b/ ·
¶ Por · ii · males et · ii · bahuz · et · iii · baz · lxx *s. t.* · et x *s. t.* por coiffes[77] nueuves ·
¶ Item · por · iiii baz · xl *s. t.* · por · ii · coffres · x b/

For one pair of leg protectors 6 b/ and 4 *s. t.* for 1 carving knife, for 1 iron blade 10 *s. t.*
Likewise, for 1 iron blade and for 2 pieces of gold embroidered silk bands, and for 1 chessboard and chess pieces sold together 9 b/
Likewise, for 3 pairs of spurs 2 b/, for 1 knife 1 b/, for 1 iron blade 1 b/
For a small gambeson and 2 pair of shin protectors 22 *s. t.*
Likewise, for 4 pairs of shin protectors 24 *s. t.*
For one white horse blanket 12 b/, for one neck protector and 2 old banners 3 b/;
For one new banner 2 b/, for 1 Boukhara cloth 3 and one half b/.
For a silver belt 10 b/ and for 2 gold belts, one old and the other new 36 b/; and for 1 Tartar cloth 12 b/.
Likewise, for 2 Tartar cloths 40 b/, for 16 cane-lengths of linen 12 b/.
For 40 lengths of cloth and for one dozen towels 28 b/.
For sashes and 4 pairs of undergarments and finished shirts, and for 3 pairs of lined gloves 5 b/,
And for another 4 pairs of undergarments and finished shirts 3 b/,
and for 4 pairs of new shoes 8 *s. t.* and for one pair of new leggings 1 and one half b/.
For one vermillion quilt 5 b/, for 2 suedeskins 2 b/.
For 2 furs of grosvair and another red fur and one fur cape
of vair 8 *l. t.*, for the boiled-leather chests where the chapel was 16 b/.
For the 2 cases and 2 domed trunks and 3 flat trunks 70 *s. t.* and 10 *s. t.* for new cases.
Likewise, for 4 flat [trunks] 40 *s. t.*, for 2 cases 10 b/.

77. Context suggests this may be a variant spelling of "coffres."

¶ Por · ii · chameloz xvi b/ · por la viez chapelle vendue · xlviii b/ ¶ Por · i · pot dargent vendu par soi · xvi b/ · ¶ Item · por · xxii · escuelles dargent et iiii · granz bacins · vii · henas · et · i · pot dargent · qui peseient[78] · lxiiii · mars et xxx · estellins · le marc vendu · viii b/ · iiii quarrobles	For 2 camlets [cloths] 16 b/. For the old chapel, [which] sold for 48 b/. For 1 silver pot sold on its own 16 b/. Likewise, for 22 silver saucers and 4 large basins, 7 goblets, and 1 silver pot that weighed 64 marks and 30 sterling, the mark trading at 8 b/ 4 q,
—Somme · v^{c} · xxiiii b/ · v quarrobles · amarcheanz · ¶ Por une tyreteinne · lxvi b/ · por · xxix queuvrechies · vi b/ · ¶ por quarraus et pilez · ix b/ et x quarrobles · ¶ Por les · ii · palefroiz et les · ii · mulaces · v^{c} · b/ · ¶ Por le cheval grile · c b/ ·	—The total, 524 b/ 5 q at market For one tiretaine [cloth] 66 b/, for 29 head coverings 6 b/, For quarrels and arrows 9 b/ and 10 q. For the 2 palfreys and the 2 mules 500 b/. For the grey horse 100 b/.
[Right margin] Ceste somme sanz ~~iii~~ les · iii · premiers · ii^{m} · vi^{c} · iiii^{xx} x b/ vi quarrobles et xix lb ix *s.* tornois ·	[Right margin] This total without ~~3~~ the first 3, 2,690 b/ 6 q and 19 *lb* 9 *s. t.*
—Ce sunt les choses vendues au Temple · ¶ Por · i · pot dor et une cope cuvesclee dor qui poisent vii · mars · xxxii estellins moins le marc lxx b/ vendu · somme · iiii^{cccc} · lxxvi b/ ·	—These are the things sold to the Temple. For 1 gold pot and one covered gold cup that weighs 7 marks less 32 sterling, the mark valued at 70 b/, for a total of 476 b/.
¶ Item por ii · poz dargent ·qui poisent ix mars · et xxxv estellins le marc vendu ix b/ somme · por ces · ii · poz iiii^{xx} · iii b/ ii · quarrobles moins ·	Likewise, for 2 silver pots that weigh 9 marks and 35 sterling, the mark valued at 9 b/; Total for these two pots 83 b/ less 2 q
Item · por · ii · barriz dargent qui poisent xiii mars · v estellins · moins · a x b/ le mars · somme por les barriz · C · et · xxx b/ · tierz moins ·	Likewise, for 2 silver containers that weigh 13 marks less 5 sterling, at 10 b/ to the mark, the total for the containers, 130 b/ less one third.
Item por une cope dargent doree a cuvescle · qui poise iiii · mars et demi v estellins moins	Likewise, for one silver gilded cup with a cover, that weighs 4 and a half marks, less 5 sterling,
a · xii · b/ le marc · somme · por la cope · Liii b/ · xv quarrobles ·	at 12 b/ to the mark, the total for the cup is 53 b/ 15 q.

78. We chose the third person plural imperfect, but variant expansions might include *pesoient* or *pesevent*.

—Somme de tot sor le temple · vii^{cc} · xlii b/ v quarrobles ·	—The total for all [charged] to the Temple, 742 b/ 5 q.
——Somme de tot cet escrit · v^{m} · C · lxxi b/ ix quarrobles et dautrepart · xix *lb* ix *s.* tournois · cilz compes fu feiz ledemain de feste Sainte-Croiz en septembre · au temple · par devant lemaistre dou temple et mon segnor Erart de Valeri et mon segnor Joffroi de Sergignes le juenne	——The total of everything written here, 5,171 b/ 9 q, and for the other part 19 *lb* 9 *s. t.* These accounts were made the day after the feast of the Holy Cross in September, at the Temple, before the master of the Temple, and my lord Érard of Vallery, and my lord Geoffrey of Sergines the younger.
Item por iiii cuillers dargent adragiee ii b/ et xxxiii *s. t.* por · xi eniaus dou Pui	Likewise, for 4 silver dessert spoons 2 b/ and 33 *s. t.* for 11 rings from Puy.
Item · por · le drap deremenant des esprevers · vi b/ ·	Likewise, for the remaining cloth from the bedding, 6 b/
—Somme de tot cest escrit · iiii^{m} · iiii^{cccc} · xxix b/ iiii quarrobles sanz le temple · —Somme de tot v^{m} · c · lxxix b/ · ix quarrobles· et xix *lb* ix *s. t.* · et puis · xxxiii *s.*	—The total for everything written: 4,429 b/ 4 q without the Temple. —The overall total 5,179 b/ 9 q and 19 *lb* 9 *s. t.* and another 33 *s.*

Roll D Back

[Dark ink, column 1]	[Dark ink, column 1]
¶ Ce sunt choses qui ne sunt pas ancor vendues ·	These are the things that are not yet sold
~~une corroie dor viez~~ apelles ~~et une neuve~~	~~one old belt of gold~~ with pearls ~~and a new [one]~~
~~xi · petiz enaus dou Pui ·~~	~~11 small rings from Puy~~
~~et i que messires Gauchers aligranz ot~~	~~and 1 large one that my lord Gaucher has~~
~~· iiii · cuillers dargent a dragiees ·~~	~~4 silver dessert spoons~~
· i · orfroi aperles · ii coilles de bievre	1 orphrey with pearls, 2 beaver testicles
une langue de sarpant ·	one serpent's tongue
~~i · henap dargent a pierres que len cuida quil fust dor~~	~~1 goblet of silver set with stones that was believed to be gold~~
Item · ii · paire de cuiraces ·	Likewise, 2 pairs of cuirasses
une male de cur · ii · paire de bouges et iii · autres viez males · et xxiiii napes viez	one leather chest, 2 pairs of chests, and 3 other old chests, and 24 old napkins
x dras de tartais · et ii espreviers · et le drap de remenant de lesprevier ·	10 Tartar cloths and 2 coverlets and the remaining cloth from the coverlet
La chapelle nueuve ·	the new chapel
une male ·	one chest
ii · tapiz nues ovrez	2 new worked hangings
La tante de Chastiau pelerin[79]	The tent from Château Pèlerin

79. This line was added in a lighter ink, slightly different script, possibly as an addition made at the same time as the totals on the other end of the parchment (inverted and in lighter ink). We believe that this represents an additional accounting and summarizing as the sale of all items was completed.

[column 2]
~~et · i · henap dargent apierres et aesmaus~~
—i chapel dor apierres et apelles
~~une cope dargent cuveselee~~
~~et ii poz dargent~~
~~i · aiguier dor~~
~~une cope dor cuveselee~~
~~ii · barriz dargent~~
[margin]
Somme ·
xxii mars et vii
estellins
dargent
et vii mars dor
moins xxxii estellins

[column 2]
~~and 1 goblet set with stones and enamels~~
—1 chapel [made] of gold with stones and pearls
~~one silver covered cup~~
~~and 2 silver pots~~
~~1 pitcher of gold~~
~~one cup of gold with a cover~~
~~2 silver containers~~
[margin]
Total
22 marks and 7
sterling
of silver
and 7 marks of gold
less 32 sterling

[Inverted: lighter ink]
¶ · Ce est ceu que li cuens avoit en deniers monaez et en besanz
au jor quil ala de vie amort · Cest asavoir xv *lb* ii *s.* tournois
et xii *l* tournois de resus · ces deniers livra Estienes li clers · quant il ot conte
et Robez livra · iii^{m} · vii^{cc} · xvi b/ · et xxxviii *lb* xix *s. t.*
et xiii · *s.* de reaus · en la main mon segnor Hugue dAugerant ·
Item · Estienes li clers bailla · xv *s.* iii *d.* de reaus ·
cilz compes fu feiz laveille de feste saint Lorant a lan · m · cc lxvi ·
par devant mon segnor Hugue dAugerant
et mon segnor Joffroi de
Sergines le juenne—

[Inverted: lighter ink]
This is what the count had in deniers currency and in bezants
on the day he went from life to death. That is to say, 15 *lb* 2 *s. t.*
and 12 *l. t.* of the realm. Étienne le Clerc disbursed these monies once he had done the accounting,
and Robet disbursed 3,716 b/ and 38 *lb* 19 *s. t.*
and 13 *s.* of the realm into the hands of my lord Hugh of Augerant.
Likewise, Étienne le Clerc paid 15 *s.* 3 *d.* of the realm.
These accounts were made the eve of the feast of Saint Lawrence in the year 1266
before my lord Hugh of Augerant
and my lord Geoffrey of
Sergines the younger.

Part II

COMMENTARY

3

Crusading in the Mid-Thirteenth Century

Eudes of Nevers (b. 1230; d. August 7, 1266) was the son of Hugh IV, duke of Burgundy (d. 1272), and Yolande of Dreux (d. 1248) (see appendix 1 and figures 13.1–13.2). He could trace his lineage through multiple crusader families going back generations.[1] In 1248, Eudes married Mahaut II of Bourbon (1234/35–62), who had inherited the county of Nevers through her mother and who also boasted a crusader lineage in her own right.[2] Once he was married, Eudes took the title of count of Nevers while Mahaut retained her title to Bourbon. Eudes's great-grandfather, Duke Hugh III of Burgundy, had taken part in the Third Crusade and died in Acre on August 25, 1192. His grandfather, Eudes III of Burgundy, joined the Fifth Crusade and died on July 6, 1218. And his father had taken part in the so-called Barons' Crusade of 1239 and joined Louis IX's first expedition east in 1248. In 1262, Hugh IV took a final

1. On the crusader lineage of the counts of Nevers, see Elizabeth Siberry, "The Crusading Counts of Nevers," *Nottingham Medieval Studies* 34 (1990): 64–70; Anne E. Lester, "Crusading as a Religious Movement: Families, Community, and Lordship in a Vernacular Frame," in *Between Orders and Heresy: Rethinking Medieval Religious Movements*, ed. Jennifer Kolpacoff Deane and Anne E. Lester (Toronto: University of Toronto Press, 2022), 127–69. Lespinasse, *Le Nivernais*, vol. 2, offers the most in-depth narrative of the Nevers family's crusade participation. See also Philippe Murat, "La croisade en Nivernais: Transfert de propriété et lutte d'influence," in *Le concile de Clermont de 1095 et l'appel à la croisade: Actes du Colloque Universitaire International de Clermont-Ferrand (23–25 juin 1995)*, Publications de l'École française de Rome 236 (Rome: École Français de Rome, 1997), 295–312.

2. Lespinasse, *Le Nivernais*, 2:261–62; and Constance Brittain Bouchard, "Three Counties, One Lineage, and Eight Heiresses: Nevers, Auxerre, and Tonnerre, Eleventh to the Thirteenth Centuries," *Medieval Prosopography* 31 (2016): 25–46.

crusade vow to aid Baldwin II in reclaiming the Latin Empire of Constantinople.[3] Whether for reasons of age or ailing health, Hugh commuted his vow and allowed his son Eudes to serve in his stead.[4] Familial and political commitments thus guided Eudes of Nevers to take the cross and propelled him to Acre.[5]

By the autumn of 1265, the situation in the Kingdom of Jerusalem had deteriorated considerably. Four years earlier, in 1261, Michael VIII Palaeologus (r. 1261–82) succeeded in taking the Latin Empire of Constantinople and restored Greek rule to the Byzantine capital. At the same time, a perceived two-pronged offensive had begun to compromise what remained of the principalities of Outremer along the Syrian coast. To the north, the Mongol armies had begun to move southward across Anatolia. To the south, the Mamluk general Baybars led his Muslim forces in a series of effective and crushing campaigns to take over crusader castles and towns along the littoral.[6] In response, Pope Clement IV (r. 1265–68) began a preaching campaign to raise a new general crusade (*passage général* or *passagium generale*) and to recruit the kings of France and England along with other major barons to undertake a cooperative and jointly funded expedition to the East in the service of Christendom.[7]

3. The crusading commitments of the dukes of Burgundy are detailed in Ernst Petit, *Histoire des ducs de Bourgogne de la race capétienne* (Dijon: Darantiere, 1885–1905), vols. 4–5. For Hugh IV's role in the Barons' Crusade and with Louis IX, see Michael Lower, *The Barons' Crusade: A Call to Arms and Its Consequences* (Philadelphia: University of Pennsylvania Press, 2005). See Rutebeuf's poems, below.

4. See Alexandre Teulet et al., eds., *Layettes du Trésor des chartes* (Paris: H. Plon, 1863–1909), 3:537–38, no. 4619 (July 6, 1260); Petit, *Histoire des ducs de Bourgogne*, 5:72–73. Hugh IV continued to harbor ambitions in the East, both in Greece and in the Regno. In the months after Eudes's departure for Acre, Hugh met with Baldwin II and began arrangements to aid him in reconquering the Latin Empire in exchange for the principality of Thessalonica, yet nothing came of such plans. See the comments in Jean Dunbabin, *The French in the Kingdom of Sicily, 1266–1305* (Cambridge: Cambridge University Press, 2005), 139–41; and Jean Richard, *Les ducs de Bourgogne et de la formation du duché, du XIe au XIVe siècle* (Dijon: Bernigaud et Privat, 1954), 294–305.

5. For this chronology, see Petit, *Histoire des ducs de Bourgogne*, vols. 4–5. See the comments below on Rutebeuf's poem "La complainte doutremeir."

6. For the general context informing the renewed crusade call in 1265, see Jean Richard, *Saint Louis: Roi d'une France féodale, soutien de la Terre sainte* (Paris: Fayard, 1983), 451–574; Richard, "La croisade de 1270, premier 'passage général'?," *Comptes rendus des séances de l'Académie des Inscriptions et Belles-Lettres* 133 (1989): 510–23; Peter Jackson, "The Crisis in the Holy Land in 1260," *English Historical Review* 95 (1980): 481–513; and Jackson, *The Mongols and the West: 1221–1410*, 2nd ed. (London: Routledge, 2018); Xavier Hélary, "Les rois de France et la Terre Sainte de la Croisade de Tunis à la chute d'Acre (1270–1291)," *Annuaire-Bulletin de la Société de l'histoire de France* 118 (2005): 21–104; Hélary, *La dernière croisade: Saint Louis à Tunis (1270)* (Paris: Perrin, 2016); Michael Lower, "Conversion and St Louis's Last Crusade," *Journal of Ecclesiastical History* 58 (2007): 211–31; Lower, *The Tunis Crusade of 1270: A Mediterranean History* (Oxford: Oxford University Press, 2018).

7. Léon Borrelli de Serres, "Compte d'une mission de prédication pour secours à la Terre Sainte (1265)," *Mémoires de la société de l'histoire de Paris et de l'Ile-de-France* 30 (1903):

With little fanfare, on October 20, 1265, Eudes departed for the Holy Land at the head of a regiment of knights, what some historians have referred to as independent crusaders.[8] His expedition left just before contingents of barons and retainers joined Charles of Anjou, who marched through the Piedmont to Rome, in a series of campaigns in Italy that would entangle the French and Flemish in the lands of the Regno—that is, southern Italy and Sicily—for generations to come.[9] Eudes's expedition had the support of both Pope Clement IV and the French king, Louis IX. Indeed, Eudes's journey anticipated Louis IX's second and final crusade, which would depart for Tunis five years later, in March 1270. Eudes's presence in Syria responded to the need to shore up defenses in and around Acre and Jaffa and to deliver funds to support what was left of crusader Outremer. His presence in the East extended the French crown's commitment to maintain a foothold in Syria and in Greece. Jean Richard identified Eudes's expedition as the first "*passage particulier*," that is, "an operation limited in effect and objectives, with the goal of reinforcing and consolidating the Christian position in the East."[10]

Eudes traveled with Érard of Vallery and Érard of Nanteuil, and together they led fifty knights "in the service of God [*au service de Dieu*]."[11] In letters to the pope and to the king, this lordly contingent referred to themselves as "*chevaliers pelerins*," or knightly pilgrims.[12] Once they arrived in the Holy Land, they were to serve in aid to the French king's forces stationed in Acre.

243–80, and Richard, "La croisade de 1270." These events compiled in succession: July 25, 1261, Constantinople fell to the Greeks; March 24, 1267, the Paris Assembly convened, and Louis IX accepted the crusader's cross from Simon of Brie, the Franciscan cardinal of St. Cecilia; 1267 the Treaty of Viterbo in which the Latin emperor, Baldwin II of Courtenay, transferred suzerainty over the Princedom of Achaea to Charles of Anjou, king of Sicily. For the transfer of titles within the Latin Empire, see Filip Van Tricht, *The Latin "Renovatio" of Byzantium: The Empire of Constantinople (1204–1228)* (Leiden: Brill, 2011), 207–10. Several of Rutebeuf's poems translated below were written in direct response to these events.

8. On independent crusaders, that is, expeditions that were not part of larger and more coordinated or general efforts led by kings and popes, see Fordham University's *Independent Crusaders Mapping Project*, March 30, 2018, https://research.library.fordham.edu/ddp_archivingdossier/5/. For aid to the Holy Land in 1265, see Borelli de Serres, "Compte d'une mission de prédication."

9. Dunbabin, *The French in the Kingdom of Sicily*; and Norman Housley, *The Italian Crusades: The Papal-Angevin Alliance and the Crusades against Christian Lay Powers, 1254–1343* (Oxford: Clarendon Press, 1982).

10. Richard, "La croisade de 1270," 515.

11. Jonathan Riley-Smith, "The Crown of France and Acre, 1254–1291," in *France and the Holy Land: Frankish Culture at the End of the Crusades*, ed. Daniel H. Weiss and Lisa Mahoney (Baltimore: Johns Hopkins University Press, 2004), 51–52n65, citing: *TdT*, 104 (para. 103 [339]); and "L'Estoire de Eracles," *RHC* 2:454. Érard of Nanteuil is difficult to identify. Most likely a relative of Philip of Nanteuil, the family probably hailed from the region for the Ainse at Nanteuil-la-Fosse. A possible seal survives that may be connected to Érard of Nanteuil, on a charter in Paris, AN, S//5035 no. 39 (1256), available at Sigilla, http://www.sigilla.org/acte/an-paris-s-5035-ndeg-39-ii-48841.

12. Gustav Servois, "Emprunts de Saint Louis en Palestine et en Afrique," *Bibliothèque de l'École des chartes* 4 (1858): 129.

Sometimes known as the *stipendarii*, this was a permanent garrison of salaried knights who had remained in Acre to shore up the defense of the city and to hold the Holy Land following Louis IX's first failed crusade (1248–54).[13] In 1254, as he departed to return home to France, the king put Geoffrey of Sergines "the elder," one of his closest crusade companions, in command of the first contingent of one hundred knights, who remained in the East following the royal campaign.[14] Many of those serving in this cohort did so as *milites ad terminum*, that is, knights who performed service for a limited period of time and who often provided for their own maintenance.[15] Geoffrey of Sergines the elder was the first to hold the appointment of "captain," and combined that post with the seneschalsy of the Kingdom of Jerusalem, a royal administrative position that gave him the authority to govern within the city. Geoffrey served in both capacities until his death in 1269.[16] Following his return to France, Louis IX "spent an average of four thousand pounds *tournois* per year from 1254 to 1270" in support of the *stipendarii*, who remained in the East, headquartered in Acre.[17] In 1265, Eudes's expedition coincided with an additional set of payments transferred from the crown, which Geoffrey's son, Geoffrey of Sergines the younger, and Érard of Vallery oversaw.[18]

13. For the garrison in Acre, see Christopher J. Marshall, "The French Regiment in the Latin East, 1254–91," *Journal of Medieval History* 15 (1989): 301–7. On the terms used and *stipendarii* specifically, see Riley-Smith, "The Crown of France and Acre," 51–52nn66–67; and Pierre-Vincent Claverie, ed., *L'ordre du Temple dans l'Orient des croisades* (Brussels: De Boeck, 2014).

14. Joinville refers to Geoffrey as "a good knight and *preudhomme*." Jean de Joinville, *Vie de Saint Louis*, ed. J. Monfrin (Paris: Garnier, 1995) [hereafter Joinville, *VSL*, cited by paragraph number]. Joinville's phrase is "preudommes chevaliers": "tiex chevaliers soloit l'en appeler *bons* chevalier. Le non de ceulz qui estoient chevaliers entour le roy sont tiex: mon seigneurs Geoffroy de Sargines, mon seigneur Mahi de Marley, mon seigneur Phelippe de Nanteul, mon seigneur Hymbert de Biaujeu." Joinville, *VSL*, para. 173, see also paras. 308–9, 369, 378, 438, and 571. For the situation in the East at this time, see Servois, "Emprunts de Saint Louis," and Riley-Smith, "The Crown of France and Acre."

15. As such they were not always part of a specific retinue, but had to maintain themselves and their own horses, squires, and pages. See Jochen G. Schenk, "Forms of Lay Association with the Order of the Temple," *Journal of Medieval History* 34 (2008): 100–103; and Alan Forey, "*Milites ad terminum* in the Military Orders during the Twelfth and Thirteenth Centuries," in *The Military Orders*, vol. 4: *On Land and By Sea*, edited by Judi Upton-Ward (London: Routledge, 2016), 23–30.

16. See Riley-Smith, "The Crown of France and Acre," 47. The position of seneschal of Arce was sometimes referred to as *bailli* or bailiff. In short, he was the highest administrative official working on behalf of the royal government in Acre.

17. William Chester Jordan, *Louis IX and the Challenge of the Crusade* (Princeton, NJ: Princeton University Press, 1979), 78; Riley-Smith, "The Crown of France and Acre"; and Joseph R. Strayer, "The Crusades of Louis IX," in Strayer, *Medieval Statecraft and the Perspectives of History* (Princeton, NJ: Princeton University Press, 1971), 159–92. See also Borelli de Serres, "Comptes d'une mission de prédication," 255n6.

18. These transactions were uncovered and discussed in Servois, "Emprunts de Saint Louis." For the papal letters addressing funds in support of Acre and the Holy Land, see Teulet, *Layettes*,

It was in this context of crusade service, at the age of thirty-six, that Eudes of Nevers died in Acre on August 7, 1266. He and his family were at the height of aristocratic prestige and connection. In June 1265 his eldest daughter, Yolande (d. 1280), married King Louis IX's youngest son, Jean Tristan (d. 1270), just as a new Mediterranean-wide crusade campaign was being planned.[19] Three years later, in 1268, Eudes's second daughter, Marguerite (d. 1308), married the king's youngest brother, Charles of Anjou (d. 1285), and became Countess of Anjou, queen of Sicily, and (titular) queen of Jerusalem. The connections with the Capetians and the crown of Sicily would persist for generations in titles and through objects passed among heirs. These connections also go some way toward explaining how and why Eudes's final Account-Inventory made its way to Paris. At the time of Eudes's death, his executors in Acre finalized his accounts and recorded his inventory as part of the process of disbursing the final payments for his debts and overseeing the partial liquidation of his movable goods. They also oversaw Eudes's final bequests, both charitable and personal, and orchestrated the care of his body, the embalming of his heart, and his final burial. His executors and legal representatives included one of Eudes's household knights, Hugh of Augerant, and his companion, Érard of Vallery, who was represented in the initial transactions by Geoffrey of Sergines the younger. Although Eudes made provisions for his goods in Acre—offering instructions, referred to in our text as *lais* (F. *legs*)—no formal testament appears to exist. Despite a growing interest on the part of the crusading nobility in creating final testaments before departure, Eudes's death, it seems, was unexpected, something no one, perhaps especially Eudes, had prepared for fully.[20]

Eudes's inventory offers a rare glimpse into the accoutrements and objects a crusader of stature carried with him to the East in the later part of the thirteenth century. It illuminates the kinds of obligations such men took on and the ways they provided for their retinue—the many layers of men (and possibly a few women) in their service. It details how such men dressed and maintained themselves, their servants, their quarters, and their kitchens. The

---

4:149 and 163–64; for the transfer of funds and loans by Érard of Vallery, 4:144 (July 1265), 4:230 (July 7, 1267, Acre), and involving Geoffrey of Sergines, 4:155–56 (October 29, 1265, Acre), 4:228–29 (June 30, 1267, Acre). For the financial and military situation in the Holy Land in the later thirteenth century, see also Judith Bronstein, *The Hospitallers in the Holy Land: Financing the Latin East, 1187–1274* (Woodbridge: Boydell, 2005).

19. Lespinasse, *Le Nivernais*, 2:267–70, 287–93.

20. It was not uncommon for some crusaders to draw up their will or testament at the last moment, or at the moment of death. Guy IV of Forez had done so as he lay dying in Brindisi in 1241; see Lester, "Crusading as a Religious Movement," 137. Likewise, Hugh of Neville and Edward I of England both wrote or dictated wills while in Acre in 1269 and 1272, respectively. See below.

inventory too sheds light on how they entertained and engaged in personal and public acts of diplomacy, devotion, and aristocratic self-presentation, as well as the many ways that wealth was made portable in the form of coinage, clothing, jewels, and plate. The surviving five *rouleaux* reflect the lively and lived documentary and fiscal culture of crusader Acre, which employed multiple strategies for record-keeping, used various currencies of account, and relied upon the copious circulation of people and goods gathered together. It is thus a rare administrative survival—one written in Acre, in Old French, and carried to, and finally archived in, Paris. As a textual object, it represents relationships that were far more complex and intertwined than have previously been considered.[21] The clerks or scribes gave careful attention to the payments and amounts recorded, which are given in three different currencies: local *bezants*, the money of account in Acre; pounds *tournois*, the currency of the royal domain of France; and the silver mark sterling, the international money of account (see figures 8–10).[22] The precise enumeration of goods and services and the checking and rechecking of summary totals and values as embedded in the text's repetitions is indicative of a set of individuals and institutions present and at work with different, and at times competing, interests, all of which made up the crusading world of a great French baron. Moreover, the Account-Inventory offers us access inside the chambers, armories, kitchens, and religious spaces of a crusader's household during the final decades of Latin rule in the East, revealing the lived material world of crusader Outremer.

21. For a marvelous analysis of a similar sort of "living text," see the discussion of Abraham's list in Elizabeth A. Lambourn, *Abraham's Luggage: A Social Life of Things in the Medieval Indian Ocean* (Cambridge: Cambridge University Press, 2018). An Account-Inventory is also, in its most basic form, a set of lists. Much has been written about inventories, the process of inventorying, and lists and list-making. For some of this scholarship, see the articles collected on the DALME website: https://dalme.org/project/bibliography/. For the poetic and political potential of lists, see also Claire Angotti, Pierre Chastang, Vincent Debiais and Laura Kendrick, eds. *Le pouvoir des listes au moyen âge: Écritures de la liste* (Paris: Éditions de la Sorbonne, 2019); and Katherine C. Little, "The Politics of Lists," *Exemplaria* 31 (2019): 117–28.

22. On the currencies and their values at the time, see Chazaud, "Inventaire," 174–76. More broadly, see Gustave Schlumberger, *Numismatiques de l'Orient latin* (Paris: Leroux, 1878); David Michael Metcalf, *Coinage of the Crusades and the Latin East in the Ashmolean Museum, Oxford*, 2nd ed. (London: Royal Numismatic Society and Society for the Study of the Crusades and the Latin East, 1995); and Alan M. Stahl, "The Circulation of European Coinage in the Crusader States," in *The Meeting of Two Worlds: Cultural Exchange between East and West during the Period of the Crusades*, ed. Vladimir P. Goss and Christin V. Bornstein, Studies in Medieval Culture 21 (Kalamazoo: Medieval Institute Publications, 1986), 85–102.

4

French Acre

The Language and Landscapes of the Rouleaux

Previous studies of Eudes's Account-Inventory have emphasized the western elements and actors mentioned in the texts with very little acknowledgement of the Outremer setting. But closer scrutiny of the *rouleaux* situates these texts firmly within the context of Crusader Acre. Unlike written products crafted solely to allow the reader to engage with and linger over the written word (such as liturgical books or historical narratives), these records were ancillary to the main proceedings. They were created to accompany the actions of those who carried them out. In this way, the rolls functioned as an *aide-compte*, that is, as an aid for accounting, and an *aide-memoire*, a memory device. Just as the *rouleaux* allow us to reconstruct the actions of the main figures of Eudes's retinue, they also render evidence of the landscapes and cultural environments where those events transpired.

The world of Acre is visible in two ways: first, in the location-specific institutions and vocabularies listed within; and second, through the Outremer-inflected language and writing styles used to describe the count's final deeds and to instruct how his affairs were to be settled. But we also see how eastern and western elements cohabitated, combined, and at times clashed in this unrehearsed and unpolished recounting of Eudes's Outremer experiences. Those aspects specific to the Holy Land, including references to Acre-based political and religious institutions, the recourse to Levantine vocabularies, and the use of Old French for documentation, all vie with currencies, ways of reckoning time, and certain graphic and toponymic norms rooted in a western Christian worldview. The imbrication of both Levantine and western European elements makes Eudes's Account-Inventory stand out clearly as a product of the Latin East's thirteenth-century capital city.

The Account-Inventory is also an invaluable list of the principal churches and other religious organizations named as beneficiaries in the document, all of which were located in and around the northwestern part of the city.[1] Whether this list reflects Eudes's choices or those of his executors we can't know, but the place-names recorded on Roll C serve as a handlist of institutions and individuals in Acre deemed worthy of aristocratic testamentary bequests. In drawing up his magisterial topographical lexicon of the churches in the crusader Kingdom of Jerusalem, Denys Pringle used Eudes's inventory as one of his key sources to map the religious landscape of Acre in the later thirteenth century.[2] Religious houses, leper hospitals, both smaller independent groups and those connected to the Order of St. Lazarus, as well as beguines and hermits are all listed on Roll C among Eudes's beneficiaries.[3] The list is both selective and securely rooted in a knowledge of Acre's social and religious topography. Not every institution in the city is named, nor are any organizations mentioned as recipients beyond those located within the city and its nearby environs, with the possible exception of one unidentified church named "St. Mary of Vamit."[4]

The locations of these institutions reveal that Eudes and his retinue had either developed ties to beneficiaries scattered throughout Acre, or had been advised, for reasons now lost to us, to donate to a geographically widespread set of recipients. Very few of Eudes's bequests were made to institutions at the heart of the city, near the port, in areas dominated by inhabitants from the Italian city-states of Venice, Genoa, and Pisa. Rather, the majority of Eudes's bequests went to religious houses, hospitals, and churches found around the perimeter of the crowded urban center, or placed well to the north, extending into the adjacent French-dominated suburb of Montmusard. The churches of St. Thomas the Martyr, St. Bartholomew, St. Martin, the Franciscan headquarters, and the Bethlehem Hospital, for example, were all located in Montmusard. St. Michael's, however, situated at the furthest edge of the old city bordering the coast and adjacent to the town's ancient walls, also benefited from the count's generosity. This was the same location where fellow crusader and author John of Joinville had convalesced in 1250 after a near brush with death.[5]

1. The location of each institution is listed in Denys Pringle, *The Churches of the Crusader Kingdom of Jerusalem: A Corpus* (Cambridge: Cambridge University Press, 1993–2009), 4:23. Our map relies on the placement of these institutions on Pringle's map, at 4:16–17.

2. See Pringle, *The Churches of the Crusader Kingdom*, 4:21–23 and 46.

3. On the charitable landscape between Acre and Jerusalem in general, see Pringle, *The Churches of the Crusader Kingdom*; for the Order of St. Lazar, see Malcolm Barber, "The Order of Saint Lazarus and the Crusades," *Catholic Historical Review* 80 (1994): 439–56.

4. Pringle, *The Churches of the Crusader Kingdom*, 4:23.

5. Pringle, *The Churches of the Crusader Kingdom*, 4:57. For monastic houses in the Crusader States more broadly, see Bernard Hamilton and Andrew Jotischky, *Latin and Greek Monasticism in the Crusader States* (Cambridge: Cambridge University Press, 2020). On Joinville's time in Acre, see Joinville, *VSL*, paras. 406–69, esp. 410.

Map 2. Religious institutions in Acre listed in Eudes's inventory, after Pringle. L. Morreale.

The long list of Acre-based institutions places this text squarely in the Crusader States' capital. Even if we are unaware of the precise locations of these religious houses and hospitals, there are other more subtle indications of the texts' context of creation. A specific Holy Land vocabulary was characteristic of the French-language documents produced at the time. Local terms used to describe Levantine geographies, military titles, or currencies were incorporated into the lexicon of western Christians during their time in the crusading East. Tyre (*Sur*), Beirut (*Bereithe*), and Château Pèlerin (*Chastiau pelerin*) were all eastern locations mentioned explicitly in the text following their Eastern usage. These names appear either on their own or as toponyms to accompany institutions found on eudes's list of beneficiaries. The title of turcopole (Account-Inventory: *trecopole*), a term of decidedly eastern origin and understood as a position equivalent to a light cavalryman, describes several of the combatants in Eudes's retinue and listed among those in his pay.[6] Words for Levantine currency denominations, the bezant and the *quarroble*, appear either written out or as well-known symbols or abbreviations on nearly every surface of the five *rouleaux*. And finally, some of the goods—especially fabrics—found in Eudes's apartments carry linguistic traces of their Levantine origins. Fabrics of eastern production described as *boqueranz*, *cameline*, or *dras de tartais* contrast with the cloth coming from the northern French towns of *Provins* (Provins) and *Troies* (Troyes) or the duchy of *Borgoingne* (Burgundy).[7]

The clearest indicator, however, of the texts' Outremer provenance is the choice of Old French as the language of record. In Acre, many individuals and corporate entities used a style of Old French that scholars now call the *French of Outremer* or *Outremer French* to record their affairs.[8] Although Eudes's inventory displays only some of the linguistic markers of Outremer French, the fact that this legal and administrative document was written in French at all in many ways aligns it more closely with the linguistic and graphic norms common to crusader Acre and to the knightly administrative elite at work there than to the Christian, Latinate West.[9] Aside from the Acre-based religious institutions to which Eudes pledged money or objects of value, the city

6. Laura Minervini, "What We Do and Do Not Know about Outremer French," in *The French of Outremer: Communities and Communications in the Crusading Mediterranean*, ed. Laura K. Morreale and Nicholas L. Paul (New York: Fordham University Press, 2018), 15–29. See also Cyril Aslanov, "Languages in Contact in the Latin East: Acre and Cyprus," *Crusades* 1 (2002): 155–81; and Aslanov, *Le français au Levant, jadis et naguère: À la recherche d'une langue perdue* (Paris: Champion, 2006).

7. See the discussion of cloth types and production below, and in the essay by Sharon Farmer.

8. Minervini, "What We Do and Do Not Know about Outremer French."

9. Cyril Aslanov, "Crusaders' Old French," in *Research on Old French: The State of the Art*, ed. Deborah L. Arteaga (Dordrecht: Springer Netherlands, 2012), 207–20. On graphic practices in Acre, see Pierre Noble, "Écrire dans le Royaume franc: La *scripta* de deux manuscrits copiés à Acre au XIIIe siècle," in *Variations linguistiques: Koinés, dialectes, français régionaux*, ed. Pierre Noble (Besançon: Presses universitaires de Franche-Comté, 2003), 33–52; and Laura Minervini, "Le français dans l'Orient latin (XIIIe–XIVe siècles): Éléments pour la caractérisation d'une *scripta* du Levant," *Revue de linguistique romane* 74 (2010): 121–98.

also served as the headquarters for several western-facing secular and ecclesiastical institutions, all of which contributed to the unique graphic culture that shaped the composition of the dying count's Account-Inventory. The list of institutions producing written texts in thirteenth-century Acre was impressive: the bishops of Bethlehem, Nazareth, and Acre all maintained residences in the city, as did the patriarch of Jerusalem and brethren of the Hospitallers, the Templars, and the Teutonic Knights, all of whom relied on writing offices or formal chanceries.[10] In addition, three different Italian city-state communities were anchored in the areas surrounding the port, and their members often worked in multiple languages, including various dialects of Italian, Ladino, and Old French. These institutions and cultural communities relied on the skills of writers and scribes whose textual products spanned several genres, including business contracts, legal statutes, translations from one language into another, pilgrim wills and bequests, liturgical texts, local history books, or works of leisure reading such as romances or song collections like the ones found in Eudes's apartments.[11] All of these Acre-based institutions produced written documents that recorded the financial and diplomatic affairs in which they were engaged, whether in the Holy Land or abroad. A significant number of these documents were produced in French rather than Latin or a local vernacular, or were written in both French and another language including Italian, the French of Italy, or Ladino.[12]

Of the Acre-based institutions that produced French-language texts, the Templars appear most prominently in the Account-Inventory as the site where the count's monies were received, exchanged, and disbursed. The Temple functioned as the bank of deposit for Louis IX on his own trip to the Holy Land, and he continued to use the Templars' services to direct funds eastward after his return to France in 1254.[13] And the duke of Burgundy sent his son, our

10. For western-oriented institutions and their placement in Acre, see Pringle, *The Churches of the Crusader Kingdom*; and David Jacoby, "L'évolution urbaine et la fonction méditerranéenne d'Acre à l'époque des croisades," in *Citta portuali del Mediterraneo, storia e archeologia: Atti del Convegno Internazionale di Genova 1985*, ed. Ennio Poleggi (Geneva: Sagep, 1989), 95–109.

11. For an overview of the types of literature produced in the Latin East, see Anthony Bale, "Reading and Writing in Outremer," in *The Cambridge Companion to the Literature of the Crusades*, ed. Anthony Bale (Cambridge: Cambridge University Press, 2018), 85–101; and Jonathan Rubin, *Learning in a Crusader City: Intellectual Activity and Intercultural Exchanges in Acre, 1191–1291* (Cambridge: Cambridge University Press, 2018).

12. For documents from Acre, see Reinhold Röhricht, *Regesta Regni Hierosolymitani (MXCVII–MCCXCI)* (Oeniponti: Libraria Academica Wageriana, 1893); for a mapping of graphic practice in Acre, see Laura Morreale, *Pilgrims and Writing in Crusader Acre*, https://scalar.lauramorreale.com/pilgrims-and-writing-in-crusader-acre/graphic-topographies-of-crusader-acre. As noted above, Eudes's Account-Inventory is exceptional in that it was not included in the *Regesta*.

13. David Michael Metcalf, "The Templars as Bankers and Monetary Transfers between West and East in the Twelfth Century," in *Coinage in the Latin East: The Fourth Oxford Symposium on Coinage and Monetary History*, ed. Peter Edbury and D. M. Metcalf, 2nd ed. (Oxford: Ashmolean Museum, 1995), 1–17; and Léopold Delisle, *Mémoire sur les opérations financières des Templiers* (Paris: Impr. Nationale, 1889), 23.

Eudes, monies by this same route. We read that "500 marks sterling were delivered from Burgundy, which the duke of Burgundy sent to the count by way of the Temple, in the August passage, which were worth, on that day in Acre, 1,387 *lb* 10 *s.* ~~. . . d~~ *t*."[14] Like the Hospitallers and Teutonic Knights, the Templars produced administrative documentation in Outremer French while headquartered in the Levant. And like their Hospitaller counterparts, they did so in greatest abundance in the decades between 1250 and 1270.[15] Members of the Templar order also wrote letters in French while stationed in Acre. The Holy Land has been provisionally identified as the production locale for one of the three surviving manuscript copies of the French-language version of the Templar's *Rule* and *Retrais* (supplementary legislation).[16] In short, the clerics and scribes who wrote the Account-Inventory and who chose French as the language of record were working in line with the documentary practices of their Templar associates.

And yet, to focus solely on the Levantine elements of these texts is to tell only half the story. What makes this set of writings stand out as a product of Outremer—that is, coming from a place that could only exist and be understood as "across the sea" from one's homeland in the West—is the imbrication of western-imported and Levantine local words, ideas, referents, and graphic practices. For example, while the names of the religious houses of Acre linked them to the western Christian canon of saints widely recognized across Christendom and the Mediterranean (e.g., St. Anne, St. Bartholomew, St. Anthony), several feast days mentioned as reference points in the account documents were saints known in northern France specifically. Whereas the feasts of Saint Lawrence, Saint Michael, and that of the Holy Cross, all used as dates of record in the Account-Inventory, were shared within the Christian calendar, the feast day of Saint Leu (Loup), probably referred to the celebration of the seventh-century bishop of Sens, also called Saint Lupus, which took place on the first of September.[17] Its inclusion as a date of record signals both the geographic connection to and an insider familiarity with this northern French saint on the

14. Edition, Roll A Front, Part 2: "Il fu aporte de borgoingne v^{c} mars destellins que li dux de Borgoingne envoia le conte par le temple au passaige daoust qui valoient au jour de lors en Acre m iii^{ccc} iiii^{xx} vii *lb* x *s* ~~. . . d~~ tornois." Chazaud, "Inventaire," 185.

15. Érard of Vallery composed a letter in French in 1267 that confirmed receipt of funds from Louis IX's Sienese creditors by way of the Templars. On Érard's correspondence, see below. See also Laura K. Morreale, "French-Language Documents Produced by the Hospitallers, 1231–1310," *Journal of Medieval History* 40 (2014): 439–57.

16. The manuscript in question is Paris, BnF, MS fr. 1977. Simonetta Cerrini, "La tradition manuscrite de la règle du temple," in *Autour de la première croisade: Actes du colloque de la Society for the Study of the Crusades and the Latin East (Clermont-Ferrand, 22–25 juin 1995)*, ed. Michel Balard (Paris: Publications de la Sorbonne, 1996), 216. A fourth manuscript of the *Rule* survived until the twentieth century, housed in Dijon, but the manuscript was stolen in 1985 just after the publication of the catalogue of the library's holdings and has yet to be recovered.

17. Not to be confused with Saint Leu (Lupus) of Troyes. See Bryan Ward-Perkins and Robert Wiśniewski, eds., "The Cult of Saints in Late Antiquity Database," http://csla.history.ox.ac.uk.

part of the compiler-accountants. Even when the texts were operating within a shared, cohesive, western Christian calendar of sanctoral references, there is a sense that each instance of saintly naming also existed alongside another western or Levantine counterpart.

Just as the Holy Land place-names evoked the near landscape in which the records were created, they could also call to mind personal identities and associations. Place-names not only designate geographic locations, they also identified people. Western toponyms that referenced locations Francophone visitors to Acre might have called *deça mer* (this side of the sea, meaning western Europe) were a reminder that *la Terre Outremer* could only exist when charted from a western perspective.[18] The texts that list Acre, Tyre, and Château Pèlerin alongside Troyes, Cîteaux, and Burgundy are a clear witness to how East met West in the Crusader States and in the surviving records that originated there. The long list of toponymic surnames among Eudes's payees in Roll A is a reminder that the majority of his retinue were displaced and very far from home while stationed in Acre. Northern French toponyms like *de Diepe*, *de Brabant*, and *le Picart* were placed side by side with other payees, such as the "valet who served the archbishop of Tyre [*Vallet qui fu a larcevesque de Sur*]."[19] This uneven pairing often jolts the reader into a confrontation with the reality of displacement for so many of those listed. The admixture is also present in vocational names; the French-language vocations *le Clerc* (the clerk) and *le Chapelain* (the chaplain) contrast with the *trecoples* found in Roll A, making the reader wonder whether the jobs of clerk and chaplain were different in the Levant than in the West. Ever-present as well is the tension that exists between the monetary denominations cited in the texts, whether Levantine (*bezant* and *quarroble*), northern French (*sous tournois*) or international (*mark sterling*). The Account-Inventory's frequent conversion of value from one denomination to another, one system of account to the next, demonstrates acutely how daily life in this context involved a constant negotiation between the worlds of *outre* and *deça mer*.

The skills visitors and inhabitants of thirteenth-century Acre developed when mediating between one set of norms and another extended to graphic and literary styles as well. From the early twelfth century, those who wrote for the knightly class in the West valued Old French as a multiform medium of expression. By the mid-thirteenth century, writers in the crusader East had become increasingly adept at doing the same for knightly readers. Several French-language manuscripts produced in Acre in the later part of the

For the history of Saint Leu in the region, see Clark Maines, *The Western Portal of Saint-Loup-de-Naud* (New York: Garland, 1979).

18. Alan Forey, "The Office of Master *deça mer* in Military Orders," in *The Templars and Their Sources*, ed. Karl Borchardt, Karoline Döring, Philippe Josserand, and Helen Nicholson (London: Routledge, 2017), 125–32.

19. Edition, Roll A Front, Part 1.

century, including histories and chansonniers similar to those found among the count's belongings, spoke directly to the interests of aristocratic readers and their desire to participate in the crusading culture of the Latin East. The Account-Inventory, therefore, can be seen as a combination of two types of emerging Outremer French-language writing styles, the documentary and knightly narrative.[20] As the documents' creators accounted for what was required to feed, house, and maintain a retinue, to ensure the spiritual routines deemed necessary for a crusader-noble's household like Eudes's, and to bequeath alms following the death of a great lord, they were also documenting the material constituents of performed crusader-knighthood.[21] Not surprisingly, since the settings and items they described were aristocratic in nature, the compilers also inserted subtle snippets of narrative style and turns of phrase that evoked knightly literatures. For example, instead of noting Eudes's date of death in relation to a certain feast day, as was the case with other dates in the text, the makers of the Account-Inventory recorded Eudes's final day as "the day the count passed from life to death." Similarly, the honorific "mon segnor" (my lord) punctuates throughout the text and, unlike in many accounting documents, is almost never omitted when they name the three principal executors, Érard of Vallery, Geoffrey of Sergines, and Hugh of Augerant.

20. Eudes's Account-Inventory was not the first Old French text written in the Latin East to combine documentary and narrative writing styles. The first prose history written in French comes from Geoffrey of Villehardouin, whose *Conquete de Constantinople* was written in the Latin East. Villehardouin's text, like that of Robert of Clari, also written in Old French, was part of an efflorescence of vernacular writing that emerged at the turn of the thirteenth century, drawing in the interests of a French reading/listening aristocracy, many of whom were women, and echoing a documentary practice that was increasingly pursued publicly in the vernacular as well. On the importance of the French vernacular tradition, see Gabrielle M. Spiegel, *Romancing the Past: The Rise of Vernacular Prose Historiography in Thirteenth-Century France* (Berkeley: University of California Press, 1993); on vernacularity in the crusade context, see Anne E. Lester, "Crusading as a Religious Movement: Families, Community, and Lordship in a Vernacular Frame," in *Between Orders and Heresy: Rethinking Medieval Religious Movements*, ed. Jennifer Kolpacoff Deane and Anne E. Lester (Toronto: University of Toronto Press, 2021), 127–69; and Marisa Galvez, *The Subject of Crusade: Lyric, Romance, and Materials, 1150 to 1500* (Chicago: University of Chicago Press, 2020). See also Theodore Evergates, *Geoffroy of Villehardouin, Marshal of Champagne* (Ithaca, NY: Cornell University Press, 2024), which sheds important light on these questions. For a wider and multilingual vernacular circulation, see Teresa Shawcross, *The Chronicle of Morea: Historiography in Crusader Greece* (Oxford: Oxford University Press, 2009), 53–114; as well as Uri Zvi Shachar, *A Pious Belligerence: Dialogical Warfare and the Rhetoric of Righteousness in the Crusading Near East* (Philadelphia: University of Pennsylvania Press, 2021).

21. Recent work on the contours of the knightly culture of Outremer and its movement between East and West demonstrates how powerful an ideal and cultural imaginary this was becoming. See, for example, Amanda R. Luyster, ed., *Bringing the Holy Land Home: The Crusades, Chertsey Abbey, and the Reconstruction of a Medieval Masterpiece* (Turnhout: Brepols/Harvey Miller, 2023).

The Account-Inventory does more than document; it represents and even reenacts an Outremer knightly ethos in real-life terms. Curiously, it is in the text that was copied twice in the Account-Inventory—once on the day of Eudes's death (on Roll B) and a second time on the parchment containing a list of all his bequests (Roll C)—that we see the strongest traces of a knightly narrative style and *courtoisie* come through. Akin to *chansons de geste* written to extol knightly models or the personalized laments (*complaintes*) Rutebeuf composed, the text elements repeated in Rolls B and C capture a scene in which the dying count bestows precious objects to his followers and ceremoniously distributes a sapphire, emeralds, and rings from Le Puy—all of which he had carried with him from his homeland—to the most loyal members of his entourage.[22] The mini-scripts of Eudes's bestowals are laced with the vocabulary of aristocratic patronage and obligation. The scribes emphasize and repeat terms of masculine relationships and endearments (brothers, a father, the *patriarches*), as well as those that reference the practice of the faith, including mentions of liturgical garb (a surplice) and other sacred treasures (a breviary, a golden cross, and a collection of relics). Even though the Account-Inventory seems to share little with the genre of elaborately rhyming chivalric French-language literature created in the Holy Land and elsewhere, the scribes chose to use similar objects, actions, and expressions to animate the *rouleaux*. This was entirely appropriate as Outremer writers and audiences were comfortable reading and writing both documentary and chivalric texts in French. The crossover from one genre to another exhibited in the inventory was common for writing originating in the Latin East.[23] Both permanent and part-time members of these communities were constantly negotiating the intermediary nature of their activities and identities, at times looking westward, at other times firmly anchored in the affairs of the Holy Land. The compositional strategies employed in this multicultural context, the materials Eudes's executors had at their disposal while living in the Latin East, and even Acre's on-the-ground sacred geographies, all rise to the surface in the text and mark it as a product of the Outremer.

Although circulation characterizes the contents of the rolls, we remain in the dark about why, when, and how they traveled from Acre to France and then into the archives in Paris. Certainly, by the later thirteenth century the crown had a vested interest in the territories that made up the fiefs of

22. Edition, Roll B Back; Roll C Back; and the discussion of these objects below.

23. See Nicholas L. Paul, "In Search of the Marshal's Lost Crusade: The Persistence of Memory, the Problems of History and the Painful Birth of Crusading Romance," *Journal of Medieval History* 40 (2014): 292–310. On the crossover among genres and ideas, see the masterful study by Barbara Newman, *Medieval Crossover: Reading the Secular against the Sacred* (Notre Dame, IN: University of Notre Dame Press, 2013). Concerning the broader circulation of ideas and practices in this context, see the essays in Stephen G. Nichols, Joachim Küpper, and Andreas Kablitz, eds., *Spectral Sea: Mediterranean Palimpsests in European Culture* (New York: Peter Lang, 2017); and Luyster, *Bringing the Holy Land Home*.

Burgundy and Nevers. In 1265, the year before Eudes's death, Louis IX's son Jean Tristan married Eudes's daughter Yolande and took the title of count of Nevers, which he held until his death in 1270 while on crusade in Tunis. It may have been useful for the young couple and then the royal administration to have a list of Eudes's knights in service in the East. After his death many of these same men were retained to serve and defend of the Kingdom of Jerusalem and continued to be paid and to reside in Acre through 1268.[24] Thus, Eudes's Account-Inventory, and certainly Roll A, could have functioned as a form of feudal register or accounting record reflecting how much each person was to be paid, much like the records maintained by the crusade leaders in the 1270s as contingents of crusaders passed through the Kingdom of Sicily in the aftermath of the Tunis crusade.[25] It is also likely that the rolls were used or perhaps even recopied in the mid-1270s as part of the ongoing disputes over the inheritances of Burgundy that ensued among Eudes's daughters and their respective husbands.[26] After 1270, and the death of Jean Tristan, Yolande married her second husband, Robert of Bethuné, the future count of Flanders. Eudes's second daughter, Marguerite, was married to Charles of Anjou and took the title queen of Sicily, which she held during her lifetime.[27] The sisters maintained close ties, fostered by visitors, relatives, and their own travel between France, Flanders, and the Regno. The movement of wealth and titles within and among the houses of Anjou, Sicily, Flanders, Nevers, and Tonnerre, among others, however, remained contentious and complex. Eudes's

24. Christopher J. Marshall, "The French Regiment in the Latin East," *Journal of Medieval History* 15 (1989): 303.

25. On the *Rôles des fiefs* for Champagne, see Theodore Evergates, *Feudal Society in the Bailliage of Troyes under the Counts of Champagne, 1152–1284* (Baltimore: Johns Hopkins University Press, 1975). In the crusade context, see the discussion of such record-keeping practices in Jean Dunbabin, *The French in the Kingdom of Sicily, 1266–1305* (Cambridge: Cambridge University Press, 2005), 78–98; and comparatively, see Dunbabin, "The Household and Entourage of Charles I, King of the Regno, 1266–85," *Historical Research* 77 (2004): 313–36. The lists of men accompanying each leader have been edited in Riccardo Filangieri et al., eds., *I registri della Cancelleria angioina* (Naples: L'Accademia, 1951–2006), vol. 6: Register XXII, item 891 (at pp. 171–72) and item 1205 (at pp. 226–27). For another example of the payments and feudal inventories of a princely court, see Erika Graham-Goering, *Princely Power in Late Medieval France: Jeanne de Penthièvre and the War for Brittany* (Cambridge: Cambridge University Press, 2020).

26. See Dunbabin, *The French in the Kingdom of Sicily*, 15–17, 41–42, 124–26.

27. Yves Sassier, "Conflit de succession entre heritieres et sentence du parlement royal au XIIIe siècle: La partition du grand comté de Nevers-Auxerre-Tonnerre (Toussaint 1273)," in *Inheritance, Law and Religions in the Ancient and Medieval Worlds*, ed. Béatrice Caseau and Sabine R. Huebner (Paris: ACHAByz, 2014), 67–74; Meredith Parsons Lillich, *The Queen of Sicily and Gothic Stained Glass in Mussy and Tonnerre* (Philadelphia: American Philosophical Society, 1998); and L. Le Maistre, "Marguerite de Bourgogne, reine de Naples, de Sicile et de Jérusalem, Comtesse de Tonnerre," *Annuaire historique du département de l'Yonne* 31 (1867): 43–109; see also Jean Richard, *Les ducs de Bourgogne et de la formation du duché, du XIe au XIVe siècle* (Dijon: Bernigaud et Privat, 1954), 318–28.

Account-Inventory offered in the 1270s, as it still does now, a model of a luxuriant court with clothing and gifts in abundance, very much of a piece with the courts of Sicily, Artois, and Flanders by the close of the century.[28] Finally, the text's descriptive quality, especially Rolls B–D, may have also, simultaneously, served a commemorative function, evoking the count in all his sartorial splendor and in the many gifts enumerated and recounted for those who read the administrative text in the West.

28. For the life of such courts, see Dunbabin, "The Household and Entourage of Charles I"; Sharon Farmer, "Aristocratic Power and the 'Natural' Landscape: The Garden Park at Hesdin, ca. 1291–1302," *Speculum* 88 (2013): 644–680; and Sarah-Grace Heller, "Revisiting the Inventories of Artois: Fashion, Status, and Taste at the Court of Mahaut, ca. 1307–1310," in *Inventories of Textiles—Textiles in Inventories: Studies on Late Medieval and Early Modern Material Culture*, ed. Thomas Ertl and Barbara Karl (Vienna: Vienna University Press, 2017), 71–87.

5

Outremer Subjects

A Crusader's Retinue

Although the count of Nevers is the principal subject of the Account-Inventory, the text makes reference to a vast array of individuals in Eudes's employ and within his household. Paramount among them are three knights, two of whom accompanied him to the East and who together coordinated the assessment and appraisal of his goods and oversaw the payments and disbursal of his wealth both in cash and in kind: Érard of Vallery, Geoffrey of Sergines the younger, and Hugh of Augerant. Surprisingly little scholarship has focused on these men, although they played critical roles in the business of the Holy Land and the Mediterranean-wide crusades planned between 1261 and 1272. Rutebeuf, the vernacular poet active around the court of Louis IX, offered detailed contemporary poetic portraits of Eudes, count of Nevers, as well as Geoffrey of Sergines the elder (father of Geoffrey the younger) and Érard of Vallery. Composed as a series of *complaintes*, that is, laments and tributes to these men as models of chivalric valor, they formed part of a corpus of crusade verse compositions possibly performed for the royal court or in related courtly circles.[1] Rutebeuf argued that Eudes, Geoffrey, and Érard gave their lives in service to the cross and extolled their commitments as exemplars, goading others to take up the cross anew on the eve of the Tunis expedition.[2] As such, Rutebeuf's poems offer valuable contemporary observations

1. See Anne Latowsky's introduction to Rutebeuf's poems below.

2. The "Complaintes" were written between 1255 and 1267 or possibly later, but before 1270. *Oeuvres complètes de Rutebeuf, Trouvère du XIIIe siècle: Recueillies et mises au jour pour la première fois*, ed. Archille Jubinal, 3 vols. (Paris: A. Delahays, 1874–1875); *Rutebeuf: Oeuvres complètes*, ed. Michel Zink (Paris: Classiques Garnier, 2001); *Oeuvres complètes*

and commentary on the actions, ambitions, and legacies of Eudes and those within his circle and provide a poetic gloss in the staccato language of the Account-Inventory.

In the late fall of 1265 **Érard of Vallery** departed with Eudes and Érard of Nanteuil for Acre. Although we do not know the precise route they took, it is likely that they set out from Lyons, on the border of Burgundy, and followed the Rhône River south to Marseille and from there sailed by way of Italy and Bari to Cyprus or directly to Acre. The Italian peninsula was deeply divided at that moment, and Charles of Anjou was mustering his own troops to face the last Hohenstaufen heirs for control of the crown of Sicily.[3] In 1266, Érard appears obliquely in the Account-Inventory overseeing the creation of the text and the distribution of salaries and bequests. He was not physically present when funds for the initial payment of salaries were paid, and the text notes that Geoffrey of Sergines the younger represented him for all remaining transactions that took place in person.

Érard was a Champenois knight (Valéry, Vallery, or Saint-Valéry is in the Yonne, in the canton of Chéroy, east of Troyes) and the son of Jean of Vallery, one of the "good knights" who served with Louis IX. Jean the father and his two sons, Jean and Érard, accompanied the king on his first expedition to Egypt and then to Outremer in 1248.[4] John of Joinville mentions Jean the father often in the *Vie de Saint Louis* in favorable terms.[5] The elder Jean

---

de Rutebeuf, ed. Julia Bastin and Edmond Faral, 4th ed., vol. 1 (Paris: Picard, 1977); *Onze poèmes de Rutebeuf concernant la croisade*, ed. Bastin and Faral (Paris: Libraire Orientaliste Paul Geuthner, 1946). For studies of the poet, see Edward Billings Ham, *Rutebeuf and Louis IX* (Chapel Hill: University of North Carolina Press, 1962); Nancy Freeman Regalado, *Poetic Patterns in Rutebeuf: A Study in Noncourtly Poetic Modes of the Thirteenth Century* (New Haven, CT: Yale University Press, 1970); and Michel Zink, "Si je t'oublie, Constantinople . . .," *Médiévales* 12 (1987): 43–46. They can be read in the context of a longer crusade lyric tradition addressed for the French context in Linda Paterson, *Singing the Crusades: French and Occitan Lyric Reponses to the Crusading Movements, 1137–1336* (Woodbridge: D. S. Brewer, 2018).

3. Jean Dunbabin, *The French in the Kingdom of Sicily, 1266–1305* (Cambridge: Cambridge University Press, 2005), 34; Steven Runciman, *The Sicilian Vespers: A History of the Mediterranean World in the Late Thirteenth Century* (Cambridge: Cambridge University Press, 1992); and Norman Housley, *The Italian Crusades: The Papal-Angevin Alliance and the Crusades against Christian Lay Powers, 1254–1343* (Oxford: Clarendon Press, 1982).

4. The most recent discussion of Érard of Vallery, with particular attention to his role in the household of Philip III, is in the masterful study by Xavier Hélary, *L'Ascension et la chute de Pierre de La Broce, chambellan du roi († 1278): Étude sur le pouvoir royal au temps de Saint Louis et de Philippe III (v. 1250–v. 1280)* (Paris: Honoré Champion, 2021). See also the remarks in Jean Richard, *Saint Louis: Roi d'une France féodale, soutien de la Terre sainte* (Paris: Fayard, 1983), 528–30, 537; *Oeuvres complètes de Rutebeuf*, ed. Jubinal, 3: note G, 39–52; Lespinasse, *Le Nivernais*, 2:272–73; Chazaud, "Inventaire," 171–72; and Bastin and Faral, *Onze poèmes*, 64–69. Henri d'Arbois de Jubainville, *Histoire des ducs et des comtes de Champagne* (Paris: Durand, 1865), 4:494–98, also briefly describes Érard's position.

5. Joinville, *VSL*, paras. (Jean) 168–69, on Jean's knowledge of the customs of Outremer; 230–32, on Jean's military advice to the king when in Damietta contrary to that of the king's

was brought into royal circles in 1230 when the king granted him an annual income of 100 *lbs.* as a fief-rent from lands in the bailliage of Escurolles (Allier, in the arrondissement of Gannat). At the time, he was also a vassal of Thibaut IV, count of Champagne, and is listed in the feudal registers of the counts between 1222 and 1229.[6] Érard accompanied his father and brother on Louis IX's crusade in 1248, and they were all at Damietta in the following year. According to Joinville, Érard's father offered Louis valuable advice at critical moments leading up to and during the Battle of Mansurah. At that time, Érard's brother was nearly taken captive, but Érard managed to save him, and the two continued to serve the king in Egypt and most likely traveled on to Acre with Louis and stayed there, at least for a time. From then on, Érard would spend much of his life traveling between France, the Kingdom of Sicily, and the Holy Land. Five years later, he served in the battle of West-Kappel (July 4, 1253) and was taken prisoner in Lorraine with Guy and Jean of Dampierre and Thibaut of Bar in their struggle against Jean of Avesnes for the title to the county of Flanders. It may have been through the Dampierre, who were related to Mahaut II of Bourbon (Eudes's wife), that Érard came to know and to serve with Eudes. In 1261, Jean and his son Érard, both described as "chevaliers," were given a fief-rent of 100 *lbs.* annual rent from Jean of Châtillon, count of Blois and Avesnes.[7] And in June 1261, Érard oversaw the exchange of rents between one Adam Genart and the prior of Braunay.[8] Then in 1264, the elder Jean seems to have retired and created an

brothers; 243, with the king as he learned of Robert of Artois's death at Mansurah; 295, 339, one of the representatives of the king sent to negotiate the French release from captivity; (Érard) 295, when he rescues his brother Jean from near captivity in Damietta.

6. See Theodore Evergates, *Feudal Society in the Bailliage of Troyes under the Counts of Champagne, 1152–1284* (Baltimore: Johns Hopkins University Press, 1975), 120, 172, 194, where he notes that Jean held only minor rear-fiefs, which "were barely distinguishable from peasant tenures" (120). In total, Jean and his wife held nineteen such small fiefs totaling an annual income of 75 *lbs.* Thus, a fief-rent of 100 *lbs.* annually represented significant upward mobility for Jean and, it seems, his family. See Auguste Longnon, *Rôles des fiefs du comté de Champagne sous le règne de Thibaud le Chansonnier, 1249–1252* (Paris: Henri Menu, 1877), in Troyes: 245–46, no. 1119; in Provins: 303, nos. 1323–25.

7. In this document, Érard is listed as Jean's son (*filz*). Alexandre Teulet et al., eds., *Layettes du Trésor des chartes* (Paris: H. Plon, 1863–1909), 4:23–24 (September 1261). The rent is in the currency of Chartres paid from Jean of Châtillon's *taille* from Chartres, collected annually on the feast of Saint Remy. Curiously, Jean notes that he shall also pay them 10 *s. t.* per pound for each week that they are late or default on the payment. In return, Châtillon receives Jean in his homage, and after his death, he will receive Érard. The charter of infeudation is in French and represents, one must assume, a relationship of mutual support built on close ties following on the crusade expedition in which both fought and served together. Indeed, Gautier of Châtillon did serve in a contingent of knights with Jean the elder and Érard of Vallery; see Joinville, *VSL*, para. 295.

8. Maximilien Quantin, *Recueil de pièces pour faire suite au cartulaire général de l'Yonne* (Paris: Durand et Pédone-Lauriel, 1878), 292, no. 600 (June 1261), written in French.

annuity with the abbey of Cluny with the consent of his son. Four years later he sold lands from his royal fief to Agnes of Dampierre (wife of John of Bourbon), Eudes's sister-in-law.[9] These families, in short, were closely connected in France and in the Holy Land and were accustomed to moving between the two with regularity.

By this point, Érard had made himself an important player in royal and comital circles with connections to the formidable counts of Champagne, Blois, and Nevers. In 1265, he was one of a handful of knights whom Louis IX charged with the transfer of funds designated for the Holy Land in support of Acre.[10] In this capacity, Érard traveled with Eudes, but then returned to France after Eudes's death in 1266. By June 1267 he was serving the king with Geoffrey of Sergines, carrying sealed letters from Louis IX concerning loans contracted with Sienese bankers in support of the Holy Land.[11] Érard then entered into the service of the king's brother, Charles of Anjou, and in August 1268 he was in Italy, serving as Charles's military advisor at the Battle of Tagliacozzo (August 23, 1268), where he coordinated the final decisive victory that won Charles the crown of Sicily.[12]

Érard may have returned to Outremer in the early fall but appears again, in late 1268, back in France, serving as constable of Champagne in the court of Thibaut V, king of Navarre and count of Champagne.[13] On March 19 he was a witness to an agreement between Count Thibaut and his brother Henry, count of Rosnay, in which Henry consented not to marry without Thibaut's agreement.[14] The following March, Érard was in Paris and represented Thibaut V in an agreement to aid Baldwin II in recovering Constantinople, for which Thibaut was promised one quarter of the Latin imperial lands should they

9. Lespinasse, *Le Nivernais*, 2:272–73; Chazaud, "Inventaire," 171–72.

10. Teulet et al., *Layettes*, 4:144 (July 1265); Gustav Servois, "Emprunts de Saint Louis en Palestine et en Afrique," *Bibliothèque de l'École des chartes* 4 (1858): 284.

11. Teulet et al., *Layettes*, 4:228–29 (June 30, 1267, Acre); and 4:230 (July 7, 1267, Acre); Servois, "Emprunts de Saint Louis," 130.

12. See *TdT*, para. 359. Interestingly, for the transmission of knowledge across Outremer, as Michael Lower notes, it was Érard who "recommended a tactic that he had seen the Mamluks use during his time leading the French regiment in Acre. Érard led his knights back toward the stream, as if to leave the field. [The enemy's] men then charged toward him, but began to lose momentum as their horses tired. Érard's knights turned . . . in the classic conclusion to a Mamluk feigned retreat, seizing his [enemy's] horse and forcing him to run away, a humiliating end." See Michael Lower, *The Tunis Crusade of 1270: A Mediterranean History* (Oxford: Oxford University Press, 2018), 67. See also Housley, *The Italian Crusades*, 154.

13. Bastin and Faral, *Onze poèmes*, 67. Érard served as constable of Champagne from 1263 to 1276, a title he held while he traveled; indeed, other men like Hugh and Eustache of Conflans also took the title. Érard, likewise, served as both constable of Champagne and chamberer of France and Navarre, positions he held simultaneously from 1270 to 1276.

14. Teulet et al., *Layettes*, 4:327–28 (March 19, 1268/69, Longjumeau).

ever be regained.[15] Over the following year, Érard continued to represent the count-king in several other transactions.[16]

By May 1270, he was in Aigues-Mortes, the port town the king had constructed in the south of France about 120 kilometers from Marseille, where Louis IX, with his family and household, gathered in preparation to depart on the crusade to Tunis.[17] Érard committed to bring thirty knights with him, each accompanied by an agreed upon number of horses and grooms (*garçons*) to tend to them. In a previous contract he made with Louis IX, he was to be paid 8,000 *lb. t.* for their wages, their passage, and that of their horses, but they were restricted from eating with the royal household.[18] On June 24, 1270, as he prepared to depart on crusade again ("*ou servise Nostre Seignor de la Terre Seinte, ou là que il verroient que il seroit plus granz profiz à m'ame*") he drew up a codicil to his testament.[19] Much like Eudes of Nevers, he provided payments for a long list of knights and squires in his service and made provision to give away his movable wealth, gold, silver, dishware, and other unspecified objects, to men close to him. The codicil does not state where it was created, but both Érard and Count Thibaut V appended their seals to the document, and it is likely that these final provisions were decided in Aigues-Mortes, just days before he departed with the king, perhaps also aboard the ship called *Monjoie*.[20] No mention is made of Érard's wife or heirs, although several charters in the *Trésor des chartes* indicate he was married to Marguerite de

15. Érard, along with Hugh of Conflans, marshal of Champagne, and a clerk of the king, represented Thibaut in the transaction and received a ring of investiture ("*per nostrum annulum . . . investimus*") as a symbol of the agreement. Teulet et al., *Layettes*, 4:331–33 (March 1–23, 1268/69, Paris).

16. By September, Érard was in Estella, Navarre, as a witness to another charter, Teulet et al., *Layettes*, 4:385–86 (September 24, 1269); and back in Troyes in February 1269/70 to oversee the transfer of a rent in Bar-sur-Aube, Teulet et al., *Layettes*, 4:417–18. In March 1269/70 the abbot of Preuilly endowed (one assumes as an annuity) a grange and all that pertains to it to the count for use during his lifetime, after which it would revert to the abbey, Teulet et al., *Layettes*, 4:429.

17. For these final months, see Lower, *The Tunis Crusade*, 102–5.

18. Dunbabin, *The French in the Kingdom of Sicily*, 260–61; Richard, *Saint Louis*, 538; Xavier Hélary, *La dernière croisade: Saint Louis à Tunis (1270)* (Paris: Perrin, 2016), 93–94, and Hélary, *L'armée du roi de France: La guerre de Saint Louis à Philippe le Bel* (Paris: Perrin, 2012), 91–94; and *RHGF*, 20:305.

19. Paris, AN, J 208, no. 6; edited in Teulet et al., *Layettes*, 4:449–50 (June 24, 1270), sealed by Érard and Thibaut of Navarre. For the seals, see Arnaud Baudin, *Les Sceaux des comtes de Champagne et de leur entourage (fin XIe – début XIVe siècle)* (Paris: Éditions Dominique Guéniot, 2012), 204. We thank Randall Pippenger for this reference. See also Teulet et al., *Layettes*, 4:450–51 (no. 5708), which establishes the amortization and fief-rent between Érard and Pierre de la Fauche. Érard may also have had a female relative, perhaps a sister, who was abbess of Notre-Dame-aux-Nonnians in Troyes.

20. For the departure from Aigues-Mortes, see Lower, *The Tunis Crusade*, 104–5. Many of those who mustered in Aigues-Mortes drew up testaments or revised their final instructions for the administration of their domains, or in the case of Louis IX, for the kingdom. This is reflected in the run of testaments kept in the royal archive and edited in Teulet et al., *Layettes*, 4:448–68.

Nemours, who had her own seal.[21] They had a daughter named Agnès, who married Savary, who became the Vicomte of Thouars after the death of his brother, Aimery. They had two sons, Gui and Renault.[22] After the king's defeat and death, Érard chose to follow Prince Edward of England to Acre, perhaps offering sage advice to the future king.[23] By June 1271, he had returned to the West and was present when Count Henry III of Champagne paid homage to King Philip III of France.

From that point onward, Érard was taken into the entourage of King Philip III, advising the new king and serving in his household.[24] He was especially valued for his expertise and experience in Outremer and no doubt offered advice to the young king, who began to plan a new crusade expedition. Érard served first as part of the royal chamber and then as chamberlain of France from 1270 until his death at some time between June 1276 and September 1277 (see figure 14).[25] In that year he drew up a final codicil to his testament that reaffirmed his commitments to the men in his service and made provisions for continued support of the Holy Land.[26] This document, although of a different legal nature, echoes Eudes's Account-Inventory in profound ways, providing for the payment of debts, covering the salaries and obligations to those in his retinue, and making provisions for his movable wealth. Érard appears, like many aristocrats within his circle, to have been a man of "action, of counsel, but also a man of culture."[27] He is the addressee of several courtly poems from the period, and after Eudes of Nevers's death it was Érard who took (or was given) Eudes's three vernacular books: two histories of the Outremer and

21. Hélary, *L'Ascension et la chute*, 212–15. After Érard's death in the fall of 1277, she sold land at Fins (near Graçay in the Berry) to Pierre de la Broce, just before his own arrest and fall. Pierre worked in the king's chamber with Érard, and the families were close. Marguerite refers to him as her "dear friend [*chier ami*]." From Paris, AN, J 730, no. 208. On the Nemours family connections, see Hélary, *L'Ascension et la chute*, 212–13n5.

22. *Oeuvres complètes de Rutebeuf*, ed. Jubinal, 3:39–40. Jubinal cites materials in the *Trésor des chartes*, cartons 174, 136, 143, and 208 and 256. For information on Érard's family at this time, see the references in Edmund Martene and Ursini Durand, *Veterum Scriptorum et Monumentorum Historicorum, Dogmaticorum, Moralium Amplissima Collectio* (Paris: Montalant, 1724–33), 5:1157. We thank Xavier Hélary for help with these details.

23. Hélary, *L'Ascension et la chute*, 79; and Reinhold Röhricht, "Études sur les derniers temps du royaume de Jérusalem: Croisade d'Edouard d'Angleterre," *Archives de l'Orient Latin* 1 (1881): 622. See the testament of Prince Edward here below.

24. See Hélary, *L'Ascension et la chute*, 77–79, 225–48, 410–18.

25. See Hélary, *L'Ascension et la chute*, 410–12; *Oeuvre complètes de Rutebeuf*, ed. Jubinal, 3:42–52. A number of charters pertaining to Érard can be found in the *Trésor des chartes*, carton 208.

26. This final codicil was drawn up Wednesday, July 1, 1276, in Paris, AN, J 208, no. 13, and has his seal attached (see figure 14). This document made provision for a sum of money to be paid for the maintenance of the Holy Land, an act that was confirmed in the same year by the king (Philip III) himself at Lorris. We thank Xavier Hélary for sharing his transcription and thoughts on this text by personal communication.

27. See Bastin and Faral, *Onze poèmes*, 67.

one chansonnier. These were fitting texts for a man who spent his life moving between Deça- and Outremer. Érard was also given several of the opulent objects from among Eudes's possessions, including the count's chapel and a tent, cloth of gold, and the cloth threaded through the count's heart.[28] When Eudes gave out rings to the men closest to him, he gave Érard "two small crosses of gold and a small silver case" that held "the relics that the patriarch had given to the count,"[29] an august gift that also suggests Érard's religious commitments. In the lament for Eudes, "La complainte dou conte Hue de Nevers" (vv. 109–20), Rutebeuf extolled Érard in his own right, dedicating a full stanza of the poem to his deeds. The tenor of events in 1265 that informed Rutebeuf's "Complainte doutremeir" illuminates the context and fervent concern that propelled Érard to return to Outremer, again and again.

Less is known about the lords of Sergines. Sergines was a small lordship in Champagne, in the archbishopric of Sens, today in the department of the Yonne. We know much more about **Geoffrey of Sergines** the elder than we do about his son, Geoffrey of Sergines the younger.[30] Young Geoffrey stands in

28. See the Account-Inventory, Roll A Front, Part 2: three vernacular books are listed by title "*li romanz des Loheranz et li romanz de la terre doutremer et li chaunconns*." There has been much speculation about the contents of the chansonnier that Eudes possessed. Riley-Smith has reiterated David Jacoby's statement that the volume must have been the songs, or *chansons*, of Thibaut IV of Navarre, Thibaut le Chansonnier, himself a renowned crusader and the father of Érard's feudal lord for his fiefs in Champagne, yet this remains unsubstantiated. Such song books took many forms and were not fixed texts, but rather unique compilations. See Paterson, *Singing the Crusades*; Marisa Galvez, *The Subject of Crusade: Lyric, Romance, and Materials, 1150 to 1500* (Chicago: University of Chicago Press, 2020); and John Haines, "Aristocratic Patronage and the Cosmopolitan Vernacular Songbook: The *Chansonnier du Roi (M-trouv.)* and the French Mediterranean," in *Musical Culture in the World of Adam de la Halle*, ed. Jennifer Saltstein (Leiden: Brill, 2019), 95–120; for readers of similar volumes, see Judith A. Peraino, "Taking *Notae* on King and Cleric: Thibaut, Adam, and the Medieval Readers of the *Chansonnier de Noailles (T-trouv.)*," in Saltstein, *Musical Culture*, 121–52. Concerning the narrative texts, Folda notes the "'*roma[n]z des lo[h]eranz*'—probably a work like Garin le Loherain—came from the West, but the '*romanz de la terre doutremer*,' which was almost certainly a copy of the History of Outremer by William of Tyre, might well have been a codex ordered by the count in Acre . . . as it was without doubt the most popular work done in Acre in the second half of the thirteenth century." Jaroslav Folda, *Crusader Art in the Holy Land, from the Third Crusade to the Fall of Acre, 1187–1291* (Cambridge: Cambridge University Press, 2005), 357. For the French-language context of Crusader Acre, see Jonathan Rubin, *Learning in a Crusader City: Intellectual Activity and Intercultural Exchanges in Acre, 1191–1291* (Cambridge: Cambridge University Press, 2018), 70–82. For the Old French translation of William of Tyre's history in Outremer, see Peter Edbury, "Ernoul, *Eracles*, and the Collapse of the Kingdom of Jerusalem," and Philip Handyside, "*L'Estoires d'Eracles* in Outremer," both in *The French of Outremer: Communities and Communications in the Crusading Mediterranean*, ed. Laura K. Morreale and Nicholas L. Paul (New York: Fordham University Press, 2018), 44–67 and 68–85 respectively. There is no way to know if this was simply the French translation of William of Tyre or, as is more likely, a continuation of that text known as the *Eracles*. We suggest it was probably the latter, or a near contemporary version known as the Ernould-Bernard *Eracles*.

29. See Roll B Back.

30. For a short biography, see Jonathan Riley-Smith, *What Were the Crusades?*, 4th ed. (New York: Palgrave, 2009), 67–73; see also *Oeuvres complètes de Rutebeuf*, ed. Jubinal, 3: note J,

the shadow of his father, whose reputation spanned the Mediterranean and who, after 1255, was presented as a model perpetual-crusader, that is, a loyal knight who dedicated himself to protecting French interests in the East and to maintaining control of Jaffa and Acre in the face of Mongol raids and Mamluk military pressure.[31] In 1254, Louis IX set Geoffrey senior at the head of the French contingent of knights the king left behind and continued to support in Acre. This is how Rutebeuf describes him in a brief poem, "La complainte de monseigneur Joffroi de Sergines," probably composed between 1255 and 1256 to recruit support and aid for the *stipendarii* in Acre under his charge.[32] In May 1259, after the death of John of Ibelin, Geoffrey of Sergines was made *bailli* of the kingdom of Jerusalem in Acre. He had a reputation as a man with a "strong sense of justice for he put to death many thieves and murderers [*fu moult fort justizier et en son tens pendy mout de larons et de murtriés*]."[33]

Geoffrey the elder is the first of his line mentioned in textual sources, and he appears in Joinville's *Vie de Saint Louis* and in William of Nangis's chronicle, both of whom share the assessment of Geoffrey as a loyal knight and companion of Saint Louis. Rutebeuf's treatment is similar and ends with a prayer for his protection ("*Or prions donques a celui*").[34] Twenty years later Rutebeuf mentions both Geoffrey and Eudes in his "Nouvele complainte doutremeir" (1277) where they are eulogized as exemplars, model crusaders crowned in paradise:

Avoir deussiez en memoire
Monseigneur Joffroi de Sergines
Qui fu tant boens et fu tant dignes
Quen paradix et coroneiz
Com sages et bien ordeneiz
Et le conte Huede de Nevers
Dont hom ne peut chanson ne vers
Dire se boen non et loiaul
Et bien loei en court roiaul.
A ceux deussiez panrre essample
Et Acres secorre et le Temple.[35]

58–69; Lespinasse, *Le Nivernais*, 2:272–73; Joinville, *VSL*, paras. 173, 302 (as a *prudhomme* knight), 308–12 (protecting Louis as he enters captivity).

31. According to the Templar of Tyre account, Geoffrey was already living and fighting in the East before 1254, and together with a contingent of Templars, they "made camp at Jaffa, and [confirmed] the truce between them and the sultan of Damascus, which gave the Christians Jerusalem and the lands on this side of the river except of Nablus and Jericho." See *TdT*, para. 245.

32. Bastin and Faral, *Onze poèmes*, 19–27.

33. *TdT*, paras. 297–98.

34. See in the present volume, "La complainte de monseigneur Joffroi de Sergines," v. 157.

35. See in the present volume, "La nouvele complainte doutremeir," vv. 124–35; and Bastin and Faral, *Onze poèmes*, 111–30, at 122–23.

Other than the letters to pope and king mentioned above, Geoffrey appears in virtually no other archival texts. He did not receive fiefs from the crown or serve in other administrative capacities in the West. In February 1262, he was given permission from Pope Urban IV (r. 1261–64) to have a portable altar to celebrate Mass for himself and his knights and retainers.[36] Perhaps this was an arrangement not unlike the chapel that Eudes had and that moved into the possession of Érard after the count's death, as noted above. Geoffrey certainly must have authored documents while serving in Acre, but there is precious little trace of such activity.

On the fifteenth of April 1263, the Templar of Tyre notes that Geoffrey was injured by "missiles [*pilés*]" when Baybars laid siege to the city.[37] In the spring of 1264, he led a contingent of knights on regular raids into the territory beyond Acre, which Baybars had taken into his control. In June of the same year, Geoffrey and his men attacked the area around Ascalon, "destroying crops and rustling livestock." In response, Baybars launched raids north of Acre—at Caesarea and Chastel Pèlerin—that November. This continual, seasonal, warfare meant that the Franks became familiar with Mamluk tactics but gained little ground as they were always outnumbered.[38] Although both Geoffrey the elder and his son are referenced in the Account-Inventory, the latter, the young Geoffrey, stands in for Érard of Vallery, representing him when debts were paid and when Érard's salary needed to be collected as noted on Roll A. This suggests a close relationship between the three men, reflected in the diplomatic correspondence from 1265 and 1267 when Érard and Geoffrey senior oversaw the transfer of subsidies to the Holy Land and again in 1268 when they wrote to the pope and the French king asking for additional aid.[39] In the spring of 1267, payments for such loans were slow in coming, and Geoffrey was forced to borrow 3,000 *lbs.* from the Temple in his own name to pay the knights in his regiment while he waited for payments from the French crown. This would be a debt that he and his heirs would carry forward for at least another decade.[40] But in the immediate aftermath of Eudes death, it was Geoffrey the son, with Hugh of Augerant, who oversaw the distribution of Eudes's goods and rendered his accounts. By 1266, Érard was already on his

36. *Les Registres d'Urbain IV (1261–1264): Recueil des bulles de ce pape publiées ou analysées d'après les manuscrits originaux du Vatican*, ed. Jean Guiraud (Paris: Thorin et fils, 1901–58), 2:19, nos. 53–55 (February 13, 1262).

37. *TdT*, para. 320.

38. See Lower, *The Tunis Crusade*, 26. It may be that the tent that came into Eudes's possession from Chastel Pèlerin was salvaged during or after one of these raids. See also *TdT*, paras. 327–53.

39. See Servois, "Emprunts de Saint Louis."

40. Alain Demurger uncovered three documents in the AN that shed further light on the family's debt. See Alain Demurger, "Pour trois mille livres de dette: Geoffroy de Sergines et le temple," in *La présence latine en orient au moyen âge*, ed. Ghislain Brunel, Marie-Adélaïde Nielen, and Marie-Paule Arnauld (Paris: C.H.A.N./Champion, 2000), 67–76.

way to Sicily to join Charles of Anjou, and Geoffrey the elder was taken up outside of Acre raiding near Tiberias.[41]

The Templar of Tyre records Geoffrey the elder's death on April 11, 1269.[42] His son went on to serve as Charles of Anjou's seneschal and died barely a year later outside of Tunis in August 1270.[43] In France, the Sergines family surfaces from time to time in administrative records and other sources. In April 1275, Pope Gregory X wrote to King Philip III of France to ask forgiveness of the debt owed in Geoffrey the elder's name, a debt that had carried over to Geoffrey the younger's wife, Isabelle.[44] Three years later, Isabelle, who is described as Geoffrey the younger's widow, was remarried to Jean d'Artier, a knight, and together they brought a plea to the Parlement of Paris to seek forgiveness of the 3,000 *lbs*. This is the first time we learn that Geoffrey the younger was married and had heirs, although they are not named. The barons of Parlement were unmoved and rejected Isabelle and Jean's plea; the debt to the Temple stood and no doubt stoked resentments.[45] The material conditions and burdens of Outremer could live on over generations, saddling widows for years to come. How and if Geoffrey's original debt was ever paid, we do not know.

The Sergines surface in other subtler forms in the West. A representation of their coat of arms, that is, the family's heraldry, appears in the glazing program at Saint-Pierre-ès-Liens in Mussy in southern Champagne, a church that Eudes's second daughter, Marguerite of Burgundy, countess of Tonnerre, wife of Charles of Anjou, and queen of Sicily, patronized.[46] This may have been a way of signaling the close connections between the families and therefore may have been a form of commemoration. In 1299, a Gilles de Sergines served as the cupbearer (*échanson*) to the queen, Jeanne of France (countess of Champagne and queen of Navarre) and was granted freedom for his heirs from servile status. Forty years later, in 1339, one Jean de Sergines rendered

41. The Templar of Tyre notes that Geoffrey and a French contingent of knights, together with Templars, Hospitallers, and some German Teutonic Knights all began raiding the plains outside the city. They were then ambushed by a contingent of Muslim forces from Safad, and the French suffered considerable losses. See *TdT*, para. 349. The author paints a miserable portrait of the French at this point, and in all likelihood, if Eudes died or was wounded on the battlefield, it may have been in this skirmish in August 1266.

42. *Oeuvres complètes de Rutebeuf*, ed. Jubinal, 3: note J, 67–68; Jonathan Riley-Smith, "The Crown of France and Acre, 1254–1291," in *France and the Holy Land: Frankish Culture at the End of the Crusades*, ed. Daniel H. Weiss and Lisa Mahoney (Baltimore: Johns Hopkins University Press, 2004), 58n23; *TdT*, para. 368; and "L'Estoire de Eracles," *RHC*, 2:457.

43. Jean Dunbabin, *Charles I of Anjou* (London: Longman, 1998), 59.

44. Demurger, "Pour trois mille livres de dette," 72–74.

45. Demurger, "Pour trois mille livres de dette," 74–76.

46. For Marguerite of Burgundy's patronage in France after her return from Sicily, see Meredith Parsons Lillich, *The Queen of Sicily and Gothic Sainted Glass in Mussy and Tonnerre* (Philadelphia: American Philosophical Society, 1998), 76 for the stained glass that could be a reference to the Sergines.

homage to the archbishop of Sens for lands in the lordship of Sergines.[47] The fact the Rutebeuf found it compelling to write of these men, Eudes, Érard, and Geoffrey, suggests that he chose—quite in keeping with his other poems—to valorize and memorialize men from his local world, from the border of Champagne and Burgundy. In doing so, he brought attention to the service of men who began their careers as lesser knights, men—with the exception of Eudes—without great lordships or fortunes but who were committed to the ideal of personal sacrifice in service to the Holy Land and who rose through the ranks of service to make a name for themselves.[48]

There are several other men who appear multiple times throughout the Account-Inventory whom we know of only through this text. **Hugh of Augerant** was a knight in Eudes's employ, probably from Langeron, a hamlet in the arrondissement of Nevers.[49] He is one of the administrators of Eudes's estate and commanded a smaller retinue of knights in his own right. He was part of Eudes's close circle and played the largest role in overseeing the dissolution of the count's apartment and the disbursal of his things. It was Hugh who was charged with carrying some of the count's most precious objects and family heirlooms back to the West to bestow on John of Bourbon, Eudes's brother, and Jean Tristan, Eudes's son-in-law. And it was Hugh who accepted the count's silver-gilt *henap*, or drinking cup, in lieu of pay and, it would seem, as a memento evocative of the count, his table, and the close relationship the two men shared.[50] After Eudes's death, Hugh was given lands at Noain as a gift for service from Robert of Flanders, Yolande of Nevers's second husband. Thus, it appears that Hugh continued to have close ties with Eudes's daughters. By 1274, he also held the lordship of Granges (near Magny-Course), and lands at Chantenay, Livry, and Riousse near Langeron.[51]

Two other men who played an official role in Eudes's household should also be noted.[52] **Étienne le Clerc** is mentioned seven times in the rolls and served as a clerk or cleric in Eudes's household, and he may have been the one to write our *rouleaux* or parts thereof. In this capacity, he would have known

47. *Oeuvres complètes de Rutebeuf*, ed. Jubinal, 3: note J, 58–69.

48. For comments on Rutebeuf's writings in the context of crusade and the Latin East, see Galvez, *The Subject of Crusade*, 186–206. These men also map onto those who were part of the group of knights around the king, his family knights or family of knights ("*ses chevaliers familiers*" ["*familiars sui milites*"]). See Hélary, *L'Ascension et la chute*, 120–21; Paul-Édouard Riant, ed., "Déposition de Charles d'Anjou pour la canonisation de Saint Louis," in *Notices et documents publiés pour la Société de l'Histoire de France à l'occasion du cinquantième anniversaire de sa fondation* (Paris: Librairie Renouard, 1884), 155–76; and Jean Dunbabin, "The Household and Entourage of Charles I, King of the Regno, 1266–85," *Historical Research* 77 (2004): 313–36.

49. Lespinasse, *Le Nivernais*, 2:271–72; Chazaud, "Inventaire," 172–73.

50. See the discussion in the essay below by Richard Leson.

51. For the reconstruction of the Angeran lineage from extant sources, see "Maison d'Angerant," Terres et Seigneurs en Donziais, July 4, 2021, http://www.terres-et-seigneurs-en-donziais.fr/wp-content/uploads/2021/07/dAngerant.pdf.

52. Lespinasse, *Le Nivernais*, 2:274–76.

Eudes's knights, retainers, serjeants, servants, household workings, goods, and tastes perhaps better than anyone and would likewise have been familiar with the writing practices of the Temple and other official institutions in Acre and in France. Étienne received a payment from Eudes's estate that seems to encompass his salary for a portion of the year (15 *lb. t.* or 45 *b.*). **Guillaume le Chapelain** is mentioned once and must have been a priest, most likely Eudes's household chaplain. He would have conducted Mass for the count and his men, heard confessions, led prayers, and maintained the count's chapel and guided his devotional life.[53] It seems reasonable to assume that both Étienne and Guillaume accompanied Eudes from Nevers to Acre, but it is possible that they met in the East. A tantalizing reference in an earlier text suggests that both men may have served in the household of the counts of Nevers for some time and may even have been familiar with the rigors of crusading. In 1241, when Guy IV, count of Nevers and Forez, second husband of Mahaut I of Nevers, Tonnerre, and Auxerre, died in Brindisi on his return from the Barons' Crusade, he drew up a final testament. He did so, as he stated, "in the presence of brother Guilleum de Vitry, my chaplain and brother Guillelmo de . . . both of the order of Friars Minor, [and] Stephan my clerk [*presentibus fratre Guillelmo de Vichiaco capellano meo et fratre Guillelmo de . . . socio ejusdem ordinis fratrum Minorum, Stephano clerico meo*]."[54] Is it possible that one of these Guillaumes or this "*Stephano clerico*" could be the same men, surfacing again in Eudes's accounts, and who remained in service to the Nevers family?

What is clear for all of the men mentioned in the text—Érard, Geoffrey, Hugh, Étienne, and Guillaume—is that French was the language of transaction. When writing to the French king in Paris and to the pope in residence in Viterbo, they wrote in French. When reading or listening to histories, *romanciers*, poems, and chansons, they did so in French. And this was the language they used to record the Account-Inventory, the same language that Rutebeuf would use to commemorate them in France.[55]

53. In 1265, presumably just before his departure for the east, Eudes attested to an arbitration between "Guillaume de Ligny-le-Châtel, son clerc," and Hugh de Souilly, a canon of Auxerre. It is possible that this Guillaume would become the count's chaplain and the two men are one and same. See Ernst Petit, *Histoire des ducs de Bourgogne de la race Capétienne* (Dijon: Darantière, 1885–1905), 5:256, no. 3459 (1265), citing AD de l'Yonne, H 1214, fonds St.-Marien d'Auxerre.

54. J.-L.-A. Huillard-Breholles and A. Lecoy de La Marche, eds., *Titres de la maison ducale de Bourbon* (Paris: H. Plon, 1867–74), 1:46–47, no. 221 (August 10, 1241) (*le jour de Saint-Laurent*, Castellaneta, near Brindisi, in the kingdom of Naples). The editor notes that the document was on cotton paper, in a contemporary (mid-thirteenth-century) Italian hand.

55. There is much debate about what dialects of French were used in Outremer, in the Romance corpus as well as in poetic and lyric texts. Two principal northern French variants emerge, Picard and the French that is used in these texts, that of Champagne-Burgundy, which favors the *z* over *s*, and which softens the *qu-* to *c-* rather than the hard *k-*. It is striking to us how similar Rutebeuf's French is to that of the Account-Inventory. For the ascendant use of French in Outremer at this time, see Jonathan Rubin "Multilingualism and the Attitude toward French in the

Many other men (and perhaps a few women) are mentioned in the Account-Inventory for whom we know nothing other than their name and form of service. When Eudes died, he supported in his household four knights, one chaplain, one clerk, eight squires, nine servants, and thirty-two pages, almost all of whom were listed and named in the account.[56] He also hired five crossbowmen (paid 105 *b.* for two months' service), and four turcopoles, that is, hired light cavalry (paid 117 *b.* for service for an unspecified amount of time), who are not named, implying they may have been local soldiers for hire rather than individuals known to the household traveling with Eudes to the East.[57] Of the four household knights listed, including Hugh of Augerant, we learn the names of Gaucher de Merry, Gui and Hervé de Chantenai, and "*mon segnor Copin*."[58] Gaucher de Merry had served in the count's retinue before departing for the Holy Land and is found in Eudes's company in June 1261, serving as a witness to an agreement between the count and the monks of Reigny in Burgundy.[59] In addition to Eudes's personal knights, the knights Reynaud of Précigné and Robert of Juennesses—both listed in Rolls A, B, and C—led two smaller groups of crusaders. Eudes's household knights received 40 *lb. t.* in pay for one quarter of the year and would have been paid four times a year.[60] By contrast, Reynaud and Robert were paid 375 *lb. t.* and 235 *lb. t.* respectively.[61] Given these sums, as Jonathan Riley-Smith has argued, this seems to imply that they supported their own contingents of two to four

Latin Kingdom of Jerusalem," in *Multilingualism and History*, ed. Aneta Pavlenko (Cambridge: Cambridge University Press, 2023), 123–37.

56. For lists of knights and household retainers as sources, see Hélary, *L'armée du roi de France*, 95. Numerous examples of similar lists survive, and lists of pay were not uncommon. See for example *RHGF*, 23:767 and following. It is possible that the rolls were retained in the archives of the duke of Burgundy, and subsequently by the crown, because such lists were useful for administrative purposes.

57. Edition, Roll A Front, Part 1; Folda, *Crusader Art*, 357.

58. Edition, Roll A Front, Part 1.

59. Lespinasse, *Le Nivernais*, 2:274–76, where brief notes are supplied for several of those listed here; Quantin, *Recueil*, 292–93, no. 601 (June 1261). Gaucher de Merry is listed alongside Gaucher Bridainne, lord of Baissy, Abbot Pierre de Châteux-Censoir, and Estienne Lietard, chanter. The latter could perhaps be our Étienne le Clerc? Ernst Petit notes that Gaucher de Merry was the lord of Merry-sur-Yonne and Bessy (or Baissy?) and the son of Geoffrey de Merry, constable of Romanie, that is, of the Greek Morea. This means that Gaucher would be part of the Villehardouin family in that his grandfather, Ascelin of Merry, from the lordship of Châtel-Censoir, was married to Marie of Villehardouin, daughter of Geoffrey of Villehardouin, who wrote the famed memoir of the Fourth Crusade. On Villehardouin, see Theodore Evergates, *Geoffroy of Villehardouin, Marshal of Champagne: His Life and Memoirs of the Fourth Crusade* (Ithaca, NY: Cornell University Press, 2023).

60. On the payment and maintenance of knights, see Hélary, *L'armée du roi de France*, 39–63.

61. To give some context, the average pay for many *baillis* in France was approximately 365 *lbs.* per annum. In short, Eudes's knights and those associated with him were extremely well paid. For salaries in France at this time, see Joseph R. Strayer, *The Administration of Normandy under Saint Louis* (Cambridge, MA: Medieval Academy of America, 1932), 96–104.

knights with them in turn.[62] Reynaud and Robert may have been knights known to Eudes and part of the larger regiment with which he traveled, but not part of his own retinue.

Several other knights appear in the text under the designation "*mon segnor*" (*mon seigneur*) or "my lord." These include William de la Tor and William Arnaut, whom the count paid 60 *b.* and 40 *b.* respectively, perhaps for lodging or for an unspecified service. "My lord" (*mon segnor*) Hervé de Chantenai's lodgings were covered by the count for 9 *b.*, more than what Eudes paid to lodge his knight Gui de Chantenai for two months (6 *b.* 16 *q.*).[63] It is possible that Hervé and Gui were related, but the text does not say.[64] The count also paid Salemon de Safforit, Lionnet de Tabarie, Homede, and Jehan le Porer for three months each, for unspecified service.[65] Similarly, the account makes it clear that Eudes knew Jaque Vidaut (that is, Jacques Vidal), an important knight and landholder in the Kingdom of Jerusalem who served as marshal of the kingdom and was recognized for his legal learning.[66] On his death, Eudes was in possession of a war horse (*granz chevax*) that had belonged to Jaque, suggesting that the marshal either sold it to Eudes or had given it to him.[67] Finally, additional knights and barons are listed in the inventory when they purchased items from Eudes's estate. Geoffrey of Sergines "the father," that is, the elder, is named when he purchased foodstuffs, presumably for the maintenance of his own household. "My lord Hugh de la Baume" acquired items from Eudes's kitchen along with table linens; whereas "my lord Hugh de Mont-Cornet" bought some of the measures of barley kept in Eudes's stores.[68] Given all the opulent objects available among Eudes's things, as we shall see, these discrete purchases are indicative of the high price of food and fodder and the desire to sell and consume what the count had with him rather than let it go to waste. The 1260s proved to be a tremendously challenging time to live in Acre and to maintain a residence in the city.[69] Providing for a knightly household, ensuring a regular supply of food stuffs, and maintaining animals

62. Edition, Roll A Front, Part 1; Riley-Smith, "The Crown of France and Acre," 51. For comparison with the amounts Louis IX paid his knights and retainers, see Joseph R. Strayer, "The Crusades of Louis IX," in Strayer, *Medieval Statecraft and the Perspectives of History* (Princeton, NJ: Princeton University Press, 1971), 166, where he notes that "knights were paid 160 *l.t.* a year (many received more), and crossbowmen and men-at-arms about 90 *l.* a year." See also Joinville's fees for retaining knights in Acre: Joinville, *VSL*, paras. 440–41.

63. Edition, Roll A Front, Part 1.

64. Lespinasse, *Le Nivernais*, 2:275.

65. Edition, Roll A Back. For the identities and roles of Salemon de Safforit and Lionnet de Tabarie, see the essay below by Jonathan Rubin.

66. On Jacques Vidal, see the essay by Jonathan Rubin below.

67. Edition, Roll B Front.

68. These purchases are tallied in Roll D Front; see the Edition. Both men, Hugh de Mont-Cornet and Hugh de la Baume, belonged to well-known knightly families in Burgundy. They may have been part of the count's regiment of fifty knights but not part of his more intimate retinue.

69. See Lower, *The Tunis Crusade*, 11–41.

and soldiers alike took careful planning. And all of these men were engaged in managing the needs of their own retinues.

In addition to the knights, the text lists the stipends paid to each of Eudes's squires, servants, and pages ("*des Escuyers*," "*des Serjanz*," and "*des garçons*") and details the costs of their housing (*ostels*).[70] The patterns of listing these lodgings may give insight into who was housed together. For example, the knights Hugh, Gaucher, Gui, and Copin appear to lodge on their own, whereas Odet de Menant and Hermenin Le Veaul are listed together under one entry, so too for Huguenin de Givri and Tierriet (Thierriaut) (all of whom were squires). Among the squires too is one Perriau de Sissy, perhaps a relative of Étienne de Sissy. Brother Étienne de Sissy was a Templar official. He had served as marshal of the Temple in Acre from 1261 to 1262, after which point Urban IV made him resign his position.[71] In 1271, after being excommunicated and then reconciling with Pope Clement IV, he was put at the head of the Templar province of Sicily-Apulia from 1271 until his death in 1273. At the time of his death in 1266, Eudes owed brother Étienne 1,000 *b.*, which his executors repaid.[72] Étienne and perhaps Perriau too were men from the same social world as Eudes and his knights, and Étienne would follow the same trajectory—from Acre to Sicily—that Érard and Geoffrey would take, all of them animating the broader networks that connected the French medieval Mediterranean.

The names of the sergeants also offer insight into how an Outremer household of knights may have functioned. Most of the sergeants were listed with two appellations, a first name and a second that in some cases, it would seem, implied a place of origin, like Jehan de Mussy, Henri de Brabant, Jehan de Bese, and Henri de Diepe. Other sergeants, or servants, have names that are more colloquial and familiar: Robet, Chauvin, Travers, and Afetie seem to need no other designation; they are there to hand. Indeed, both Robet and Bossu appear later in the inventory for other duties and larger sums that the count owed them, implying that they had been in Eudes's service for a longer period of time or had been employed for additional extraordinary tasks. There are several men who seem to have attended to the count's personal needs and were associated with specific rooms and therefore duties within the count's household, including Huet de la Chambre, Perrinet de la Chambre, and Renaut de la Chambre, who may have served the count in his own room (*chambre*) or wardrobe, or so their names imply. Perrinet dou For perhaps worked in the kitchen, baking possibly (*for* or *fur* close phonetically to *four*, meaning oven, or to bake, in French). Then there may have been servants

70. On such lists and the place of the "*hôtel*" in the maintenance of knights and their retinues, see Hélary, *L'armée du roi de France*, 90–94. Edition, Roll A Front, Part 1.

71. On "L'affaire Sissy," see Pierre-Vincent Claverie, *L'ordre du Temple en Terre Sainte et à Chypre au XIIIe siècle* (Nicosie: Centre de Recherche Scientifique, 2005), 2:140–43.

72. Edition, Roll A Front, Part 1; and Claverie, *L'ordre du Temple en Terre Sainte*, 2:142.

of repute: "Tastepeire" (Blockhead), "Char de Beuf" (Beefsteak), and "Boen home" (Good Man) have names, or maybe nicknames, that could connote affection or perhaps disrespect. We cannot know. But the names do suggest the familiarity of a retinue and a household that traveled, labored, and lived together. The count also paid small amounts to the valet of the Viscountess of Limoges (Marguerite of Burgundy, Eudes's sister) and the valet of the archbishop of Tyre, perhaps for short errands between or among the households.[73] Finally, there are a number of servants listed whose names suggest the possibility that there may have been a few women in Eudes's household, including Luile, Jannet le Flament, Jannet de Nichiz, Jannet de Talan, and Jehannin de la Ferrae. It is possible that the suffix *-net* or *-nin* could be feminine, or it could simply be a diminutive. We are left to speculate as the list gives us no other context to expand either hypothesis.

Additional one-time payments to specific individuals or functionaries, sometimes left unnamed, give insight into the needs and obligations contingent with a baron's death in the East. The scribes recorded payments to agents for securing loans of cash and for selling cloth and silver items as well as for arranging for travel, specifically "passage," one presumes back to France.[74] The executors also paid a spicer (*lespicie*) for embalming the count's heart, and purchased a box (*escrin*) to transport it, relic like, to the Cistercian abbey of Cîteaux in Burgundy where the count instructed he should be commemorated in the West.[75] The same men also set up payments to cover the cost of the count's tomb in the cemetery of St. Nicholas in Acre (60 *b.*).[76] Finally, at the margins of the text, evident especially when totals were summed or summarized, there is the presence of the treasurer and the grand master of the Temple.[77] By the 1260s, the Templar order had become indispensable for

73. The archbishop of Tyre in 1266 was Gilles de Saumur (1253–66), who had been a close confidant of Louis IX and who continued to work closely with the French court in support of Outremer. See Pierre-Vincent Claverie, ed., "De l'entourage royal à l'entourage pontifical: L'exemple méconnu de l'archevêque Gilles de Tyr (d. 1266)," in *À l'ombre du pouvoir: Les entourages princiers au moyen âge*, ed. Alain Marchandisse and Jean-Louis Kupper (Geneva: Droz, 2003), 57–76; and Lower, *The Tunis Crusade*, 36–38. The Viscountess of Limoges at this time was Eudes's older sister, Marguerite, lady of Molinot, who married Guy VI, viscount of Limoges, in 1258 or 1259. This suggests the smaller often hidden networks and connections among family members and their staff and paid servants. For bibliography on Margaret, see the (actually quite excellent) Wikipedia entry, https://fr.wikipedia.org/wiki/Marguerite_de_Bourgogne_(morte_en_1277).

74. Edition, Roll A Front, Part 1.

75. Edition, Roll A Front, Part 1: "*escrin*"; "*por lespicier qui acira le cuer le conte por [um] guelient et por choses quil [i] m[i]st et por sa peine*"; "*drap qui i estoit dor en fu percez sor le cuer le conte*." See Rutebeuf, "La complainte dou conte Hue de Nevers," v. 85: "*Li ceurs le conte est a Citiaux*."

76. Edition, Roll A Front, Part 1.

77. The Templar treasurer is a challenge to identify. This may have been one Bienvenu who was active with Thomas Béraud in 1262. The grand master of the Temple at this time was Thomas Béraud (master from 1256 to 1273). See Jochen Burgtorf, *The Central Convent of Hospitallers and Templars: History, Organization, and Personnel (1099/1230–1310)* (Leiden: Brill, 2008), 500.

all transactions involving large sums or transfers of money, especially from France to Outremer. Eudes had at least one loan of 3,000 *lb. t.*, which he drew from and attempted to have repaid after his death.[78] And he appears to have borrowed a similar amount from the Hospitallers.[79] By contrast, no mention is made of Italian merchant-bankers, like those from whom the king of France had drawn loans.[80] Eudes's household was financially obliged, as far as this record is concerned, to the Templars and the Hospitallers alone, and it appears his debts were cleared after his death.

The household that emerges from the Account-Inventory was distinctively Burgundian. Most of the knights in Eudes's retinue hailed from lands within the duchy or along its border with Champagne. Similarly, the other figures who circulated within Eudes's orbit, both after his death and one presumes during his life, also had connections to the duchy of Burgundy, to Nevers, to southern Champagne, and to related territories, or to extended family members, such as Eudes's sister. And for those whose careers we can follow after 1266, it is clear that these networks continued to hold as knights and retainers moved to serve in the employ of Charles of Anjou in Sicily, or under the king of France or count of Champagne upon returning to France. Thus, we can imagine that the contours of Eudes's aristocratic household-on-the-move were to some extent maintained after his death, just as his memory lived on through the objects and things that moved with them, out of Acre and beyond Outremer.

78. Edition, Roll A Front, Part 1, and Roll D Front.

79. Provision in the account in Roll A is made for payments "for the agent who negotiated the loan of 3,000 *l. t.* that the Hospital lent to the count [*Por i corretier qui porchaca lemprunst des iii*^{m} *l. tornois que li Opitauz presta le conte xxii b/ et quart*]." Edition, Roll A Front, Part 1.

80. William Chester Jordan, *Louis IX and the Challenge of the Crusade* (Princeton, NJ: Princeton University Press, 1979), 100–104; A. Sayous, "Les Mandats de saint Louis sur son trésor et le mouvement international des capitaux pendant la septième croisade (1248–1254)," *Revue historique* 167 (1931): 254–304; and Housley, *The Italian Crusades*.

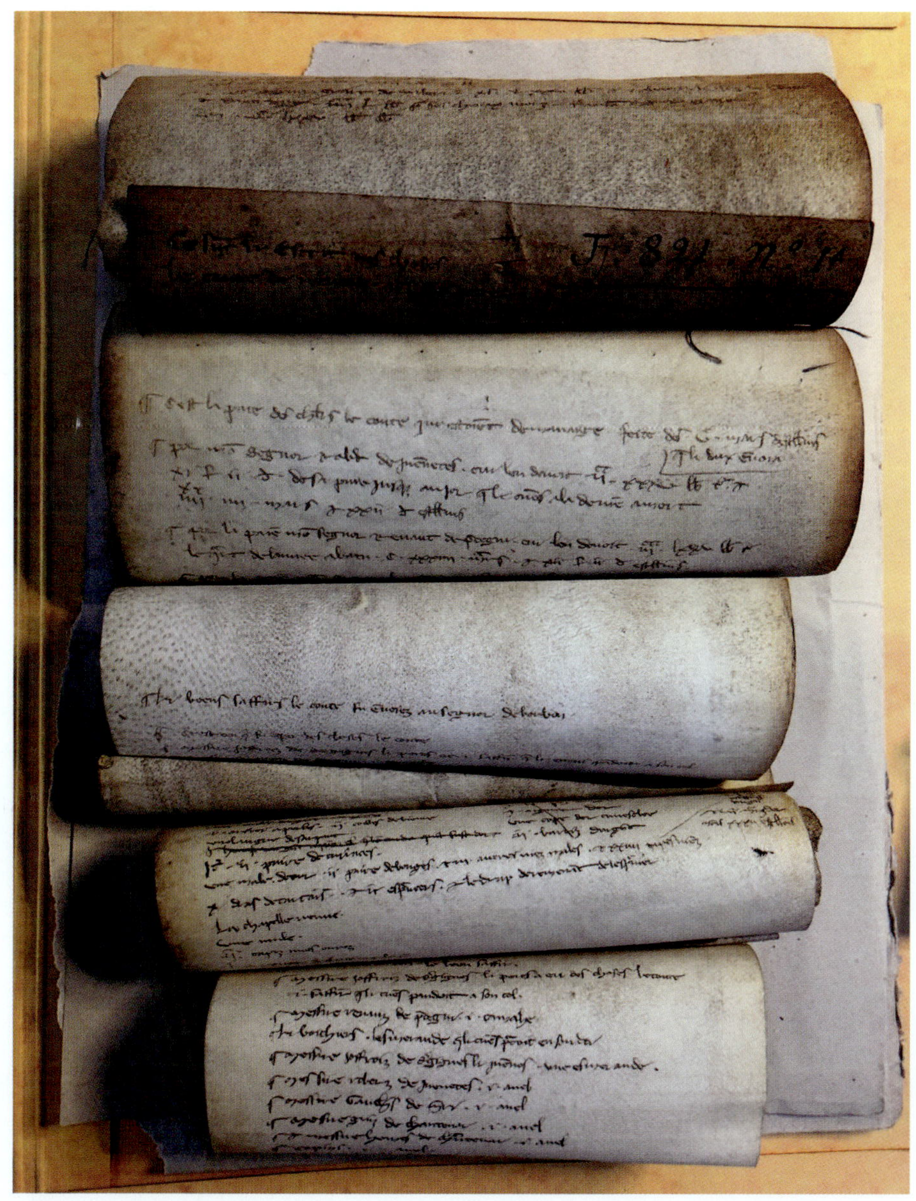

Figure 1. Paris, AN, series J 821, no. 1, Rolls A–D in order of size. Photo: A. E. Lester.

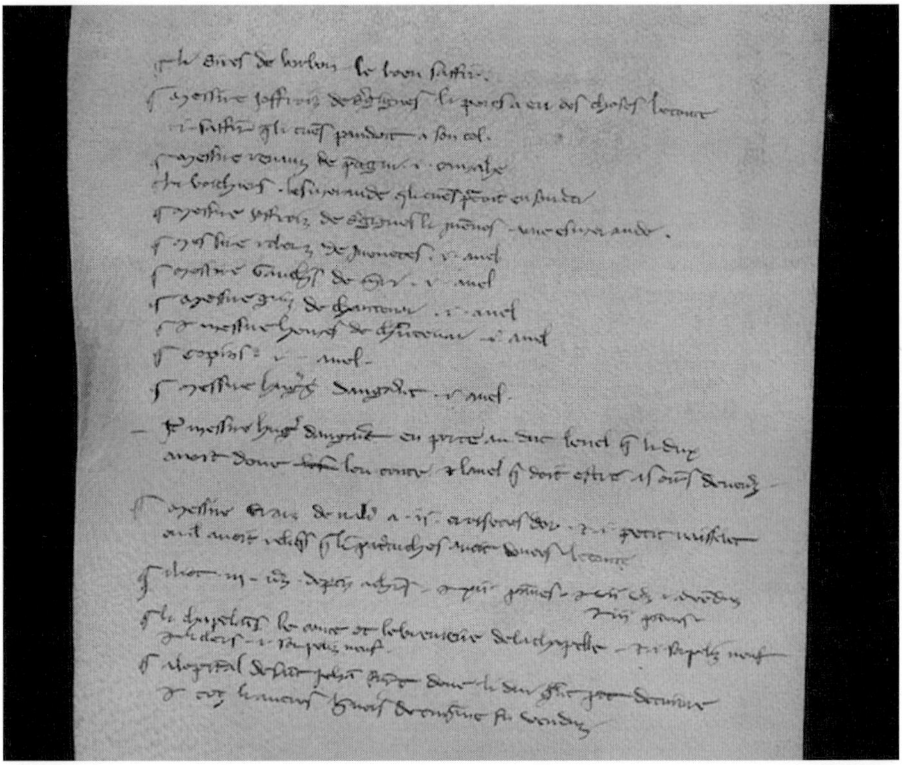

Figure 2. Detail, Paris, AN, series J 821, no. 1, Roll C (verso/dorsal). Photo: AN.

Figure 3. Paris, AN, series J 821, no. 1, Rolls A–D as stored together. Photo: A. E. Lester.

Figure 4. Paris, AN, series J 821, no. 1, Roll A, held in the hand for scale. Photo: A. E. Lester.

Figure 5. Paris, AN, series J 821, no. 1, Roll A, held in the hand. Photo: A. E. Lester.

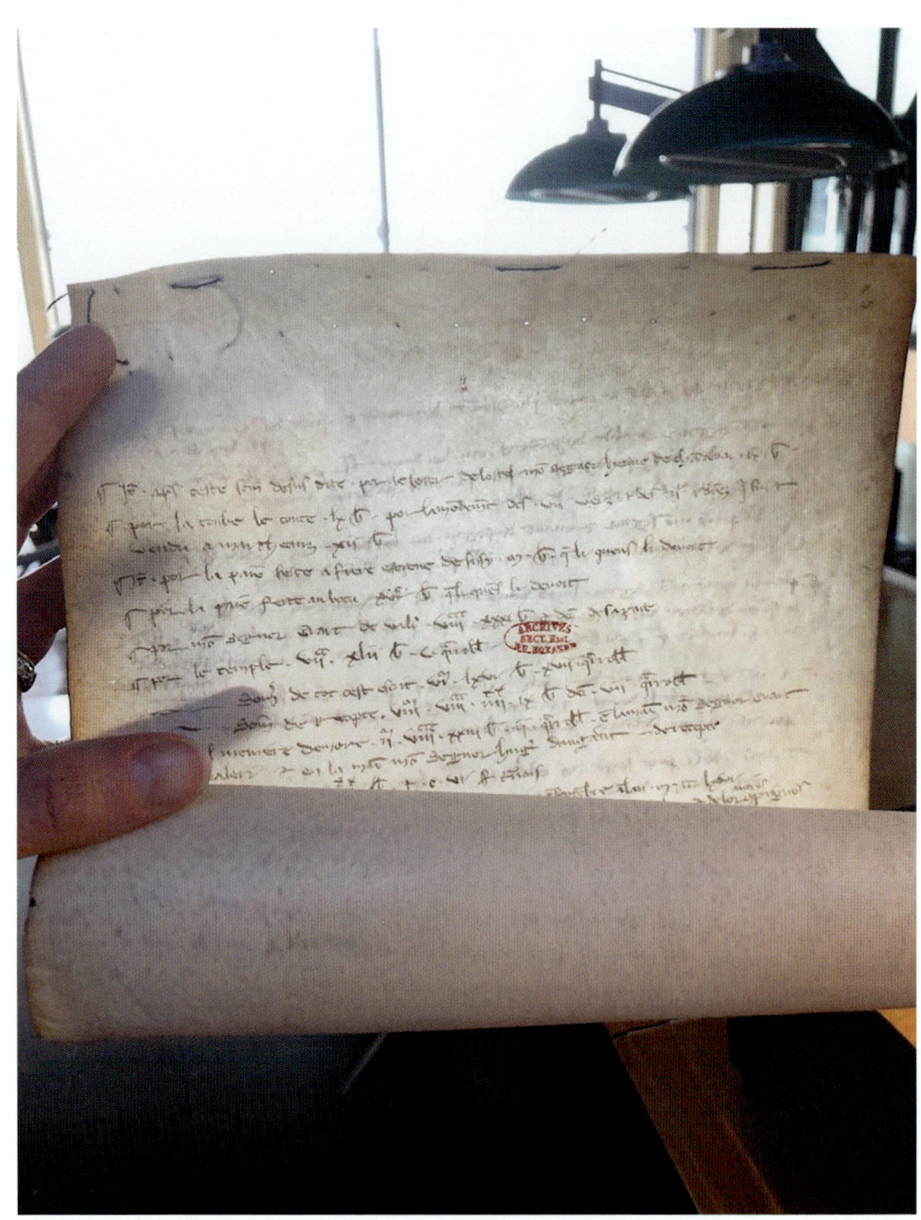

Figure 6. Paris, AN, series J 821, no. 1, Roll A with stitching visible. Photo: A. E. Lester.

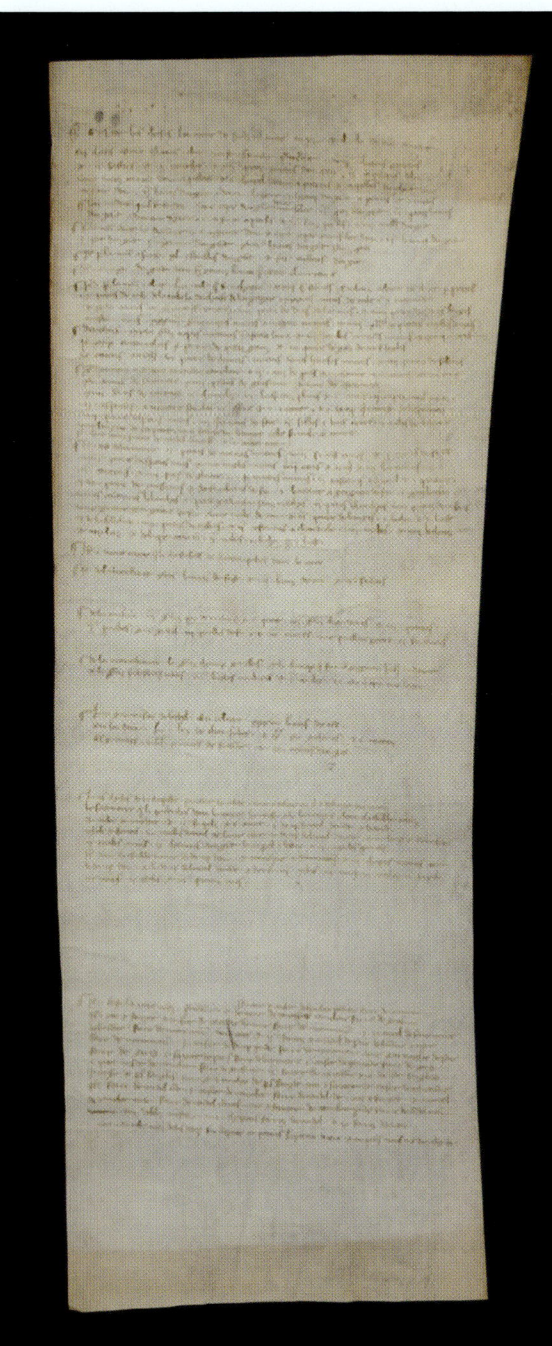

Figure 7. Paris, AN, series J 821, no. 1, Roll B (recto) unrolled showing full text. Photo: AN.

Figures 8.1 and 8.2. France, *gros tournois*, silver coin equivalent to roughly 12 *deniers tournois*, or 1 *sous tournois*, reign of Louis IX, (1226–1270), issued after 1265. Linked visually with the coinage of the East. See below, figure 11, which also shows concentric circles of text. Princeton University Numismatic Collection, France 321, Laf. 198c. Obverse and reverse. Photo: A. E. Lester.

Figures 9.1 and 9.2. Coin, France, *denier tournois*, silver penny of Tours, later reign of Louis IX, 1266–70. Princeton University Numismatic Collection, France 846, Laf. 201. Obverse and reverse. Photo: A. E. Lester.

Figures 10.1 and 10.2. Jerusalem, silver *denier* of Damietta, John of Brienne, 1210–25. Princeton University Numismatic Collection MPS.43.748.5. Obverse and reverse. Photo: A. E. Lester.

Figures 11.1 and 11.2. Alexandria, gold *dinar*. Princeton University Numismatic Collection, Fl Fatimid 9195, al-Mustansi 1085, ACFC 1685. Obverse and reverse. Photo: A. E. Lester.

Figures 12.1 and 12.2. Crusader Acre, Kingdom of Jerusalem, imitation gold *dinar*, ca. 1148/59–1187. An imitation of Egyptian dinars in the name of Caliph Al-Amir. Princeton University Numismatic Collection. Obverse and reverse. Photo: A. E. Lester.

Figures 13.1 and 13.2. Seals of Eudes of Nevers (Eudes de Bourgogne), Paris, AN, J 256, no. 56 (1255), and Dijon, AD CdO Ad 21. B 304—ps 428 (1265). Photo: AN. Plaster cast from seal mold, Louis Douët-d'Arcq 447: http://www.sigilla.org/empreinte/eudes-bourgogne-an-paris-j-256-ndeg-56-51974; and http://www.sigilla.org/empreinte/eudes-nevers-ad-21-b-304-ps-428-18917.

Figure 14. Seal of Érard of Vallery, Paris, AN, J 208, no. 13 (1276). Photo: AN. Plaster cast from seal mold, Louis Douët-d'Arcq 3811: http://www.sigilla.org/sceau-type/erard-valery-sceau-47766.

Figure 15. Illumination of King Arthur and his retinue. Robert de Boron, *Romans arthuriens*, France (possibly St.-Omer or region of Thérouanne), ca. 1270–90. Paris, BnF, MS fr. 95, fol. 345v. Note the vair-lined outer capes or houppelandes, and the gloves and caps. Photo: Paris, BnF.

Figure 16. From Genesis 42–48, showing Joseph's reception of his brothers with a feast and baggage train on the move. New York, Pierpont Morgan Library, MS M.638, fol. 6v. Old Testament miniatures, Paris, France, ca. 1244–54. The Morgan Library & Museum. Purchased by J. P. Morgan (1867–1943) in 1916. Shows a table lavishly set and multiple cases and trucks of baggage on the move. Photo: Morgan Library.

Figure 17. Ring with small sapphire, England, 14th century. Gilded silver, sapphire; diameter: 2.9 cm (1 1/8 in.). The Cleveland Museum of Art, Purchase from the J. H. Wade Fund 1950.383. Photo: CMA (CC0), https://www.clevelandart.org/art/1950.383.

Figure 18. Ring Brooch, German, ca. 1340–49, Middle Rhineland, Germany. Gold, spinels, and sapphires and rubies (2.2 x 0.5 cm). New York, Metropolitan Museum of Art, The Cloisters Collection, 2006.257. Photo: The Cloisters 2006, https://www.metmuseum.org/art/collection/search/477239.

Figures 19.1, 19.2, and 19.3. Silk Robe made of "Tartar cloth of gold," 13th century, Central Asia. Silk, woven; 142 cm. Aga Khan Museum, Toronto, ON, Canada. AKM816. © The Aga Khan Museum.

Figure 20. Cloth of gold with winged lions and griffins, ca. 1225–75, Central Asia. Silk and gold thread: lampas; 124 x 48.8 cm. The Cleveland Museum of Art, Purchase from the J. H. Wade Fund 1989.50. Photo: CMA (CC0), https://www.clevelandart.org/art/1989.50.

Figure 21. Illumination of Saint Martin. From *Images de la vie du Christ et des saints*. France, ca. 1250–1300. Paris, BnF, MS NAF 16251, fol. 89r. St. Martin's cloak is lined with vair and he is wearing a gold brooch and gloves sitting on a great horse. Photo: Paris, BnF.

Figure 22. A hunter and a beaver, from a bestiary. Unknown illuminator, possibly made in Thérouanne, northern France, ca. 1270. Tempera colors, gold leaf, ink on parchment; 7 ½ x 5 5/8 in. Los Angeles, J. Paul Getty Museum, MS Lugwig XV 3 83.MR.173, fol. 83r. Photo: The Getty, CC, https://www.getty.edu/art/collection/object/103SAY.

Figure 23. Coral tree with serpent's tongues hanging. Germany before 1562. Gold, silver-gilt, coral, fossilized shark teeth. Vienna, Treasury and Museum of the Teutonic Order, inv. no. K-037. Photo: Schatzkammer und Museum des Deutschen Ordens, Vienna.

Figure 24. Illumination of Abraham and Melchisedek (Genesis 14:18–20). From *Psautier dit de Saint Louis*, France, ca. 1270–74. Paris, BnF, MS lat. 10525, fol. 106r. Shows a precious box or *escrin* like that purchased for transport of Eudes's heart. Photo: Paris, BnF.

Figure 25. Coffret of the Blessed John of Montmirail or the Longpont Coffret, Limoges, ca. 1270 (or 1242?). Copper, engraved, stippled, and gilt champlevé enamel; 15 x 78.7 x 17.5 cm. Treasury of the Abbey of Longpont (Aisne), France. Photo: Thierry Lefébure, Ministère de la culture, Inventaire général, Département de l'Aisne, AGIR-Picardie.

Figure 26. Illumination of knights setting up tents outside of Camelot. Robert de Boron, *Romans arthuriens*, France (possibly St.-Omer or region of Thérouanne), ca. 1270–90. Paris, BnF, MS fr. 95, fol. 324v. Photo: Paris, BnF.

Figures 27.1 and 27.2. Silver-gilt drinking cup, possibly northern France, near Amiens/Coucy, ca. 1190–1219, profile and interior. Syria National Museum, Damascus (Inv. Nr. 29313/14). Photo: Courtesy of the Deutsches Archäologisches Institut.

Figure 28. Reliquary Cross, ca. 1180, Limoges France, possibly from the Abbey of Grandmont. Silver gilt, rock crystal, glass cabochons, wood core. New York, Metropolitan Museum of Art, The Cloisters Collection, 2002.18. Photo: The Cloisters, https://www.metmuseum.org/art/collection/search/474199.

Figure 29. Pyx, ca. 1250. France, Limousin, Limoges. Gilded copper, champlevé enamel. The Cleveland Museum of Art, Purchase from the J. H. Wade Fund 1952.328. Photo: CMA (CC0), https://www.clevelandart.org/art/1952.328.

Figure 30. Illumination bottom margin, *Mon Seigneur Jehan de Lens* playing chess with his friend. *Psalter*, Amiens, France, ca. 1280–90. Paris, BnF, MS lat. 10435, fol. 61r. Photo: Paris, BnF.

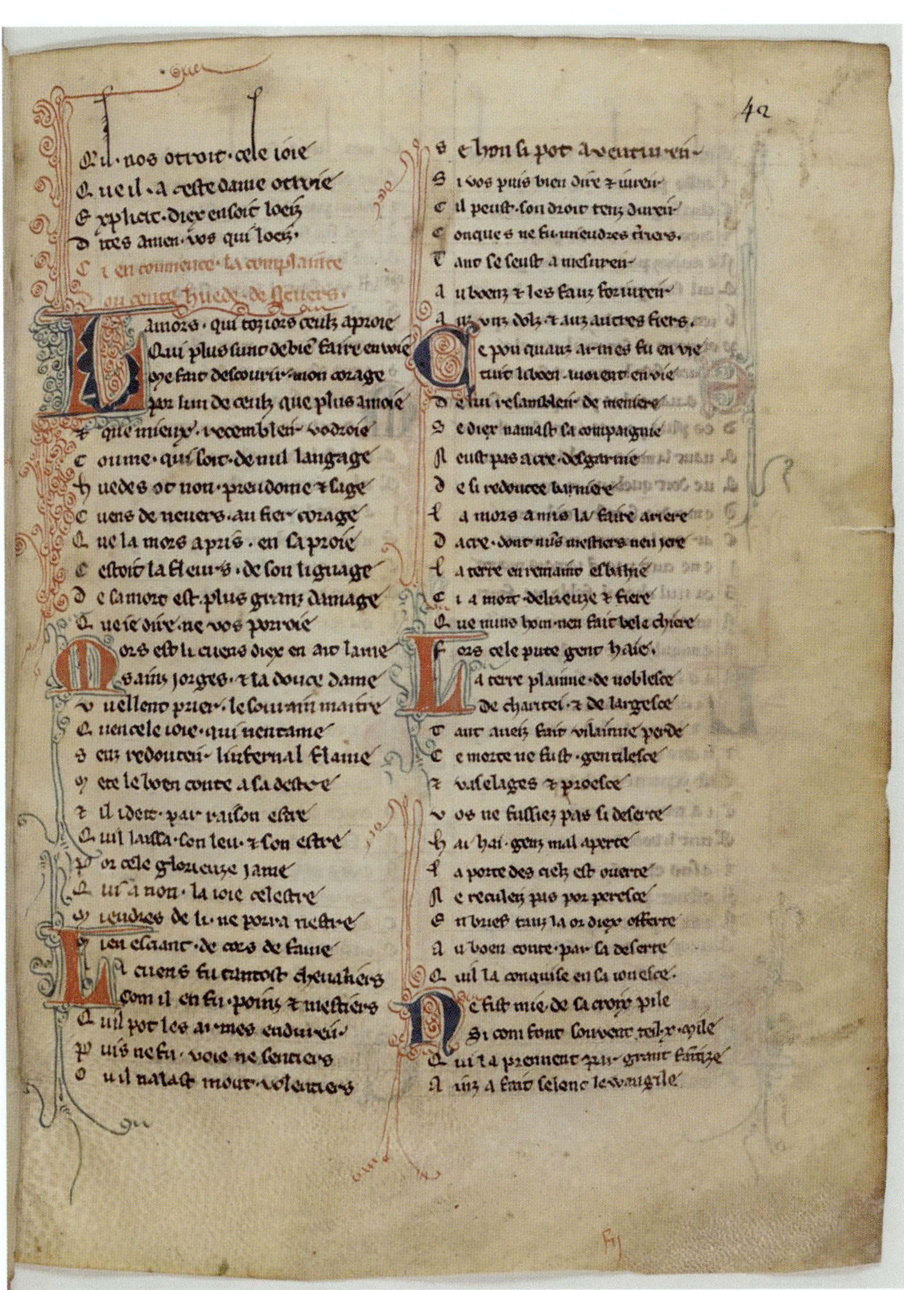

Figure 31. Rutebeuf, "La complainte dou conte Hue de Nevers," Paris, BnF, MS fr. 1635, fol. 42r. France, possibly Champagne or Burgundy, ca. 1201–1300. Photo: Paris, BnF.

Figure 32. Illumination of the Siege of Acre from Rutebeuf, "Li complainte daccre" ("La nouvele complainte doutremeir"). Brussels, KBR, MS 9411–9426, fol. 34r. Photo: Brussels, KBR.

6

Outremer Objects

A Documentary Archaeology of Crusader Possessions

Whereas the account that makes up most of Roll A lists individuals in Eudes's household and tracks when knights and servants were paid for services, the inventories that form Rolls B and C reveal the workings of the household itself and the religious houses and individuals in Acre that received the count's goods as they were given out after his death. To read these rolls is to move through the domestic spaces of Eudes's lodgings and out into the religious and charitable landscape of French Acre. In this way we can see Acre through the eyes of a French crusader. Geographically, Eudes's inventory is oriented toward Outremer and its holy sites. The only religious house mentioned outside of Acre is Cîteaux, the Cistercian monastery in Burgundy where Eudes's heart was sent and where he was commemorated, alongside generations of the crusader-counts of Burgundy and Nevers.[1] The inventory

1. See the obituary from Cîteaux in appendix 3 of Ernst Petit, *Histoire des ducs de Bourgogne de la race capétienne* (Dijon: Darantière, 1885–1905), 5:396–411, at 403. It is notable that between the 2 nones and 8 ides of August, that is, August 3–25, three successive counts of Burgundy and Nevers who died while on crusade were commemorated at Cîteaux, which functioned as the necropolis for the dukes of Burgundy. Hugh III of Burgundy (Eudes's grandfather) died in Acre on August 25, 1192, after having taken part in the Third Crusade. Jean Tristan, count of Nevers through marriage (Eudes's son-in-law), died on August 3, 1270, in Tunis. And Eudes, who like his grandfather died in Acre, was partially buried at Cîteaux. A large tomb was constructed at Cîteaux for Hugh III that was subsequently destroyed in 1552 during the Wars of Religion. Eudes's brother Robert II of Burgundy stipulated in his will from 1297 that he wished to have his heart buried at Cîteaux and his body *deça mer*, in Acre, in both cases next to his brother ("*delès . . . mon frere*"). See Bastin and Faral, *Onze poèmes*, 65n8. For Robert II's testament, see Urbain Plancher, *Histoire générale et particulière du duché de Bourgogne* (Dijon: A. de Fay, 1739–81), 2: Preuves, xci–xcvi, no. 145, at xcii.

links places—descriptively, relationally, and personally—to and with objects; in doing so, it represents networks that once existed in space and time. Rolls B and C list items in the spaces where they were kept and used. In this way, the inventory seems to follow the movement of its scribes as they progressed through rooms filled with things that were themselves afforded values, histories, associations, and future trajectories as they were enumerated, given over, sold off, and distributed in turn.

Those who have studied the *rouleaux* or used them to illuminate the crusading histories of the counts of Burgundy and Nevers have been awed by the sheer abundance of things listed and by what we learn of the intimate and opulent details of Eudes's life and domestic setting in the East. Chazaud, the text's first editor, as well as Ernst Petit, René Lespinasse, Jaroslav Folda, and Jonathan Riley-Smith have all noted the vivid qualities of the inventory and its evocation of the seemingly everyday details of life in Acre. In Petit's words, "we find in this precious document the exact descriptions of all the baggage and *matériel* that a knight of this stature would need in the later thirteenth century for such an expedition."[2] Something of the richness of quotidian life seeps through the text, leaving most readers with a sense that they have glimpsed into the personal world of a noble crusader in Acre. Overflowing with Eudes's "stuff," his surroundings seem almost tangible.[3]

Roll B, in particular, gets us as close as we can come to the voice of Eudes himself. Drawn up on "the day he went from life to death [*au jor quil ala de vie amort*]," it reflects Eudes's final wishes and directives as he assigned specific objects to precise people either to keep for themselves, to hold until a final sale or compensation could be made, or—in ways that lie beyond the limits of our text—to give away at another point in time.[4] The inventory begins in what must be Eudes's own intimate chambers, with objects known to him in quantity, value, history, and provenance. And it begins with those things of greatest value. Eudes's servant Robet takes in hand eight rings, two sapphires, one cameo, twelve small rings from Puy (most likely, Le Puy), two small crosses of gold, a gold belt with pearls, a chapel of gold with stones and pearls, yet more plate including two silver basins to hold water, one silver goblet set with stones and enamels, which is believed to be of gold, additional pots, goblets, and silver spoons (see for examples figures 16–17 and 25).

2. "On trouve dans ce précieux document des indications exactes sur les bagages et le matériel, dont se faisait suivre au XIIIe siècle un chevalier de cette importance partant pour une telle expédition." Petit, *Histoire des ducs de Bourgogne*, 5:74–76, at 76; and Réne de Lespinasse, *Le Nivernais et les contes de Nevers* (Paris: Honoré Champion, 1909–14), 2:270–86.

3. On what we can and cannot see, "glance," or "gaze" at in these texts, see Shirin A. Khanmohamadi, *In Light of Another's Word: European Ethnography in the Middle Ages* (Philadelphia: University of Pennsylvania Press, 2013). On empiricism and its limits, see Gabrielle M. Spiegel, "The Limits of Empiricism: The Utility of Theory in Historical Thought and Writing," *Medieval History Journal* 22 (2019): 1–22.

4. Edition, Roll B Front.

Robet must have been charged with distributing these items, for all of them surface again in later rolls when they were sold, purchased, or in some cases given away as a form of salary compensation or personal remembrance.[5] While still in the same space, two other servants, Odet le decannat, a squire, and Afetie, a page, received into their hands additional stores of silver including pitchers, basins, containers, pots, goblets, saucers, and spoons. Some of these items were weighed and valued and were later purchased by the Temple (see figures 16 and 27.1 and 27.2).[6] Through the late nineteenth century, silver objects, especially tablewares like pitchers, cups, and plates, were a common way to store and keep wealth for those who had it. For those objects that passed to friends, family, or religious institutions, they carried the memory and marks of their donors.[7]

The scribes then move to record the vast troves of cloth in the count's possession. Eudes or his executors again charged Robet with taking these in hand (*par la main*). There are ten measures of cloth purchased in Troyes, which Simon Ysanbars bought, ten measures of linen cloth from the duchesses of Burgundy, two measures of striped cloth from Provins, and dozens more ells or measures of cloth, some plain, some worked, some embroidered and used for tablecloths or wall hangings.[8] Then dozens of hand towels are listed, old and new, small and large, as well as twenty-nine head coverings (*cuevrechies*) (most likely pieces of cloth to be wrapped around the head as a shield to the sun), ten pairs of small gloves, three pairs of deerskin gloves, daggers, leggings, and four pairs of shoes. There are also fur pieces—vair (grey squirrel), and *miniver* (white squirrel)—camel hair cloth, or camlet, as well as Boukhara cloth, Tartar cloth, quilts, hangings, coverlets, and four silk cushions, an embroidered coverlet of red taffeta and two whistles (see figures 19.1–19.3,

5. Edition, Roll B Front. This is the case with Érard of Vallery, who was paid in part with objects that belonged to Eudes, including the gold chapel with stones and pearls, and the decorations for the new chapel, two new cloth hangings, the nine Tartar cloths, and the cloth of gold threaded through or around the count's heart, two large romances, and one chansonnier, all of which was valued at 206 *lb. t.* 13 *s.* 4 *d. t.* See Edition, Roll A Front, Part 2.

6. See Roll B Front.

7. Laurence Delobette, "'Faites ceci en mémoire de moi': Calices et testaments du diocèse de Besançon XIIIe–XVe siècles," in *Le miracle de Faverney (1608) l'eucharistie: Environnement et temps de l'histoire*, ed. Corinne Marchal and Manuel Tramaux (Besançon: Presses Universitaires de Franche-Comté, 2010), 95–125; and Brigitte Buettner, "Le système des objets dans le testament de Blanche de Navarre," *Clio*, no. 19 (2004), https://doi.org/10.4000/clio.644. For later resonances of silver and plate in this way, see for example, Michael Gorra, *The Saddest Words: William Faulkner's Civil War* (New York: Liverlight, 2020), 202–29.

8. Edition, Roll B Front. For the use of cloth in similar spaces, see Frédérique Lachaud, "Documents financiers et histoire de la culture matérielle: Les textiles dans les comptes des hôtels royaux et nobiliaires (France et Angleterre, XXIe–XVe siècle)," *Bibliothèque de l'école des chartes* 164 (2006): 71–96; Lachaud, "Les tentes et l'activité militaire: Les guerres d'Edouard Ier Plantagenet (1272–1307)," *Mélanges d l'École française de Rome: Moyen-Âge* 111 (1999): 443–61; and Françoise Piponnier, "Linge de corps et linge de maison au Moyen Âge d'après les inventaires bourguignons," *Ethnologie française* 16 (1986): 239–48.

20, and 21).[9] And finally there are items that must come from what we can only call Eudes's toilet or medicine chest, including "1 shaving basin, 2 beaver's testicles, one serpent's tongue; a vial of balm [*i bacin arere; ii coilles de bievre une langue de serpent une fiolete de baume*]" (see figures 22 and 23).[10]

Eudes's personal rooms were opulent spaces, covered in cloth, and decorated with gold and silver objects, wall hangings, and silk cushions. Even if all of this cloth and plate was not used, it was clearly on hand. We can infer Eudes's role here because the details used to describe the objects were drawn from memories and known associations or attributions that reflected the provenance of cloth, whether from the East (Tartar or Boukhara) or the West (Troyes, Provins, Burgundy). Likewise, knowledge of who purchased or gave certain items to the count was still associated with some of the objects when the list was drawn up.[11] We can envision a bed with multiple coverlets, some silk and decorated, some plain; towels in abundance with which to wash and wipe; and medicines and tinctures for promoting health or in healing wounds. Beaver testicles were used for the oil they contained, castor oil, which may have aided in digestion. Or—as some bestiaries conveyed—beaver testicles were also thought to have a stimulant effect, sometimes called a medieval Viagra.[12] Serpent's tongue is harder to identify with precision. This may have been an herb believed to function as an antidote in case of poisoning or to stanch bleeding. But serpent's tongue could also refer to petrified sharks' teeth, ornamented and used—often by servants or pages—to test food and drink for

9. Edition, Roll B Front. For the cloth described here, see the essay by Sharon Farmer in this volume, below.

10. Edition, Roll B Front.

11. For a well-known parallel, see Joinville, *VSL*, para. 323, where he describes the blanket made of scarlet and lined with fine *vair* that had been given to him by his mother. On Eastern cloth and its use and meaning, see E. Jane Burns, *Sea of Silk: A Textile Geography of Women's Work in Medieval French Literature* (Philadelphia: University of Pennsylvania Press, 2006); and for connections beyond the Mediterranean, see Sharon Farmer, *The Silk Industries of Medieval Paris: Artisanal Migration, Technological Innovation, and Gendered Experience* (Philadelphia: University of Pennsylvania Press, 2017); Farmer, "Global and Gendered Perspectives on the Production of a Parisian Alms Purse, c. 1340," *Journal of Medieval Worlds* 1 (2019): 45–85; and Anne E. Lester, "Intimacy and Abundance: Textile Relics, the Veronica, and Christian Devotion in the Aftermath of the Fourth Crusade," in "Material Religion in the Crusading World," ed. William Purkis, special issue, *Material Religion* 14 (2018): 533–44.

12. See Ranya Halbouni, "The Treasured Testicles of the Medieval Beaver," *The Iris* (blog), Getty, May 7, 2018, https://blogs.getty.edu/iris/the-treasured-testicles-of-the-medieval-beaver/; Melissa Lo, "Recasting the *Castor*: From *The Book of Beasts* to Albertus Magnus's *On Animals*," *Thresholds* 35 (2009): 92–95; Efraim Lev, "Healing with Animals in the Levant from the 10th to the 18th Century," *Journal of Ethnobiology and Ethnomedicine* 2 (2006): https://doi.org/10.1186/1746-4269-2-11; and Kenneth Gouwens, "Emasculation as Empowerment: Lessons of Beaver Lore for Two Italian Humanists," *European Review of History: Revue européenne d'histoire* 22 (2015): 536–62. According to Christian tradition, the beaver's willingness to sacrifice part of himself was a sign of his devotion to Christ. Such self-sacrifice paralleled the sacrifices that crusaders were asked to take up.

"toxic contamination" or poison.[13] Some late medieval "serpent's tongues" still exist in museum collections, like the stunning example held today in the treasury of the Viennese chapter of the Teutonic order (see figure 23). Finally, balm may have been used to treat any number of ailments from aches to wounds to irritants.

From the intimacies of Eudes's rooms, the scribes moved into the armory. Eudes possessed four coats of armor, three banners, as well as leg protectors, a helmet and iron neck cover, a pair of white horse blankets, reins, and eight pairs of spurs, among other items for horses, two knives, four iron blades, and two new axes (see figure 24). Save for swords and lances, bows and arrows, which one might expect, the count was well equipped for the skirmishes and raids that had come to characterize crusading warfare by the late 1260s.[14] In addition, payments were made to one Jehan de Dijon "for the count's armor," implying that Jehan had either made pieces of armor at Eudes's request or repaired armor; either way, Jehan was part of Eudes's local, Acre-based, network.[15] Those inventorying then went on to the chamber where they recorded trunks and chests of many sizes and shapes, presumably used to store and move the objects detailed above (see figures 16 and 24–25).[16] The pantry came next, and the scribes list yet more trunks, alongside a tent, given to the count from "the castellan of Château Pèlerin [*une tante que li chastelains de Chastiaupelerin dona le conte*]," that is, the nearby Templar stronghold (see figure 26).[17] This detail of provenance suggests a personal knowledge of this object and its history, which itself created a shared space for life on campaign or on the move.[18]

13. See the discussion in Brigitte Buettner, *The Mineral and the Visual: Precious Stones in Medieval Secular Culture* (University Park: Pennsylvania State University Press, 2022), 116–17; and George Zammit-Maempel, "Fossil Sharks' Teeth: A Medieval Safeguard against Poisoning," *Melita Historica* 6 (1975): 391–410.

14. Edition, Roll B Front.

15. Edition, Roll A Front, Part 1 and Back. Eudes paid Jehan de Dijon presumably to make or repair armor and weapons. But it is surprising that no store of weapons of war is listed, especially swords, nor are they exchanged, passed on, or sold, or specifically mentioned in the inventory. This absence may indicate that there were additional rolls that are no longer extant where such information could have been recorded.

16. Edition, Roll B Front.

17. Edition, Roll B Front. Also known as Pilgrim Castle or 'Atlit Castle, today on the northern coast of Israel, not far (13 km south) from Haifa. Baybars's forces had raided as far north as Caesarea and were at Château Pèlerin between 1264 and 1265. It may be that this tent was recovered and given to Eudes after one of these skirmishes. See Michael Lower, *The Tunis Crusade of 1270: A Mediterranean History* (Oxford: Oxford University Press, 2018), 26–28. For maintenance and the fall of Château Pèlerin, see Pierre-Vincent Claverie, "Un nouvel éclairage sur le financement de la première croisade de saint Louis," *Mélanges de l'École française de Rome: Moyen-Age* 113 (2001): 621–35.

18. Joinville describes the painted chapel tent that Louis IX had made and sent to the Mongols in the hopes of their conversion; Joinville, *VSL*, para. 471. And tents are depicted throughout the lavish imagery of the Morgan Picture Bible, especially in scenes of warfare. See New York,

Through the hands of the scribes, the inventory moves next into the cellar, where wooden barrels, flasks, and casks are accounted for; then to the kitchen where copper pots, large and small, cauldrons, pans, grills, iron pans, perforated pans, and forks are listed.[19] Then, perhaps just adjacent in space, the inventory moves into the stables, where the scribes enumerated the animals Eudes possessed including the large grey war horse that belonged to Jaque Vidaut, a large palfrey, three pack animals, and "a mule used for carrying water [*et i asne qui aportoit laigue*]" (see figure 21).[20] Again, the attributed genealogy of ownership personalized even the animals, and the inventory makes clear that Jaques and Eudes must have known, or at the very least known of, each other. Finally, we learn of the "supply for the lodging [*la garnison de lostel*]," that is, the provisions in the cellar and the larder that included significant stores of food: three dozen butts of wine, fifty sides of salted meat, 195 chickens, one sheep, and 170 measures of wheat and 200 of barley.[21] Enough food stuff to maintain a retinue of knights for several months.[22]

Although none of these details is especially surprising, the objects are organized and listed in a telling manner. The inventory text was clearly ordered in a way that reflected Eudes's living spaces. As we read, we move through the rooms of Eudes's residence—from the intimacy of his personal wardrobe and chambers, to the pantry, the cellar, the kitchen, and then outside among the animals and the stores of food. Daniel Lord Smail has shown that this sort of spatial recording of possessions was a common way of creating an inventory, of transferring physical objects and spaces onto a written list, rendering them in textual form. Such descriptions and movement through space was a

Morgan Library, MS M 638: https://www.themorgan.org/collection/Crusader-Bible. Tents were certainly part of the shared and mobile aristocratic spaces that formed the material Outremer.

19. Edition, Roll B Front.

20. Edition, Roll B Front.

21. As Jordan notes, Joinville discusses salted meat (pork, which would have been difficult to obtain from Muslim traders), grain, and wine and the work of provisioning an army on the move. See William Chester Jordan, *Louis IX and the Challenge of the Crusade* (Princeton, NJ: Princeton University Press, 1979), 76–78; and Joinville, *VSL*, para. 130. In contrast, Joinville also notes the foods eaten locally supplied by the Nile; see paras. 187–90. Later, Joinville comments that when the army was captured the Muslim forces made two piles, "one of the salted pork and one of the bodies of the Christian dead [*un lit de bacons et un autre de gens mors*]," "which they were meant to look after since they do not eat pork [*et les chairs salees que il devoient garder, pour ce que il ne manjurent point de porc*]," and "they set fire to both; there was such a blaze that it lasted throughout Friday, Saturday and Sunday [*et mistrent le feu dedans; et y ot si grant feu que il dura le vendredi, le samedi, et le dymanche*]" (para. 370).

22. While living in Acre, Joinville provisioned his own retinue in almost exactly the same fashion; Joinville, *VSL*, paras. 502–3. He notes that after the feast of Saint Remy he had foodstuffs (*garnison de l'ostel*) (the same term used in the inventory), readied for the winter because "supplies became more expensive in winter due to the sea, which is more treacherous than in summer [*ce fesoi je pour ce que les danrees enchierissent en yver, pour la mer qui est plus felonnesce en yver que en esté*]" (para. 502).

common way of recording and then unfurling the contents of a life.[23] This process was "something more akin to an act of translation," of tagging the charismatic three-dimensional things in the world to descriptive phrases that would stand in and be pressed to re-create on the flat page what was once very much alive.[24]

Equally revealing is what was not inventoried.[25] Furniture is never mentioned. We hear nothing of chairs, tables, bed frames, or mattresses.[26] If they were in the lodgings Eudes rented, they were not his to give away. Swords and other weapons of war are also conspicuously absent, a surprising omission for a crusader's household. And although some objects make reference to women, there is nothing inventoried that was evidently or descriptively gendered female or intended for use by women. Eudes's was a decidedly masculine space, in which male solidarities were reinforced through naming, gifts, and personal memories.[27] Present, however, is luggage—dozens of trunks, chests, caskets, barrels, casks, and the like—and what they contained. We are among the goods of a traveler, someone with a temporary house and a store of valued and mundane objects, some of which were saved and treasured, and others that had to be consumed, as we shall see.[28]

Without doubt the two most opulent spaces in Eudes's *ostel* were the chapel and the wardrobe. They were inventoried last and reflect the vast quantity and quality of what they held. The chapel—whether a dedicated room, consecrated space, or corner of a hall made sacred though the things with which it was furnished—had on hand all that was needed for a priest or chaplain to perform the Mass and to say the hours. Although no altar is specifically mentioned, the count did have a chalice, a small cross with a relic of the True Cross (see figure 28), and what is called "the sanctuary [*le saintuaire*]" that the patriarchs gave to the count. We take this to be a portable altar, or possibly a reliquary that was given to the count by a bishop or archbishop, even the archbishop of Tyre himself or the patriarch of Jerusalem.[29] There

23. Daniel Lord Smail, *Legal Plunder: Households and Debt Collection in Late Medieval Europe* (Cambridge, MA: Harvard University Press, 2016); see his analysis of inventorying as a process, 31–35. Smail notes that "the contents of a life unfurl as you move from room to room" (31).

24. Smail, *Legal Plunder*, 67.

25. Smail, *Legal Plunder*, 76–88.

26. See Benjamin Z. Kedar, *Cultures of the Medieval Kingdom of Jerusalem: Frontier Inventiveness in the Age of the Crusades* (Ithaca, NY: Cornell University Press, 2025).

27. We thank Sarah McNamer for pointing this out.

28. Elizabeth Lambourn makes this point beautifully in her evocative analysis of a merchant-traveler's list found in the Geniza records. See Lambourn, *Abraham's Luggage: A Social Life of Things in the Medieval Indian Ocean* (Cambridge: Cambridge University Press, 2018).

29. William II of Agen was the Latin patriarch of Jerusalem from 1261 to 1270, and the relics could have been a gift from him or perhaps his predecessor, Jacques Panthaléon, who became Pope Urban IV in 1261. A portable altar such as this was not uncommon. As noted above, Geoffrey of Sergines the elder was given permission by Pope Urban IV to have and to use a portable altar as needed. See above, chapter 5, n. 36. See the comments in Denys Pringle, *The Churches of*

were numerous altar cloths, some for the front of the altar and some for the back, and sets of old and new liturgical vestments—chasubles, albs, tunics, dalmatics, cloaks, amices, rochets, stoles, and maniples.[30] The scribes also list an ivory box, linen hand cloths, a corporal and a monstrance, two decorated pyxes (see figure 29), as well as a missal and breviary. Eudes possessed everything needed for a chaplain, presumably Guillaume le Chaplain, to say Mass on the move.[31] Interestingly, for a world obsessed with conversion and baptism in the East, no baptismal basin is listed.[32] Eudes, of course, could have had recourse to his two silver basins in his chamber, if needed, but this was not the space for a public ceremony. Rather, this was an aristocratic chapel, equipped for domestic devotion, for confession, contrition, prayer—both and communal—and for the Mass. Such portable objects would also have been useful as Eudes lay dying, and if and when he took the Eucharist in his final moments.[33]

Whether by association with vestiture and vestments or proximity in Eudes's lodgings, the scribes moved next to record the contents of Eudes's "*old* wardrobe [*la robe viez*]."[34] What the term *viez*, or old, means here is not clear. It may be that these are the items of clothing Eudes had carried with him to Acre, implying that they were already made, stitched, and ready to wear, or had been used, and hence old, in contrast to the ells of cloth itemized in the account that appear to be unfinished, that is, that could be made into clothing, vestments, and livery, as needed. The old wardrobe contained over three dozen articles of clothing, some in matching sets. The scribes record a tunic (*cote*), with overcoat (*serecot*) and corset (*corset*) of brown tiretaine (*tireteinne*), for example, and a tunic, two overcoats, and a mantel (*mantel*) of red serge trimmed with beaver and miniver, or *vair*—clearly garments all made from the same cloth.[35]

---

the Crusader Kingdom of Jerusalem: A Corpus (Cambridge: Cambridge University Press, 1993–2009), 4:46; and the essay by Maureen Miller below.

30. Edition, Roll B Front. Concerning ecclesiastical vestiture, see Maureen C. Miller, *Clothing the Clergy: Virtue and Power in Medieval Europe, c. 800–1200* (Ithaca, NY: Cornell University Press, 2014).

31. Again, Eudes's lordly chapel can be compared to Joinville's situation in Acre, where the latter had two chaplains to say the Mass every day. Joinville, *VSL*, para. 501.

32. On conversion and baptism in the East and specifically during the reign of Louis IX, see William Chester Jordan, *The Apple of His Eye: Converts from Islam in the Reign of Louis IX* (Princeton, NJ: Princeton University Press, 2019), 56–57. Jordan also speculates that in the period after the king had departed Acre, Geoffrey of Sergines the elder may have overseen and facilitated the conversion and baptism of Muslims seeking to convert to Christianity (see 50–51).

33. For comparison, see the description of the death of Pierre d'Alençon in Xavier Hélary, "La mort de Pierre, comte d'Alençon (1283), fils de Saint Louis, dans la mémoire capétienne," *Revue d'histoire de l'église de France* 94 (2008): 5–22.

34. Edition, Roll B Front.

35. On woven cloth, dyes, fabrication, and trim, see Farmer, *The Silk Industries of Medieval Paris*. For what was known as *tiretaine* specifically, a lightweight cloth made with a linen warp and a weft of wool, produced in Europe and in Paris specifically, see Farmer, "*Biffes*, *Tiretaines*, and *Aumonières*: The Role of Paris in the International Textile Markets of the Thirteenth

Many of the robes were opulent, like the tunic and bright iridescent red corset trimmed with miniver, or the indigo tunic and overcoat made of camelin and lined with black taffeta. Indigo, aquamarine, and black were favored colors for wool blends and camelin, whereas green, vermillion, and black were used for silk blends and taffeta linings (see figures 19.1–19.3).[36] A variety of furs were favored for linings and trim ranging from *grosvair* (grey squirrel), to *menuvair* or miniver (white squirrel), to lynx and beaver fur (see figures 16 and 21). The types of clothing varied too. We hear little of undershirts or chemises of cotton or linen, like those kept from among Saint Louis's garments as relics.[37] Rather it is the outerwear that is listed: overcoats, tunics, and what were called corsets, which were akin to long wool-blend vests rather than the women's undergarments from the eighteenth and nineteenth centuries with a similar name.[38] Eudes also had a number of *garnaiche*, later known as *garde-corps*, or houppelandes, also an outer garment, perhaps worn in more formal settings.[39] These garments could also be used as portable stores of wealth, an affordance of their material and function (see figure 15).

After they were inventoried on Roll B in the spatial context of Eudes's chambers on the day he died, the scribes then created a corresponding list of the count's garments copied on Roll C that recorded an appraisal of the monetary value of each garment. Roll C then lists the religious house or person who

and Fourteenth Centuries," in *Medieval Clothing and Textiles*, ed. Robin Netherton and Gale R. Owen-Crocker (Woodbridge: Boydell, 2006), 2:73–89. The combination of linen and wool may have made it an especially suitable fabric for the climes of Outremer, warm but not too heavy.

36. For similar garments worn in the East, see Joinville, *VSL*, paras. 467–68, where he outfits his retinue of Champenois knights "in *cotes* and green *herigauts* [*je leur fiz tailler cotes et hargaus de vert*]." During his captivity in Egypt the sultan gave Louis IX clothes made of black samite, lined with *vair* and grey fur, with a great many buttons made all of gold ("*les robes que le soudanc li avoit fet bailler et tailler, qui estoient de samit noir forré de vair et de griz, et y avoit grant foison de noiaus touz d'or*," para. 403). For such opulent textiles, see Lisa Monnas, *Merchants, Princes and Painters: Silk Fabrics in Italian and Northern Paintings, 1300–1500* (New Haven, CT: Yale University Press, 2009); Monnas, *Renaissance Velvets* (London: V&A Publications, 2012); and Monnas, "Silk Cloths Purchased for the Great Wardrobe of the Kings of England, 1325–1462," *Textile History* 20 (1989): 283–307. For similar opulent garments but used as livery, see Frédérique Lachaud, "Liveries of Robes in England, ca. 1200–1330," *English Historical Review* 111 (1996): 279–98.

37. They do appear among the things sold en masse in Roll D. It seems the Templars were willing to buy Eudes's remaining things almost in total, either to pay off his debts or because they could be repurposed rather easily and were well suited for the brethren, who were knight-pilgrims, in effect like Eudes himself. On these sorts of intimate textiles kept as relics, see Lester, "Intimacy and Abundance." See also Tina Anderlini, "The Shirt Attributed to St. Louis," in *Medieval Clothing and Textiles*, vol. 11, ed. Robin Netherton, Gale R. Owen-Crocker, and Monic L. Wright (Woodbridge: Boydell, 2015), 49–78.

38. Daniel Lord Smail, "A Fur Corset as Daily Wear," DALME, May 1, 2021, http://dalme.org/features/fur-corset/.

39. On houppelandes, see the discussion in Smail, *Legal Plunder*, 70–72.

received each piece as part of Eudes's final charitable bequest.[40] Whether Eudes indicated who was to receive which garment, we cannot know.[41] The appraisal and recipient list copied in Roll C is the only undated roll of the five parchments. Smaller gifts, like the gift of a fur hood and small fur corset for two hermits, or the single dress-doublet given to a beguine, and the four doublets and leggings for four of the poor, are tantalizing references to individuals whom the count may have seen or known. But there is no confirmation of this.

If we read the inventory of the old wardrobe with Roll C—the appraisal and bestowal of the same items—we can follow the count or his executors through the space of Acre itself. As the inventory and appraisal proceeds, the scribes appear to move in concentric circles within the northern quarters of the city, the area most familiar to the French and where a higher proportion of French-affiliated religious houses and associated monastic orders were located. No clear pattern is discernable, but it is possible the gifts correspond to known routes in the city or to a sequence of institutions and individuals Eudes preferred or visited. It is likewise hard to know why specific garments were given to specific institutions (see map 2). Most, as noted above, were probably reused, remade into altar cloths or vestments, or given to residents of the hospitals or religious foundations.[42] In doing so—in divesting himself of his worldly possessions—as Rutebeuf reminds his listeners, Eudes died "as one with the very poor [*quavec les plus povres samort*]," hoping "to be counted among the poorest [*Des plus povres vot estre el conte*]."[43]

In terms of documentation and documentary practice there is a notable redundancy between Rolls B and C. Why recopy information about clothing in such detail? Why not rework the inventory and add to it the objects' appraised values? Perhaps Roll C was used as a walking text, that is, a useful list that Hugh or Érard or Geoffrey the younger, or more likely Robet the servant, had on hand while giving out these final charitable donations. In its preservation, however, it is also a quasi-religious text, a sort of testament that carries out Eudes's plans after his death. And it is, or becomes, a way for institutions and individuals to recall his generosity. A roll in this fashion works well. It functions as "an instrument of performance"; unfurled, it presents the full extent of Eudes's largesse.[44] Moreover, by the mid-thirteenth century, the

40. Edition, Roll C Front.

41. On reading textiles though and in inventories, see Thomas Ertl and Barbara Karl, eds., *Inventories of Textiles—Textiles in Inventories: Studies on Late Medieval and Early Modern Material Culture* (Göttingen: Vandenhoeck & Ruprecht, 2017).

42. On the reuse of such textiles, especially linen in the context of hospitals, see Carole Rawcliffe, "A Marginal Occupation? The Medieval Laundress and Her Work," *Gender and History* 21 (2009): 147–69.

43. See Rutebeuf, "La complainte dou conte Hue de Nevers," below, vv. 74–75.

44. For an excellent discussion of the *rotulus* as presentation and performance page, see Marina Rustow, *The Lost Archive: Traces of a Caliphate in a Cairo Synagogue* (Princeton, NJ: Princeton University Press, 2020), 381–401.

public performance of last bequests, especially gifts of alms and objects for the poor, often required executors to bestow such donations personally with their own hands, in the name of the testator (see figure 21).[45] Such performed piety and penance mattered, for after his death miracles were reported to have occurred at Eudes's tomb in the cemetery of St. Nicholas in Acre.[46] The text authored by the Templar of Tyre is even more explicit about Eudes's holiness. In the short note recounting the count's expedition, the author states—in a manner that is almost an echo of Rutebeuf—that

> it was the will of Our Lord that this *prud'homme*, that count of Nevers, should die at Acre. In his will he stipulated that everything that was found to belong to him, whether money or equipment, should all be given to the poor, for the sake of God. Know that Our Lord worked miracles for him, for any sick persons who touched his bequests were immediately healed of their ailments [*Et plost a Nostre Seignor que se prodome conte de [Ne]veres morut a Acre et fist son testament de tout ce qui se trova dous sien, de monoie et de harneis, douner tout pour Dieu as povres gens, et sachés que Nostre Seignor fist pour luy miracles, car tous maladies quy atouchoi[en]t a son monyment estoient tant tost guaris de lor maladie*].[47]

Might Roll C have been copied in preparation for a hagiographic dossier to make an argument for Eudes's possible canonization? Perhaps, but we cannot know.

Rolls B and C both preserve one other shared list, an addition to the inventory of Eudes's things. On the reverse, that is, on the dorsal side of both rolls, the scribes recorded a nearly identical, and therefore repetitive, list of the rings, jewels, and relics that the count gave to his closest companions

45. See the example of the will of Gaucher of Châtillon, lord of Donzy: Nevers, AD Niève 43 H 5 (1248), ed. H. de Flamare, "La charte de départ pour La Terre-Sainte de Gaucher de Châtillon," *Bulletin de la Société Nivernaise* 13 (1886–89): 174–82; and discussed by William Chester Jordan, "Rituals of War: Departure for Crusade in Thirteenth-Century France," in *The Book of Kings: Art, War, and the Morgan Library's Medieval Picture Bible*, ed. William Noel and Daniel Weiss (London: Third Millennium, 2002), 102; and Anne E. Lester, "Crusading as a Religious Movement: Families, Community, and Lordship in a Vernacular Frame," in *Between Orders and Heresy: Rethinking Medieval Religious Movements*, ed. Jennifer Kolpacoff Deane and Anne E. Lester (Toronto: University of Toronto Press, 2021), 151–52. More broadly, on royal gifts to the poor, especially gifts of vestments, see Priscille Aladjidi, *Le Roi père des pauvres, France XIIIe–XVe siècle* (Rennes: Presses Universitaires de Rennes, 2008).

46. See "L'Estoire de Eracles," *RHC*, 2:455; Jonathan Riley-Smith, "The Crown of France and Acre, 1254–1291," in *France and the Holy Land: Frankish Culture at the End of the Crusades*, ed. Daniel H. Weiss and Lisa Mahoney (Baltimore: Johns Hopkins University Press, 2004), 51. The cemetery itself was recognized as a special place of holiness: Jonathan Riley-Smith, "The Death and Burial of Latin Christian Pilgrims to Jerusalem and Acre, 1099–1291," *Crusades* 7 (2008): 165–79. For the services in commemoration arranged by the lady of Sidon, sister of the Count of Reynel, for Count Walter of Brienne, who was killed in Egypt and whose bones were returned to the French and buried in the same cemetery, see Joinville, *VSL*, para. 466.

47. *TdT*, para. 339.

(see figure 2).[48] This list—copied on the back of the roll and positioned almost on its own—offers a suggestion of how and by whom Eudes was to be remembered through and within specific small objects, some of which, like his clothes, were connected to specific individuals and previous crusading experiences.[49] These objects are crusader heirlooms, or heirlooms in the making.[50] The action here and the list itself is jumbled and requires careful parsing. It begins by stating simply "the count's good sapphire has been sent to the lord of Bourbon [*Li boens saffirs le conte fu envoiez au segnor de Borbon*]"; this was his brother Jean, lord of Bourbon (for example, figure 17). Then, as if a paused afterthought, as if the scribe realized what was to come next, a note is made: "These are the things that were given away [*fu departie*] from among the count's possessions."[51] This is only the second instance of the phrase *fu departie*. All the other objects listed before were simply put "in the hand of," or listed but not let go of, purposefully bestowed, or given away. One exception is the note that ends Roll B recto explaining that "everything that is in the old wardrobe mentioned above was given [*fu departie*] to the poor hospitals of Acre and to the poor religious houses."[52] The dorsal list of personal bequests continues: My lord (*messire*) Geoffrey of Sergines, the father, that is, the elder, has or is to have the one sapphire that the count wears around his neck; *messire* Reynaud of Précigné one cameo; "the Boichiers," his brother (not Eudes's brother, but Reynaud's perhaps, or is this Bossu? It is unclear) received the emerald that the count wore on his finger; *messire* Geoffrey of Sergines the younger, another emerald. Then in turn, *messire* Robert of Juennesses, *messires* Gaucher de Merry, *messires* Gui de Chantenai and *messires* Hervé de Chantenai, *messire* Copin, and *messires* Hugh of Augerant, each received a ring (*i anel*). In addition, Hugh received "the ring that the duke [of Burgundy] had given the count and the ring that should be [given] to the heirs of Nevers" (that is, to Jean Tristan, son of the king of France, and to the heirs he was presumed to have with Eudes's daughter Yolande). *Messire* Érard of Vallery is given the two small crosses of gold and the small case of silver (*vaisselet*) that

48. Edition, Roll B Back; Roll C Back. Chazaud omitted the repetition of the list between Rolls B and C; however, Roll C's notes are slightly longer and elaborated. We have corrected for this and retained the repetitions in our edition.

49. Here again we must underline the fact that the dorsal is not a rough draft of the recto as Chazaud suggested, but functioned quite differently, perhaps as an addendum or aide-mémoire, if not a fully performative text: a script for the presentation of Eudes's most personal objects.

50. On such objects meant to be sent back from Outremer, see Nicholas L. Paul, *To Follow in Their Footsteps: The Crusades and Family Memory in the High Middle Ages* (Ithaca, NY: Cornell University Press, 2012), 90–170; Anne E. Lester, "What Remains: Women, Relics and Remembrance in the Aftermath of the Fourth Crusade," *Journal of Medieval History* 40 (2014): 311–28; and Lester, "Remembrance of Things Past: Memory and Material Objects in the Time of the Crusades, 1095–1291," in *Remembering Crusades and Crusading*, ed. Megan Cassidy-Welch (London: Routledge, 2017), 73–94.

51. Edition, Roll B Back.

52. Edition, Roll B Front.

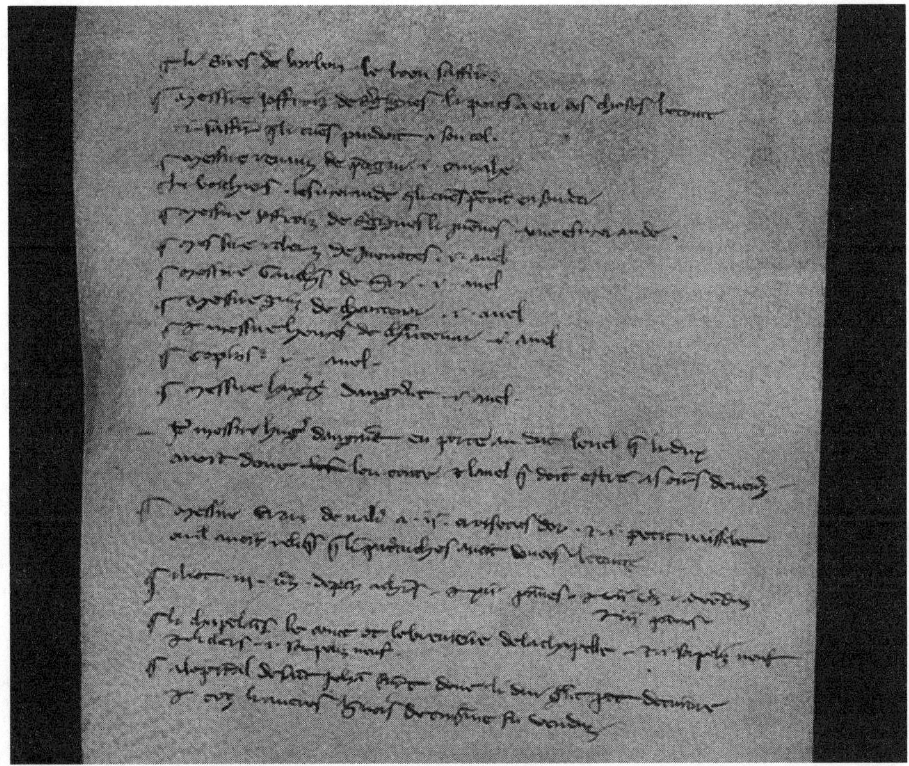

Figure 2. Detail, Paris, AN, series J 821, no. 1, Roll C (verso/dorsal). Photo: AN.

holds the relic that the patriarch gave the count. Finally, there are additional panels of cloth and furs given to the knights. The count's chaplain was to have the breviary, the chapel, and one new surplice, and one surplice was to go to Étienne le Clerc as well. And the Hospital of St. John received the two large copper pots from the kitchen.[53]

As is clear from this list and what is known from other examples, crusader rings and jewels were a transmissible mode of participation in the knightly culture of Outremer. Eudes gave away objects—emeralds, cameos, and rings—that had belonged to his father and father-in-law, both crusaders in their own right.[54] Moreover, he gives them to specific family members from his own family lines: the good sapphire to the lord of Bourbon (Eudes's brother) ("*li boens saffirs le conte fu envoiez au segnor de Borbon*") and the ring for the

53. Edition, Roll B Back.

54. It may be that some of the same jewels mentioned in the inventory also appear in the testament of Guy IV of Forez, count of Nevers from 1241; see above, chapter 5, n. 54. These objects are also discussed in Lester, "Crusading as a Religious Movement."

heirs of Nevers (his son-in-law, Jean Tristan) ("*lenel qui doit estre as oirs de Neverz*"). Hugh of Augerant received and perhaps first wore these objects when he was charged with carrying them back to France and to Eudes's heirs. The other single rings—given to the knights (*messires*) Eudes has assembled close to him—went forward as objects tied to Eudes's expedition in 1265, to his death in Acre, and to the material world of Outremer.[55] That Érard of Vallery was not among those who received rings may be explained by the fact that he was not personally present at the time of Eudes's death and was represented in these earlier transactions by Geoffrey of Sergines the younger. Nevertheless, objects set aside for him, and other items he purchased later or received as compensation, were equally significant and personalized, including the reliquary and gold crosses and the three vernacular manuscript volumes, which passed to him in part as payment and in part as a sign of shared closeness with the count.[56] Evident in these short lists is not only the transfer of wealth but also the transfer of a set of ideas, memories, experiences, and ideals: the transfer of an ideology of aristocratic crusading embedded within things.

To have been present when a crusader-baron like Eudes of Nevers passed from life to death in his apartment in Acre, sick from illness perhaps or wounded but not recognized for valiant deeds performed on the battlefield, was also an experience carried in these small objects. Eudes's private death, if that was in fact what occurred, paralleled the deaths of many crusaders who died of disease, languishing, penitent, but not victorious in battle as a martyr for the faith. This is how Louis IX would die in August 1270, on the floor of his tent in Tunis, in a circle of ash, as a penitent.[57] We can see in these relics and rings the possibility for the circulation of a whole set of vernacular crusade ideas and experiences all of which lie outside of texts strictly speaking even if we can hear echoes of them in Rutebeuf's "Complaintes" and Joinville's reminiscences. In Eudes's case, we can sense that the bestowal of such objects meant a great deal, for the items and their recipients were copied twice on the reverse or dorsal side of two different rolls of parchment. There is a commitment to remembering these details. Finally, the repeated refrain in these lists—"messires . . . messires . . . messires"—echoes Rutebeuf's poetic cadence, and one can hear the spoken text performed, recorded on a roll almost like a

55. It is hard to know what "the good sapphire [*li boens saffirs*]" may have looked like. Perhaps, although this seems unlikely, it was a single jewel. More reasonable is to assume it was a large "beautiful" sapphire set either in a ring or on a pendant. A possible later comparable object could be the so-called Middleham Jewel from the second half of the fifteenth century depicting an engraved crucifixion scene with a large sapphire set above. Such jewels were often worn attached to a necklace or on a collar. See C. M. Woolgar, *The Great Household in Late Medieval England* (New Haven, CT: Yale University Press, 1999), 175. For a discussion of Eudes's jewels and other valuable heirlooms, see the essay by Richard Leson below.

56. Edition, Roll B Back; and Roll A Front, Part 2.

57. Joinville, *VSL*, paras. 755–59.

pseudo-play script, possibly to be read again, aloud, before other audiences of family and kin in the West.

Different people remembered and commemorated Eudes through his objects and through the material experiences of Outremer. For the poor and sick of Acre and especially for those cured after touching his bequests, he must have seemed a saint, or saintly. The Templar of Tyre was clear, moreover, that Eudes's holiness moved through his things. In France, such objects carried other layers of associations. Memories of a young father must have been passed down and glossed orally by those who knew Eudes. His brothers and father surely shared in cultivating his memory as would his daughters, especially Marguerite, who returned to Burgundy at the end of her life and built a lavish hospital complex at Tonnerre, an act that was a formal recognition of the ways that charity, service, and crusading were intertwined and that echoed her father's actions and spiritual commitments.[58]

58. See Meredith Parsons Lillich, *The Queen of Sicily and Gothic Sainted Glass in Mussy and Tonnerre* (Philadelphia: American Philosophical Society, 1998), 68–95; and Lynn Courtenay, "The Hospital of Notre Dame des Fontenilles at Tonnerre: Medicine as *Misericordia*," in *The Medieval Hospital and Medieval Practice*, ed. Barbara S. Bowers (Aldershot: Ashgate, 2007), 77–106.

7

The Threaded Heart

Converted Objects and Return Journeys

Lamors—the word would have hung in the air; phonetically it could mean both "Love" and "Death." The poet Rutebeuf begins his lament, his *complainte*, for Eudes of Nevers with "Lamors."[1] *Lamors* has its own cadence in the poem, returning as a refrain in nearly every stanza, carrying its twin each time—"Death/Love." With this word the poet found a powerful singular term to characterize Eudes's loss and his enduring legacy. Those who knew him, we are told, loved him and lamented his death. The rolls—objects carried in their own right—were a testament to Eudes's material munificence on display in the East, but also to his connections with those in his retinue, those in France, and those in Acre. As is always the case, objects, especially when enumerated in an inventory, carry with them far more than their individuated specificity: they convey value of many kinds, networks of making and use, memories both public and private, and futures yet to unfold.

Our final task, as it was Eudes's, is to consider what remained in Outremer and what returned to France. Roll D offers some insight into this, for it records ("*Cest li escriz*") "the count's things that were sold [*des choses le conte vendues*]."[2] Are we to imagine the count is present for these sales, or is this a posthumous list? Unlike Rolls B and C, which are not dated, Roll D notes that the accounts were made on September 15, 1266, thus over a month after Eudes's death. It could be that the sales were made while Eudes was alive and the accounting finalized later, although that seems less likely. Rather, we are witness to the process of dissolving a baron's material household, to the legal

1. See the transcription and translation below.
2. Edition, Roll D Front.

and financial resolutions at the end of a life. Certainly, Roll D seems our most worksheet-like in that a scribe, or possibly two, at different times, has used the back, the dorsal, of the roll to make two different notes. One in the same hand and ink as Roll B, written upside down, calculates "what the count had in deniers currency and in bezants" on the day he died, noting that this account, that is, this discrete cash sum, was made August 9, 1266, two days after the count's death. This total appears again incorporated into the full and final sum total of Eudes's estate at the bottom of Roll D recto. Also on the dorsal side of Roll D is a short list in a different ink, more a note without itemized values, of "the things that are not yet sold [*choses qui ne sunt pas ancor vendues*]" with a total value given in marks sterling and gold.[3] We believe that the dorsal lists were preparatory and thus ancillary to the longer more carefully compiled lists made on Roll D recto.

Six buyers are listed; five are knights, but not all in Eudes's retinue. Érard of Vallery purchased an assortment of items; most were from the kitchen, including pots, pans, a fork, saucers, goblets and platters, table coverings, and hand towels. He also purchased items from the larder and from among Eudes's personal things including ten pairs of small gloves, a whistle, and unadorned fabrics. And he bought the donkey, forty chickens, and half of Eudes's barley stores.[4] Érard was most likely providing for his own household and his own lodgings, taking over where Eudes has left off. And there must have been some urgency, for unlike gold, silver, or cloth, barley, chickens, and salted meat cannot last forever. Similarly, Geoffrey of Sergines the elder buys from Eudes's kitchen and stores, including cauldrons, pans, sides of salted meat, and casks of wine. He certainly had a permanent household in Acre and here is seen to provision it, to buy up Eudes's stocks that would otherwise have been wasted or given away.[5] Hugh de la Baume and Hugh de Mont-Cornet, both knights, made similar small purchases.[6]

Finally, a vast assortment of objects were sold off from among those things remaining in Eudes's household: an array of cloth and clothing, food stores, wood for fuel, cases and chests for transport, some armor, many things that were not listed among Eudes's more public-facing wardrobe items—like undergarments, pairs of shoes, and blouses—as well as the two palfreys and two mules, the one grey horse, and "1 chessboard and chess pieces sold together [*i eschaquier et les eschas vendu ensemble*]" (see figure 30).[7] These items were purchased, but the inventory does not list who bought them. They entered into the material economy of Acre. The Temple, that is, the Templars of Acre, are listed last as purchasers of a series of silver and gold vessels—pitchers, cups,

3. Edition, Roll D Back.
4. Edition, Roll D Front.
5. Edition, Roll D Front.
6. Edition, Roll D Front.
7. Edition, Roll D Front.

pots—either for their own use, perhaps, or to be repurposed for use in their chapel, or as transportable, pawnable, wealth.[8] This final list of transactions was concluded in the presence of the master of the Temple and, as noted on Roll A, the treasurer, and in the presence of Érard of Vallery and Geoffrey of Sergines the younger. Here the Temple is the beneficiary, in a way, of Eudes's death. They purchased his valuable goods, though it is hard to know how or if the values were reckoned, and finally they collected on his debts. This exchange is illuminating, for the Temple was not a recipient of Eudes's bequests as listed in Roll C, as the Hospitallers were, but it does receive a large share of his movable goods and portable wealth through purchases. All of these items remained in Outremer, with Eudes's flesh and bones, not far off in the cemetery of St. Nicholas.

What returned to the West? It is possible that Roll D's dorsal list of things "not yet sold" made their way west with Hugh of Augerant or Érard of Vallery, both of whom have the cost of return passages noted in Roll A and both of whom, we know, returned to France within the year. The things not yet sold were for the most part small, portable, and of high value. Most were made of gold and silver—including goblets, rings, a chapel of gold, a gold or gilded pitcher, silver and gold cups, and two silver carafes—but they also included opulent cloth, specifically Tartar cloth, hand-worked hangings, coverlets, and the tent from Château Pèlerin, as well as two pairs of trunks and three old chests, which may have been able to contain these items, but we cannot know for certain.[9]

Two final objects certainly did return to the West: Eudes's heart and the parchment rolls studied here. In the days after his death, a surgeon and embalmer removed Eudes's heart from his body. They treated and spiced it, which is to say embalmed it, and threaded and wrapped the heart with cloth of gold ("*drap qui i estoit dor et fu percez sor le cuer le conte*").[10] His executors purchased a special box (*escrin*) for 3 and one half bezants to contain

8. For similar examples of reuse, see Laurence Delobette, "'Faites ceci en mémoire de moi': Calices et testaments du diocèse de Besançon XIIIe–XVe siècles," in *Le miracle de Faverney (1608) l'eucharistie: Environnement et temps de l'histoire*, ed. Corinne Marchal and Manuel Tramaux (Besançon: Press Universitaires de Franche-Comté, 2010), 95–125.

9. Edition, Roll D Back.

10. Edition, Roll A Front, Part 2; see also Roll A Front, Part 1: "*por lespicier qui acira le cuer le conte por [un]guelient et por choses quil [i] m[i]st et por sa peine, vi b*l." The entry in the inventory for this is especially descriptive, almost a narrative, and thus calls attention to itself. On the practices of embalming and removal of the heart during this period, see Patrice Georges, "L'exérès du cœur dans l'embaumement médiéval occidental," in "Il cuore / The Heart," special issue, *Micrologus: Natura, Scienze e Società Medievali* 11 (2003): 279–86; Katherine Park, *Secrets of Women: Gender, Generation, and the Origins of Human Dissection* (New York: Zone, 2006), 15–20, and for the case of Chiara of Montefalco, who was also embalmed and whose heart was removed and placed in a box, 39–76. See also Romedio Schmitz-Esser, *Der Leichnam im Mittelalter: Einbalsamierung, Verbrennung, und die kulturelle Konstrukion des toten Körpers*, Mittelalter-Forschugen 48 (Ostfindern: Thorbecke, 2014); in English: *The Corpse in the Middle Ages: Embalming, Cremating, and the Cultural Construction of the Dead Body*, trans. Albrecht

it for the return journey to France (see figure 24).[11] And someone, possibly Hugh or Érard, carried his heart, relic like, to Cîteaux. There the monks placed Eudes's heart into a tomb, joining his remains with those of his ancestors, the crusader dukes of Burgundy who had died before him.[12] Eudes's heart moved—separated from his body and his bones—within a narrative and imaginative space built into and upon the penitent ambitions of the crusader's separated self.[13] The circulation of people and objects, of bodies *as* objects, and of worldly things that became secular relics suffused the crusading Mediterranean and generated what we are calling the material Outremer, constituted by habits of thought, embodied practices of behavior, ritual, comportment, and profound acts of devotion and penance all done in an "other" space, across the sea. Eudes's death in the East, burial in Acre, and the movement of his embalmed and translated heart served as a pious model for King Louis IX of France, the Count-King Thibaut V of Champagne and Navarre, and Jean Tristan, among other lords who would die on campaign in Tunis in 1270, and whose hearts were likewise separated from their bones and viscera for commemorative burial in the West.[14]

Might we then imagine Eudes's father, Duke Hugh IV of Burgundy, present with Eudes's daughter Yolande and son-in-law Jean Tristan, assembled at Cîteaux to mourn the count? Might they have been there with other family members, knights, and retainers, listening perhaps to Rutebeuf's *complainte* performed as a commemoration and celebration of Eudes of Nevers (see figure 31)?[15] And someone must have carried the *rouleaux* into France at this time too, where they served an administrative and memorial function (see figures 1–4).

Classen and Carolin Radtke (Turnhout: Brepols/Harvey Miller, 2020), 229–31, 240–74, 636–42 for the removal and separate burial of the heart.

11. Edition, Roll A Front, Part 1: "*Por i escrin achete por porter a Cytiaus iii l/ demi.*"

12. Eudes's brother Robert II of Burgundy stipulated in his will from 1297 that he wished to have his heart buried at Cîteaux and his body *deca mer*, in Acre in the cemetery of St. Nicholas, in both cases "next to [his] brother [*delès . . . mon frere*]." See above, note 1 in chapter 6.

13. Much more should be said about the movement of Eudes's heart in relation to the complex and fascinating contemporary romance *Le Roman du castelain de Couci et de la dame de Fayel* (Jakemés, ca. 1280) and the German analogue, *Herzmaere*, for Eudes's is a historical example of such separation. Marisa Galvez offers a marvelous discussion of this text and its crusading context, Marisa Galvez, *The Subject of Crusade: Lyric, Romance, and Materials, 1150 to 1500* (Chicago: University of Chicago Press, 2020), 87–97, and she treats the themes more broadly throughout. For the text, see Jakemés, *Le Roman du Castelain de Couci et de la Dame de Fayel par Jakemes*, ed. John E. Matzke and Maurice Delbouille (Paris: SATF, 1936). The fundamental study is Helen Solterer, "Dismembering, Remembering the Châtelain de Coucy," *Romance Philology* 46 (1992): 103–24. On the German tradition, see Claire Taylor Jones, "Relics and the Anxiety of Exposure in Konrad von Würzburg's *Herzmaere*," *Journal of English and German Philology* 116 (2017): 286–309.

14. Elizabeth A. R. Brown, "Authority, the Family, and the Dead in Late Medieval France" *French Historical Studies* 16 (1990): 803–32.

15. Rutebeuf, "La complainte dou conte Hue de Nevers," in Bastin and Faral, *Onze poèmes*, 69–75; and here below.

The persistence of these five parchment rolls, which contain so many things whose material imprint and meaning have endured over time, makes this scene worthy of at least some historical imaginative indulgence. It may have been useful for those in the West to have an account and inventory of all the things the count of Nevers had given away that in the words of the Templar of Tyre, "worked miracles . . . [curing] any sick person who touched his bequests."[16] The material rolls themselves also carry the realities of *Lamors*: the affective trace of death and love—Eudes's and those for him—joined together in serial acts of writing, accounting, and remembrance.

16. *TdT*, para. 339.

Part III

CONTEMPORARY SOURCES

8

Crusade Poems of Rutebeuf

Rutebeuf, Crusade Poet and Social Critic

Anne Latowsky

Between 1255 and 1277, the poet writing under the name Rutebeuf penned eleven poems related to the contemporary crusading movement, one of which eulogizes Eudes of Nevers.[1] Described variously as a minstrel, poet-preacher, poet-journalist, propagandist, and pamphleteer, Rutebeuf left behind fifty-five poems that range in tone from the playful and humorous to the moralizing and religious.[2] Although now recognized as a major figure in thirteenth-century French poetry, there is no contemporary mention of him, and anything to be gleaned about the poet himself derives exclusively from the scant and unreliable evidence provided by his own poems.[3] Rutebeuf delights in mocking

1. Dates for Rutebeuf's crusade poems, given below, are adapted from *Onze poèmes de Rutebeuf concernant la croisade*, ed. Julia Bastin and Edmond Faral (Paris: Librairie Orientaliste Paul Geuthner, 1946), 144–45.

2. *Oeuvres complètes de Rutebeuf*, ed. Julia Bastin and Edmond Faral, 4th ed., vol. 1 (Paris: Picard, 1977), 60; Nancy Freeman Regalado, *Poetic Patterns in Rutebeuf: A Study in Noncourtly Poetic Modes of the Thirteenth Century* (New Haven, CT: Yale University Press, 1970), 6; Jean Dufournet, *L'univers de Rutebeuf* (Orléans: Paradigme, 2005), 30; Michel Zink, "Poète sacré, poète maudit," *Recherches et Rencontres* 1 (1990): 235–36; Sung-Wook Moon, "Engagement difficile: Les poèmes de croisade de Rutebeuf," *Loxias* 54 (2016): 5; Jacques E. Merceron, "Rutebeuf, marchand de croisades et le système de la comptabilité spirituelle: Le dit et le non-dit," *Romania* 131 (2013): 383; Anne-Lise Cohen, "Exploration of Sounds in Rutebeuf's Poetry," *French Review* 40 (1967): 658.

3. Bastin and Faral, *Oeuvres complètes*, 32.

others, often irreverently, but also makes light of his own poetic persona. In an elaborate ten-verse digression, the poet plays with the rustic coarseness suggested by his name using repetition of the words *rude*, *beuf*, and *euvre* as in "rude," "ox," and "work." His ironic expression of poetic humility ends with his famous pronouncement, "but Rutebeuf is as rude as an ox [*mais Rutebués est ausi rudes coume bués*]."[4] His origins are unknown, although it is evident that he was well educated and seems to have spent his adult life in Paris. His poems, in particular those that memorialize Eudes of Nevers and Geoffrey of Sergines, suggest a strong affinity for the aristocratic milieu in the regions east of Paris, especially Champagne. One mention by a character in a single poem led many to believe that Rutebeuf was actually from Champagne, an idea refuted by Edmond Faral and Julia Bastin in their monumental edition of Rutebeuf's complete works.[5] Paris was not a center of aristocratic literary patronage at the time, and in 1261, Louis IX had closed the royal court to all entertainers for reasons of moral and financial austerity.[6] Had he been attached to the court, it appears that he was cut loose after that point. Rutebeuf's livelihood would therefore have depended on commissions from patrons beyond the royal court, and indeed he devoted the latter part of his career to writing propagandistic crusade poetry, although for whom remains a mystery.[7]

Rutebeuf's crusade poems reveal a poet engaged in the historical moment through the creation of a poet-preacher persona charged with exhorting the faithful to mend their ways and save the Holy Land.[8] As a poet, he was involved in two major contemporary causes, the great polemic at the University of Paris from 1255 to 1261 and the crusades.[9] In the university quarrel, Rutebeuf sided with the secular masters against the preachers of the mendicant orders, which proved to be a vote for the losing side. His participation, which included verses openly hostile to the king, likely tarnished his name, so his turn toward crusade exhortation may well reflect a bid to regain favor in royal circles.[10] His poetry shows signs of inspiration from papal crusade promotion and appears to respond directly, in some instances, to public criticism

4. "La vie de sainte Elyzabel," vv. 2005–6, in *Rutebeuf: Oeuvres complètes*, ed. Michel Zink (Paris: Classiques Garnier, 2001), 748.

5. Bastin and Faral, *Oeuvres complètes*, 32, 35, 37; Regalado, *Poetic Patterns*, 8.

6. Merceron, "Rutebeuf, marchand," 382.

7. Regalado, *Poetic Patterns*, 6; Dufournet, *L'univers*, 26–27; Linda Paterson, *Singing the Crusades: French and Occitan Lyric Reponses to the Crusading Movements, 1137–1336* (Woodbridge: D. S. Brewer, 2018), 224.

8. Estelle Doudet, "Rhétorique en mouvement: Rutebeuf, prêcheur et polémiste de la Croisade," *Méthode! Revue de littératures* 9 (2006): 16; Moon, "Engagement difficile," 5.

9. Moon, "Engagement difficile," 8.

10. Edward Billings Ham, *Rutebeuf and Louis IX* (Chapel Hill: University of North Carolina Press, 1962), 33; Arié Serper, "Le Roi Saint Louis et le poète Rutebeuf," *Romance Notes* 9 (1967): 134; D. A. Trotter, *Medieval French Literature and the Crusades (1100–1300)* (Geneva: Droz, 1987), 213 and 218.

such as that of the preacher Humbert of Romans in 1266–68.[11] Here too, the circumstances of his career remain obscure to us, although in a burgeoning culture of literature related to current events, his poems may have been part of a world of leaflets and booklets that circulated after public recitations.[12]

The Translations

Rutebeuf's eleven crusade poems can be roughly divided into eulogies of individual crusaders, direct exhortations to save the Holy Land, poems related to events in Apulia in the mid-1260s, and a well-known debate poem between two knights, one in favor of crusading and one skeptical.[13] Of the eleven, we selected seven to transcribe as a single-text edition and translate from Old French into English. They include the two poems memorializing Eudes of Nevers and Geoffrey of Sergines, the four crusade exhortations, and the debate poem. Of the four not translated, two relate to Apulia and Charles of Anjou and two are laments for fallen crusaders on the ill-fated expedition that ended at Tunis in 1270. Interesting as they are, those individuals and events sit outside the scope of Eudes of Nevers's experiences in the East, and therefore we chose not to include them here. Our transcriptions are of the poems found in Paris, Bibliothèque nationale de France (BnF), manuscript français (MS fr.) 1635. This manuscript is one of the twenty manuscripts that Faral and Bastin used for their edition. We chose BnF, MS fr. 1635 because it contains eight of his poems that appear in no other manuscript, all related to crusading, and because it is closest in time to Rutebeuf's own lifetime.[14]

Our English translations of Rutebeuf's crusade poems, most of which were composed in the octosyllabic verse typical of the era, are rendered with no attempt to preserve syntax or rhyme scheme. We tried to remain relatively close to the Old French text, except for when an English idiom better captured the often rhetorically complex meaning. A major challenge in translating Rutebeuf into English is his frequent use of wordplay based on similar sounds including homonyms, rhymes, puns, and alliteration, a rhetorical device known as *annominatio*. For instance, in the space of the first eight verses of the "Lament for My Lord Geoffrey of Sergines [*Complainte de monseigneur Joffroi de Sergines*]" he uses the following words suggesting variations on concepts of endings or refinement: *fin*, *defineroit*, *afineroit*, *defineir*, *finement*, *fineir*, *fine*, *fin*, and *fine*. In another recurring example, death, *la mort*, rhymes or appears in proximity to words related to biting and, by extension, regret such as *mord*

11. Regalado, *Poetic Patterns*, 40; Paul Rousset, "Rutebeuf, poète de la croisade," *Zeitschrift für schweizerische Kirchengeschichte* 60 (1966): 110; Doudet, "Rhétorique en mouvement," 11.

12. Regalado, *Poetic Patterns*, 106; Merceron, "Rutebeuf, marchand," 387.

13. Trotter, *Medieval French Literature*, 171.

14. Bastin and Faral, *Oeuvres complètes*, 17–20. See the preface, above, for the methods we employed in transcribing and translating the text collaboratively.

and *remord*. Some scholars have disparaged Rutebeuf for his wordplay, accusing him of undermining the solemnity of his crusade poems, but there is evidence that medieval audiences would not have shared this view. Scorn toward punning and rhymes was a later development, and in fact, these devices were in vogue during Rutebeuf's era.[15] Moreover, vernacular poetry at the time was strongly influenced by Latin oratory, and the establishment of sound patterns using rhetorical devices would have been familiar from Latin hymns. Poetry was created for the ear and not the eye, Nancy Freeman Regalado reminds us, and the similar sounds often pointed to deep metaphorical relationships between the rhyming words and sounds in question, as in the case of remorse and death's deadly bite.[16] For those translating from Old French into Modern French, it is possible to reproduce or at least approximate Rutebeuf's frequent sound-based wordplay since the syntax can often be preserved and the phonetic similarities remained relatively stable over time. This is not the case when translating into English.[17] Needless to say, we have not attempted to re-create Rutebeuf's continual play of sound and meaning in English.

Reading the Crusade Poems

Throughout his poems promoting the crusade cause, the primary objects of Rutebeuf's moral outrage are not the infidels abroad, but the inhabitants of the world around him, in France.[18] He spares almost no one in his denunciations of moral failings, especially those of lazy clergymen, who, as he predicts, will soon have grown so fat that no burial shroud will fit around their paunches when they die.[19] He rarely alludes to Muslims beyond the occasional reference to "the Saracen people [*la gent sarrazine*]" as ferocious enemies, or to a sultan in the lament for Eudes who exists in the bold fantasies of those who, in a state of drunkenness, promise to go on a crusade only to lose courage once sober in the morning.[20] He saves the majority of his swipes and barbs for the members of his own society, whether lazy knights happy to stay in France and joust, merchants who cheat their neighbors, or prelates who choose a warm bed over defense of the Holy Land.[21] His rhetorical techniques are often adapted from preaching and include themes such as the scorn for earthly possessions, the evils of greed, and the promise of heaven and the threat of hell.[22] Other recurring themes include the inexorable passage of time, the uncertain

15. Cohen, "Exploration of Sounds," 660.
16. Regalado, *Poetic Patterns*, 205–7 and 216–17; Cohen, "Exploration of Sounds," 664–65.
17. Zink's 2001 edition and translation, with its detailed critical apparatus, has been an invaluable guide.
18. Moon, "Engagement difficile," 14.
19. "The Complaint of Outremer," vv. 100–101.
20. "Lament of Geoffroy," v. 115, "Lament of Eudes," 157–61.
21. Edward B. Ham, "Rutebeuf—Pauper and Polemist," *Romance Philology* 11 (1958): 236.
22. Doudet, "Rhétorique en mouvement," 12–14.

destination of the soul after the body is gone, the guarantee of judgment before God, and the crusade as an instrument of salvation and purification of the soul.[23] Rutebeuf also employs metaphors related to accounting.[24] Using a language of mortgage and credit, the poet exhorts his audience to leave behind family and possessions and take the "deal," that is, the promise of heaven for the reasonable payment of crusade. In other words, God is a merchant who is selling at a bargain, but the deal will not be on the table for much longer. More often redemption through crusade will come at a painful financial and physical price, requiring great suffering, if not martyrdom: the sacrifice of the body to save the soul.[25]

Scholars sometimes ponder the occasional mixed messages lurking in Rutebeuf's verses.[26] A growing hostility toward further sanctioned war marked the era of his crusade promotion, and although still an object of great respect, Holy Land crusading seemed to be an increasingly lost cause.[27] Rutebeuf's debate poem, most likely written between 1268 and 1269 while the expedition called in 1267 remained stalled in its preparations, dramatizes the opposing sides of the discussion, but with a surprising twist. After some predictable back and forth between the two knights, the noncrusader, who is loath to give up everything and risk his life to go on crusade, suddenly declares himself the loser and announces his intention to take the cross. As multiple critics have remarked, however, the arguments of the noncrusader are notably more compelling. As a paid propagandist, Rutebeuf could not have allowed the noncrusader to win, but social critic that he was, he may have simply allowed the superior arguments of the noncrusader to be aired publicly without comment.[28]

For whatever doubts he harbored about the viability of the movement, Rutebeuf never abandoned his task of promoting crusading, and he continued to the last to hold up Eudes of Nevers as an ideal Christian knight who had made the ultimate sacrifice. He writes in his final poem, "The New Complaint of Outremer [*La nouvele complainte doutremeir*]," that no one could ever recite songs or verses about Eudes that were not full of praise for his good qualities, including the esteem he enjoyed at the royal court (vv. 129–32). This is self-referential, no doubt, as Rutebeuf trades here on his most valuable currency, his power to memorialize in verse, which he had done for Eudes and others. By portraying the count as the subject of praise-filled songs, Rutebeuf places Eudes among the ranks of Charlemagne, Roland, Godfrey, and Tancred, heroes whose deeds are remembered thanks to the verses of poets. He

23. Regalado, *Poetic Patterns*, 48; Rousset, "Rutebeuf," 107; Caroline Smith, *Crusading in the Age of Joinville* (Farnham: Ashgate, 2006), 79.

24. Merceron, "Rutebeuf, marchand," 391.

25. Merceron, "Rutebeuf, marchand," 398–99.

26. Ham, "Rutebeuf—Pauper and Polemist," 237; Moon, "Engagement difficile," 7.

27. Rousset, "Rutebeuf," 104; Doudet, "Rhétorique en mouvement," 11; Paterson, *Singing the Crusades*, 223.

28. Merceron, "Rutebeuf, marchand," 402; Trotter, *Medieval French Literature*, 225.

offers similar future poetic glory in "The Poem of the Route to Tunis [*Li diz de la Voie de Tunes*]" (vv. 270–73), when he exhorts his listeners to go rob the sultan of all his joy and pleasure so that great songs will then be sung of them.

Rutebeuf finished his career as a crusade propagandist with one final call for future action in the Holy Land. In one of his most widely discussed verses, which appears twice, the poet exhorts his listeners "to begin a new chapter [*Reconmanciez novele estoire*]." The phrase appears early in "The Complaint of Outremer [*La complainte doutremeir*]" (v. 16) after a vision of a bloodied Christ at the Last Judgment and again in his last poem, "The New Complaint of Outremer [*La nouvele complainte doutremeir*]" (v. 341), with a final memento mori about the unknown hour of one's death and a gruesome reminder of Saint Paul's decapitation. Michel Zink makes a distinct choice here by translating *novele estoire* as "nouvelle épopée," thereby alluding to the Old French epic cycles that included songs about the First Crusade.[29] Yet the word *estoire* evokes both the word "story," a tale in the literary sense, and *historia* as in a narrative of a historical event often included in the liturgy. *Estoire* also suggests a naval flotilla, thus implying a renewed military effort.[30] It is no accident, then, that in his final exhortation Rutebeuf evokes the leaders of the First Crusade, Godfrey, Bohemond, and Tancred, whose recovery of the Holy Land, long since squandered, still demanded a new iteration.[31]

In 1277, seven years after Louis's death at Tunis, Rutebeuf was still waiting for another generation to rise to the occasion. In "The New Complaint of Outremer," some twenty verses after his second call for a "novele estoire" with his work now complete, the poet announces that he is ending his sermon ("*Rutebues son sarmon define*") (v. 366).[32] For the poet-preacher-propagandist, Eudes of Nevers had been the ideal inheritor of the mantle of a crusade hero: a man for whom rumors of sanctity circulated, a knight worthy of being named alongside the likes of Godfrey of Bouillon. Eudes was a *prudhomme* to be emulated should Rutebeuf's ever-more-leery public decide to heed his warnings about the perils of final judgment and write a new chapter in the story of the Holy Land.[33]

29. Zink, *Rutebeuf*, 847 and 997. In Jessalynn Bird, Edward Peters, and James M. Powell, eds., *Crusade and Christendom: Annotated Documents in Translation from Innocent III to the Fall of Acre, 1187–1291* (Philadelphia: University of Pennsylvania Press, 2013), at 389, the editors of "Rutebeuf's 'Lament of the Holy Land,' ca. 1266," follow Zink's lead by translating "novele estoire" as "a new epic tale." See also Regalado, *Poetic Patterns*, 53; Doudet, "Rhétorique en mouvement," 16; Moon, "Engagement difficile," 9.

30. Zink, *Rutebeuf*, 845n1; Philippe Buc, *Holy War, Martyrdom, and Terror: Christianity, Violence, and the West* (Philadelphia: University of Pennsylvania Press, 2015), 284; Doudet, "Rhétorique en mouvement," 16; Marisa Galvez, *The Subject of Crusade: Lyric, Romance, and Materials, 1150 to 1500* (Chicago: University of Chicago Press, 2020), 202.

31. Rousset, "Rutebeuf," 108; Buc, *Holy War*, 284; Galvez, *The Subject of Crusade*, 202.

32. For this verse and the word "sermon," see note 158.

33. According to Dufournet, *Prudhomie* as embodied by Geoffrey and Eudes was a combination of courage, a sense of honor, generosity, a spirit of hospitality, sociability, friendship, charity,

Poems

Translated by Anne Latowsky, Anne E. Lester, Laura K. Morreale, and Caroline Smith

Rutebeuf's crusade poems are presented here in the order in which they were written between the mid-1250s and the late 1270s. Although we know nothing of the circumstances of their earliest dissemination, the poems would likely have been shared in performance before being written down and fair-copied in Paris, BnF, MS fr. 1635, the late thirteenth-century manuscript that we have used for our transcription.[34] Although Rutebeuf wrote in the Parisian dialect of Francien, the contents of BnF, MS fr. 1635 strongly suggest that the scribes were from the regions to the east of Paris that included Champagne.[35] As indicated by the folio numbers, Rutebeuf's crusade poems were spread throughout the manuscript, interspersed with poems of religious satire and devotion, verse miracle stories, personal poems on the poet's marriage and poverty, and sayings attributed to Aristotle. The crusade poems address the period of the crusade movement that followed King Louis IX of France's return, defeated, from Acre in 1254 and continue spanning the fall of the Latin Empire of Constantinople (1261), the rise of the Mamluks in Egypt and Syria (1258–68), and Louis IX's second crusade expedition to Tunis (1270), then taking up the future of Acre, which would eventually fall in 1291. In this way, Rutebeuf offers both a biting critique of crusading culture and ambitions and a call for knights, prelates, lords, and kings to account and atone for their wrongs and to renew their aid to the Holy Land. Situated as both a critique of and a call to crusade, Rutebeuf's poems offer a blunt assessment of the state of the movement, quite different from the formal preached sermons and papal encyclicals that called in ever more hyperbolic language for new military efforts across the Mediterranean. Rutebeuf's descriptions align strikingly well with the Account-Inventory, as he is especially attuned to the financial and material hardships everyday French men, women, and children would have to endure to support the call to crusade. Loans, mortgages, and unfair financial dealings are a special concern for him and no doubt mirrored the worries of French families of all social backgrounds. Similarly, the hypocrisy of the clergy, whether friars, priests, bishops, or abbots, galled him and seemed an especial evil when

---

loyalty, fair not venal justice, equity in distribution of gifts, and defense of causes. See Dufournet, *L'univers*, 33.

34. We relied principally on the digitized images of Paris, BnF, MS fr. 1635 to establish the text for translation. The digitized images can be found at Gallica, https://gallica.bnf.fr/ark:/12148/btv1b105253083. However, there were instances when the reading from MS fr. 1635 was nonsensical, at which point we referenced Brussels, KBR MS 9411–9426 (especially regarding "La nouvele complainte doutremeir," in this manuscript called "Li complainte daccre," fols. 34r–36r). When adjustments were made to the Paris manuscript for comprehension, we note this in the French text.

35. Bastin and Faral, *Oeuvres complètes*, 18–19.

compared with the personal sacrifices vowed crusaders—men like Geoffrey of Sergines and Eudes of Nevers—had made.

Several terms reoccur throughout Rutebeuf's corpus of crusade poems that require some explanation. First, the titles of six of the seven poems here include the word ***complainte***. The Old French *complainte* is a genre of lament, often in honor of a subject whose deeds were memorable. The genre is characterized by frequent direct exclamations and exhortations to the audience called apostrophes.[36] The Latin term for a formal poetic lament is a *planctus*. Laments, like the Latin *planctus*, were often composed after someone's death, to be read aloud and to lament their loss and thereby to memorialize them. Laments were also written for the loss of places as much as people. After 1187, following the Christian loss of Jerusalem to Saladin, clerics and monks in the West composed several *planctus* hymns and poems.[37] In the context of the poems about Geoffrey of Sergines and Eudes of Nevers, we think "lament" is the appropriate translation rather than the closer English cognate, "complaint." By contrast, for the poems focused on places like Outremer, Constantinople, and Tunis, especially in the context of calling a new crusade to aid those locales, we used the English word "complaint" since the poet is also admonishing and indeed complaining about the lack of sincerity or effort put toward aiding those places and their inhabitants.

Other terms that run throughout the poetic corpus of Rutebeuf's crusade poems that are difficult to translate with ease include the following: ***Courtoisie***, or courtesy, which is to say, courtliness, is the quality of being well-versed in the appropriate behaviors of courtly life, having good and generous manners, being well-meaning, and holding a positive bearing. ***Chevalerie***, or chivalry in a general sense, is related to *courtoisie* in that it describes a code of knightly conduct central to medieval aristocratic culture. Rutebeuf also frequently uses the terms ***preux*** and ***prudhomme***, to signify the embodiment of noble and chivalric qualities and to praise men who were wise, well-governed, and showed prudence and discernment in their behavior and affairs. More than simply describing a "wise man" *prudhomme* connoted an individual who had a noble bearing even if not of noble descent, a man who was upright and judicious.[38] ***Gentillesse*** was similarly a quality that a *prudhomme* might possess or enact, that is, to be genteel, in the sense of governing oneself and one's relations with others with kindness, respect, and decorum. This was how men were to act at court, how they were to run their households and relate to family, and how they were to comport themselves publicly, with kindness, generosity, and goodwill. All of these terms encompassed a mindset, a way of being in the world, and a set of positive physical attributes that signaled a knight of

36. Regalado, *Poetic Patterns*, 3, 53.

37. See M. Cecilia Gaposchkin, *Invisible Weapons: Liturgy and the Making of Crusade Ideology* (Ithaca, NY: Cornell University Press, 2017), 192–225.

38. For more on *prudhomme*, see Anne Latowsky's introduction above.

esteem or the character of a man who could be extolled. For the most part, nearly all of these characteristics pertained to men, and therefore there is a degree to which ideals of masculinity come into view in these poems.[39]

Rutebeuf's Selected Crusade Poems

"The Lament for My Lord Geoffrey of Sergines" (1255–56)
"The Complaint of Constantinople" (1262)
"The Complaint of Outremer" (1265–66)
"The Lament for Count Eudes of Nevers" (1266)
"The Poem of the Route to Tunis" (1267)
"The Disputation between the Crusader and the Noncrusader" (1268–69)
"The New Complaint of Outremer" (1277)[40]

39. On *prudhomme*, *prudefemme*, and courtly conduct, see David Crouch, *The Chivalric Turn: Conduct and Hegemony in Europe before 1300* (Oxford: Oxford University Press, 2019).
40. Dates adapted from Bastin and Faral, *Onze poèmes*, 144–45; and Zink, *Rutebeuf*.

The Lament for My Lord Geoffrey of Sergines

La complainte de monseigneur Joffroi de Sergines (17v–19r)

Composed in the wake of Louis IX's failed crusade expedition (1248–54), this poem was written in honor of Geoffrey of Sergines, the commander of the garrison that King Louis IX maintained in Syria to oversee the cities of Jaffa and Acre following his return to France (April 25, 1254). The king would continue to provision the French garrison for the next decade. Geoffrey of Sergines is extolled here as an ideal knight and leader ("bon chevalier et prudhomme"), a model crusader to be emulated. It has been suggested that Rutebeuf and Geoffrey may have both hailed from Champagne and shared in the patronage of the king and other barons. The poet is clearly deeply moved by and sympathetic to Geoffrey's example and notes how he had become the liegeman of the king of France after having been first the vassal of Hugh of Châtillon, count of St.-Pol. Rutebeuf's "Lament" is directed at the seemingly futile struggle to defend Acre, and the lack of funds and support for the Holy Land more generally. The poem must have been finished before April 11, 1269, when Geoffrey of Sergines died, for he was certainly still alive at the time of composition. Because of the reference to Jaffa, and the series of truces signed by Geoffrey in an attempt to hold the remaining cities under French dominion, it seems most probable that the "Lament" was composed and delivered or performed between the end of 1255 and 1256.[41]

41. See Zink, *Rutebeuf*, 123; Bastin and Faral, *Onze poèmes*, 19–21.

Ci en coumence la complainte de mon seigneur Joffroi de Sergines

[17v] Qui de loiaul cuer et de fin
loiaument juques en la fin
a dieu servir defineroit
Qui son tens · i afineroit
de legier devroit defineir
Et finement vers dieu fineir.
Qui le sert de pensee fine
Cortoisement · en la fin fine
Et por ce le sunt rendu maint
Quenvers celui qui la sus maint[42]

Puissent fineir · courtoizement
Sen vont li cors · honteuzement
Se di ge por religieux
Car chacuns deulz · nest pas prieulz
et li autre · ront getei fors
[18r] Le preu des armes · por les cors

Qui riens plus · ne vuelent conquerre
Fors le cors · honoreir seur terre
Ainsi est partie · la riegle[43]
De ceulz dordre et de ceulz du siecle

Here begins the Lament of my lord Geoffrey of Sergines

[17v] He who is loyal and pure of heart,
would choose to loyally serve
God up until the end.
He should reach the end
of his life with ease,
and, facing God, perfectly meet his end.
He who serves Him with elegant thought
in the end, ends his days with *courtoisie*.[44]
And for this reason, many offer themselves up[45]
so that they might end their days with *courtoisie*

in the sight of Him who lives on high
while their bodies shamefully decay.
I say this about the religious,[46]
since not every one of them is a prior.
The latter have rejected
[18r] the interests of the soul in favor of those of the body.

They wish to obtain nothing
outside of honoring the body on earth.
There are two different rules;[47]
one for those in orders and one for those in the world.

42. We elected to transcribe the poems almost exactly as they appear in BnF, MS fr. 1635, which means there are no added apostrophes or other punctuation marks. Here in verse 10, for instance, what should be read as *qu'envers* remains as *quenvers*. On occasion we note that we have deferred to another manuscript following Faral and Bastin when our scribe had clearly made an error, and in some places, we use parentheses or em dashes to indicate poetic asides. We have numbered the Old French verses according to our transcription of BnF, MS fr. 1635, so they are not always identical to those of Zink or Bastin and Faral, whose editions are based on multiple manuscripts. In the English translation the verse numbers represent our best approximation of the corresponding verses in the Old French text rather than actual line numbers of the English text.

43. The rhyme here is slightly awkward, "*riegle*" and "*siecle,*" but we have verified against the manuscript and there may have been variations of pronunciation that elided differences audible in modern French.

44. *Courtoisie*, including its adverbial form *cortoisement*, is difficult to translate because it encapsulates an entire set of values including generosity, lack of avarice, openness, nobility, solicitousness, and respectability. See the comments above in the introduction to the poems and in the glossary.

45. A few lines later, Rutebeuf clarifies this statement by telling the reader that he is referring to those who join religious orders.

46. This is a reference to canons and monks and vowed religious as opposed to their leaders, whom he calls out below.

47. For more on Rutebeuf's attitudes toward the religious life, see his "Le Dit des règles," in Zink, *Rutebeuf*, 167–79.

Mais qui porroit · en lui avoir
Tant de proesse · et de savoir
Que larme fust · et nete et monde

Et li cors honoriez au monde
Ci auroit trop bel aventage
Mais de ceux · nen sai je cun sage

Et cil est plains · des dieu doctrines
Mes sires Joffrois de Sergines
A non li preudons · que je noume

Et si le tiennent a preudoume ·
Empereour · et roi et conte
Asseiz plus · que je ne vos conte
Touz autres · ne pris. ii. espesches
Envers li · quar ces bones tesches
Font bien partout a reprochier
De ces teches vos voel touchier
Un pou celonc ce · que jen sai
Car qui me metroit a lessai
De changier · arme · por la moie
Et je a leslire venoie
De touz ceulz · qui orendroit vivent
Qui por lor arme · au siecle estrivent
Tant quierent pain · trestot deschauz
Par les grans froiz et par les chauz
Ou vestent haire · ou ceignent corde

Ou plus fassent · que ne recorde
Je panroie · larme de lui
Plus tost asseiz · que la nelui
dendroit dou cors · vous puis je dire
Que qui me metroit · a leslire
Luns des boens chevaliers de france
Ou dou roiaume · a ma creance
Ja autre · de lui nesliroie
Je ne sai · que plus vos diroie

But whoever might have
such prowess and knowledge within himself
that the soul would be both pure and unstained,
and the body honored in the world;
that man would have a great advantage.
Yet among these men, I know but one so worthy,
and he is full of God's teachings.
My lord, Geoffrey of Sergines
is the name of the *prudhomme* of whom I speak.[48]
Emperors, kings, counts, and many more—
more than I can even tell you—
deem him to be a *prudhomme*.
All others are not even worth two cents
compared to him, for his good qualities
are cited as examples to others far and wide.
Allow me to describe these qualities for you
a bit, based on what I know.
For whoever would challenge me to exchange
his soul for mine,
and if I were to choose
among all those living right now
who battle for their soul in the world—
whether they beg for bread, go shoeless
through great cold and heat,
or wear a hairshirt, or gird themselves with a cord,[49]
or go to greater lengths than I can even say—
I would take his soul first,
far more so than anyone else's.
As for the body, may I tell you,
if anyone would ask me to choose
one from among the good knights of France
or of the kingdom,[50] in my opinion
I would choose none other than his.
I do not know what more I might say.

48. Martino da Canale also addresses Geoffrey in the introduction to book 2 of *Les Estoires de Venise*, written between 1267 and 1275. Martino da Canale, *Les estoires de Venise: Cronaca veneziana in lingua francese ale origini al 1275*, ed. Alberto Limentani (Florence: L. S. Olschki, 1972), 157.

49. A reference to the mendicants, and to the Franciscans specifically, who were known as *cordeliers*, named for the simple cord they used to secure their brown tunics.

50. A reference to the Kingdom of Jerusalem, or to the Kingdom of France as opposed to the Île-de-France, that is, the region associated with the heart of France.

Tant est preudons si comme moi cemble
Qui a ces · ii · choses encemble
Valeur de cors · et bontei darme
Garant li soit · la douce dame
Quant larme dou cors partira
Quele sache quel part ira
Et le cors ait en sa baillie

Et le maintiegne en bone vie
Quant il estoit · en cest pais
Que ne soie · por folz naïz
De ce que jai le lolz tenu
Ni estoit jones · ne chenuz
Qui tant peust · des armes faire
Dolz et cortoiz et debonaires
Le trovoit hon · en son osteil
Mais aulz armes · autre que teil
Le trovast · li siens anemis
Puis quil ci fust · mesleiz et mis
Mult amoit Dieu et sainte esglise
Si ne vousist · en nule guise
Envers nelui · feble ne fort
A son pooir · mespanrre a tort
Ses povres voizins ama bien
Volontiers · lor dona dou sien
Et si donoit · en teil meniere
Que mieulz valoit · la bele chiere
Quil fassoit · au doneir le don
Que li dons · icist boens preudons
Preudoume crut · et honora
Ainz entour · lui ne demora
Fauz lozengiers · puis quil le sot
[18v] Car qui ce fait jel teing[52] a sot
Ne fu mesliz ne mesdizans
Ne vanterres · ne despizans

Ainz que jeusse · racontei
Sa grant valeur ne sa bontei
Sa cortoisie ne son sens
Torneroit · a anui se pens
Son seigneur lige · tint tant chier
Quil ala avec li vengier
La honte dieu outre la meir
Teil preudoume doit hon ameir

He is truly a *prudhomme*, it seems to me,
who embodies these two things at once:
valor of body and goodness of soul.
May our sweet Lady be the guarantor
when his soul leaves his body,
and may she know where it is going
and may she have his body under her protection
so that she will ensure its safekeeping.
When he was in this land[51]—
may I not seem foolishly naive
because of how I have praised him—
there was no one, young or old,
who could accomplish such feats of arms.
Those within his household found him
to be gentle, courteous, and gracious,
but once armed and in the thick of it
his enemies deemed him
to be otherwise.
He loved God dearly, and the Holy Church.
Therefore, whenever possible,
he did not wish to mistreat
anyone, strong or weak, in any way.
He loved his poor neighbors
and willingly shared what he had,
giving in such a manner that as he gave the gift,
his pleasing countenance
was worth more than the gift itself.
This fine *prudhomme* trusted
and honored other *prudhommes*.
Never did false flatterers remain in his midst
once he found out about them;
[18v] whoever would do that, I deem a fool.
He was not quarrelsome, nor slanderous
nor boastful, nor contemptuous.

Were I to recount all his
great qualities and his goodness
and his *courtoisie* and his good sense
it would become tedious, I think.
He held his liege lord so dear
that he accompanied him beyond the sea
to avenge God's shame.
One should love such a *prudhomme*—

51. We think this means France, before he departed for the Holy Land.

52. MS fr. 1635 reads "teig." This is a scribal error; we have made the correction and translated the text accordingly.

Avec le roi · demora la ·	he remained there with the king,
Avec le roi · mut et ala	he set out and travelled with the king,
Avec le roi prist bien et mal	he weathered the good and the bad with the king—
Hom nat pas toz jors tenz igal	one day is never the same as the next.
Ainz pour painne ne por paour	Despite pain and fear, he never
Ne corroussa son Sauveour	angered his Savior.
Tout prist engrei · quanquil soffri	Everything he suffered, he did so willingly;
Le cors et larme · a Dieu offri	he offered his body and soul to God.
Ses consoulz fu · boens et entiers	His counsel was good and wholehearted;
Tant com il fu · poinz et mestiers	when the time and the necessity arose,[53]
Ne ne chanja · por esmaier	he did not change it out of fear.
De legie devra · Dieu paier	He will easily pay what he owes to God
Car il le paie chacun jour	because he pays Him every day.[54]
A Jasphes · ou il fait sejour	In Jaffa, where he is stationed,
Cil at se jour de guerroier	if there is a pause in the fighting
La vuet il · son tens emploier	he wishes to make use of his time.
Felon voizin et envieuz	The Saracen people find him
Et cruel et contralieuz	to be a cruel, covetous, and
Le truevent · la gent sarrazine	hostile neighbor,
Car de guerroier · ne les fine	for he is never done waging war upon them.
Souvant lor fait · grant envaie	He often launches such powerful assaults against them
Que sa demeure i est haie	that his presence there is hated.
Des or croi ge · bien cest latin	Now I truly believe this saying:
Maulz voizins · done mau matin	"bad neighbors make for bad mornings."
Son cors · lor presente souvent	He continuously offers up his body to them,
Mais il at trop petit couvent	but his retinue is too meager.
Se petiz est · petit sesmaie	Though their numbers are small, so too is their fear,
Car li paierres qui bien paie	for the payer who pays well
Les puet bien · cens doute paier	is no doubt able to pay them handsomely;
Que nuls · ne se doit esmaier	and so none should fear that
Quil nait coroune de martir	he will not receive the martyr's crown
Quant dou siecle · devra partir	when he must depart from this world.[56]
Et une riens · les reconforte	And one thing comforts them:
Car puis quil sunt fors de la porte	if they are outside the gates
Et il ont · mon seigneur Joffroi	and they have my lord Geoffrey with them,
Nunz doulz niert ja puis en effroi ·	none among them will ever be afraid.
Ainz vaut li uns · au besoing[55] quatre	For when the need arises, a single one of them is worth four,

53. Rutebeuf uses the same language in his "Lament for Count Eudes of Nevers," at stanza 3, line 2; see below.

54. See chapters 1 and 7 of the commentary for more on Geoffrey's payments.

55. MS fr. 1635 reads "besoig" This is a scribal error; we have made the correction and translated the text accordingly.

56. The words in this passage might call to mind the recent actions of Louis IX. Louis "pays well," for he maintains the garrison in Acre and Jaffa, and pays Geoffrey. The crown of the cult of martyrs may also allude to King Louis IX, who had acquired the crown of thorns and paid well for it. He established a cult of martyrs' crowns in the Sainte-Chapelle to complement the crown

Mais cens lui ne sozent combatre
Par lui jostent · par lui guerroient

Jamais cens lui · ne ce verroient
En bataille ne en estour
Quil font de li · chastel et tour
A li sasennent et ralient
Car cest · lor estandars ce dient.
Cest cil qui dou champ · ne se muet

El champ le puet · troveir qui vuet
Ne ja por fais · que il soutaigne
Ne partira · de la besoigne
Car il seit bien · de lautre part
Se de sa partie · se part
Ne puet estre · que sa partie
Ne soit tost sans li departie
Sovent asaut et va en proie
Sor cele gent qui Dieu ne proie
Ne naime · ne sert · ne aeure
Si com cil · qui ne garde leure
Que Dieux · en fasse son voloir
Por Dieu fait mult · son cors doloir

Ainsi soffre · sa penitence.
[19r] De mort · chacun jor en balance ·

Or prions donques · a celui
Qui refuzeir · ne seit nelui
Qui le vuet priier · et ameir
Qui por nos ot · le mort ameir

De la mort · vilainne · et ameire
En cele garde · quil sa meire
Commanda a lesvangelistre
Son droit maistre · et son droit menistre
Lou cors a ce preudoume gart
Et larme resoive en sa part

Explicit

but without him, they dare not fight.
Because of him they joust, because of him they fight,

without him they would never see
a battle or melee.
For they make of him a castle and a tower.
They rally to him and gather around,
for they say he is their standard.
He is the one who does not quit the field of battle.

Whoever so wishes can find him on that field.
Whatever charge he takes up,
he never abandons the cause.
On the other hand, he is well aware
that if he were to abandon his party,
there is no doubt that his group
would quickly fall apart without him.
He often attacks and preys upon
those people who do not pray to God,
who neither love, nor serve, nor praise Him,
just as one who is always ready
to do what God wills of him.
For God he makes his body endure great pain.

Thus he suffers his penitence;
[19r] each day death hangs in the balance.

So let us now pray to Him
who is unable to refuse anyone
wishing to pray to and love Him.
Let us pray to the One who, on our behalf, received the

bitter bite of evil and bitter death, that
under that protection—by which His mother
was entrusted to the Evangelist,
His rightful master and rightful servant—
He may preserve the body of this *prudhomme*
and receive his soul at His side.

The End

---

of thorns. See Robert Branner, "The Painted Medallions in the Sainte-Chapelle in Paris," *Transactions of the American Philosophical Society* 58 (1968): 1–42.

The Complaint of Constantinople

La complainte de Coustantinoble (13r–14v)

Written just after the fall of the city of Constantinople to the Greek ruler Michael VIII Paleologus on July 25, 1261, this poem is both a lament, that is, a doleful remembrance, and a complaint and indictment about how this state of affairs could have occurred. From April 1204, when a combined force of French, Flemish, and Venetian crusaders took the Byzantine capital of Constantinople, much of the former Byzantine Empire, as well as the Greek Morea and Peloponnese, had been under Latin, and principally French, Flemish, and Champenois, control. The loss of the city in 1261 signaled the end of this Latin Empire, although claims to its titles and dominion would persist for generations, passing to the Courtenay family and eventually the Angevins. Rutebeuf complains about the lack of interest and support—both financial and material—for Constantinople, for those who remain in the former Latin Empire, and for the Holy Land in general. He criticizes the clergy who grow fat and lazy, while Greece—the place where knighthood and chivalry first flourished—suffers disgrace and neglect. This poem aired grievances and critiques that aligned with that of the papacy, which had attempted to channel support to aid the Latin Empire for two decades. The poem was most likely composed in the summer or fall of 1262 following the promulgation of Pope Urban IV's commission to the Franciscans (May 21, 1262) to preach a new crusade against Michael Paleologus. In some key respects—the mention of Crete, Cyprus, and "the Islands [les Iles]," references to the menacing movements of the "Tartars," and a nostalgia for Achaea and the Morea—it seems clear that Rutebeuf knew of, or had heard read aloud, and followed the language of the papal letter. Moreover, he often referred to himself in his poems as "a sermonizer" or as offering up a "sermon," in the guise of a poem.[57]

57. See Zink, *Rutebeuf*, 401; Bastin and Faral, *Onze poèmes*, 28–35. For the repeated calls to aid the Latin Empire leading up to 1261 and a close reading of the papal documents, see Michael Lower, *The Barons' Crusade: A Call to Arms and Its Consequences* (Philadelphia: University of Pennsylvania Press, 2005).

Ci en coumence la complainte de Coustantinoble

[13r] Sopirant pour lumain linage
Et pencis au
crueil damage
Qui de jour en
jour i avient
Vos wel descovrir mon corage
Que ne sai autre · laborage
Dou plus parfont do cuer me vient
Je sai bien · et bien men souvient
Que tout a avenir covient
Quan cont dit li prophete sage
Or porroit estre · se devient
Que la foi qui feble devient
Porroit changier nostre langage

Nos en sons bien · entrei en voie
[13v] Ni at si fol · qui ne le voie

Quant Coustantinnoble est perdue
Et la Moree se ravoie
A recevoir teile escorfroie
I sainte eglize · est perdue
Quen cors at petit datendue
Quant il at la teste fendue
Se Jhesucriz · ni fait aiue
A la Sainte Terre absolue
Bien li est esloigniee joie

Dautre part viennent li Tartaire
Que hom fera · mais a tart taire
Com navoit cure daleir querre
Diex gart Acre · Jaffes · Cezeire
Autre secors ne lor puis feire.
Car je ne sui · mais hom de guerre
Ha Antioche · Sainte Terre
Qui tant coutastes a conquerre
Ainz con vos peust · a nos trere
Qui des ciels cuide ovrir la serre,

Conment puet teil doleur sofferre
Cil at Dieu · ciert donc par contrere

Here begins the Complaint of Constantinople

[13r] Sighing for humankind
and mindful of
the cruel suffering
that befalls it day
after day,
I wish to reveal what is in my heart,
for I know no other way to work;
it comes from the deepest part of my heart.
I know truly and remember well
that everything to come must happen
just as the wise prophets said.
Now it may be, perhaps,
that the faith, which grows weak,
may change the way we speak.

We are already well on our way down this path.
[13v] There is no one so foolish that he does not see that,
ever since Constantinople was lost,
and the Morea is on its way
to a similar onslaught.
The Holy Church is thus in despair,
for there is little hope in the body
when the head has been cleaved in two.
If Jesus Christ does not grant aid
to the blessed Holy Land,
all joy is truly gone from there.

The Tartars are coming from the other side;[58].
it will be too late to silence them now,
for no one did enough to seek them out.
May God preserve Acre, Jaffa, and Caesarea.
I cannot offer them any more help
since I am not a man of war.
Oh! Antioch, oh! Holy Land,
You, who cost so much to conquer
before we could make you our own.
He who believes he can open the gates of heaven
how can he tolerate such suffering?
If that man were to reach God, then all would be turned on its head.

58. See the glossary for an explanation of the term "Tartars."

Isle de Cret · Cosse · Sezile
Chipre · douce terre · et douce isle
Ou tuit avoient · recovrance
Quant vos seroiz · en autrui pile

Li rois tanra · desa concile
Conment Ayoulz · sen vint en France
Et fera · nueve remenance
A cex qui font · nueve creance.
Novel Dieu· et nueve Evangile
Et laira semeir · par doutance
Ypocrisie · sa semance
Qui est dame de ceste vile

[Se li][60] denier · que hon at mie
En celx qua Dieu · ce font amis

Fussent mis · en la Terre Sainte
Ele en eust · mains danemis
Et mains tost ce fust entremis

Cil qui la ja brisie et frainte

Mais trop a tart · en fais la plainte
Quele est ja si forment empainte
Que ces pooirs · nest mais demis

De legier · sera mais atainte
Quant sa lumiere est ja etainte.
Et sa cire devient remis·
De la Terre Dieu · qui empire
Sire Diex · que porront or dire
Li rois et li cuens de Poitiers

Diex resueffre · novel martyre
Or faissent large cemetyre
Cil dAcre · quil lor est mestiers
Touz est plains derbe · li santiers·
Com suet batre si volentiers

Isle of Crete, Corsica, and Sicily,
Cyprus—sweet land and sweet isle
where everyone once had safe harbor—
when you find yourself crushed under another's dominion
the king will hold a council on our shores
on how Ayoul[59] came to France.
And he will establish new foundations
for those who are creating a new faith,
a new God, and a new Gospel,
and, out of fear, he will allow
Hypocrisy to sow Her seed, for
She is the lady who rules over this city.

If the money that had been given
to those who make themselves out to be friends of God
had instead been sent to the Holy Land,
She would have had fewer enemies,
and those who had already broken and shattered Her
would have been slower to undertake their task.[61]
But I made my complaint too late,
for She is already under such intense attack
that Her powers are now but half of what they were.
Now [the Holy Land] will be easily attained,
since Her light is already extinguished
and Her candle is burning low.
Lord God, now what will
the king and the Count of Poitiers be able to say
about the worsening condition of God's land.
God is once again suffering a new martyrdom.
It is time to break ground on a large cemetery
for the people of Acre, for they need it now.
Wholly overgrown is the pathway
that men once beat so willingly,

59. Ayoul or Aiol is the eponymous hero of a *chanson de geste* from the early thirteenth century. Some have posited that *Aiol* was presented at the court of Philip Augustus in 1212 on the occasion of his marriage to Jeanne of Constantinople, the daughter of Baldwin of Flanders. See *Aiol: A Chanson de Geste, Modern Edition and First English Translation*, ed. and trans. Sandra C. Malicote and A. Richard Hartman (New York: Italica Press, 2014).

60. The first letters of this verse are obscured in BnF, MS fr. 1635, but they appear in BnF, MS fr. 837, fol. 326r as "Se li." See also Bastin and Faral, *Oeuvres complètes*, 426.

61. We have capitalized the pronouns in the above stanzas that refer to Hypocrisy and the Holy Land because the poet is personifying both.

Por offrir sarme · en leu de cÿre.
Et Diex na mais · nuns cuers entiers ·
Ne la terre na nuns rentiers ·
Ansois se torne · a desconfire

offering their soul in lieu of a candle.
God no longer has a single heart devoted to Him,
nor does anyone pay their dues to the Holy Land
and so She is driven to destruction.

Jherusalem · ahi · hai ·
Com ta blecie · et esbahi
Vainne gloire · qui toz maux brace
Et cil qui ceront envaÿ
Si cherront lai · ou cil chaÿ ·
Qui par orguel · perdi sa grace
Or dou foir la mors les chace
Qui lor fera · de pie eschace
Tart crieront · trahi trahi·
Quele at ja entesei sa mace
Ne jusquau ferir ne menace
Lors harra Diex qui le haÿ ·

Alas, alas, Jerusalem,
how you have been wounded and laid low
by vainglory, which is the sum of all evils.
Those who will be invaded
will fall to the same place where he who
lost his grace due to pride fell.
Now is the time to flee! Death is chasing them,
and will cause them take to their heels.
They will cry, "betrayed, betrayed"
for she [Death] has already brandished her mace;
she will give no warning before she strikes.
Now, God will despise the one who despised Him.

[14r] Or est en tribulacion
La Terre · de Promission ·
A pou de gent · toute esbahie
Sire Diex · por quoi loblion
Quant por notre redemption
I fu · la chars · de Dieu trahie
Hom lor envoia · en aïe
Une gent despite · et haïe[62]
Et ce fut · lor destrucion
Dou roi durent avoir la vie
Li rois ne la pas a sa vie (assouvie)[63]
Or guerroient sa nacion

[14r] With so few people remaining,
the Promised Land is now
being tested and is in shock.
Lord God, why do we forget this,
when for our redemption,
God's own flesh was betrayed there.
We sent to help them
despised and hated people,
and that was their destruction.
Their lives should have been safeguarded by the king,
but the king did not do his part, and
they are now fighting people of their own nation.[64]

62. When confronting the harsh realities of war, some crusaders felt compelled to renounce their Christian faith in favor of Islam. This in turn made them both traitors and criminals, and therefore hated by those who remained Christian. Evidence for such conversions comes from chapter 23 of the *Livre au roi*, a legal text from the Crusader States that may date to the late twelfth century but was recopied in Cyprus at approximately the same time Rutebeuf composed his poems. The chapter includes a series of regulations about how territories should be forfeited if a landholder "renounces the law of Jesus Christ for that of Mohammed." *Le livre au roi*, ed. Myriam Greilsammer (Paris: Académie des Inscriptions et Belles-Lettres, 1995), 201.

63. In BnF, MS fr. 837, fol. 326r, we read "assouvie," as do Bastin and Faral, *Oeuvres complètes*, 420, and Zink, *Rutebeuf*, 410, in their editions of the poem.

64. Bastin and Faral, *Oeuvres complètes*, 423–24. This may also be a critique of the negotiations and truce that Louis IX brokered with the Muslims in Egypt, in exchange for the release of French captives, or following the conversion either of Christians to Islam or of Muslims in Syria, many of whom Louis then brought to France after 1254. See William Chester Jordan, "*Etiam Reges*, Even Kings," *Speculum* 90 (2015): 613–34; and Jordan, *The Apple of His Eye: Converts from Islam in the Reign of Louis IX* (Princeton, NJ: Princeton University Press, 2019).

Hom sermona · por la croix prendre	Some sermonized on taking the cross,
Que hom cuida · paradix vendre	for they believed they were selling paradise
Et livreir · de par lapostole	and delivering it on behalf of the pope.
Hom pot bien · le sermon entendre	Others may well have paid attention to the sermon,
Mais a la croix · ne vout nuns tendre	but were in no way moved
La main · por piteuze parole	by such heart-rending appeals to take up the cross.
Or nos deffent · hon la quarole	Now they forbid us from dancing the *carole*,
Que cest ce · que la terre afole	for they say that is what wounds the Holy Land;
Se nos welent li frere[65] aprendre	this is what the brothers wish to teach.
Mais fauceteiz · qui par tot vole	But Falsity, who flies around everywhere,
Qui crestiens · tient a escole	who becomes the instructor of Christians,
Fera · la Sainte Terre rendre	will cause the Holy Land to be lost.
Que sunt li denier devenu	What has become of the money
Quentre · Jacobins et menuz	that Jacobins and Minors[66]
Ont receuz · de testamens	received from the wills of
De bougres por loiaux tenuz	heretics deemed to be faithful,
Et duzeriers vielz et chenuz	from old and white-haired usurers
Qui se muerent soudainnement	who die suddenly,
Et de clers · ausi faitement	and likewise from clerics?
I il ont grant aunement	They have a great stash, and
I li oz Dieu · fust maintenuz	they might have supported God's army from it,
Mais il en font · tot autrement	but they do the complete opposite.
Quil en font lor granz fondemenz.	They use it to build their own grand foundations,
Et Diex remaint · la outre nuz	while over there, God remains exposed.
De Grece vint · chevalerie	Knighthood first came from Greece long ago,
Premierement · danceserie	then it made its way
Si vint en France et en Bretaingne	to France and Britain,
Grant piece I at estei chierie.	and has long been cherished there.
Or est a mainie escherie	Now its company is few in number,
Que nuns nest teiz quil la retaingne	for there is no one who can maintain it.
Mort sunt Ogiers · et Charlemainne	Ogier and Charlemagne are dead.[67]
Or sen vont · que plus ni remaingne	Now they have all departed; no one remains here.
Loyauteiz est · morte et perie	Loyalty is dead and gone:
Cestoit · sa monjoie · et sensaingne	it was once the knighthood's rallying cry and standard;
Cestoit · sa dame · et sa compaingne	it was its lady and companion,
Et sa maistre · habergerie	and its chief abode.

65. *Frere* in this instance refers to the friars. Given the context and papal commission this was most likely the Franciscans.

66. Jacobins and Minors refer to the Dominicans and Franciscans respectively. See the glossary.

67. Rutebeuf is employing a version of the topos of *translatio studii et imperii* (transfer of learning and empire) found notably in the twelfth-century verse romance of Chrétien de Troyes, *Cligès* (lines 27–35), in which the poet writes that *chevalerie* had come from Greece and then moved to Rome and finally to France. For Rutebeuf, Ogier and Charlemagne are heroes of a mythic bygone era when *chevalerie* still flourished.

Coument amera · sainte Eglize
Qui ceux nainme · par con la prize.
Je ne voi pas · en queil meniere
Li rois ne fait · droit ne justize

A chevaliers · ainz les desprize
Et ce sunt cil · par quele est chiere
Fors tant quen prison · fort et fiere.
Met lun avant et lautre arriere
Ja tant niert hauz hom · a devise

En leu de Nainmon de Baviere
Tient li rois · une gens doubliere
Vestuz de robe ·blanche et grise
Tant fas je bien ·savoir le roi
Scn Francc sorsist. I. dcsroi
Terre ne fu · si orfeline
Qui les armes · et le conroi
Et le consoil · et tout lerroi
Laissast hon · sor la gent devine
Lors si veist hon · biau couvine
De cex qui France · ont en saisine
Ou il na mesure · nelroi
Sou savoient · gent tartarine.
[14v] Ja por paor · de la marine

Ne laisseroient · cest aroi

How will he love the Holy Church
who does not love those who have esteemed her?
I do not see how.
The king neither upholds the law nor renders justice
for the knights, except for when he places them,
one after the other,
into a harsh and cruel prison
no matter how distinguished they may be.
Thus, he dishonors them even though it is they who bring esteem to her.[68]
Rather than a Naime of Bavaria[69]
the king keeps a duplicitous people
dressed in white and grey robes.[70]
I wish to alert the king that should
a crisis arise in France,
never would there be a land left so defenseless
because its weapons, equipment,
planning, and the entire operation
would be left to the so-called righteous people.
In that case, one might see the lovely conclave
of those who would take possession of France—
where there is neither order nor a king.[71]
If the Tartars knew this,
[14v] they would never—even if they feared the sea—
let this opportunity pass them by.[72]

68. This may be a reference to the very public trial of Enguerrand of Coucy, which took place only three years earlier, in 1259. On the trial and its reception, see Dominique Barthélemy, "L'affaire Enguerran de Coucy (1259)," in *Affaires, scandales et grandes causes: De Socrate à Pinochet*, ed. Nicolas Offenstadt and Stéphane Van Damme (Paris: Stock, 2007), 59–77; and William Chester Jordan, *Louis IX and the Challenge of the Crusade* (Princeton, NJ: Princeton University Press, 1979), 204.

69. Naime is a trusted counselor of Charlemagne in the Old French epic tradition, a *vieux sage* (wise old man), who, unlike Ganelon, would never betray him.

70. White and grey robes were the colors of the monastic or religious habits worn by the Jacobins or Dominicans as well as the Cistercians (white) and the Franciscans (grey, hence the Greyfriars in England). For contemporary associations with cloth of this color, see Jordan, *Apple of His Eye*, 72–75.

71. On April 10, 1261, an Assembly was called in Paris to discuss concerns about the "Tartars," that is, the threat of Mongol expansion into Europe. See Jacques Paviot, "England and the Mongols (c. 1260–1330)," *Journal of the Royal Asiatic Society* 10 (2000): 305–18.

72. This is a striking phrase and may refer to the perception that the Mongols were reticent to cross the Black Sea or the Mediterranean, as some Europeans feared they would. This popular perception of fear of the sea may in fact correspond to the preference among the Mongols for a nomadic way of life far from seaports. See the comments in John Ross Sweeney, "'Spurred on by the Fear of Death': Refugees and Displaced Populations during the Mongol Invasion of Hungary," in *Nomadic Diplomacy, Destruction and Religion from the Pacific to the Adriatic: Papers Prepared for the Central and Inner Asian Seminar, University of Toronto, 1992–93*, ed. Michael Gervers and Wayne Schlepp (Toronto: Joint Centre for Asia Pacific Studies, 1994), 34–62; and Ulf Büntgen and Nicola Di Cosmo, "Climatic and Environmental Aspects of the Mongol Withdrawal from Hungary in 1242 CE," *Scientific Reports* 6, no. 1 (2016): 1–9.

Li rois · qui païens asseure
Pence bien · ceste encloeure
Por ce tient il · si pres son regne.

Teiz at alei · simple aleure
Qui tost li iroit · lambleure
Seur · le destrier a lasche regne
Corte folie · est plus seigne
Que longue · de fol consoil pleigne
Or se teigne · en sa teneure
Soutremeir · neust fait estreigne
De li miex en vausist li reignes
Cen fust la terre · plus seure

Mes sires Joffrois · de Sergines.
Je ne voi · par desa nul signes
Que hon · orendroit vos secore
Li cheval · ont mal enz eschines
Et li riche home · en lor poitrines
Que fait Diex que nes par aqueure.

Ancor vanra · tot a tenz leure
Que li maufei · noir comme meure
Les tanront en · lor decepline
Lors auront il non chantepleure
Et senz secours · lor corront seure.

Qui lor liront · longues matines ·

Explicit

The king, who appeases the pagans,
grasps this vulnerability well.
For this reason, he keeps a tight rein on his kingdom.

He who went at only a footpace
would soon go at a trot
on a warhorse if the reins were loosened.
A short folly is wiser
than a long one full of foolish council.
Now may he remain in his domain.
If he had not given himself over to Outremer,
the kingdom would be in a better state,
and the lands more secure.

My lord Geoffrey of Sergines,
I see no sign at this moment
that anyone is sending you aid.
The horses have pain in their backs,
and the rich men evil in their breasts.
What is God doing, that he does not penetrate their hearts?

For soon, the hour will come
when the demons, dark as blackberries,
will inflict their punishments upon them.
Then they will be called *chantepleure*,[73]
and with no help in sight, those who will read them long

Matins will trample them underfoot.[74]

The End

73. The idea here, based on Luke 6:25, is that the *pleurechantes* will cry and then sing by suffering in life and then singing in heaven, while the *chantepleures* will sing first in life and then weep in hell. This verse certainly alludes to the poem "La chantepleure" from the 1230s by an anonymous supporter of the grand inquisitor Robert le Bougre who terrorized France from 1232 to 1239, and which also appears in BnF, MS fr. 837, fols. 335v–336v close to the last Rutebeuf poem, which ends at 332v. Achille Jubinal reproduced "La chantepleure" in a long note in his *Oeuvres complètes de Rutebeuf, Trouvère du XIIIe siècle: Recueillies et mises au jour pour la première fois* (Paris: Edouard Pannier, 1839), 1:398–405. The poem describes the torments inflicted by devils that are "noirs comme meure" (v. 8) or dark as blackberries. See Jean-Marie Fritz, "La clepsydre et l'oxymore: Variations sur la 'chantepleure,'" *Romania* 134 (2016): 373nn91, 92.

74. "Reading long Matins," figuratively speaking, means to inflict a long painful trial on someone, because Matins entailed waking in the middle of the night for sometimes lengthy liturgical offices. See the comment in Bastin and Faral, *Oeuvres complètes*, 430.

The Complaint of Outremer

La complainte doutremeir (8v–9v)

This poem can be dated to the end of 1265 or early 1266. It aligns with a new papal call to crusade in the Holy Land, rather than in Sicily, where so much attention and support had been focused in the years leading up to Charles of Anjou's victory over the Hohenstaufen heirs and his coronation (January 5, 1266) as king of the Regno, that is, over the Kingdom of Naples and the Island of Sicily. The campaigns in Sicily, supported if not engineered by the papacy, were called as crusades against the German rulers and received severe critique as a consequence.[75] *With Charles's victory, however, attention turned once again to Jerusalem and to Outremer. In the spring of 1265, Pope Clement IV composed an exhortation to the Dominican and Franciscan friars of France to encourage the king, Louis IX, and the knights of the realm to take the cross. King Louis would do so only in 1267, but Hugh of Burgundy, Eudes of Nevers's father, took a crusade vow at this point, which was commuted and taken up by Eudes in his father's stead some time before October 1265, when Eudes departed for Acre. The allusions to the Gospel of Matthew, to renounce one's ties to family and worldly positions and to follow Christ and secure his patrimony, as well as pointed calls to the king of France and to Alphonse, the count of Poitiers, the king's brother, to take the cross, render this poem a vernacular pseudo-sermon. Rutebeuf seeks both to shame and to intimidate kings, prelates, knights, and especially tourneyors—those who only play at war in tournaments rather than on crusade—to take the cross and thus to do what was right for Outremer. In this way, the poem is both a complaint about the behavior of those who refuse to hear the call and a lament for Outremer itself. The poet goes one step further and evokes Geoffrey of Sergines, whom Rutebeuf had extolled in an earlier verse composition. He reminds his listeners at the close of the poem that "Geoffrey is asking for aid." Eudes of Nevers and those in his entourage would clearly have been a target audience for such a poem, if he was not already on his way to the East when it was performed.*[76]

75. Although we do not translate them here, Rutebeuf's two short poems "La Chanson de Pouille" (ca. 1264–65) and "Le Dit de Pouille" (mid-1265) both address the campaign or crusade in Apulia, in the far southeast of the Italian peninsula.

76. Zink, *Rutebeuf*, 845; Bastin and Faral, *Onze poémes*, 52–57.

Cest la complainte doutremeir

[8v] Empereour et roi et conte
Et duc et prince a cui hom conte
Romans divers por eux esbatre
De cex qui se[77] suelent combatre
Sa en arrier por sainte eglise
Car me dites par queil servise
Vos cuidiez avoir paradix
Cil le gaaignerent ia diz
Dont vos oeiz ces romans lire
Par la poinne par le martyre.
Que li cors soffrirent sus terre
Veiz ci le tens diex vos vient querre

Braz estanduz de son sanc tainz
Par quoi li fex vos iert estains
Et denfer et de purgatoire
Reconmenciez novele estoire
Serveiz dieu de fin cuer entier
Car dieux vos moustre le sentier
De son pays et de sa marche
Que hom cens raison[78] le sormarche
Por ce si devriiez entendre
A revangier et a deffendre
La terre de promission
Qui est en tribulacion
Et perdue ce Diex nem pence.
Se prochainnement na deffence
Soveigne vos de dieu lo peire
Qui por soffrir la mort ameire
Envoia en terre son fil
[9r] Or est la terre en grant peril.
Lai ou il fut et mors et vis
Je ne sai que plus vos devis
Qui naidera a ceste empointe
Qui ci fera[79] le mesacointe
Pou priserai tout lautre afaire
Tant sache lou papelart faire
Ainz dirai mais et jor et nuit
Nest pas tout ors quanque reluit

This is the Complaint of Outremer

[8v] Emperors, kings, counts,
dukes, and princes, for your entertainment
varied tales are told of those who
in bygone days engaged in combat
on behalf of the Holy Church.
Tell me then, by what service do
you believe you will attain paradise?
You hear tales read about those who
have already gained it
by the pain and martyrdom
that their bodies suffered on earth.
The moment has arrived when God is coming to seek you,

arms outstretched, stained in his blood
by which the fires of hell and purgatory
were extinguished for you.
It is time for you to begin a new chapter.
Serve God with your whole heart,
for God is showing you the path
toward his land and its frontiers that are
being trampled by ignorant men.
You must try, therefore,
to avenge and to defend
the promised land,
which is in turmoil
and will be lost if God does not attend to it
and if it is not defended soon.
Remember God the Father
who sent his Son to earth to
suffer a cruel death.
[9r] Now the land where He both
lived and died is in great peril.
I do not know what else to share with you.
And to him who will not support this struggle
and dismisses it,
I will accord little value to his other claims,
no matter how well he plays the devotee.[80]
Thus, I will say again, day and night,
"all that glitters is not gold."

77. MS fr. 1635 reads "ce." This is a scribal error; we have made the correction and translated the text accordingly.

78. Rutebeuf creates a deliberate play of sound and meaning here with "*hom cens raison*," which would have sounded enough like *hom sarrasin* to suggest to a listener that men without reason and Saracen men were trampling the Holy Land.

79. Lines 33–34, scribe has "naiderat" and "ferat," which are mostly likely scribal variants.

80. The word *papelart* means a hypocrite, in this case the slippery-tongued sort who is not truly devout.

Ha · rois de France rois de France
La loiz la foiz et la creance
Vat presque toute chancelant
Que vos iroie plus celant
Secorez la quor est mestiers
Et vos et li cuens de poitiers
Et li autre baron encemble

Natendeiz pas tant que vos emble
La mort larme por deu seigneur
Mais qui vorra avoir honeur
En paradix si la deserve
Car je ni voi nule autre verve

Jhesucriz dist en lewangile
Qui nest de truffe ne de guile
Ne doit pas paradix avoir
Qui fame et enfans et avoir
Ne lait por lamour de celui
Quen la fin iert juges de lui

Asseiz de gens sunt mout dolant
De ce que hom trahi rollant
Et pleurent de fauce pitie
Et voit ax eux lamistie

Que Deux nos fist qui nos cria
Qui en la sainte croix cria
Au Juys que il moroit de soi
Ce nert pas por boivre a guersoi
Ainz avoit soi de nos raiembre.
Celui doit hon douteir et criembre
Por teil seigneur doit hom ploreir
Quensi se laissat devoreir
Quil ce fist percier le costei
Por nos osteir de mal hosteil
Dou costei issi sancz et eigue
Qui ces amis netoie et leive
Rois de France qui aveiz mis
Et votre avoir et voz amis
Et le cors por dieu en prison.
Ci aurat trop grant mesprison

Ah, King of France, King of France,
religion,[81] faith, and belief
are all on the brink of collapse.
Why would I hide this from you any longer?
Send help—
you, and the Count of Poitiers,
as well as the other barons together—for it is needed now.

My lords, do not wait
until death takes your soul, by God!
For he who wishes to have honor
in paradise, may he be worthy of it.
For I have no other words to say.

Jesus Christ says in the Gospels—
which is neither a joke nor a ruse—
he will not attain paradise
who does not leave his wife and children
for the love of Him who
will judge him at the end.

Many people are very sad
that Roland[82] was betrayed,
and they weep with fake pity.
And yet they see, with their own eyes, the affection

that God who created us shows us,
the one, who on the holy cross, cried out
to the Jews that He was dying of thirst.
But this was no drinking game,
for He thirsted to redeem us.
He is the one we should fear and dread,
and we should weep for such a Lord
who allowed Himself to be so tormented
that He let his side be pierced
to deliver us from the house of evil.
From His side flowed blood and water that
washed and cleansed his friends.
King of France, you who have placed
your belongings and your friends
and your own body in prison for God,
it would be a great mistake

81. This word is usually translated as "law," but in this context it is better understood as religious law.

82. In the Old French epic tradition, Roland is the beloved nephew of Charlemagne who dies alongside the emperor's finest knights at the Battle of Roncevaux after his stepfather Ganelon betrays the Frankish troops in a deal with Marsile, the Muslim king and last holdout in Spain. The two most famous versions in the French tradition are the *Song of Roland* and *Chronicle of Pseudo-Turpin*. Rutebeuf is criticizing those who lament the loss of a character of popular poetic tradition rather than the true suffering of Jesus.

Ce la sainte terre failliez
Or covient que vos i ailliez
Ou vos i envoiez des gent
Cens apairgnier or et argent.
Dont li droiz dieu soit chalangiez
Diex ne wet faire plus lons giez
A ces amis ne longue longe
Ansois i wet metre chalonge
Et wet cil le voisent veoir
Qua sa destre vorront seoir

if you abandoned the Holy Land.
Now it is time for you to go
and to send people there
sparing neither gold nor silver.
Where the rights of God are challenged,
God does not wish to extend further credit
to his friends, nor a longer leash.
Thus he wishes to put forward a challenge.
He wishes that those who want to sit
at his right side should come to see him.

Hay prelat de saint eglise
Qui por gardeir les cors de byse

Alas, prelates of the Holy Church
who, to protect their bodies from the cold north wind,

Ne voleiz leveir aux matines
Messires joffrois de sergines.
Vos demande de la meir
Mais je di cil fait a blameir
Qui nule riens plus vos demande
Fors boens vins et boenne viande
Et que li poivres soit bien fors
Cest votre guerre et votre effors
Cest vostre diex cest votre biens
Votre peires[83] itrait le fiens
[9v] Rutebues dit qui riens ne soile
Quasseiz aureiz · dun poi de toile[84]

do not wish to arise for Matins.
My lord Geoffrey of Sergines
is calling you from beyond the sea.
But I say that he is blameworthy,
who asks no more of you
than good wine and good food
and that the pepper be good and spicy.
It is your war and your effort.
It is your God and your possession,
yet it is your Father who toils in the fields.[85]
[9v] Rutebeuf will give it to you straight:
soon you will need nothing more than a small burial cloth

Se les pances ne sont trop graces
Et que feront les armes lasses
Elz iront lai ou dire noze
Diex iert juges de ceste choze
[4 *lines missing*]

unless your stomachs have grown too fat.
And what will these wretched souls do?
They will go to the place I dare not mention.
God will be the judge of this affair.
[4 *lines missing*]

Hai grant clerc grant provendier
Qui tant estes grant vivendier
Qui faites Dieu de votre pance
Dites moi par queil acointance
Vos partireiz au Dieu roiaume
Qui ne voleiz pas dire. I. siaume
Dou sautier tant estes divers
Fors celui ou na que ii vers
Celui dites apres mangier
Diex wet que vos laleiz vengier
Sanz controuver nule autre essoinne.

So, great clerics, great prebenderies—
you who are living large,
you who make a God of your fat bellies—
tell me by what means
you will take part in the Kingdom of God.
You who do not wish to recite a single psalm
in the psalter—so contrary are you—
outside of the one that has but two verses,
the one you say after dinner,
God wants you to go and avenge him
without concocting any more excuses.

83. This line can be interpreted in different ways: Father could refer to Father in heaven, i.e., God, or to the king.

84. On "toile," see the glossary.

85. Faral and Bastin note the difficulty of this passage and underline the contrast between the dining pleasures of lazy prelates and, in the reading they suggest, God working the land, Bastin and Faral, *Oeuvres complètes*, 447.

Ou vos laissiez le patrimoinne
Qui est dou sanc au crecefi
Mal le teneiz jou vos afi
Se vos serveiz Dieu a leglise
Dieux vos resert en autre guise
Quil vos paist en votre maison
Cest quite a quite par raison
Mais ce vos ameiz le repaire
Qui sanz fin est por joie faire
Achateiz le car Diex le vent
Car il at mestier par couvent
Dacheteours et cil sengignent
Qui orendroit ne le bargignent
Car teil fois le vorront avoir
Com ne laurat pas por avoir

Or, you should renounce the patrimony
that comes from the blood of the crucified one.
You are maintaining it poorly, I assure you.
If you serve God in the church,
God serves you in other ways,
since he nourishes you in your house.
By that logic, everything evens out.
But if you love the abode
that brings joy without end,
then buy it! Because God is selling it.
For He needs committed buyers, and those who do not
make a deal right away cheat themselves,
for a time will come when they wish to have it,
and they will not be able to obtain it for any price.

Tornoieur et vos que dirois
Qui au jor dou juise irois
Devant Dieu que porroiz respondre
Car lors ne se porront repondre
Ne genz clergies ne gens laies.
Et Dieux vous monterra ces plaies
Ce il vos demande la terre
Ou por vos vout la mort soffere
Que direiz vos je ne sai quoi
Li plus hardi seront si quoi
Com les porroit panrre a la main
Et nos navons · point de demain
Car li termes vient et aprouche
Que la mort nos clourat la bouche
Ha antioche · terre sainte
Con ci at delireuze plainte
Quant tu nas mais · nuns godefrois
Li feux de charitei est frois
En chacun cuer de crestiien
Ne jone home ne ancient
Nont por Dieu cure de combatre
Asseiz se porroit ja debatre
Et jacobins et cordeliers
Quil trovassent · nuns angeliers

And you, tourneyers, what will you say
when you go to the day of judgment?
Before God, how will you be able to respond?
For then, they will not be able to hide
neither clergy nor laity.
And God will show you his wounds.
If He asks you about the land
where He wished to suffer death on your behalf,
what will you say? I don't know.
The bravest among them will be so tame
that you could catch them with your bare hand.
And there will be no tomorrow,
because the end draws near
when death will close our mouths.
Alas, Antioch, Holy Land,
oh you have such a painful lament
since you have no more Godfreys.[86]
The fire of devotion has gone cold
in each Christian heart;
no man, neither young nor old,
cares to fight for God.
Dominicans and Franciscans alike
could go to great lengths
and not find a single Angeliers,[87]

86. Godfrey of Bouillon was a hero of the First Crusade and the subject of multiple Old French epic songs written beginning in the late twelfth century. See Anne Latowsky, "Charlemagne, Godfrey of Bouillon, and Louis IX," in *The Cambridge Companion to the Literature of the Crusades*, ed. Anthony Bale (Cambridge: Cambridge University Press, 2018), 202–5; Galvez, *The Subject of Crusade*, 202–3.

87. Angeliers (Engelers), duke of Aquitaine, is mentioned among the dead at the mythic eighth-century Battle of Roncevaux in various texts including the *Song of Roland* and the Old French translations of the popular *Chronicle of Pseudo-Turpin*.

Nuns tangreiz · ne nuns bauduÿns.
Ansois lairont aux beduÿns
Maintenir la terre absolue
Qui par defaut nos est tolue
Et Dieux lat ja dune part arse
Dautre part vienent cil de tarse
Et coramin et chenillier
Revanrront por tot escillier
Ja ne serat qui la deffande
Ce mes sires joffrois demande
Secours si quiere qui li fasse
Car je ni voi nulle autre trasce ·
Car com plus en sarmoneroie
Et plus lafaire empireroie
Cils siecles faut: qui bien fera
apres la mort le trovera

Explicit

nor a Tancred nor a Baldwin.[88]
They would sooner leave the Bedouins
in charge of the Holy Land,
which was taken from us due to our neglect.
God has already seen it burned on one side,
and from the other, those from Tarsus,
the Khwarazmians and the Chananians,[89]
will return to destroy everything.
Then there will be no one there to defend it.
If my lord Geoffrey is asking
for aid, let him seek someone who will render it,
for I do not see any other course.[90]
For, the more I might sermonize,
the worse the situation would become.
This world is failing: he who will do good now
will then reap it after death.

The End

88. Like Godfrey, Tancred and Baldwin were also heroes of the successful First Crusade, but without the vernacular literary afterlife that Godfrey inspired.

89. Both the Khwarazmian and Chananians were Turco-Persian peoples who were part of the Persianate Sunni Muslim empire of Mamluk origin that stretched across the region encompassing Iran and Afghanistan, between Tabriz, Shiraz to the south, and Kabul to the east. The association with those from Tarsus (on the coast of south-central Turkey, in the region of Cilicia) suggests that Rutebeuf, like many of his contemporaries, amalgamated a common Muslim-Persian-Turkic enemy.

90. See Alexandre Teulet et al., eds., *Layettes du Trésor des chartes* (Paris: H. Plon, 1863–1909), 4:228–29, no. 5293 (June 1267), for a letter from Geoffrey asking for funds and support.

The Lament for Count Eudes of Nevers

La complainte dou conte Hue de Nevers (42r–43r)

Composed in the months following the death of Eudes of Nevers (August 7, 1266, in Acre), this poem can be dated with certainty to the autumn of 1266 (see figure 31). Eudes was born in 1230, the son of Duke Hugh IV of Burgundy. He was well connected with the major baronial families of the day, and in 1265, the year before he died, his eldest daughter, Yolande, was married to the son of the king of France, Jean Tristan. The poem was clearly written before March 1267—the year Louis IX took the cross for a second time—because Rutebeuf is still exhorting Louis and his brother, Alphonse of Poitiers, to take the vow. Moreover, Rutebeuf mentions the fact that Eudes's heart, which had been extracted and embalmed for transport across the Mediterranean, was sent to the monks of Cîteaux, where the crusading dukes of Burgundy had their family tomb. The poem not only praises Eudes as a flower of chivalry and a knight and lord of unmatched renown, it also laments his loss for the East and for France. In addition, several stanzas praise those close to Eudes, including his companion and friend Érard of Vallery, who served as one of the executors of the Account-Inventory. Érard would no doubt also have been the subject of a similar poem had he died young. He was one of a cadre of knights who worked in service first to Eudes, then as the constable of the Count of Champagne, then under the king of Sicily, Charles of Anjou, finally serving as military and political advisor to King Philip III.[91] *Any insight we have about Eudes's character and how he was perceived by others comes principally from Rutebeuf's poem. Indeed, in many respects this "Lament" reads like a public funeral oration, although there is no definitive proof that it was read in this way. The poem is an invaluable complement to the Account-Inventory, which gives insight into the ways Eudes styled himself through his material possessions and the networks such things created.*[92]

91. Érard died on August 11, 1276, almost exactly a decade after Eudes. See Xavier Hélary, *L'Ascension et la chute de Pierre de La Broce, chambellan du roi († 1278): Étude sur le pouvoir royal au temps de Saint Louis et de Philippe III (v. 1250–v.1280)* (Paris: Honoré Champion, 2021), 77–79, 410–12.

92. Zink, *Rutebeuf*, 859; Bastin and Faral, *Onze poèmes*, 64–69.

Ci en coumence la complainte dou conte huede de Nevers

[42r] Lamors · qui tozjors ceulz aproie
Qui plus sunt de bien faire en voie
Me fait descovrir · mon corage
por lun de ceulz que plus amoie
Et que mieux · resemble vodroie
Coume · qui soit · de nul langage

Huedes ot non · preudome et sage
Cuens de neuers · au fier corage
Que la mors apris · en sa proie
Cestoit la fleurs · de son lignage.
De sa mort est plus granz damage
Que je dire · ne vos porroiė

Mors est li cuens diex en ait lame
Sainz Jorges · et la douce dame
Vuellent prier · le sovrain maître
Quen cele joie · qui nentame
Senz redouteir linfernal flame
Mete le boen conte a sa destre
Et il ideit · par raison estre
Quil laissa · son leu et son ester
Por cele glorieuze jame
Qui a non · la joie celestre
Mieudres de li · ne porra nestre
Mien esciant · de cors de fame

Li cuens fu tantost chevaliers
Com il en fu poinz et mestiers
Quil pot les armes endureir
Puis ne fu · voie ne sentiers
Ou il nalast mout · volentiers
Se hon si pot aventureir
Si vos puis bien dire et jureir
Cil peust son droit tenz dureir
Conques ne fu · mieudres terriers[94]
Tant se seust amesureir
Au boenz et les fauz forjureir
Auz unz dolz et auz autres fiers
Ce pou quaux armes fu en vie

Here begins the Lament for Count Eudes of Nevers

[42r] Death, which always preys upon those
who stay true to the path of good deeds,
reveals to me my feelings for
one among them whom I loved the most
and whom I would most like to resemble,
more than any man who exists, among speakers of any tongue.[93]
His name was Eudes, a *prudhomme* and wise,
the Count of Nevers, brave of heart,
whom death has taken as its prey.
He was the flower of his lineage.
His death is such a great pity
that I could not describe it to you.

The count is dead, may God receive his soul.
May Saint George and the sweet Lady,
pray to the Sovereign Master
that He place the count at His right side,
into that joy, which cannot be corrupted,
and without the fear of the flames of hell.
And he must rightly be there,
since he left his home and way of life
for this glorious gem
that is called celestial joy.
In my opinion, it will not be possible for a better man than him to be of woman born.

The count was quickly knighted,
when the time and necessity arose,
as soon as he was able to bear arms.
Then, there was neither a course nor a path
that he did not take most eagerly
if one were able to venture thereupon.
If I might tell you truly and swear to it,
had he been able to live out the full measure of his days,
never would there have been a better lord of his lands;
so well did he know how to administer justice to the good
and to renounce the deceitful.
To the former he is mild, and to the latter, harsh.
During the brief period of his life that he bore arms,

93. This mention of "speakers of any tongue" is an example of hyperbole used to convey that there is no man anywhere in the world whom the poet would more like to resemble than Eudes.

94. A *terriers* was a landlord, literally, and as such, someone who carried out justice.

Tuit li boen avoient envie	all the good men wanted
De lui resambleir de meniere	to resemble him in their bearing.
Se Diex namast sa compaignie.	If God did not love his company,
Neust pas Acre desgarnie	He would not have deprived Acre
De si redoutee baniere	of such a formidable standard.[95]
La mors a mis la faire ariere	Death has set back the cause of
Dacre · dont nuns mestiers nen iere	Acre, which was the last thing it needed.
La terre en remaint esbahie	That land remains dumbstruck.[96]
Ci a mort · delireuze et fiere	In that place there is death, so painful and terrible
Que nuns · hom nen fait bele chière	that no one can put a brave face on it
Fors cele pute gent haie ·	except for that vile, hated people.
La terre plainne de noblesce	Oh Land, full of nobility,
De charitei et de largesce	charity, and generosity,
Tant aveiz fait vilainne perde	you have suffered such a dreadful loss.
Ce morte ne fust gentilesce	If *gentillesse* were not dead,
Et vaselages et proesce	as well as courage and prowess,
Vos ne fussiez pas si deserte	you would not be so desolate.
Hai hai · genz mal aperte	Alas, alas, you ill-mannered men,
La porte des cielz est overte	the gate of heaven is open.
Ne reculeiz pas por peresce	Do not back away out of laziness.
En brief tanz la or Diex offerte	God did not hesitate to present this opportunity
Au boen conte · par sa deserte	to the good count as his reward,
Quil l'a conquise en sa jonesce ·	which he seized during his youth.
Ne fist mie de sa croix pile[97]	He did not turn his back on his cross,
Si com font souvent teil. x. mile	as do tens of thousands who so often
Qui la prennent par grant faintize	take it with great insincerity.
Ainz a fait selonc levangile	Thus, he did it according to the Gospel:
[42v] Quil a maint borc et mainte vile	[42v] for he left behind many towns and many villages
Laissie por morir au servize	to die in the service of
Celui Seigneur · qui tot justize	that Lord who renders justice to all.
Et Diex li rent · en bele guize	And God repays him handsomely—
Ne cuidiez pas · que se soit guile	do not think this is a trick—
Quil fait granz vertuz a devize	for He performs many great miracles.
Bien pert · que Diex a sarme prise	It truly appears that God took his soul
Por metre en son roial concile	to place him in his royal council.
Encor fist li cuens a sa mort	The count arranged that at his death
Quavec les plus povres samort	he would be as one with the very poor.
Des plus povres · vot estre el conte	He wished to be counted among the poorest.

95. A standard in this case refers to the flag or banner carried in battle to represent opposing forces.

96. *La terre* (that land) is a reference to the Holy Land.

97. There is a play on words here involving the term "cross" (*croix*), which is also a reference to a coin, the French *denier tournois*, which bore the image of a cross on its obverse and was also the symbol of a promise to go on crusade. To turn your coin from heads to tails meant to be deceitful, or to abandon your vow to crusade. Here, Eudes remained true to his commitment to go on crusade. See figures 9.1 and 9.2: French *denier tournois*.

Quant la mors .I. teil home mort	When Death bites such a man,
Que doit quele ne ce remort	how can she have no remorse for
De mordre · si tost un teil conte	devouring such a count so early in life?
Car qui la veritei nos conte	For, if truth be told,
Je ne cuit pas que jamais monte	I think that no man
Sor nul cheval feble ne fort	has ever mounted a horse, weak or strong,
Nuns hom · qui tant ait doutei honte	who so feared shame,
Ne mieulz seust que honeurs monte	or better understood the meaning of honor.
Na ci doleur · et desconfort ·	Is this not a tale of sadness and pain?
Li cuers le conte · est a Citiaux.	The heart of the count is at Cîteaux,
Et larme la sus en sains ciaux	and his soul in the saintly heavens above,
Et li cors en gist outre meir	and his body lies beyond the sea.
Cist departirs est boens et biaux	This division is good and beautiful,
Ci a trois precieulz joiaux	for we now have three precious jewels
Que tuit li boen doivent ameir	that every good person should revere.
La sus elz cielz fait boen semeir	There, up in heaven, it is a good time to plant;[98]
Nestuet pas la terre femeir	one need not fertilize the soil,
Ne ne ci puet repaitre oiziaux	nor can birds feed upon the seeds.
Quant por Dieu se fist entameir	Since he allowed himself to be torn apart in God's name,
Que porra Diex · sor li clameir	what claim can God make against him,
Quant il jugera · boens et maux ·	when He judges the good and the evil?
Ha cuens Jehan biau tres dolz sire	Ah, Count John,[99] fine, sweet lord,
De vos puisse hon · tant de bien dire	may as many great things be said about you
Com hon puet dou conte Huede faire	as one can say about Count Eudes.
Quen lui a si bele matyre	For in him, we have such good material[100]
Que Diex cen puet joer et rire	in which God can rejoice and delight,
Et sainz paradix cen resclaire	and by which saintly paradise is brightened.
A iteil fin · fait il bon traire	It is good to pursue such an end,
Que hon nen puet nul mal retraire	for no one can find any wrong in it;
Teil vie · fait boen eslire	it is good to choose that kind of life.
Doulz et pitouz et debonaire	People found him to be
Le trovoit hon · en toz afaires	sweet and pious and noble in all regards;
Sages est · quen ces faiz ce mire	wise is the one who sees himself in his [Eudes's] deeds.
Mes sire Erart · Diex vos maintiegne	My lord, Érard, may God preserve you
Et en bone vie vos tiegne	and keep you well,
Quil est bien mestiers en la terre	for in that Land[101] there is great need.
Que cil avient que tost vos preigne	But should He take you early,

98. There is a temporal element to the idiom "fait boen semeir" meaning that now is the time to go on crusade.

99. This is most likely a reference to Jean Tristan, son of Louis IX, who had married Eudes's daughter Yolande in 1265. Jean took up the title of count of Nevers following Eudes's death.

100. The word *matyre* here refers both to Eudes's own person, as well as to material or subject matter, meaning things that could be sung and written about him, as in the French term "matière." This bit of typical Rutebeufian play of sound and meaning allows the poet to suggest that God is an audience for the very sorts of poems of praise that he himself is writing.

101. A reference to the Holy Land, where Eudes's body was buried.

Je dout li pais · ne remeigne
En grant doleur et en grant guerre
Com li cuers · el ventre vos serre
Quant Diex a mis · si tost en serre
Lou conte · a la doutee enseigne

I fear those lands would remain
in a state of great suffering and war.
Oh, how your heart tightens in your chest
knowing that God brought the count,
with his much-feared standard, to His side so soon.

Ou porroiz teil compaignon querre
En France ne en Aingle terre
Ne cuit pas com le vos enseingne.

Where might you seek a companion like him?
Whether in France or in England,
I do not think anyone could show you one.

Ha · rois de france · rois de france
Acre est · toute jor en balance
Secoreiz la · quil est mestiers
Serveiz Dieu · de vostre sustance
Ne faites plus ci remenance
Ne vos ne li cuens de poitiers
Diex vos i verra · volentiers
Car toz est herbuz · li santiers
Con suet batre · por penitance
Qua Dieu sera · amis entiers
Voit destorbeir · ces charpentiers
Qui destorbent notre creance ·

Ah! King of France, King of France
Acre hangs in the balance daily.
Send help to her, for it is needed.
Serve God with all you have.
Do not remain here any longer,
neither you nor the Count of Poitiers.
God will be pleased to see you there,
for the path that others were able
to clear as penance has become overgrown.
He who will be a wholehearted friend of God,
go then, and confront those who wield the axe
and undermine our faith!

Chevalier · que faites vos ci
Cuens de Blois · sire de Couci
[43r] Cuens de Saint Pol · fils au boen Hue
Bien aveiz avant · les cors ci
Coument querreiz a Dieu merci
Se la mors · en voz liz vos tue
Vos veeiz · la terre absolue
Qui a voz tenz · nos ert tolue
Dont jai · le cuer triste et marri
La mors ne fait · nule estandue
Ainz fiert a massue estandue
Tost fait nuit · de jor esclarci
Tornoieur · vos quatendeiz
Qui la Terre · ne deffendeiz
Qui est a votre creatour
Vos aveiz bien les yex bandeiz
Quant ver Dieu ne vos desfendeiz
Nen vos ne meteiz nul atour
Pou douteiz · la parfonde tour
Dont li prison nont nul retour
Ou par peresce · descendeiz

Knights, what are you doing here?
Count of Blois, Lord of Coucy,
[43r] Count of Saint-Pol, son of the good Hugh,[102]
Since your bodies are still here before us,
how then will you seek the mercy of God
if death kills you in your beds?
You see, the Holy Land
in your time has been taken from us,
which makes my heart sad and dismayed.
Death does not wait,
rather she wields her club and strikes,
quickly making night of a clear day.
Tourneyers, what are you waiting for?
You who are not defending the Holy Land,
who is your Creator?
Your eyes are truly blindfolded,
since you are neither defending yourself
nor have you prepared yourself to face God.
You scarcely fear the deep tower
from which prisoners have no escape
and into which you are descending through sloth.

102. According to Zink, who follows Bastin and Faral (above), these named persons are John of Châtillon, son of Hugh of Châtillon (count of Blois), Guy of Châtillon the count of Saint-Pol, and Enguerrand IV of Coucy.

Ci na plus ne guanche ne tour
Quant la mors vos va si entour
A Dieu · cors et arme rendeiz ·

There is no way to avoid it nor to turn back
when death is closing in on you.
You offer up your body and soul to God.

Quant la teste est · bien avinee
Au feu · deleiz la cheminee
Si nos croizonz de plain eslaiz
Et quant vient · a la matinee
Si est ceste voie finee
Teil coutume a · et clers et lais
Et quant il muert · et fait son lais
Si lait sales · maisons palais
A doleur · a fort destinee
Lai sen va · ou na nul relais
De lavoir · rest il bone pais
Quant gist mors · desus lechinee

When the head is tipsy with wine,
around the fire, near the hearth,
then we leap with great verve.
And when the morning comes
this journey ends.
Such is the habit of both the cleric and the layman.
When he dies and writes his will[103]
he leaves behind halls, houses, and palaces
in sadness, because of this cruel fate.
He goes there where there is no relief.
Wealth is no longer a concern
when one lies dead on one's back.

Or prions · au roi glorieux
Qui par son sanc esprecieulz
Nos osta · de destrucion
Quen son regne delicieuz
Qui tant est doulz ·et gracieuz
Faciens la nostre mansion
Et que par grant devocion
Ailliens en cele region
Ou Diex soffri · la mort crueulz.
Qui lait en teil confusion
La terre de promission ·
Pou est de sarme curieulz

Now let us pray to the glorious King
who by his precious blood
delivered us from destruction,
that we may make our home
in His exquisite kingdom,
so sweet and filled with grace.
And with great devotion,
let us go to that land
where God suffered cruel death.
Whoever leaves the promised land
in such a state of disarray
has little regard for his soul.

Explicit.

The End.

103. See note 1 of the Account-Inventory for an explanation of *lais*.

The Poem of the Route to Tunis

Li diz de la voie de Tunes (56v–58v)

On March 25, 1267, Louis IX took a second crusade vow following nearly two years of papal and mendicant organization and preaching. He was joined in this commitment by his brother, Alphonse, count of Poitiers, and two of his sons, Philip (who would become Philip III) and Jean Tristan, who held the title of Count of Nevers, as well as his nephew Robert, count of Artois. On June 5 (at Pentecost), 1267, his son-in-law, Thibaut V, count of Champagne and king of Navarre, also took the vow. It was not clear yet at that point that the crusade expedition was destined for Tunis. There was some consideration of Egypt as a strategic goal toward regaining Jerusalem, and the poet's references to the "desert" underline that such ideas were circulating. The title of the poem, "the Route to Tunis," was most likely appended after the poem was first composed and performed, thus after 1270, when it was fair-copied into the manuscript tradition. Even if Rutebeuf could not know where the king and his crusade would end up, the themes developed in the poem—of service to God and to courtoisie, *of the sacrifices one must make especially regarding the body to win paradise, and of the unavoidable "bite" of death—were almost prescient of the outcome. For Louis IX, his son-in-law Thibaut V, daughter Isabelle, and son Jean Tristan would all die on campaign in Tunis or in the protracted funeral cortège that returned to France by way of the Kingdom of Sicily. Rutebeuf surely could not have known this when he wrote; however, the fact that his verse aligns with broader associations uniting crusading with martyrdom, self-sacrifice, and the inevitability of death suggests that such ideas circulated widely and certainly beyond the royal court. The poem must have been composed then between June 5, 1267, and August 25, 1270, the day Louis IX died in Tunis. More likely is that it was written in connection with the June 5 celebration of the knighting of Louis's two younger sons, Pierre, future count of Alençon (a title he would take up in March 1269), and Jean Tristan, which coincided with Pentecost and was the occasion of a public celebration and preaching all directed toward the new crusade.*[104]

104. Zink, *Rutebeuf*, 875; Bastin and Faral, *Onze poèmes*, 76–78. On the Tunis crusade, see Michael Lower, "Louis IX, Charles of Anjou, and the Tunis Crusade of 1270," in *Crusades: Medieval Worlds in Conflict*, ed. Thomas Madden, James Naus, and Vincent Ryan (Farnham: Ashgate, 2009), 173–93; Xavier Hélary, *La dernière croisade: Saint Louis à Tunis (1270)* (Paris: Perrin, 2016); and Lower, *The Tunis Crusade of 1270: A Mediterranean History* (Oxford: Oxford University Press, 2018).

Ci en coumence li diz de la voie de tunes.[105]

[56v] De corrouz et danui
De pleur et damistie
Est toute la matiere
dont je tras mon ditie
Qui na pitie en soi
Bien at Dieu fors getie
Vers Dieu ne doit trouveir
amour ne amistie

Evangelistre · apostre
martyr et confesseur
Por Jhesucrit soffrirent
De la mort · le presseur
Or vos i gardeiz bien
Qui estes successeur
Con nat pas paradyx
Cens martyre plus eur

On ques en paradix
nentra nuns fors par poinne
Por cest il · foulz cheitis
Qui por larme ne poinne
Cuidiez que Jhesucris
En paradyx nos mainne
Por norrir en delices
La char nest pas sainne

Sainne nest ele pas
De ce ne dout je point
Or est chaude · or est froide
Or est soeiz · or point
Ja niert en. i. estat
Ne en un certain point
Qui sert Dieu de teil char
Mainne il bien sarme a point

Here begins the poem[106] **of the route to Tunis.**

[56v] Anger and frustration,
sadness and attachment,
all are themes upon which
I draw for my verses.
He who does not have pity
within himself has rejected God.
He should find neither
love nor friendship with God.

Evangelists, apostles,
martyrs, and confessors
suffered the torment of death
for Jesus Christ.
Now be well aware,
you who are their successors,
one does not attain paradise
without intense suffering.

No one ever enters paradise
except through pain.
For he is a miserable fool
who does not suffer for his soul.
Do you think Jesus Christ
leads us to paradise
for having fed with delicacies
our unhealthy flesh?

And it [the flesh] is not healthy—
of that, I have no doubt.
At times it is warm, at times it is cold,
sometimes it is at ease, other times not at all;
never will it be in a single state,
nor in a stable condition.
He who serves God with that sort of flesh,
does he guide his soul well?

105. We have transcribed this poem as it appears in BnF, MS fr. 1635 rather than rendering it in quatrains of twelve-syllable Alexandrine verse as Jubinal did in his 1839 edition of the poem also based on BnF, MS fr. 1635, a format that Faral and Bastin and then Zink retained in their subsequent complete works of Rutebeuf.

106. A *dit* is a poem that is spoken, not sung, which is what separates it from lyric. There is no particular form that defines a *dit*; however, it was a phenomenon distinctive to the thirteenth and fourteenth centuries. The term *voie* can mean route or way and is occasionally translated as "crusade." Audiences would have understood this term to refer to the planned crusade expedition led by Louis IX in 1270 that was directed to Tunis. This title may have been given to the poem after the full text was composed, and possibly after Louis IX's death.

A point la moinne il bien
A cele grant fornaize
Qui est dou puis denfer
Ou ja nuns naura aise
Bien se gart qui i vat
Bien se gart qui i plaise

Que Dieux ne morra plus
Por nule arme mauvaise

Dieux dist en lewangile
Se li preudons seust
A queil heure li lerres
Son suel chaveir deust
[57r] Il veillast por la criente
Que dou larron eust
Si bien qua son pooir
De rien ne li neust[107]

Ausi ne savons nos
Quant Dieuz dira veneiz
Qui lors est mal garniz
Mult iert mal aseneiz
Car Dieux li sera lors
Com lions forceneiz
Vos ne vos preneiz garde
Qui les respis preneiz
Li rois ne le prent pas
Cui douce France est toute
Qui tant par ainme larme
Que la mort nen redoute
Ainz va par meir requerre
Cele chiennaille gloute
Jhesuchriz par sa grace
Si gart lui et sa route

Prince prelat baron
Por Dieu preneiz ci garde
France est si grace terre
Nestuet pas com la larde[108]
Or la wet cil laissier [qu][109]

He is certainly leading it directly
to that great furnace,
into the pits of hell,
where no one will be comfortable.
Beware, he who goes there,
beware, he who enjoys it [the pleasures of the flesh],
for God will not die again
for any evil soul.

God said in the Gospel:
"if the *prudhomme* had known
at what time the thief
would breach his threshold,
[57r] out of fear of the thief,
he would have kept watch
as best he could
so the thief would do him no harm."

Also we do not know
when God will say "Come!"
He who is poorly prepared at that time
will be sorely out of luck.
Because God will
rage at him like a lion.
You are failing to take heed, you
who are taking your time.
The king, to whom sweet France is everything,
is not delaying.
He loves his own soul so much
that he does not fear death.
Rather, he will cross the sea
to attack this vile pack of dogs.
May Jesus Christ, by His grace,
protect him and his expedition.

Princes, prelates, barons,
take heed of this, for God's sake.
France is so well-fatted a land
that it should not be further larded.
And so, he who maintains and protects it

107. See Matthew 24:43.

108. Regarding the word *grace*, Zink, *Rutebeuf*, 880n1, notes that a fatty meat requires no larding. The verb *larder* means to lace with strips of bacon, while *arder* means to destroy by burning. The couplet reads "France is such a fatty land that there is no need to lard it" but, with some adjustments for grammar, can sound like "France is such a blessed land that one ought not destroy it."

109. We believe this is a scribal error. An extra set of letters is repeated here that belongs at the head of the next line.

Qui la maintient et garde
Por lamor de celui
Qui tout a en sa garde

wishes to leave it
for the love of Him
who has all under His protection.

Desor mais se deust
Li preudons sejorneir
Et toute sa tendue
A sejour atourneir
Or wet de douce France
Et partir et tornei
Dieux le doint a paris
A joie retorneir
Et li cuens de Poitiers
Qui. i. pueple souztient
Et qui en douce France
Si bien le sien leu tient
Que. xv. jors vaut miex
li leux par ou il vient
Il sen va outre meir
Que riens ne le detient

From now on that *prudhomme* [the king]
ought to stay home and rest
and turn all his attention
to his respite.
And yet he wishes to
take off and leave sweet France behind.
May God grant that
he return to Paris with joy.
And the Count of Poitiers—
who oversees an entire people
and who in sweet France
plays his role so well that
any place he passes through
is then better off for a fortnight[110]—
is going overseas
and nothing will hold him back.

Plus ainme Dieu que home
Qui emprent teil voiage
Qui est li souverains
De tout pelerinage
Le cors mettre a essil
Et meir passer a nage
Por amor de celui ·
Qui le fist a symage
Et mes sires Phelipes
Et li boens cuens dartois
Et li cuens de Nevers·
Qui sunt preu et cortois
Refont en lor venue
A Dieu biau serventois
Chevalier qui ne suit
Ne pris pas. i. nantois

He loves God more than his fellow man,
who undertakes such a voyage
which is the greatest of
all pilgrimages.
He puts his body in peril
and sails across the sea
out of love for Him
who made him in His image.
And my lord Philip,
and the good Count of Artois,
and the Count of Nevers,[111]
who are wise and *courtois*
render a beautiful service to God
by their journey.[112]
A knight who does not follow them
is not worth a penny to me.

Li boens rois de Navarre
Qui lait si bele terre
Que ne sai ou plus bele
Puisse on troveir ne querre

The good king of Navarre—
who leaves behind such beautiful lands
that I do not know where
one might seek or find any more beautiful,[113]

110. This is a reference to itinerant aristocratic courts that would set up for a short period of time and then move on to the next locale. See Bastin and Faral, *Oeuvres complètes*, 464–65n43.

111. See Roll C Back of the Account-Inventory for an echo of this passage.

112. The play on words here suggests that these men had inspired songs of praise. The *serventois* is a genre of poetry influenced early on by the satirical and political Occitan *sirventes* but had evolved by Rutebeuf's time into a genre of pious praise.

113. The king of Navarre at this time was also the count of Champagne, Thibaut V.

Mais hom doit tout laissier
Por lamor Dieu conquerre
Ciz voiages est cleis
Qui paradix desserre

(but then one must leave it all behind
to attain the Love of the God since
this journey is the key
that unlocks paradise)—

Ne prent pas garde a choze
Quil ait eu a faire
[57v] Sa il asseiz eu
Et anui et contraire
Mais si con Dieux trouva
Saint Andreu debonaire
Trueve il le roi Thiebaut
Doulz et de boen afaire

does not worry about the things
that he might have had to do
[57v] even though he has had many
troubles and afflictions.
But just as God found
Saint Andrew[114] to be benevolent[115]
so too does he find King Thibaut
well-intentioned and kind.

Et li dui fil le Roi
Et lor couzins germains,
Ce est li cuens dArtois ·
Qui nest mie dou mains
Revont bien enz dezers
Laboreir de lor mains
Quant par meir vont requerre
Sarrazins et Coumains

And the two sons of the king
and their first cousin—
that is, the Count of Artois
who is in no way the lesser—
are themselves going into the desert
to labor with their hands.[116]
For they are going by sea to attack
the Saracens and Cumans.

Tot soit qua moi bien faire
Soie tardiz et lans
Si ai je de pitie
Por eulz le cuer dolant
Mais ce me reconforte
Quiroie je celant
Quen lor venues vont
En paradix volant
Sains Jehans eschiva
Compaignie de gent
En sa venue fist de sa char
Son serjant
Plus ama les desers
Que or fin ne argent
Quorgueulz ne li alast
Sa vie damagent

Although for me, they are
late and slow to do the right thing,
nonetheless my heart
aches with pity for them.
But what comforts me
(and why would I hide it?)
is that by their journey they
go on the wing to paradise.
Saint John, eschewing the
company of men,
in his turn made a servant
of his flesh.
He loved the desert
more than gold or silver
and he avoided pride, lest
it mar his life.

Bien doit ameir le cors
Qui en puet Dieu servir

He who can serve God
must love his own body

114. Saint Andrew was a patron saint of the crusades, so Rutebeuf is encouraging his audience to follow his example.

115. The word *debonair* suggests nobility, gentility, kindness, and generosity of spirit.

116. The reference to the desert and "to labor with their hands" may evoke monks laboring with their own hands and thus also refer to the religious vow crusaders took, which was akin to the monastic vow. But this may also be a nod to the destination of the crusade, to the "desert" landscapes of either North Africa or Syria and Palestine.

Quil en puet paradix
Et honeur deservir
Trop par ainme son aise
Qui lait larme aservir
Quen enfer sera serve
Par son fol mes servir

so that he can merit paradise
and honor.
The one who loves comfort too much
allows his soul to be in servitude,
such that it will be a serf in hell
because of his foolish disservice.

Veiz ci mult biau sermon
li rois va outre meir
Pour celui roi servir
Ou il n'a point dameir
Qui ces. ij. rois vodra
Et servir et ameir
Croize soi voit apres
Mieulz ne puet il semeir

Here is a very beautiful appeal:[117]
the king is going overseas
to serve that King
in whom there is no bitterness.
Whoever wishes to serve
and love these two kings,
may he take the cross and go after them;
he can sow no better seed.

Ce dit cil qui por nos
Out asseiz honte et lait
Nest pas dignes de moi
Qui por moi tot ne lait
Qua pres moi wet venir
Croize soi ne delait
Qui apres Dieu nira
Mal fu norriz de lait

He, the one who
endured shame and ugliness for us, says:
"He is not worthy of Me who
does not leave everything behind for Me.
He who wishes to come to Me,
may he take the cross and not delay."
He who does not go toward God
was nourished with the milk of evil.

Vauvaseur bacheleir
Plain de grant non savoir
Cuidiez vos par desa
Pris ne honeur avoir
Vous vous laireiz morir
Et porrir votre avoir
Et ce vos vos moreiz
Diex nou quiert ja savoir
Dites aveiz vos pleges
De vivre longuement
Je voi aucun riche home
Faire maisonnement
Quant il a assouvi
trestout entierement
Se li fait hon. i. autre
de petit coustement

Vavasors, young knights
full of great ignorance,
do you think you have gained honor
back here on this side?
You will allow yourself to die
and your fortunes rot,
and if you are dying,
God will pay no heed.
Tell me, do you have a guarantee
of a long life?
I see some rich men
who build houses for themselves.
When the work
is complete
someone makes another for them,
at little cost.[118]

117. In Old French, *sarmon* or *sermon*, with the related verb *sermoner*, means a long talk or discourse, likely rooted in the idea of joining together. It often involves moralizing speech or exhortation and, by extension, the most common modern understanding of the term as a form of religious preaching. Rutebeuf interweaves all these meanings.

118. This most likely refers to making a coffin, a final resting place made of cheaper wood.

[58r] Ja coars nenterra
en paradyx celestre
Si nest nuns si coars
Qui bien ni vouxist estre
Mais tant doutent mesaize
Et a guerpir lor estre
Quil en adossent Dieu
Et metent a senestre

[58r] A coward will never enter
heavenly paradise,
but there is no one so cowardly
that he does not wish to be there.
But they so dread discomfort
and abandoning their way of life,
that they turn their backs on God
and leave Him aside.

Des lors que li hons nait
a il petit a vivre
Quant il a. xl. ans
Or en a mains on livre
Quant il doit servir Dieu
Si saboivre et enyvre
Ja ne se prendra garde
Tant que mors le delivre

From the moment a man is born,
he has little time to live.
When he is forty years old
there is even less time on the ledger.
When he ought to serve God
he drinks too much and gets drunk.
He will never be mindful
until death delivers him.

Or est mors · qua il fait
Quau siecle a tant estei
Il a destruiz les biens
Que Dieux li a prestei
De Dieu ne li souvint
Ne yver ne estei
Il aura paradix
Ce il la conquestei

Now he is dead, and what has he accomplished,
he who was in this world for so long?
He has destroyed the goods
that God lent him.
He never remembers God,
neither in winter nor in summer.
He will gain paradise
if only he strives for it.

Foulz est qui contre mort
Cuide troveir deffence
Des biaux · des fors · des sages
Fait la mors sa despance
La mors mort Absalon
Et Salomon et Sance
De legier despit tout
Quades a morir pance

He is a fool who believes
he has found a defense against death.
Death feeds on the
handsome, strong, and wise.
Death bit Absolom,
and Solomon, and Samson.
He easily holds all things in contempt
who thinks endlessly about death.

Et vos a quoi penceiz
Qui naveiz nul demain
Et qui a nul bien faire
Ne voleiz metre main
Se hom va au moustier
Vos dites je remain
A Dieu servir dou votre
I estes vos droit romain

And you, what do you think about,
you who have no tomorrow,
you who do not wish to lift a finger
to do the slightest good?
If another man goes to church
you say, "I am staying home."
In serving God with what is yours,
you are a true Roman.[119]

119. Rutebeuf is playing here with the double meaning of *droit Romain*, which suggests both Roman law and acting like a "a true Roman." Since he is moralizing about lack of service to God, the reference is likely to the stereotype of Roman avarice. See Bastin and Faral, *Oeuvres complètes*, 467n112, and Zink, *Rutebeuf*, 888–89n1.

Se hom va au moustier
La naveiz vos que faire
Nest pas touz dune piece
Tost vos porroit maufaire
A ceux qui i vont dites
Quailleurs aveiz a faire
Sans oir messe sunt
Maint biau serf embiaire

If another man goes to church,
you want nothing to do with that place:
it is not built of one single piece,
it could easily injure you.[120]
To those who attend, you say
you have business elsewhere:
why go to Mass when
there are many beautiful stags at Bierre.[121]

Vous vous moqueiz de Dieu
Tant que vient a la mort
Si li crieiz merci
Lors que li mors vos mort
Et une consciance
Vos reprent et remort
Si nen souvient nelui
Tant que la mors le mort

You mock God
until the moment of death.
Then you cry out for mercy
as death bites you,
and your conscience
seizes and gnaws at you.
And yet no one remembers this
until death has him in her maw.

Gardeiz dont vos venistes
Et ou vous revandroiz
Diex ne fait nelui tort
Nest nuns juges si droiz
Il est sires de loiz
Et cest maitres de droiz
Touz jors le trovereiz
Droit juge en toz endroiz

Look where you came from
and to where you will return.
God does wrong to no one.
There is no judge who is as just.
He is the lord of laws
and the master of justice.
Every day and everywhere
you will find Him to be a fair judge.

Li besoins est venuz
Quil a mestier damis
Il ne quiert que le cuer
De quanque en vos a mis
Qui le cuer li aura
Et donei et promis
[58v] De resouvoir son reigne
Ciert mult bien entremis

The time has come
when He will need friends.
Despite how much He has given you,
He seeks only your heart.
Whoever gives and
promises Him his heart,
[58v] will be well placed
to inherit His kingdom.

Li mauvais demorront
Nes convient pas eslire
Et cil sunt hui mauvais
Il seront demain pire
De jour en jour iront

The wicked ones will stay behind.
They should not be chosen;
if they are bad today,
they will be worse tomorrow.
Day after day, they will go from

120. The poet is criticizing negligent Christians who come up with excuses to avoid going to church, in this case the fear that because the building is not complete it could fall down, injuring or killing those inside. See Zink, *Rutebeuf*, 890n1.

121. A reference to the forest of Fontainebleau, which was well known as a place to hunt stag, especially among vavassors and bachelors, that is, among younger knights and men at arms. See Zink, *Rutebeuf*, 890n2.

de roiaume en empire
Se nos nes retrouvons
Si nen ferons que rire

kingdom to empire.[122]
If we do not retrieve them,
all we can do is ridicule them.

Li rois qui les trois rois
en belleem conduit
Conduie touz croisiez
Qui a mouvoir sunt duit
Quosteir au soudant puissant
et joie et deduit
Si que bonnes en soient
Et notes et conduit

May the King, who led
the three kings to Bethlehem,
compel all crusaders
who are set to embark
so they may deprive
the sultan of joy and pleasure,
and so that good music and
song may come of it.[123]

Explicit.

The End

122. The verb *empirer* means "to get worse." This is a play on words, suggesting that those who do not answer God's call are going from bad to worse.

123. Like the *serventois*, the *conduit* is also a poetic genre. Here too, the poet finds a single word that evokes both the act of crusade and its role in providing material for poets.

The Disputation between the Crusader and the Noncrusader

La desputizons dou croisie et dou descroizie (10r–11v)

Like the "Diz de la voie de Tunes," the "Desputizons" was composed in the period between March 25, 1267, the year in which Louis IX, together with his sons—Jean Tristan, count of Nevers; Pierre, count of Alençon; and Philip the future king—took his second crusade vow, and March 1270, when the king and his entourage departed for the southern port of Aigues-Mortes. Most likely Rutebeuf wrote closer to the earlier date as internal references to the extreme proximity of "the enemies" to Acre (so close they could shoot their arrows into the city) suggest that he had heard news of the attack on the city by Mamluk forces under the command of Sultan Baybars on May 2, 1267. If the allusion to the feast of Saint Remy in the first line is taken literally, the poem could be dated to just after October 1 (the feast of Saint Remy), 1267.[124] *The debate of the title may also allude to the debates that ensued, albeit privately within court circles, concerning the objective of the crusade expedition itself. Should a crusade return to Syria or Egypt, or go to Tunis as a strategic objective? Pushed by Mongol advances to the east, Baybars and his forces menaced the last remaining French strongholds on the Syrian coast, principally Acre and Jaffa, while the emir of Tunis, Al-Mustansir, continued to try to thwart the efforts of Charles of Anjou and his attempted dominance of Sicily and the western Mediterranean. As Michael Lower has shown, the choice of Tunis was complicated and probably overly optimistic and ambitious. Indeed, in August 1270, the king and many in his retinue died from disease on the Tunisian beach before any real military action was taken. The debate of the poem may have mirrored the debate over a crusade destination that must have occupied Louis IX and his court for much of the ensuing period between 1268 and 1270 as the political, religious, and diplomatic situation in the Mediterranean continued to be negotiated among the leading powers, Angevin, Mamluk, Hafsid, and Aragonese.*[125]

124. Zink, *Rutebeuf*, 895; Bastin and Faral, *Onze poèmes*, 84.

125. See Lower, "Louis IX, Charles of Anjou, and the Tunis Crusade of 1270,"; and Lower, *The Tunis Crusade*, 71–99.

Ci coumence la desputizons dou croisie et dou descroizie

[10r] Lautrier entour
la Saint Remei
Chevauchoie
por mon afaire
Pencix car trop sunt agrami
La gent dont Diex at plus a faire
Cil dAcre qui nont nul ami
Ce puet on bien por voir retraire
Et sont si pres lor anemi
Qua eux pueent lancier et traire

Tant fui pancis a ceste choze
Que je desvoiai de ma voie
Com cil qua li meismes choze
Por le penceir que gi avoie
Une maison fort et bien cloze
Trouvai dont je riens ne savoie
Et cestoit la dedens encloze
Une gent que je demandoie

Chevaliers i avoit teiz quatre
Qui bien seivent parleir fransois
Soupei orent si vont esbatre
En un vergier deleiz le bois
Ge ne me voulz sor eux embatre
Que ce me dist · uns hom cortois
Teiz cuide compaignie esbatre
Qui la toust cest or sans gabois

Li dui laissent parleir les deux
Et je les pris a escouteir
Qui leiz la haie fui touz seux
Si descent por moi acouteir
Si distrent entre gas et geux
Teiz moz con vos morreiz conteir
Siecles i fut nomeiz et Deus
De ce pristrent a desputeir

Li uns deux avoit la croix prise
Li autres ne la voloit prendre
Or estoit de ce lor emprise
Que li croiziez voloit aprendre

Here Begins the Disputation between the Crusader and the Noncrusader

[10r] The other day, around
the feast of Saint Remy,
I was riding along,
minding my own business,
troubled, because those for whom God has
the greatest task are in deep distress:
the people of Acre are friendless
—this is easily proved—
and their enemies are so close
they can draw their bows and shoot at them.

I was so deep in thought about this matter
that I lost my way,
like someone quarreling with himself
over the thoughts that were on my mind.
Then I came upon a house,
tightly locked up,
about which I knew nothing, and there inside
were the sort of people whom I was seeking.

There were four knights there,
who knew how to speak French well.[126]
Having dined, they were off to amuse themselves
in an orchard near the woods.
I did not want to intrude upon them,
for a courtly man once said to me:
"He who thinks he is delighting the crowd
is the one who ruins the fun." Now that's no joke.

Two of them allowed the other two to speak,
and I, all alone next to the hedge,
started to listen to them.
Then I dismounted to get closer.
Between jokes and pleasantries, they exchanged
these words that you will hear me say.
They spoke of the world, and God;
this was the subject they began to debate.

One of the two had taken the cross;
the other did not want to take it.
This was the topic of their debate,
for the crusader wanted to instruct

126. See chapter 4 of the commentary for more information about French speakers of this class, that is, those who are learned and know how to speak rightly accented and correct French.

A celui qui pas ne desprise

La croix ne la main ni vuet tendre
Quil la preist par sa maitrize
Ce ces sans ce puet tant estendre

the other one—who, although he did not disdain the cross
did not want to take it in hand—
to accept it on account of his expertise;
that is, if his meaning could be grasped.

Dit li croisiez premierement
Entens a moi biaux dolz amis
Tu seiz moult bien entierement
Que Diex en toi le san a mis
Dont tu connois apertement
Bien de mal amis danemis
Se tu en euvres sagement
Tes loiers ten est promis

The crusader spoke first:
"Listen to me, dear, sweet friend.
You know very well
that God has given you good sense,
with which you distinguish clearly
good from evil, and friends from enemies.
If you employ it wisely,
your reward is promised to you.

Tu voiz et parsois et entens
Le meschief de la Sainte Terre
Por quest de proesse vantans
Qui le leu Dieu lait en teil guerre
Suns hom pooit vivre cent ans
Ne puet il tant doneur conquerre
Com se il est bien repentans
Daleir le Sepuchre requerre

You see and perceive and understand
the suffering of the Holy Land.
How is it that a man, who leaves God's land
in such a state of war, can boast of prowess?
If a man could live a hundred years,
he could not gain as much honor
as he would if he were to go, truly repentant, to
reconquer the Sepulcher."

Dit li autres jentens moult bien
Por quoi vos dites teiz paroles
Vos me sermoneiz que le mien

Doingne au coc et puis si men vole
Mes enfans garderont li chien
Qui demorront en la parole (pailliole)[127]
Hon dit ce que tu tiens si tien
Ci at boen mot de bone escole

The other one said. "I understand very well
why you say these things.
You are preaching to me that I should hand over all I have
to the rooster and then fly the coop.
The dogs will look after my children,
who will be left to live in the straw.[128]
As they say, 'hold on to what you have.'
These are some good and wise words.

[10v] Cuidiez vos or que la croix preingne
Et que je men voize outre meir
Et que les. c. soudees deingne
Por. xl. cens reclameir
Je ne cuit pas que Deux enseingne
Que hom le doie ainsi semeir
Qui ainsi senme pou i veigne

Car hom le devroit asomeir

[10v] Do you think that I will now take the cross
and set off overseas,
and that I will give up 100 sous in rent
and then ask for only 40 in return?
I do not think that God teaches
that a man must sow his seeds like this.
Anyone who plants in this way had better hide his face,
since he will deserve what he gets."

127. Faral and Bastin supply *pailliole* based on the version in KBR, MS 9411–9426, fols. 24r–25v, Bastin and Faral, *Oeuvres complètes*, 472. See note 128 below. *Parole* is clearly an error, so we have translated accordingly.

128. See above, note 127, for choice of straw, *pailliole*, rather than speech, *parole*.

Tu naquiz de ta mere nuz
Dit li croisiez cest choze aperte
Or iez juqua cet tens venuz
Que ta chars est bien recoverte
Quest Dieus ne quest lors devenuz
Qua cent dobles rent la deserte
Bien iert por mescheanz tenuz
Qui ferat si vilainne perde

"You were born naked from your mother,"
said the crusader: "that is clear.
Now you have reached a point
where your flesh is well covered.
What is God for you now,
He who repays you a hundredfold?
Anyone would be seen as truly unlucky
who had suffered such a humiliating loss.

Hom puet or paradix avoir
Ligierement Diex en ait loux
Asseiz plus, ce poeiz savoir

One can easily get to paradise now,
praise be to God!
You should know, the price was much higher when

Lacheta sainz Piere et sainz Poulz
Qui de si precieux avoir
Com furent la teste et li coux
Laquistrent ce teneiz a voir
Icist dui firent. ii. biaux coux

Saint Peter and Saint Paul purchased it,
for they obtained it for something as precious
as their heads and necks;
believe me! Those two men
made two great coups!"[129]

Dit cil qui de croizier na cure
Je voi merveilles dune gent
Qui asseiz sueffrent poinne dure
En amasseir. i. pou dargent
Puis vont a Roume ou en Esture
Ou vont autre voie enchergent
Tant vont cerchant bone aventure
Quil nont baesse ne sergent

The one who did not care about crusading said:
"I marvel at people
who go to such great pains
to gather up a little money,
and then go off to Rome or to Asturias,[130]
or take up other routes.
They are so intent on great adventure
that they take along neither maid nor servant.

Hom puet moult bien en cet payx
Gaiaignier Dieu cens grant damage
Vos ireiz outre mer layʼs
Qua folie aveiz fait homage
Je di que il est foux naÿx
Qui se mest en autrui servage
Quant Dieu puet gaaignier saÿx
Et vivre de son heritage

One can certainly reach God
right here in this country, without great suffering.
You go there to Outremer
because you have sworn homage to folly.
I say he is a born fool who
places himself in servitude to another,
when he can reach God from here
and live off his inheritance."[131]

129. The double entendre of ".ii. biaux coux" is "two beautiful necks" and "two lovely feats." Zink suggests that there is also an echo of the *coups* of a game of dice here, Zink, *Rutebeuf*, 903n1. Likewise, *coux* also echoes the French *coup*, that is, to cut or offer a blow of an axe, referencing perhaps the cutting off of a head. Here therefore *beaux coux* or *beau coup* could also refer to beautiful cuts that render them martyrs.

130. This is meant to evoke the pilgrimage route to Santiago de Compostela, in Spain.

131. The meaning is surely deliberately ambiguous here since "his" inheritance may refer to the material inheritance of the noncrusader, or to the legacy left to man by God. This would capture both laymen and clergy who stay behind and do nothing. See v. 223 of "La nouvele complainte" about clergy living well off the patrimony of the Crucified One.

Tu dis si grant abusion
Que nus ne la porroit descrire
Qui wes sans tribulacion
Gaaignier Dieu por ton biau rire
Dont orent fole entencion

Li saint qui soffrirent martyre
Por venir a redempcion
Tu diz ce que nuns ne doit dire

"You are talking such complete nonsense
that no one could even describe it,
you who wish, without any hardship,
to reach God, relying on your pretty face.
So then, did the saints who suffered martyrdom,
have a foolish plan
for obtaining their redemption?
You are saying things no one ought to say.

Ancor nest pas digne la poingne
Que nuns hom puisse soutenir
A ce qua la joie sovrainne
Puisse ne ne doie venir
Por ce se rendent tuit cil moinne
Qua teil joie puissent venir
Hom ne doit pas douteir essoinne
Con ait pour Dieu juquau fenir

Such as that there is no pain
that a man might endure
that would be worthy enough
to earn him sovereign joy.[132]
This is why all these men become monks,
so that they may reach such joy.
One should not fear the hardships
that we must take on for God up until the end."

Sire qui des croix sermoneiz
Resoffreiz moi que je deslas
Sermoneiz ces hauz coroneiz
Ces grans doiens et ces prelaz
Cui Diex est toz abandoneiz
Et dou siecle toz li solaz
Ciz geux est trop mal ordeneiz
Que toz jors nos meteiz es laz

"Sir, you who are sermonizing about crosses,
you should let me off the hook.
Preach to the crowned ones,[133]
the grand doyens and the prelates,
to whom God gives everything
and who have all the comforts of this world.
This contest is rigged,[134]
and every day you ensnare us in your net.

Clerc et prelat doivent vengier
La honte Dieu quil ont ces rentes
Il ont a boivre et a mangier
Si ne lor chaut cil pluet ou vente
Siecles est touz en lor dangier
Cil vont a Dieu par teile sente
[11r] Fol sunt cil la welent changier
Car cest de toutes la plus gente

Clerics and prelates must avenge
God's dishonor, since they receive his revenues.
They have plenty to eat and drink,
they do not care whether it is rainy or windy.
The world is completely under their sway.
If they are taking this path toward God,
[11r] then they are crazy if they want to change course,
for this one is the most pleasant of them all."

132. This refutation of the excuse that even the most extreme pain and suffering would not be enough to win God's grace also appears in Rutebeuf's "Le Dit des règles," vv. 61–64. The passage is also a paraphrase of Paul's Letter to the Romans 8:18, which states that present suffering is not worthy of comparison with future glory to be revealed by God. See Zink, *Rutebeuf*, 907n1.

133. Here again is a double entendre that allows the poet to speak to the laity and the clergy at the same time, referring both to those who wear royal crowns as well as those belonging to religious orders, who are tonsured.

134. *Geux* means "game," but this verse also alludes to the genre of medieval lyric poetry known as the *jeu-parti*, a two-part debate in verse between two poets.

Laisse clers et prelaz esteir
Et te pren garde au roi de France
Qui por paradix conquesteir
Vuet metre le cors en balance
Et ces enfans a Dieu presteir
Li pres nest pas en aesmance
Tu voiz quil se vuet apresteir
Et faire ce dont a toi tance

"Set aside the clerics and prelates
and consider the king of France,
who in order to conquer paradise,
wishes to place his own body in the balance
and lend his children to God.
The value of that loan cannot be estimated.
You see that he wishes to prepare himself
and do exactly what I am arguing with you about.

Moult a or meillor demoreir
Li rois el roiaume que nos
Qui de son cors wet honoreir
Celui que por seignor tenons
Quen crois se laissa devoreir

The king has much better reasons to stay
here in the kingdom than we do, and yet
he wishes to honor with his own body Him
whom we hold to be our Lord,
who, on the cross, allowed Himself to be devoured.

Ce de lui servir ne penons
Helas trop avrons a ploreir
Que trop fole vie menons

If we do not suffer to serve Him,
alas, we will have much to lament,
for the lives we lead are far too foolish."

Je wel entre mes voisins estre
Et moi deduire et solacier
Vos ireiz outre la meir peistre

"I want to be among my neighbors
and to have fun and take pleasure in life.
You will go and find [spiritual] nourishment beyond the sea

Qui poeiz grant fais embracier
Dites le soudant vostre meistre
Que je pri pou son menacier
Cil vient desa mal me vit neistre
Mais lai ne lirai pas chacier

since you can bear these great burdens.
Tell your master the sultan
that I take little heed of his threats.
If he comes here, I will see that he pays,
but I will not go there to hunt him down.

Je ne faz nul tort a nul home
Nuns hom ne fait de moi clamour
Je cuiche tost et tien grant soume
Et tieng mes voisins a amour
Si croi par saint Pierre de Roume
Quil me vaut miex que je demour
Que de lautrui porter grant soume
Dont je seroie en grant cremour

I am not doing anyone any harm;
no one is complaining about me.
I go to bed early and sleep well,
and I have love for my neighbors.
And so I believe, by Saint Peter of Rome,
that it is better for me to stay here
than to carry someone else's heavy load,
a task that would cause me great fear."

Desai bees a aise vivre
Seiz tu se tu vivras asseiz
Di moi ce tu ceiz en queil livre
Certains vivres soit compasseiz
Manjue et boif et si ten yvre
Que mauvais est de pou lasseiz
Tuit sont. i. saches a delivre
Et vie doume et oez quasseiz

"And so, you aspire to live here in comfort?
Do you know whether you will live a long time?
Tell me if you know in what book
certain lives are measured?
Eat and drink, and then get drunk,
for a poor wretch is soon exhausted.
Know this well: a man's life and broken eggs
are one and the same.

Laz ti dolant la mors te chace
Qui tost tavra lassei et pris
Desus ta teste tient sa mace
Viex et jones prent a un pris

Alas, you poor soul, Death is chasing you
and soon she will have ensnared and trapped you.
Death wields her club above your head.
Young and old, she takes for the same price.

Tantost at fait de pie eschace
Et tu as tant vers Dieu mespris
Au moins enxui. i. pou la trace
Par quoi li boen ont loz et pris

She has quickly turned a foot into a peg leg.
And you! You have so much contempt for God.
Try to follow, at least a little bit, the path
by which good men have earned praise
and esteem."

Sire croiziez merveilles voi
Moult vont outre meir gent menue
Sage large de grant aroi
De bien metable convenue
Et bien i font si com je croi
Dont larme est por meilleur tenue
Si ne valent ne ce ne quoi
Quant ce vient a la revenue

"Lord crusader, I marvel at what I see!
Many humble people are going beyond the sea.
They are a wise, generous, upstanding,
and trustworthy company,
and they are doing some good there, I think,
for which their souls are held in higher regard.
Yet they are worth nothing at all
when it comes to their return.

Se Diex est nule part el monde
Il est en France cet sens doute
Ne cuidiez pas quil se reponde
Entre gent qui ne lainment goute
Et vostre meir est si parfonde
Quil est bien droiz que la redoute
Jaing mieux fontainne qui soronde
Que quen estei sesgoute

If God is anywhere in the world,
he is in France, without a doubt.
Do not think he is hiding over there
among people who do not love him one bit.
And your sea is so deep
that it is quite right that I fear it.
I prefer a fountain that runs over
to one that runs dry in the summertime."

Tu ne redoutes pas la mort
Si seiz que morir te couvient
Et tu diz que la mers tamort
Si faite folie dont vient
[11v] La mauvaistiez quen toi samort
Te tient a lostel se devient
Que feras se la mors te mort
Que ne ceiz que li tenz deviant

"You do not fear death,
yet you know you will have to die.
And you say that the sea frightens you?
Where does such foolishness come from?
[11v] The villainy that takes hold of you
is what keeps you at home, perhaps?
What will you do if death bites you,
since you do not know what the future holds?

Li mauvais desa demorront
Que ja nuns boens ni demorra
Com vaches en lor liz morront
Buer iert neiz qui delai morra

The wretches will remain here—
and no good man will be left—
like cows they will die in their beds;
he who dies over there was born under a
lucky star.

Jamais recovreir ne porront
Fasse chacuns mieux quil porrat
Lor peresce en la fin plorront
Et sil muerent nuns nes plorra

They will never revive;
let each man try as he might.
They will end up lamenting their laziness,
and if they die, no one will cry for them.

Ausi com par ci le me taille
Cuides foir denfer la flame
Et acroire et metre a la taille
Et faire de la char ta dame
A moi ne chaut coument quil aille
Mais que li cors puist sauver lame
Ne de prison ne de bataille
Ne de laissier enfans ne fame

While others do the work for you,
you imagine you will flee the fires of hell,
buying on credit, living in debt,
and making your flesh your mistress.
As long as I can use my body to save my soul,
I don't care how it plays out,
whether I am taken prisoner or face battle or
leave my wife and children behind."

Biaux sire chiers que que dit aie
Vos maveiz vaincu et matei
A vos macort a vos mapaie
Que vos ne maveiz pas flatei
La croix preing sans nule delaie
Si doing a Dieu cors et chatei

Car qui faudra a cele paie
Mauvaisement avra gratei

En non dou haut Roi glorieux
Qui de sa fille fist sa meire
Qui par son sanc esprecieux
Nos osta de la mort ameire
Sui de moi croizier curieux
Por venir a la joie cleire
Car qui a same est oblieux
Bien est raisons quil le compeire

Explicit

"Dear sir, whatever I was able to say,
checkmate, you have bested me!
I agree and make my peace with you,
for you did not sugarcoat things for me.
I am taking the cross without further delay,
and thus give my body and my possessions
to God.
For the one who defaults on this payment
will have made a bad deal.

In the name of the great glorious King
who made of His daughter His mother,
who by His precious blood
delivered us from a bitter death,
I long to go on crusade
to attain such radiant joy.
For if a person forgets his soul,
it is only right that he pay the price."

The End

The New Complaint of Outremer

La nouvele complainte doutremeir (54r–56v)

In this late poem, Rutebeuf returns once again to the tone of a lament, or complaint, as the title evokes (see figure 32). Taking the form of a verse sermon, a harangue, and call to action, the poet begins the second stanza with a quotation, as sermons would have, from Saint Paul. This new complaint of Outremer articulates Rutebeuf's extreme frustration with courtly life, the distracted nobility, and bourgeois townsmen gone soft and lazy. He critiques their ongoing procrastination while the Holy Land hangs in the balance. As he sees it, Acre is in such a fragile state that it will be lost within the year. But which year? The poem was composed sometime between June 24, 1274, when the great barons of France took the cross (including Philip III, the new king of France; the Duke of Burgundy; and the king's son, Robert II of Béthune who held the title to Flanders and Nevers), and June 24, 1277, when they planned to depart. In the intervening three years, a robust papal correspondence called vowed crusaders to action, condemned the sins of usury, and offered indulgences to clerics and laymen who would take up the cross. The mention of William of Beaujeu, the newly elected master of the Temple, and the references to holding Acre and the Temple suggest that it was composed after June 1275 when William departed France for the East.[135] The poet closes by presenting an offer of salvation in Christian terms, recalling the benefits of sacrifice and martyrdom for those who are brave and worthy: "No one reaches paradise if he does not suffer pain." Echoing the sermon genre he imitates, he closes with a prayer, offering us a sober poetic voice rather than the more sarcastic persona he presents in his satirical poems. Rutebeuf's frustrations were entirely justified, as no crusade to the East ever departed from France during the reign of Philip III; rather the new king's interests—political and diplomatic—turned south, to a crusade against Aragon.[136]

135. Zink, *Rutebeuf*, 975; Bastin and Faral, *Onze poèmes*, 111–17.

136. Joseph R. Strayer, "The Crusade against Aragon," *Speculum* 28 (1953): 102–13, repr. Strayer, *Medieval Statecraft and the Perspectives of History* (Princeton, NJ: Princeton University Press, 1971), 107–21.

Ci en coumence la nouvele complainte doutremeir

Here begins the New Complaint of Outremer

[54r] Pour lanui et por le damage

Que je voi· en lumain linage·
Mestuet mon pencei descovrir
En sospirant mestuet ovrir
La bouche · por mon voloir dire.
Com hom corrouciez et plains dire
Quant je pens · ala sainte terre
Que picheour doient requerre
Ainz quil aient pascei jonesce
Et jes voi entreir en viellesce
Et pius aleir de vie a mort
Et pou envoi qui sen amort
A empanrre la sainte voie
Ne faire par quoi diex les voie·

Sen sui iriez par charitei
Car sains poulz dist par veritei
Tuit sons ·i· cors en Jhesucrit
Dont je vos monstre par lescrit
Que li uns est · membres de lautre[137]
Et nos sons ausi com li viautre
Qui se combatent · por · i · os
Plus en deisse · mais je noz ·

Vos qui aveiz sans et savoir
Entendre vos fais et savoir
Que de dieu sunt bien averies
Les paroles · des prophecies ·
En crois morut por noz mesfais
Que nos et autres · avons fais ·
Ne morra plus ce est la voire
Or poons sor noz piauz a croire
Voirs est que David nos recorde
Diex est plains de misericorde ·
Mais veiz ci trop grant restrainture
Il est juges plains de droiture ·
Il est juges fors et poissans
Et sages et bien connoissans ·
Juges que on ne puet plaissier
Ne hom ne peut sa cort laissier
Fors si fors fox est qui cesforce
A ce que il vainque sa force

Poissans que riens ne li eschape
Por quoi quil at tot soz sa chape

[54r] On account of the suffering and the wretchedness

that I see in humankind,
I must reveal my thoughts.
Sighing, I must open
my mouth to say what I want to say
as an angry man, full of wrath.
When I think of the Holy Land
that sinners ought to retake
before they move beyond their youth,
and I see them enter into old age,
and then go from life to death,
and I see so few people commit themselves
to undertake the holy journey,
and do nothing to attract approval in the eyes of God,

my sense of charity fills me with anger.
Because Saint Paul says, in truth,
“We are all one body in Jesus Christ.”
So I demonstrate to you through Scripture
that each one of us is a part of the other.
And yet we are also like boarhounds
who fight over a bone.
I would say more, but I dare not.

You who have sense and wisdom,
I will have you know and understand
that the words of the prophecies
are rendered true by God:
He died on the cross for the
misdeeds that we and others have committed.
He will not die again, that is for sure.
Now it is we who mortgage our hides.
It is true what David says to us:
God is full of mercy,
but take note, there is a major restriction.
He is a judge full of righteousness.
He is a judge, strong and powerful,
and wise and very learned.
He is a judge whom no one can bend,
nor can any man escape His court.
He is strong, so strong
that anyone who tries to best his strength is crazy.

He is so powerful that nothing escapes Him.
Why? Because He has everything under His mantle:

137. Romans 12:5.

Sages con non puet desovoir
Se peut chacuns aparsovoir
Connoissans quil connoist la choze
Avant que li hons la propoze
Qui doit aleir devent teil juge
Sens troveir recet ne refuge
Cil at tort paour doit avoir
Cil a en lui sans ne savoir

Prince baron tournoieur
Et vos autre sejorneour
Qui teneiz a aise le cors
Quant larme serat mise fors
Queil porra elle osteil prendre
Sauriiez le me vos aprendre
Je ne le sai pas diex le sache
Mais trop me plaing de votre outrage
Quant vos ne penceiz a la fin
Et au pelerinage fin
Qui larme pecheresse afine
Si qua dieu la rent pure et fine

Prince premier qui ne saveiz
[54v] Combien de terme vos aveiz
A vivre en ceste morteil vie
Que naveiz vos · de lautre envie
Qui cens fin est por joie faire
Que nentendeiz a votre afaire
Tant com de vie · aveiz espace
Natendeiz pas que la mors face
De larme et dou cors desevrance
Ci auroit trop dure atendance
Car li termes vient durement
Que dieux tanrra son jugement
Quant li plus juste dadam nei

Auront paour destre dampnei
Ange et archange trembleront
Les laces armes que feront
Queil part ce porront elz repondre
Qua dieu nes estuisse responder
Quant il at le monde en sa main
Et nos navons point de demain.

wise, for no one is able to deceive Him,
as anyone can see;
knowledgeable, for He understands the case
before a man has even stated it.
Whoever should go before such a judge,
finding neither refuge nor place to hide,
should be afraid if he is in the wrong,
if he has any common sense.

Princes, barons, tourneyers,
and you other layabouts,
who tend to the comforts of your body,
when your soul is cast out
what refuge will it take?
Can you tell me that?
I don't know; God knows.
But I am complaining too much of your excesses
while you think neither of your own demise,
nor of the ultimate pilgrimage[138]
that refines the sinful soul,
so that it is rendered to God, more pure and perfect.

First of all, princes, you who do not know
[54v] how much time you have
to live in this mortal life,
why do you not desire the other life
which is joy without end?
Why do you not attend to your affairs
while you still have time in your life?
Do not wait until death severs
your soul from your body.
There will be terrible anticipation
because the painful moment will come
when God renders his judgment.
When the most righteous, who were born of Adam,

are afraid of being damned,
and the angels and archangels tremble,
what will the wretched souls do?
Where can they hide
so they will not have to answer to God
when He has the world in His hand
and we have no tomorrow?

138. In the second part of this stanza Rutebeuf plays with the term *fin* or end. Here the "pelerinage fin" could be a reference both to the crusade's end or final destination, its terminus in Acre and Jerusalem, but also to the end of one's pilgrimage on earth and thus a final end, which is death.

Rois de France rois dAingleterre
Quen jonesce deveiz conquerre
Loneur dou cors le preu de lame

King of France, King of England,[139]
while you are young, you ought to win
honor for your body and advantage for your soul,

Ains que li cors soit soz la lame
Sans espairgnier cors et avoir
Sor voleiz · paradix avoir
Si secoreiz la Terre sainte
Qui est perdue a seste empainte
Qui na pas un an de recours
Sen lan meimes na secours
Et cele est a voz tenz perdue
A cui tens ert ele rendue

before your body lies beneath your tombstone;
you must offer up your body and your wealth
if you truly wish to attain paradise.
Go rescue the Holy Land,
which was lost in this[140] assault
and which has no more than a year left
if no aid is sent this year.
And if it is lost in your time,
in whose time will it be regained?

Rois de Sezile par la grace
de dieu qui vos dona espace
de conquerre · Puille et Cezille
Remembre vos de lEwangile
Qui dist qui ne lait peire et meire
Fame et enfans et suers et freires
Possessions et manandie
Quil na pas · avec li partie

King of Sicily, by the
grace of God, who gave you the opportunity
to conquer Apulia and Sicily,
remember the Gospel, which says that
he who does not leave behind father and mother,
wife and children, sisters and brothers,
possessions and domains,
has no share in His inheritance.[141]

Baron quaveiz vos en pancei
Seront jamais par vos tensei
Cil dAcre qui sunt en balance
Et de secorre en esperance
Cuens de Flandres dus de Bergoingne
Cuens de Nevers con grant vergoinge
De perdre la Terre absolue
Qui a voz tenz nos iert tolue
Et vos autre baron encemble
Quen dites vos que il vos cemble
Saveiz vos honte si aperte
Com de soffrir si laide perde

Barons, what are your intentions?
Will you ever go to the defense of
those in Acre, whose lives hang in the balance
and who are hoping for succor?
Count of Flanders, Duke of Burgundy,
Count of Nevers, what a great shame
to lose the Holy Land,
which was taken from us in your time.
And all you other barons,
what do you say? How does it look to you?
Can you think of a more overt disgrace
than the suffering of such a hideous loss?

Tournoieur vos qui aleiz
En yver · et vos enjaleiz
Querre places a tournoier
Vos ne poeiz mieux foloier
Vos despandeiz et sens raison
Votre tens et votre saison

Tourneyers, you who go
in winter, and freeze yourselves
seeking places to tourney,[142]
you could not commit a greater folly.
You thoughtlessly waste
your time, your opportunity,[143]

139. The king of France is Philip III (b. 1245; r. 1270–85), and the king of England is Edward I (1239–1307). Both were in their thirties.

140. It is unclear which campaign is being referenced here.

141. From Matthew 19:29.

142. This refers to locations in which to hold a tournament.

143. Here "votre saison," which we interpret as one's moment to take action, could refer both to the season of one's life, that is, one's age, or to the ideal season of the year when one might go on campaign, typically in the summer.

Et le votre et lautrui entasche
Le noiel laissiez por lescraffe
Et paradix · pour vainne gloire
Avoir deussiez · en memoire
Monseigneur Joffroi de Sergines
Qui fu tant boens et fu tant dignes
Quen paradix est coroneiz
Com sages et bien ordeneiz
Et le conte Huede de Nevers
Dont hom ne puet chanson ne vers
Dire se boen non et loiaul
Et bien loei en court roiaul
A ceux deussiez panrre essample
[55r] Et Acres secorre et le Temple

your money and that of others, all at once.
You abandon the nut in favor of its shell,
and likewise, paradise in favor of vainglory.
You ought to remember
my lord Geoffrey of Sergines,
who was so good and so worthy,
that he is crowned in paradise
among the wise and steadfast.
And Count Eudes of Nevers,
about whom no man can recite songs or verses
unless they are of his goodness, loyalty,
and esteem in the royal court.
You ought to follow the examples of these men
[55r] and rescue Acre and the Temple.

Jone escuier au poil volage
Trop me plaing de votre folage
Qua nul bien faire · nentendeiz
Ne de rien ne vous amendeiz
Si fustes filz a mains preudoume
Teiz com jes vi je les vos nome
Et vos estes muzart et nice
Que nentendeiz a votre office
De veoir preudoume aveiz honte
Vostre esprevier sunt trop plus donte
Que vos niestes cest veriteiz
Car teil i a quant le geteiz
Seur le poing aporte la loe
Honiz soit · qui de lui se loe
Se nest Diex ne vostre pays
Li plus sages est foux nayx

Downy-faced young squire,
I greatly lament your folly,
for you have no plans to do good
and no intention of mending your ways.
Yet you are the sons of great *prudhommes*,
(I know them and name them as such)
and you are lazy and half-witted,
and you do not concern yourself with your duties.
You are ashamed to encounter a *prudhomme*.
Your sparrowhawks are better trained
than you are, that is true.
For there are those that, when you release them,
bring a lark back to your hand.
Shame on him who praises you,
since neither God nor your country does so.
The wisest among you is a true fool.

Quant vos deveiz aucun bien faire
Qua aucun bien vos doie traire
Si le faites tout autrement
Car vos toleiz vilainnement
Povres puceles lor honeurs
Quant ne pueent avoir seigneurs
Lors si deviennent · dou grant nombre
Cest. i. pechiez qui vos encombre
Voz povres voizins soz marchiez
Ausi bien at · leans marchiez
Vendre voz bleiz et votre aumaille
Com cele autre · povre pietaille
Toute gentilesce effaciez ·
Il ne vous chaut que vous faciez
Tant que viellesce vos efface
Que ridee vos est la face
Que vos iestes viel et chenu
Por ce quil vos seroit tenu

When you ought to do something good
that would be to your benefit,
you do the complete opposite.
For you vilely take the
honor of poor young girls.
Then, they can no longer have honorable men
and they become one of the many.
That is but one of the sins that weighs upon you.
You trample upon your poor neighbors:
you even go to the market
to sell your wheat and livestock
alongside these other poor wretches.
You wipe away all *gentillesse*.
You do not care about what you do
until old age renders you invisible,
when your face is wrinkled and
you are old and grey-haired.
Because of this, people will say you are

A Gilemeir dou parentei
Non pas par vostre volentei
Sestes chevalier leiz la couche
Que vous douteiz. i. poi reproche
Mais se vous amissiez honeur
Et doutissiez la deshoneur
Et amissiez votre lignage
Vous fussiez et proudome et sage
Quant vostre tenz aveiz vescu
Quainz paiens ne vit votre escu
Que deveiz demandeir celui
Qui sacrefice fist de lui
Je ne sais quoi se Diex me voie
Quant vos ne teneiz droite voie

of Gilemeir's lineage,[144]
which is something you would not want.
You were born into knighthood
and therefore, you have some fear of reproach.
But if you loved honor
and feared dishonor
and loved your lineage,
then you would be a wise man and a *prudhomme*.
When you have lived out your time and
no pagan[145] has ever seen your shield,
what might you ask of Him who
made a sacrifice of Himself?
With God as my witness, I do not know,
since you are not keeping to the right path.

Prelat clerc chevalier borjois
Qui trois semainnes por. i. mois
Laissiez aleir a votre guise
Sens servir Dieu et sainte Eglise
Dites saveiz vos en queil livre
Hom trueve combien hon doit vivre
Je ne sai je nou puis troveir
Mais je vos puis par droit proveir
Que quant li hons commence a nestre
En cest siecle a il pou a estre
Ne ne seit quant partir en doit
La riens qui plus certainne soit
Si est que mors nos corra seure
La mains certainne si est leure

Prelates, clerics, knights, bourgeois,
who let three weeks of a month
go by at your whim,
without serving God and the Holy Church,
tell me, do you know in which book
one finds how long a man will live?
I do not know, I cannot find it.
But I can rightly prove to you
that once a man is born
he has little time to be in this world.
He does not know when he will have to depart.
What is more certain
is that death will run us down.
Less certain is at what hour.

Prelat auz palefrois norrois
Qui bien saveiz par queil norrois?
Li filz dieu fu en la crois mis
Por confondre ces anemis
Vos sermoneiz aus gens menues
Et aus povres vielles chenues
Quelz soient plaines de droiture
[55v] Maugrei eulz · font ele penance
Queles ont sanz pain ·asse painne
Et si nont pas · la pance plainne ·

Prelates on your Norwegian palfreys,
you who know well by what barbaric deed
the son of God was put on the cross
to confound his enemies,
you sermonize to the little people
and the poor grey-haired old ladies
that they should be full of righteousness.
[55v] They do penance in spite of themselves
for, without bread, they do not have a full belly
and suffer greatly.

144. "Gilemeir" is said to be the uncle of Ganelon from the *Song of Roland*. See Zink, *Rutebeuf*, 986–87n1. For verses 169–71, there is some debate. Zink thinks this refers to Ganelon; others think Guinevere or a totally different interpretation is warranted. In the copy of the text owned and annotated by Edward Billings Ham, he notes next to Guilemeir that this is "comme une tromperie," that is, suggesting a play on words related to *guiler*, to trick or to fool, therefore suggesting that one is a trickster, a pretender, or dishonest. Ham's volume is in the collection of Caroline Smith.

145. The word "pagan" was often used to refer to Muslims in Old French epic poetry.

Naiez paour ·je ne di pas	Do not fear; I am not saying
Que vos meueiz isnele pas	that you should set out this minute
Por la sainte · terre deffendre	to defend the Holy Land.
Mais vos poeiz · entor vos prendre	But you can gather up plenty of
Asseiz de povres · gentilz homes	poor gentlemen who have
Qui ne mainnent soumiers ne soumes	neither beasts of burden nor burdens for them to carry,
Qui doient · et nont de quil paient	who owe, yet have nothing with which to pay,
Et lor enfant de fain semaient	while their children are fainting from hunger.
A cex doneiz · de vostre avoir	Donate your wealth to these people,
Dont par tens · porreiz pou avoir	for, in the end, you might have very little left,
Ces envoiez outre la meir	and send these people across the sea
Et vos faites · a Dieu ameir	and make yourselves loved by God.
Montreiz · par bouche et par example	Demonstrate by word and by example,
Que vos ameiz Dieu et le Temple	that you love God and the Temple.
Clerc · a aise · et bien sejornei	Comfortable, well-rested clerics,
Bien · vestu · et bien sejornei (conraei)[146]	well-dressed and well-tended,[148]
Dou patrimoinne · au Crucei	living off the patrimony of the Crucified One,
Je vos promet · e vos afi	I promise and assure you
Se vos failliez · Deu orendroit	that if you let God down now,
Quil vos faudra · au fort endroit	He will let you down at the crucial moment.
Vos sereiz · forjugie en court	You will be convicted at His court
Ou la riegle faut qui or court	where the rule that applies now is no longer in force:
Por ce te fais · que tu me faces	"I am doing this for you, so that you will do it for me,
Non pas por ce · que tu me haces	not so that you will hate me."
Diex vos fait bien · faites li donc	God does good for you, so give Him
De quoi (de cors) · de cuer et darme don[147]	the gift of your body, heart, and soul.[149]
Si fereiz que preu · et que sage	In doing so, you would behave decorously and wisely.
Or me dites · queil aventage	Tell me now, what good
Vos puet faire · vostres tresors	can your wealth bring to you
Quant larme iert · partie dou cors	when your soul has left your body?
Li executeur · le retiennent	The executors hold onto it
Ju qua tant qua lor fin reviennent	until the time of their deaths,
Chacuns son eage a son tour	each in his own turn.
Cest maniere · dexecutour	This is how it is with executors.

146. Bastin and Faral supply *conraei* rather than repeating *sejournei* based on the version in KBR, MS 9411–9426, fols. 33r–35r, Bastin and Faral, *Oeuvres complètes*, 504. See note 148 below regarding translation.

147. Bastin and Faral supply *de cors* rather than repeating *de quoi* based on the version in KBR, MS 9411–9426, fols. 33r–35r, Bastin and Faral, *Oeuvres complètes*, 504. See note 149 below regarding translation.

148. The doubling of *sejournei* was likely a scribal error. In our translation we chose a meaning closer to that of *conraei*, although all four descriptors in the couplet are related to comfortable living.

149. See note 146 above regarding the decision to translate using "body" based on *de cors* rather than *de quoi*.

Ou il avient par mecheance	When the time comes,
Quil en donent · por reparlance	they will give away
Xx. paire de solers · ou trente	twenty or thirty pairs of shoes,
Or est sauve · larme dolante	just for show, and then a wretched soul is saved.[150]
Chevaliers · de plaiz et daxises	You knights, who preside at the judicial court and assises,
Qui par vos faites vos justices	who render verdicts on your own behalf,
Sens jugement · aucunes fois	sometimes even without good judgment—
Tot i soit · sairemens · ou foiz	regardless of oaths or sworn testaments—
Cuidiez vos · toz jors · einsi faire	do you think you can always behave this way?
A un chief · vos covient il traire	Things will come to a head for you.[151]
Quant la teste est · bien avinee	When your head is full of wine
Au feu · deleiz la cheminee	by the fire, next to the hearth,
Si vos croiziez · sens sermoneir	that is when you take the cross without being preached to;
Donc verriez · grant coulz doneir	then you envision yourself
Seur le sozdant · et seur sa gent	striking the sultan and his people with powerful blows,
Forment les aleiz · damagent	and inflicting great damage upon them.
Quant vos · vos leveiz au matin	When you awake in the morning,
Saveiz changie vostre latin	then you change your tune,
Que gari sunt tuit li blecie	and all the wounded are healed
Et li abatu · redrecie	and those cut down are upright once more.
Li un vont au lievres chacier	Some will go hunting for hare,
Et li autre · vont porchacier	and the others will try to capture
Cil panront. i. mallart ou deux	a mallard or two, if they can,
Car de combatre nest pas geux	for making war is no game.
Par vos faites voz jugemens	You make your judgments for your own benefit,
Qui sera vostres dampnemens	which will be your damnation
Se li jugemens · nest loiaus	if the judgment is not loyal,
Boens · et honestes et feaus	good, honest, and faithful.
Qui plus vos done · si at droit	For you, whoever gives you the most is in the right.
Ce faites · que Diex ne voudroit	You are doing what God would not want.
Ainsi defineiz · vostre vie	This is how you are ending your life,
Et lors que li cors · se devie	and when the body becomes lifeless,
Si trueve larme · tant a faire	then the soul finds so much to do
[56r] Que je ne porroie · retraire	[56r] that I cannot even describe it.
Car Diex vos rent · la faucetei	God will repay your hypocrisy
Par jugement · car achatei	with judgment; since you have purchased
Aveiz enfer · et vos laveiz	hell, now you have it.
Car ceste choze · bien saveiz	In this matter, as you well know,

150. The poet is criticizing those who make only a paltry gift of alms in their wills for the remission of their sins, thinking it will suffice to save their souls. Similar criticisms appear elsewhere in Rutebeuf's polemical literature against the mendicants. See Zink, *Rutebeuf*, 77, 991.

151. A version of the following scenario of drunken promises appears in "La complainte dou conte Hue de Nevers," vv. 157–61.

Diex rent de tout · le guerredon	God renders payment for all,
Soit biens · soit maux · il en a don	whether good or bad; that is His gift.
Riche borjois · dautrui sustance	Bourgeois, you get rich off what others need to survive,
Qui faites Dieu · de vostre pance	and make a God of your belly,[152]
Li povre Dieu · chiez vos saunent	while God's poor are gathering at your house,
Qui de fain muerent · et geunent	dying of hunger and starvation,
Por atendre · vostre gragan	waiting for your scraps,
Dont il nont pas a grant lagan	which are not plentiful,
Et vos entendeiz · au mestier	and you go about your business,
Qui aux armes · neust mestier	which renders no service to souls.[153]
Vos saveiz · que morir convient	You know you have to die,
Mais je ne sai · cil vos souvient	but I do not know whether you recall
Que luevre ensuit · lome et la fame	that deeds follow both man and woman.[154]
Cil at bien fait · bien en a larme	He who has done good has goodness in his soul,
Et nos trovons bien en escrit	and we find this clearly in the scriptures:
Tout va fors lamour JhesuCrit	"Everything falls away except for the love of Jesus Christ."
Mais de ce · naveiz vos que faire	But you do not care about this.
Vos entendeiz · a autre afaire	You attend to other matters.
Je sai toute · vostre atendue	I know everything you are up to.
Dou bleis ameiz · la grant vendue	You like to close the big deal on your wheat,
Et chier vendre · de si au tans	and then sell it at a high price in installments
Seur lettre · seur plege · ou	by letter [of credit], by pledge,
seur · nans.	or collateral.
Vil acheteir et vendre chier	Buying low and selling high,
Et uzereir et gent trichier	charging usurious rates and cheating people,
Et faire · dun deable Deus	and making one devil into two,
Por ce · que enfers · est trop seux	because hell is too lonely.
Jusqua la mort · ne faut la guerre	This battle endures until death.
Et quant li cors · est mis en terre	And when the body is put in the ground
Et hon est · a losteil venuz	and people have returned home,
Ja puis nen iert · contes tenuz	from then on, no one will take any account.
Quant li enfant · sunt lor seigneur	When children become their own lords,
Veiz ci conquest · a grant honeur	behold their most valued pursuit:
Au bordel · ou en la taverne	who can steer himself to the brothel
Qui plus tost puet · plus ci governe	or the tavern the fastest?
Cil qui lor doit · si lor demande	He who is in their debt comes calling;
Paier covient ce com commande	one must pay for what one has ordered.
Teiz marchiez font · com vous eustes	They bargain the way you did
Quant en vostre autoritei fustes	when you were in charge.
Chacuns en prent · chacuns en oste	Each one takes some and each removes a little.
Enz osteiz pluee sen vont li oste	It rains in the house, and the tenant
Les terres demeurent en friche	leaves, the lands remain uncultivated,
Sen sunt li hom estrange riche	and the foreigners get rich off it.[155]

152. Philippians 3:19.

153. Note the double entendre of "aux armes" as "souls" or "arms" as military service.

154. Revelation 14:13.

155. This may be a reference to the mounting indebtedness of the crown and the aristocratic class to Italian lenders and the social anxiety that accompanied it.

Cil qui lor doit paier nes daingne
Ansois convient · que hon en daingne
Lune moitie · por lautre avoir
Veiz ci la fin · de vostre avoir
La fin de larme · est tote aperte
Bien est qui li rant · sa deserte
Maistre doutre meir et de France
Dou temple · par la Dieu poissance
Frere Guillaume de Biaugeu
Or poeiz veioir le biau geu
De quoi li siecles · seit servir
Il nont cure de Dieu servir
Por conquerre · sainz paradis
Com li preudome de ja diz
Godefroiz · Buemons · et Tancreiz
Ja niert lor ancres · a encreiz
En meir · por la neif rafreschir
De ce ce vuelent · il franchir
Ha bone gent Diex vos sequeure
Que de la mort ne saveiz leure
Recoumanciez · novele estoire
Car Jhesucriz · li rois de gloire
vos vuet avoir · et maugre votre
[56v] Sovaingne vos · qui li apostre
Norent pas · paradix por pou
Or vos remembre de saint Pou
Qui por deu ot ·copei la teste
Por noiant · nen fait hon pas feste
Et le saveiz bien · que sains peires
Et sains Andreuz ·qui fu ces freres
Furent por dieu ·en la coix mis
Por ce fu dieux·lor boens amis
Et li autre saint·ausiment
Que vos iroie · plus rimant
Nuns na paradix ·cil na painne

Por cest cil sages · qui san painne

Or prions au roi glorieux
Et a son chier fil · precieux
Et au saint esperit ·ensemble
En cui toute bonteiz ·sasemble
Et a la precieuze dame

He who owes them does not deign to pay them,
so it becomes necessary to give over
one half of it [the debt] to keep the other.
This is how your fortunes are lost.
The fate of your soul is clear;
indeed, someone will render it what it is due.
Master of the Temple in Outremer
and in France, by the power of God
Brother William of Beaujeu,[156]
now you can see the clever game
the world knows how to play.
They have no interest in serving God
to obtain holy paradise
like the *prudhommes* of old:
Godfrey, Bohemond, and Tancred.
They will never drop their anchors
at sea to resupply their ship;
they wish to be free of all that.
Ah! Good men, may God help you,
for you know not the hour of your death.
Begin a new story,[157]
for Jesus Christ, the King of Glory
wants you at his side, in spite of yourself.
[56v] Remember that the apostles
did not reach paradise for a trifle.
Indeed, think of Saint Paul,
who had his head chopped off for God;
we do not celebrate him for nothing.
You know well that Saint Peter
and Saint Andrew, who was his brother,
were put upon the cross for God.
Therefore, God was their good friend,
just as He was to the other saints.
What more can I rhyme about for you?
No one reaches paradise if he does not suffer pain.
For this reason, he is wise who takes this on.

Let us pray to the Glorious King
and His dear, precious Son,
together with the Holy Spirit
in whom all goodness is gathered,
and to the precious Lady

156. Note the play on words here between the name *Biaugeu* or *Beaujeu*, which also sounds like "good game," the subject of the subsequent verse with *biau geu*.

157. For the appearances and significance of the phrase "novele estoire," see Anne Latowsky's introduction above.

Qui est saluz de cors et darme
A touz sainz·et a toutes saintes
Qui por dieu ·orent painnes maintes
Quil nos otroit· la joie fine
Rutebues · son sarmon define.

Explicit

who is the salvation of body and soul,
to all the saints, male and female,
who have endured many pains for God,
may they grant us pure joy.
Rutebeuf ends his sermon.[158]

The End.

158. Rutebeuf ends his crusade poems as he began them, using *annominatio* to play with the sound [fin], evoking both endings and perfection. In his final gesture, he announces the end of his *sarmon*, a word that allows him to, once again, convey multiple meanings in a single term, and to sum up in four words his endlessly intertwined roles of self-reflexive poet and paid preacher for the cause of crusading.

9

Two Wills from Acre, 1267–1272

In Eudes of Nevers's time, taking the cross meant confronting the possibility of a glorious death in battle or perhaps a more ignominious one resulting from the everyday dangers that arise during far-flung travel. The risks that accompanied crusading inspired many who undertook the journey east to make provisions for what might happen if they did not return home, to arrange for the final resting place of their bodies, to prepare for the commendation of their souls, and to communicate the distribution of their worldly goods once they had died. Although we have no formal written version of Eudes's last wishes—what we would now call a will—his Account-Inventory details the postmortem actions taken by his most trusted companions as they tended to his bodily, spiritual, and financial affairs. In doing so, his executors carried out the instructions the count had given to them before his death in what the Account-Inventory refers to as his *lais*.[1] The Account-Inventory thus records the execution of Eudes's final intentions that may have been recorded in some lost document or only have been spoken aloud among the members of his crusading household.

When Eudes died in 1266, expressing one's postmortem intentions as he may have done—that is, formally, orally, and in the company of witnesses—was already a well-established practice. But as the thirteenth century wore on, crusaders began to memorialize their postmortem intentions in writing rather than in purely oral expressions of intent. Since written wills were often extensions of the documented bequests made to religious institutions, they took on

1. See the Account-Inventory, note 1.

a specific format to ensure that all the necessary details were included for the legal transfer of assets and that witnesses were listed to corroborate the testator's intentions. Each will began with a statement of the identity of the testator, that is, the person making the will, followed by a declaration of his or her state of mind, a commendation of the soul to God, an acknowledgment of debts and how they might be fulfilled, and instructions for how the decedent's assets were to be distributed and by whom. The wills were then signed and sealed in a formal process to ensure the document's authenticity.

These same elements appear in the crusader wills written in Acre that record the intentions of two prominent English lords, Hugh de Neville and Prince Edward of England, both of which provide meaningful points of comparison with the Account-Inventory. The will of Hugh de Neville, a knight from a well-known English family, was compiled in 1267 and features payment to religious houses for the safekeeping of his soul, but also looks to more quotidian matters, including the debts he owed to the person charged with caring for his horse. On the other hand, the will of Prince Edward, the future king of England, written while he was on crusade in 1272, is primarily concerned with matters of state, ensuring that his many territories would be appropriately bequeathed to his children and that his wife would recoup her dowry upon his death. Although neither of these testators died in Acre, the postmortem actions they instructed their agents to take were similar to those that Eudes's executors undertook on his behalf in 1266 and therefore represent a documented version of what the count may have expressed orally before he died. Even if Edward's will is oriented toward his holdings in England and Hugh's is anchored in the East, both state clearly that the wills were produced in Acre and make mention of western Christian institutions in the East. Like the Account-Inventory, both wills were written in Old French, and both are translated into English here.[2]

2. For information on medieval wills, see Henri Auffroy, *Evolution du testament en France des origines au XIIIe siècle* (Paris: A. Rousseau, 1899), 423–29; Michael M. Sheehan, *The Will in Medieval England, from the Conversion of the Anglo-Saxons to the End of the Thirteenth Century* (Toronto: Pontifical Institute of Mediaeval Studies, 1963); and Sheehan, "A List of Thirteenth-Century English Wills," in *Marriage, Family, and Law in Medieval Europe*, ed. James K. Farge (Toronto: University of Toronto Press, 1997), 8–15.

The Will of Sir Hugh de Neville (1267)

Edited and translated by Caroline Smith

Introduction

Considering the relatively small number of wills that survive from the thirteenth century, it is remarkable that two of the extant examples were made for crusaders visiting Acre within a few years of each other, and in the period soon after Eudes of Nevers's death and the creation of the Account-Inventory. The first of these was made in 1267 for Hugh de Neville, a knight from a prominent English family who had inherited lands in Essex. The will survives in the National Archives of England and was first made available in print in 1899 by M. S. Giuseppi, whose work to identify Hugh and explain the circumstances of his crusade remain invaluable.[3]

Hugh had taken part in the Montfortian rebellion against the English king Henry III, and in the wake of the king's victory at Evesham in 1265 his lands were confiscated.[4] Although Hugh was reconciled to the king the following year and his lands were partially restored to him before he left on crusade, his position appears not to have been secure. A letter sent by his mother, Hawisa, around the same time this will was made expresses her belief that his rights and possessions at home remained precarious.[5] Hawisa urged Hugh to return home, and her pleas may have been instrumental in his decision to cut short his stay in the Kingdom of Jerusalem. A surviving document of uncertain date (but probably later than his Acre will) absolved Hugh of his crusade vow on behalf of the patriarch of Jerusalem.[6] Another, made in Viterbo in August 1269 and concerning the execution of a will, makes it apparent that he died in Italy (where his mother had encouraged him to seek papal support for his claims in England) during his return journey.[7]

Giuseppi was confident that the will referred to in this last document was one that had superseded the will made for Hugh in Acre that is transcribed and translated here. This makes sense because Hugh's Acre will is concerned

3. Kew, National Archives, MS DL 25/177. M. S. Giuseppi, "On the Testament of Sire Hugh de Nevill, Written at Acre, 1267," *Archaeologia* 56 (1899): 351–70. An edition of Hugh's will is to be published in Timothy S. Haskett and Sarah B. White, eds., *The Wills of Medieval England, 1066–1300* (Toronto, forthcoming). I am grateful to Dr. White for providing me with the text of this edition, which has been of great assistance in preparing the edition and translation presented here.

4. Charles R. Young, *The Making of the Neville Family in England, 1066–1400* (Woodbridge: Boydell and Brewer, 1996), 57; C. H. Knowles, "The Resettlement of England after the Barons' War, 1264–67," *Transactions of the Royal Historical Society* 32 (1982): 28–29.

5. Kew, National Archives, MS DL 34/1/2. This letter is edited and translated in Giuseppi, "On the Testament," 358–61.

6. Kew, National Archives, MS DL 25/1317; Giuseppi, "On the Testament," 362.

7. Giuseppi, "On the Testament," 363.

only with people and things with him in the Kingdom of Jerusalem, and with the religious institutions and projects that were relevant to him in that context. Although Hugh's household was more modest than that of Eudes of Nevers, his will, like the Account-Inventory drawn up by Eudes's executors, gives us a sense of the range of people he relied on during his time on crusade (three knightly companions are named, a squire, a chaplain, a clerk, and servants who attended to Hugh's horses, among others), some of the valued possessions he had with him (horses, weapons, a decorative cup, gold and jeweled buckles, rings), and the numerous religious institutions (military orders, hospitals, mendicant communities) and charitable causes (care for lepers, widows, orphans) in Acre he wished to support with gifts of money, knightly equipment, and precious objects. Most of the institutions to which he designated bequests were also favored by Eudes of Nevers.

These religious and charitable bequests reflect a concern for the fate of one's soul ubiquitous among Hugh's contemporaries. His will suggests more personal worries too. Money, or the lack of it, was clearly on Hugh's mind, and he was waiting for funds to be sent from England. He mentioned that he was hoping for "my money" to arrive, as well as referring to a sum the pope had said would be set aside for him from English crusade funds; these appear to have been different potential injections of cash, but it is not clear that any of it ever arrived. His mother's letter lamented his financial prospects and said he should not hold out much hope of receiving money from the English crusade funds in particular.[8] Alongside these money worries, Hugh was also preoccupied by potential dangers facing him as a crusader. It is not known whether Hugh ever saw military action against Muslims while he was in the Kingdom of Jerusalem, but he was concerned about the prospect of being taken captive by them. Hugh's last instruction before naming his executors was to say that they should use his possessions to pay his ransom if the need arose.

The transcription below was made in accordance with the principles laid out by Lester and Morreale for the transcription of the Account-Inventory of Eudes of Nevers in this volume, with the exception that abbreviations/contractions have been expanded in italics.

Edition

Co est le testament sire Huue Nevile chivaler en le non del pere el fiz · et de le seint espirit · Jo cu*m*maund ma alme a deu omnipotent e a nostre dame seinte Marie e a tuz seinz · e mun cors a la seinte sepult*ur*e ṣẹịṇ[9] de le cimit*er*ie sein Nicholas · Jo divis a labur de la vile de Acre q*ua*rante sols de st*erling* · A la

8. Giuseppi, "On the Testament," 360.

9. The punctus marks below the letters of this word indicate a scribal error that should be deleted.

maisun sein Thomas de Cantirbir en Acre mun palefrei feraunt e mes armures · ke apendent a vne p*er*sone · Jo divis au temple de Acre vn hanap a pe · des armes le Roi de Engelt*ere* · Jo divis al hospital p*or* sustinir le malades · q*uar*ante sou de · st*erling* · Jo divis al hospital de Bethlee*m* chink · ℔ · Al hospital sein Lazer treis · ℔ · Al hospital seinte Bride vn · ℔ · A la maisun de la t*ri*nite · vn · ℔ · A frere du Carme treis · ℔ · A freres del penaunce ih*es*u c*ri*st · treis · ℔ · A frere preschures · chink · ℔[·] A frere menures · dis · ℔ · A la frarie sein dionis · un · ℔ · Jo divis a sire Randouf de Munchensi ma petite espeie e vn fermeil oue ameraudes a sire Rob*ert* de Bridishale vn fermeil oue ameraudes a sire Rauf de Ekleshale · vn anel de or · A Jakke mun vallet le paumer le chival Bai ke fu a Will*aume* le fiz Symon ke jo li dunai oue tute les armures[10] ke appendent a vn gentil home · e q*ui*nze mars de st*er*ling · A Wat*er* mun chapelein p*or* chant*er* p*or* ma alme vn an · oct · mars de st*erling* · A colin le clerk dis mars pur sun servise · a Lucel le cu · q*ua*rante souz · e sun passage utre la mer de Grece · A Pain mun homme si il venge de ca mer amoi · sis mars e sun passage vtre la mer de Grece · A Beuerle sis mars e sun passage utre la mer de Grece · A thomas ke Gard mun chival · q*ua*tre · ℔ · p*or* sun servise · e vn · ℔ · por deu · A Will*aume* le Bretun q*ua*rante souz de st*erling* · e jo li pardoins vint cink sous ke il me doit · A Joan le marescal p*or* sun servise · vint souz de st*erling* · A mest*re* Reimund le mareschal por sun servise · vn mark de st*erling* · A plu[11] pouere meseus de Acre · treis · ℔ · Jo diuis a Esteuene le Draper q*ua*trevint · ℔ · e cink ke jo li doi p*or* sire Ingra*m* de Humframuile · e a Leanard le chaniur q*ua*tre vint · ℔ · ke jo li doi p*or* le vaundit Ingra*m* · Jo diuis a poueres orfanins · e veues en la Cite de Acre · set marz de st*erling* · A fere mun servise le jur de obit · q*ui*nze mars de st*erling* · e co ke demort seit done a poueres a sein Nicholas en pain chaut · Jo diuis a sein Nicholas · cink · ℔ · A p*ri*ur de sein Gile · vn fermeil de or · A cest testame*n*t parfere e me dettes a q*ui*ter jo voil e deuis ke me chiuaus e mes armueres e tute mes autre choses seint venduz · De aut*re*part si me deners ven*g*ent de Engelt*ere* jo voil e deuis ke chechun article de mun diuis la u greinur mester soit · par le ordeineme*n*t de mes essechetures seit en oite de vne partie · e de le remenant voil ke ma meine soit sustenuz · vn an en la tere seinte en cu*n*tre le enemis ih*esu* c*ri*st · e si eus ne volent · jo diuis ke mes exeketures p*or*veint ailures la u il [p]urun meuz fere · de cinkcent mars ke la postoile me *gar*unta de la cruserie de Engelt*ere* si il me vengent jo voil e deuis ke gent de armes soint sustenuz en cunt*re* les enemis de la Croix ausi longement c[oe] puru*n*t d[u]rer p*or* moi e p*or* eus des queus cel auer leua e coe tuteueirs par la despositm*en*t de mes executurs · e si[12] il avenge ke jo soi p*ri*s en le meins de sarazins jo voel ke coe ke jo ai diuise demorge en le meins de mes executurs le kes eus sacent si jo puse estre reins par coe v nun · ces sunt mes essecutures mun sire Randouf de Munchensi · le p*ri*ur de sein Gile du

10. This word inserted below the line above to amend a scribal error.
11. This word inserted below the line above to amend a scribal error.
12. This word inserted below the line above to amend a scribal error.

Temple sire Rob*ert* de Brideshale e Walt*er* mun chapelin · Le cu*m*maundur de sein Thomas · e Jakke le Paumer mun valet · tut le remenaunt utre mun testa*ment* jo diuis a poueres veues e a orphanins en la Cite de Ac*re*. Escr*it*es en Ac*re* le lundi devaunt[13] feste sein Symon e sein Jude le an de le incarnaciun Jh*es*u cr*is*t m*illesim*o.cc.lx.vii.

Translation

This is the testament of lord Hugh Neville, knight, in the name of the Father and of the Son and of the Holy Spirit. I commend my soul to almighty God and to Our Lady Saint Mary and to all the saints, and my body to the holy burial-place of the cemetery of Saint Nicholas.[14] I bequeath to the works of the city of Acre[15] forty *sous* sterling; to the house of Saint Thomas of Canterbury in Acre[16] my light gray palfrey and my arms, appropriate for one person. I bequeath to the Temple of Acre[17] a footed cup with the arms of the king of England. I bequeath to the Hospital,[18] for care of the sick, forty *sous* sterling. I bequeath to the Hospital of Bethlehem[19] five bezants; to the

13. A slit made in the document in order to attach a seal appears to obscure a word here. The seal itself is now lost; the strip of parchment used to attach it remains.

14. The cemetery of St. Nicholas, outside the eastern walls of the city, was the burial site for most Latin Christians who died in Acre during the twelfth and thirteenth centuries. Denys Pringle, *The Churches of the Crusader Kingdom of Jerusalem: A Corpus*, vol. 4 (Cambridge: Cambridge University Press, 2009), 151–55, no. 138; hereafter all citations are to vol. 4.

15. Giuseppi suggested these "works" might be the construction of a new church for the Order of Saint Thomas, but Pringle interprets this as a bequest to support the construction of walls of Acre. Giuseppi, "On the Testament," 357; Pringle, *The Churches of the Crusader Kingdom*, 23.

16. The Order of Saint Thomas of Canterbury had its origins in the English contingent present in the city at the time of the Third Crusade. Plagued by underfunding from the outset, in the late 1220s it was reformed as a military order, with its headquarters in the Montmusard suburb of Acre, to the north of the old city. Eudes of Nevers bequeathed to the order a tunic and overcoat. Pringle, *The Churches of the Crusader Kingdom*, 161–64; Denys Pringle, "The Order of St Thomas of Canterbury in Acre," in *The Military Orders*, vol. 5: *Politics and Power*, ed. Peter W. Edbury (London: Routledge, 2012), 75–82. For Eudes's bequests to this and other religious institutions, see Roll C Front in the Account-Inventory.

17. The military order of the Temple (the Templars) had a presence in Acre since at least the mid-twelfth century, centered on a castle and church complex in the southwest of the city's peninsula. Pringle, *The Churches of the Crusader Kingdom*, 166–72, no. 451.

18. The military order of the Hospital of St. John (the Hospitallers) had a presence in Acre from the early twelfth century, with extensive property, primarily in the northern part of the old city, where its church, hospital, and principal buildings were located. Eudes of Nevers bequeathed copper cooking pots to the Hospitallers. Pringle, *The Churches of the Crusader Kingdom*, 82–114, nos. 410–11.

19. The Hospital of the Brothers and/or Sisters of Bethlehem provided a hospital for female lepers (possibly located in the suburb of Montmusard, to the north of the old city of Acre), to

Hospital of Saint Lazarus[20] three bezants; to the Hospital of Saint Brigid[21] one bezant; to the house of the Trinity[22] one bezant; to the Carmelite friars[23] three bezants; to the friars of the Penance of Jesus Christ[24] three bezants; to the Friars Preacher[25] five bezants; to the Friars Minor[26] ten bezants; to the Friary of Saint Denis[27] one bezant. I bequeath to lord Ralph de Munchensy[28]

---

which Eudes of Nevers also made a bequest of an overcoat and a fur-lined cape. Pringle, *The Churches of the Crusader Kingdom*, 44–45, no. 377.

20. The Order of St. Lazarus appears to have established a house in Acre by the mid-twelfth century, which became their head of operations by the end of that century. Eudes of Nevers made a bequest of an overcoat and a cape in favor of the order. Pringle, *The Churches of the Crusader Kingdom*, 121–23, no. 418.

21. A church and hospital dedicated to St. Brigid (or St. Bride) of Kildare were attested in the mid-thirteenth century, located near the sea in Montmusard. Pringle suggests that the popularity of this saint in Ireland and western England makes it likely that this house was founded by crusaders from that region, probably after the Third Crusade. Pringle, *The Churches of the Crusader Kingdom*, 72, no. 398.

22. The Order of the Holy Trinity, founded in the late twelfth century with the primary aim of ransoming captives held by Muslims, had a presence in Acre from the early thirteenth century. Their house, by the time of Hugh de Neville's visit at least, was in Montmusard. Eudes of Nevers made a bequest of a fur-trimmed overcoat to the order. Pringle, *The Churches of the Crusader Kingdom*, 56–57, no. 387.

23. The church of St. Mary of the Carmelites is attested in the early 1260s, although the order may well have had a presence in Acre before that time. The church was situated in Montmusard, close to the sea. Eudes of Nevers left the Carmelites a tunic and a fur-trimmed corset. Pringle, *The Churches of the Crusader Kingdom*, 130–13, no. 423.

24. A mendicant order, the Brothers of the Penitence of Jesus Christ (Friars of the Sack) had established a house located in the old city of Acre no later than 1264. Eudes of Nevers left them an overcoat and a cape. Pringle, *The Churches of the Crusader Kingdom*, 50, no. 382.

25. The Dominicans (Friars Preacher) were a presence in Acre by the late 1220s, with their convent in the old city, near the sea on the west side of the peninsula. Eudes of Nevers made a bequest of a silk garnache to the Dominicans. Pringle, *The Churches of the Crusader Kingdom*, 46–48, no. 380.

26. The Franciscans (Friars Minor) were a presence in Acre since the visit of Saint Francis himself in 1219–20. Their house appears to have been located in the eastern part of Montmusard. Eudes of Nevers left the Franciscans a fur-lined mantle. Pringle, *The Churches of the Crusader Kingdom*, 48–50, no. 381.

27. The church of St. Denis, situated in Montmusard, also benefited from bequests from both Hugh de Neville and Eudes of Nevers. Eudes, who identified this religious house as a hospital, left it a fur-trimmed tunic and overcoat. Pringle, *The Churches of the Crusader Kingdom*, 76, no. 403.

28. The first three individuals who would have benefited from this will appear to have been Hugh's knightly companions in Acre. It is not possible to identify these men with any certainty, but I am very grateful to Dr. Sophie Ambler for sharing her expertise, which has been invaluable in producing the suggestions for identifying Ralph de Munchensy presented here. The English inquisitions postmortem record two men named Ralph de Munchensy who might have been in Hugh's company in Acre. Of one of them, who died in 1292, all we know is that he held lands at Rettendon in Essex, "Inquisitions Post Mortem, Edward I, File 63," in *Calendar of Inquisitions Post Mortem*, vol. 3: *Edward I*, ed. J. E. E. S. Sharp and A. E. Stamp (London: His Majesty's Stationery Office, 1912), 30–54; available at *British History Online*, http://www.british-history.ac.uk/inquis-post-mortem/vol3/pp30-54. The other Ralph de Munchensy is recorded as having died in 1311, "Inquisitions Post Mortem, Edward II, File 20," in *Calendar of Inquisitions Post*

my small sword and a buckle with emeralds; to lord Robert of Birdsall[29] a buckle with emeralds; to lord Ralph of Ecclesall[30] a gold ring; to Jack the Palmer,[31] my squire, the bay horse (which belonged to William, son of Simon), which I gave to him with all the arms appropriate to a gentleman, and fifteen marks sterling; to Walter, my chaplain, to chant for my soul for one year, eight marks sterling; to Colin, the clerk, ten marks for his service; to Lucel le Cu[32] forty *sous* and his passage beyond the sea of Greece; to my man Pain, if he should come across the sea to me, six marks and his passage beyond the sea of Greece; to Beverly six marks and his passage beyond the sea of Greece; to Thomas, who keeps my horse, four bezants for his service and one bezant for God; to William the Breton forty *sous* sterling, and I forgive him the twenty-five *sous* that he owes me; to John, the farrier, for his service twenty *sous* sterling; to master Raymond the farrier for his service one mark sterling; to the most impoverished of Acre's lepers three bezants. I bequeath to Stephen the Draper eighty-five bezants that I owe him for lord Ingram de Umfraville.[33]

Mortem, vol. 5: *Edward II*, ed. J. E. E. S. Sharp and A. E. Stamp (London: His Majesty's Stationery Office, 1908), 135–45; available at *British History Online*, http://www.british-history.ac.uk/inquis-post-mortem/vol5/pp135-145. This Ralph appears to have been the vassal of William de Munchensy of Edwardstone in Suffolk; both men are mentioned in an entry in the calendar of inquisitions miscellaneous for October 1265 for having seized lands of adherents of the Montfortian rebellion, *Calendar of Inquisitions Miscellaneous (Chancery)*, vol. 1 (London: His Majesty's Stationery Office, 1916), 269–70.

29. "Bridishale" is probably Birdsall in Yorkshire. No identification can be made with confidence, but a "Robertus de Brydeshale" is named in a charter of the Augustinian priory at Healaugh Park in that county; the charter is itself undated but appears alongside other documents of the mid-thirteenth century in the priory's cartulary; J. S. Purvis, ed., *The Chartulary of the Augustinian Priory of St John the Evangelist of the Park of Healaugh* (Cambridge: Cambridge University Press, 1936), 158–59.

30. "Ekleshale" could be Eccleshall, Staffordshire, or Ecclesall, south Yorkshire. Again, no certain identification can be made, but a "Radulfus de Ecleshall" (Ralph of Ecclesall) appears several times in the charters of the abbey of Beauchief (south Yorkshire) for the second half of the thirteenth century; D. Hey, L. Liddy, and D. Luscombe, eds., *A Monastic Community in Local Society: The Beauchief Abbey Cartulary* (Cambridge: Cambridge University Press, 2012), nos. 111–16, 119–25.

31. This bequest to Jack suggests he was being prepared for knighthood; Christopher Tyerman has described him as doing his "in-service knighthood training" on crusade with Hugh; Christopher Tyerman, *How to Plan a Crusade: Reason and Religious War in the High Middle Ages* (London: Alan Lane, 2015), 161.

32. "Le Cu" probably means the cook; Tyerman, *How to Plan a Crusade*, 158.

33. A knight of this name was known for his role in the Scottish Wars of Independence. As the work of Amanda Beam suggests, it seems unlikely (although perhaps not impossible) this was the same man as is named in Hugh's will, and there may have been more than one man named Ingram de Umfraville active in the late thirteenth and early fourteenth centuries. It seems plausible that the Ingram mentioned in Hugh's will was the man who would later be identified as heir to the lands of a William de Umfraville in Essex in 1296. The inquisition postmortem into William's estates said his heir, Ingram de Umfraville, was at least sixty years old. A. Beam, "'At the Apex of Chivalry': Sir Ingram de Umfraville and the Anglo-Scottish Wars," in *England and Scotland at War, c.1296–c.1513*, ed. Andy King and David Simpkin (Leiden: Brill, 2012), 55–56. If this

And to Leonard the money changer eighty bezants that I owe him for the aforementioned Ingram. I bequeath to poor orphans and widows in the city of Acre seven marks sterling. For the performance of my service on the day of my death fifteen marks sterling, and any sum left over should provide warm bread to the poor of Saint Nicholas. I bequeath to Saint Nicholas five bezants; to the prior of Saint Giles[34] a gold buckle. To fulfill this testament and to settle my debts I will and direct that my horses and my arms and all my other possessions should be sold. Alternatively, if my money arrives from England I will and direct that each article of my testament (according to the greatest need as determined by my executors) be taken from it in the first instance, and with the remainder I will that my company be maintained in the Holy Land against the enemies of Jesus Christ for one year. And if they [the men of Hugh's company] do not wish to do this, I direct that my executors should make provision where they might have the best effect. Concerning the five hundred marks that the pope promised me from the crusade [funds] of England (if they should reach me), I will and direct that men at arms be maintained against the enemies of the cross for as long they should last, to benefit me and those from whom they were raised; all this, however, is subject to the disposal made by my executors. And if it should happen that I am taken into the hands of Saracens I will that those things I have bequeathed should remain in the hands of my executors, who should discover if I might be ransomed by them, or not. These are my executors: my lord Ralph de Munchensy; the prior of Saint Giles of the Temple; Robert of Birdsall; and Walter, my chaplain; the commander of Saint Thomas; and Jack the Palmer, my squire. All that remains after my testament has been accomplished I leave to the poor widows and orphans in the city of Acre. Written in Acre the Monday before [the] feast of Saint Simon and Saint Jude in the year of the incarnation of Jesus Christ 1267.[35]

Ingram was around sixty in the mid-1290s he would have been in his early thirties in 1267; shared connections in Essex might help explain why Hugh knew Ingram and felt a desire or obligation to assist him. In her letter to him during his absence in Acre Hugh's mother, Hawisa, bemoaned his potentially costly support for Ingram; Giuseppi, "On the Testament," 360.

34. St. Giles was a church and hospital in Montmusard. Later in his will Hugh refers to this same person as "the prior of Saint Giles of the Temple"; the Templars had asserted a claim (disputed by the patriarch of Jerusalem) to be able to appoint the prior of St. Giles. Pringle, *The Churches of the Crusader Kingdom*, 80–81, no. 408.

35. October 24, 1267.

The Will of Prince Edward I of England (1272)

Edited and translated by Laura K. Morreale and Anne Latowsky

Introduction

The only extant will and testament of Edward I of England was written on June 18, 1272, when Edward was not yet king and he and his wife Eleanor of Castile were stationed in Acre on crusade. Composed in French just a few months before Edward inherited the throne in November of that same year, the will survives in only one, fifteenth-century copy, now housed at the National Archives of England.[36] A print version was published in the early eighteenth century as a part of Thomas Rymer's monumental documentary collection, the *Foedera*, and copies have appeared in several publications thereafter, though subsequent versions often replicate the misreadings first disseminated in the earliest print editions.[37] The following transcription and translation is based on the manuscript version and reinterprets several of those early renderings.

The circumstances surrounding the writing of Edward's will were well reported, though the facts have certainly been embellished over time. According to eighteenth-century historian Rapin de Thoyras, the document was drawn up shortly after an attempt was made on Edward's life in early June 1272, when a would-be assassin, wielding a poisoned knife, entered the prince's tent, lunged at him, and stabbed him in the arm.[38] Although Edward was able to fend off the attacker with a kick to the chest, the wound festered; it is said that Edward's beloved Eleanor sucked the poison from the wound, thereby saving her husband's life.[39] Whether this story is true or not, Edward's desire to record his last wishes shortly after the attack occurred attests to the danger he felt while on crusade and his desire to arrange for the possibility that he might not return. In fact, he remained in Acre only a few more months after the will was written and, along with his entourage, began his trip back to England by way of the Sicilian court of Charles of Anjou in late September 1272.

Edward's will addressed the prince's duties as lord, landholder, husband, and father, set forth his obligations in these roles, identified the individuals whom he empowered to meet them, and designated how they ought to be met. Naturally, his first debt was to God, to whom he pledged his soul and bodily remains. But unlike Hugh de Neville's will or Eudes of Nevers's Account-Inventory, both of which made provisions for distributing alms to religious

36. The will is kept in an Exchequer miscellany, catalogued as Kew, National Archives, E 36/274, fols. 341–42v.

37. Thomas Rymer, ed., "Testimentum Domini Edwardi primogeniti Regis conditum apud Acres," in *Foedera*, vol. 1 (London: J. Tonson, 1726), 885–86.

38. Rapin de Thoyras, *The History of England*, trans. N. Tindal, 2nd ed. (London: Printed for James John and Paul Knapton, 1732–47), 345.

39. Other sources suggest it was his friend Otto de Grandson, though this too is suspect. Michael Prestwich, *The Three Edwards* (London: Routledge, 1980), 7.

houses and other beneficiaries in the Holy Land, Edward's will was decidedly westward-looking and made little mention of his time in the Levant. On the contrary, he staked his claim as the son of the king of England in the testament's opening lines and referred to his landed estates in England, Ireland, and Gascony as his sources of income. With these resources at hand, Edward set forth what was owed to the members of his household for their service, and after making the arrangements for these payments, he turned to the financial well-being of his children and wife with a series of pragmatic provisions.

Edward named his closest companions and members of his household, Roger de Clifford, Payn de Chaworth, Robert Tibetot, and Anthony Bek, as executors of these provisions.[40] He instructed them to tend to his lands and keep an accounting of revenues that were to be remitted to his children once they reached the age of majority. His close attention to the administrative details of land tenure, rent collection, and English inheritance law suggests that he was far more attuned to his affairs at home than he was to those of the Holy Land, even if he included the archbishop of Tyre as well as the grand masters of the Hospitallers and the Templars among his witnesses. Edward would never return to the Holy Land, but in the years after he became king, he continued to receive letters from these same testators who decried the situation in the East, requested his aid, and implored him to return and take the cross once again.[41] When Edward finally died in 1307, no other will was present, and certain unsubstantiated reports suggest that his deathbed wish was to have his heart taken back to the Holy Land; other more reliable sources indicate that his last instructions were for his closest confidants, including the same Roger de Clifford named in this will, to look after and care for his son, the future Edward II, as he assumed the throne.[42]

Edition

En nun du pere du finz e du seynt esp*ri*t, amen · Nus Edward eisnsne filz au noble rey dengletere ·fesoins nostre testament en nostre bon sen e en nostre bone memorie le samedy p*ro*rocheyn apres la Pentecouste · en le an de nostre seygnur mil deu cent · setannt secund en ceste manere En p*ri*mes nus divisoms a deu e a nostre dame seinte marie e a tuz seyns nostre alme & nostre cors ensevelir· ou nos esseketurs · ceo est a saver sire Johan de bretayne · sire William de Valence · sire Rog*er* de Clifford Sire payn de Chaurtos · sire Roberd Tibetot · sire Otes de Grauntson · Robert Burnell, & Antoyne Beks · o aukuns

40. For members of Edward's household, see Michael Prestwich, *Edward I* (London: Guild, 1988), 68–69.

41. Charles-Victor Langlois and Charles Kohler, "Lettres inédites concernant les croisades (1275–1307)," *Bibliothèque de l'Ecole des chartes* 52, no. 1 (1891): 46–63.

42. Prestwich, *Edward I*, 557.

de eus aurunt devise le queus nus donoms & grauntoms plener poer ke il pusint ordiner p*or* nostre alme de tuz nos beyns moebles e noun moebles · cum en rendre nos dettes · e redrecher les tort ke nus avoms fet par nus ou par nos baliz e rendre a nostre gent lur s*er*vise sillom ceo ke il verrunt ke bon seyt E p*or* ceo ke nus savoms ben ke noz moebles ne purrunt pas suffire a ceo · vuluns e ot*r*oms ke noz avaunt diz exseketurs eyent plener poer le quel nus les grauntoms si avaunt ke nus poims de ordiner establir de tutes nos teres dengletere · de Irelaunde, de Gascoine e de tutes nos aut*re*s teres ke il en pusent ovrir en memes la manere ke nus feymes qu*ant* eles furent en nostre meign saunz vendre ou doner e en lur meyns tenir ensemblement o la garde de nos enfaunz jusque au plener age de eus pur nostre testament acomplir · & nos aumones fere en englet*ere* & aillurs sillu*m* ceo ke nos esseketurs verrunt ke seyt a fere · as queus fere nus ordinoms ceynt milie mars & ap*re*s nostre devis fet & nos aumons acomplies volums ke les issues des avaunt dites teres turgent au p*ro*fit de noz enfaunz e demurgent en les meyns des avauntdiz exseketurs juskes alage de noz enfaunz avaunt nomes · & si aventure avenge ke nostre seygnur rey nostr*e* pere murge dedenz le age de nos enfauns ke deu defende · nos voloms ke le reaume denglet*ere* & tutes les autres teres ke porrunt eschair a noz enfaunz demorgent en les meyns de nos esse keturs avaunt nomes ensemblement ov*es*que nostre cher piere le Erceuesk de Ev*er*wyk e sire Rog*er* ovesk & aut*re*s p*ro*deshom*m*es · du reaume ke il akondrunt · fi mesti*er* seyt jekes al plen*er* age de nos enfaunz sus nomez · e keles issues des avaunt dites teres feyent cuilliz e gardez p*er* les meyns de nos exseketures avaunt diz & liverez a nos enfaunz qu*an*t il serrunt de plener age a lur p*ro*fist E sur ceo nus voloms e ordinoms ke deus ou plus de noz esseketurs eyent poer de oiir nos acuntes e de receyvere de tuz nos baliz ou ke il seyent · devaunt nostre departir dengletere e puis se il ne poent muster ke il eyent leal acunte rendue · e si nul de noz balif seyt mort ke ses heirs seyent tenuz a rendre la cunte pur luy Endreyt de dowarie de n*ost*re chere femme Alianor volums ke ele eyt pleynement ceo ke fut nome q*ua*nt n*us* les pusams · e si de ceo ne se tent pas a pae nus voloms ke ele eyt ceo ke dreyt e ley la dorra · sulom les usages e le leys dengletere E voloms ausi ke la ou tuz noz · esseketurs ne porrunt estre pur fere le execution de nostre testament avaunt dit ke quatre ou plus en num des autrys eyent poer p*er* eus e pur les autrys pur acomplir les choses susdites E pur ceo p*r*iums a nostre seynt pere lapostle ke il wyle ceste chose tenir & fere tenir e confirmer · e ke il voyle prier nostre cher pere ke il voyle tenir estable e fere tenir par tut son reaume e tot son poer quel part ke il seyt · les choses avant nomes En testimoniaunce de la queu chose a ceo testament avoms fet mettre nostre sel · & avoms p*rie* sire Johan Erceveske de Sur & vicarie de la seinte eglise de Jerusalem · & les honurables bers frere Hue Revel Mestre de lhospital · & frere Thomas Berard mestre du Temple ke a cest escrit meisent ausi lur seus · les quieus si le vut fet ensemblement o nos esseketurs avaunt nomes en tesmoyaunce des choses sus dites · Donez a Acre, le samedy avaunt nome le disutime Jur de Juen lan du regne le rey nostre pere · cinkaunt e si*xie*me.

Translation

In the name of the Father, the Son, and Holy Spirit, amen. We Edward, first son of the noble king of England, of sound mind and good memory, make our testament the Saturday following Pentecost in the year of our Lord one thousand two hundred seventy-two. First, therefore, we dedicate our soul and our bodily remains to God and Our Lady Blessed Mary and to all the saints. Whereas our executors, namely Lord John of Brittany, Lord William de Valence, Lord Roger de Clifford, Lord Payn de Chaworth, Lord Robert Tibetot, Lord Otto de Grandson, Robert Burnell, and Anthony Bek, each have the authority that we give and grant fully such that they can arrange for our soul and all our belongings, movable and immovable, in order to settle our debts and redress the wrongs committed by us or by our bailiffs, and render to [members of] our household [compensation for] their service according to what they deem appropriate.

And since we know that our assets will not be enough to [cover] all this, we desire and authorize that our aforementioned executors have that full power, which we grant to them to the extent that we are able, to arrange for it to be established regarding all our lands in England, Ireland, Gascony, and all our other lands, that they be able to work them in the same way that we did when they [the lands] were in our hands without selling or donating, and [be able to] hold [them] in their hands jointly with the custody of our children until they reach the [full] age to carry out our will and to pay our alms in England and elsewhere according to that which our executors view as necessary. To this end, we conscript one hundred thousand marks.

And after our debts are settled and our alms paid, we desire that the proceeds of the said lands be remitted to our children and remain in the hands of the named executors until our above-named children reach the age of majority. And if it so happens that our lord the king, our father, should die within the lifetime of our children—God forbid—we desire that the kingdom of England and all other lands that can escheat to our children remain in the hands of the aforementioned executors, together with our dear father the archbishop of York, and Lord Roger, bishop, and with other *prudhommes* of the kingdom, that they keep whatever accounting is needed until the age of majority of our aforementioned children, and that the proceeds of the abovementioned lands be collected and retained in the hands of our named executors and submitted to our children, for their benefit, when they reach the age of majority.

And concerning this, we wish and command that two or more of our executors be able to hear our accounts and collect from all our bailiwicks wherever they were [located] before our departure from England, and then, if they are unable to demonstrate that they have rendered a faithful account, and if any one of our bailiffs should die, then may his heirs be responsible for rendering the account on his behalf. By right of dower for our dear wife Eleanor, we desire that she have in full that which was stated when we put this [document] in place, and if this is not sufficient, we desire that she have that which by right and law is granted to her according to the customs and the laws of England.

And we desire, in the event that all our executors cannot be present for the execution of our aforementioned will, that four or more, in the name of the others, have the power, for themselves and for the others, to carry out the aforementioned things. For this reason, we pray to our Holy Father, the pope, that he so desire to hold and bind and confirm all of this and that he request of our dear father that he so desire to hold firm and maintain throughout his entire kingdom and all his domain, wherever he may be, the abovementioned things. In witness to this matter, we have affixed our seal to this will and we have requested of Lord John, archbishop of Tyre and vicar of the Holy Church of Jerusalem, and the honorable, noble brother Hugh Revel, master of the Hospital, and brother Thomas Berard, master of the Temple, that they also affix their seals to this document; they did so, jointly with our aforementioned executors, as witness to the aforementioned matters.

Given in Acre the Saturday before noon, the eighteenth day of June in the fifty-sixth year of reign of the king our father.

Part IV

INTERPRETATIONS

10

The Landscapes of Acre

Andrew Jotischky

When Eudes of Nevers arrived at Acre in late fall of 1265, the landscape and topography of the city and its surrounding region were very different from the scene that his grandfather and father, crusaders in 1217–18 and 1239, had encountered. Power, population, and wealth in the Kingdom of Jerusalem had always been concentrated on the urban littoral. Although Jerusalem was the seat of symbolic royal and ecclesiastical power, Acre, Tyre, Sidon, and Beirut were the economic heart of the kingdom. Acre had seen dramatic expansion of both population and physical size after the loss of most of the territory of the Kingdom of Jerusalem to Saladin's conquest in 1187. Although much of the extent of the pre-1187 kingdom was restored through a combination of military action and diplomacy from the 1190s to the 1240s, this situation began to unravel from 1250 onward with the rise of Mamluk power.

The political frontiers of the Kingdom of Jerusalem, stable until 1244, shrank with alarming speed after the rise of the Mamluks, and especially with the campaigns Sultan Baybars launched in the 1260s. Only three years before Eudes's arrival, Baybars had attempted an assault on Acre. Although he failed to take it, his pillaging raids on Nazareth and Mount Tabor, which looked to Acre for their security, showed the reach of Mamluk power.[1] As the territories controlled by the Franks receded, the cities along the coast expanded to accommodate refugees emigrating from Mamluk-controlled regions. The area covered by the city of Acre doubled in size during the thirteenth century as the new faubourg of Montmusard developed beyond

1. "L'Estoire d'Eracles," *RHC*, 2:446–47.

the limits of the twelfth-century city walls. The earliest description of the enclosure of this suburb, written by Wilbrand of Oldenbourg in 1211, testifies to a double wall fortified with towers. Louis IX completed the fortifications in 1250 at the start of his sojourn in Acre.[2] The twelfth-century extent of the city was about 1,300m (west–east) x 325m (north–south).[3] Montmusard ran about 600m north–south along the sea front, but running inland its walls at their easternmost point were only about 300m north of the old city wall. The full extent of its west–east axis was probably about 500m (see map 2).

Acre was an important trading entrepot, with revenues from taxes worth fifty thousand pounds in silver annually to the king of Jerusalem.[4] Within the city the major commercial powers—Genoa, Venice, and Pisa—controlled proprietorial zones. The origins of these quarters, not only in Acre but also in the other major ports of the kingdom, went back to the original conquests of the coastal cities, which were achieved with the naval help of the mercantile republics. Within their quarters, the republics exercised jurisdictional rights over their citizens and owned municipal and commercial buildings and churches. Representatives from the home cities ran these quarters and rented out properties to merchants and other colonists. A Venetian inventory divides the quarter into four districts. In the middle was the *fondaco*, a large building combining warehouse and sixteen retail spaces with lodgings on upper floors, including those for the parish priest and court clerk. The *bailli* had a house of two or three stories with six shops at ground level and apartments for rent on other floors. The church of St. Mark stood next door, and grouped around it outside were pitches for stalls. The Genoese inventory of 1249 shows that the republic maintained four houses and six larger buildings divided into rental apartments.[5] The built environment of cities in the Kingdom of Jerusalem presented a dramatic contrast to what Eudes would have known in the West. In Outremer, houses were built of stone rather than wood and might comprise three or more stories. As can still be seen in the street layout of the largely medieval old city of Acre today, buildings were next to and across from each

2. David Jacoby, "Montmusard, Suburb of Crusader Acre: The First Stage of Its Development," in *Outremer: Studies in the History of the Crusading Kingdom of Jerusalem Presented to Joshua Prawer*, ed. Benjamin Z. Kedar, Hans E. Mayer, and R. C. Smail (Jerusalem: Yad Izhak Ben-Zvi Institute,1982), 213–14.

3. Denys Pringle, *The Churches of the Crusader Kingdom of Jerusalem: A Corpus*, (Cambridge: Cambridge University Press, 2009), 4:4-5; hereafter all citations are to vol. 4.

4. Jonathan Riley-Smith, *The Feudal Monarchy and the Kingdom of Jerusalem* (London: Macmillan, 1973), 64.

5. David Jacoby, "Crusader Acre in the Thirteenth Century: Urban Layout and Topography," *Studi medievali* 20 (1979): 1–45; Jacoby, "New Venetian Evidence on Crusader Acre," in *The Experience of Crusading*, vol. 2, *Defining the Crusader Kingdom*, ed. Peter W. Edbury and Jonathan Phillips (Cambridge: Cambridge University Press, 2003), 240–56; Jacoby, "Aspects of Everyday Life in Frankish Acre," *Crusades* 4 (2005): 73–105.

other in narrow streets, so close together that inhabitants of upper floors could reach across and hold hands. Jacques de Vitry, whose episcopal palace was to the north of the Arsenal, says that he could see the slopes of Mount Carmel from his window, so he must have occupied rooms on an upper story.[6]

The port of Acre faced south into the Bay of Haifa. Seawalls ran the length of the city from the north to the corner tower built by the Templars, and then west–east, curving to the north to follow the natural bend of the coast before running southeast. At the point where the coastline curved north, a levee mole ran into the bay from west to east, while another, longer one ran north–south from the Arsenal, on the west–east axis of the coastline. At the end of this longer mole, on the same axis as the west–east one, stood a defensive tower, known as the Tower of the Flies. A chain could be stretched across the gap between the Tower of the Flies and the shorter mole, so that access to the inner harbor by ships could be controlled.[7] To the east of the longer mole was the outer anchorage. The Venetian quarter occupied what must have been an advantageous position with waterfront access to the inner harbor, while the Pisan quarter stood between the Templars' corner tower and the west–east mole, and the Genoese just to the north of this with no direct access to the harbor. The Hospitallers' palace lay north of the Genoese quarter against the old twelfth-century city wall, which in the 1260s marked the boundary between the old city and Montmusard. In the 1260s the Hospital had its headquarters in this building, whereas the Templars had moved their center of operations to Château Pèlerin, along the coast south of Haifa, in 1218.

Western visitors such as Eudes and his household often found material standards of living in the cities of the eastern Mediterranean higher than at home. Many of the luxury goods in high demand among western elites either originated in or were more readily to be found in a city such as Acre. Local products for export to the West included sugarcane, cotton, soap, glass, and the raw materials for glass making, but Acre also served as a mediator of the overland trade from Asia and as a warehouse for goods destined for Europe from Egypt and its trade in the Indian Ocean. This meant that luxury goods such as spices (pepper, cinnamon, ginger), silks, and worked metals, which had by the mid-thirteenth century become an important indicator of high status, were more plentiful in Acre. Not all visitors or new immigrants found the change of diet easy at first, as Jacques de Vitry noted in his letters, when he lamented that it was "with some difficulty [that he had] taken some food—for

6. *Lettres de Jacques de Vitry*, ed. R. B. C. Huygens (Leiden: E. J. Brill, 1960), 79–97, no. 2.

7. By the thirteenth century, the eastern mole, which comprised masonry supported on timber rafts, was subsiding into the seabed, with the result that there were gaps through which smaller craft could find their way. Ruth Gertwagen, "The Crusader Port of Acre: Layout and Maintenance," in *Autour de la première croisade: Actes du colloque de la Society for the Study of the Crusades and the Latin East (Clermont-Ferrand, 22–25 juin 1995)*, ed. Michel Balard (Paris: Publications de la Sorbonne,1996), 553–82.

I have lost my appetite for eating and drinking since I entered this land beyond the sea." His avowal of being unable to digest the rich food may owe as much to his disapproval of the general environment he found as to the food.[8]

By the time of Eudes's residence in Acre, the years of apparently unbridled prosperity were in the past. The long-term consequences of disruption to overland trade with Asia were exacerbated by the War of St. Sabas (1258–61), a conflict between the two major commercial rivals in the eastern Mediterranean, Venice and Genoa. The other political and economic powers, notably the military orders, were drawn into the conflict. The Venetian victory over the Genoese altered the topography of the city considerably: the Genoese fortifications were destroyed, and between 1261 and 1270 Genoese citizens were expelled.[9]

The upgrading of the city's defenses in the face of the Mongol advance in 1260 had also changed the visual appearance of the city, as trees in gardens and orchards near the defensive walls were cut down. In 1263 Baybars's raid damaged properties in outlying suburbs, and further damage was caused a year later. Outlying defensive fortifications at Tell al-Fukhkhar were taken. In 1265, the year Eudes left France, buildings in the district of Daʿuk, including a mill tower, had been demolished by the inhabitants who feared their presence would provide raiders with a foothold from which to attack the city. Eudes's brief period of residence in the city thus came at a time when the built environment was changing as the city experienced low-level but constant threat of attack.

Crusaders, pilgrims, and visitors to the Holy Land from northern Europe were confronted with an urban landscape that was unfamiliar and unnerving. Famously, Jacques de Vitry, appointed bishop of Acre in 1216, described his impressions of life in his cathedral seat in a letter home to friends in the West. Acre was "a horrible city . . . full of countless disgraceful acts," he complained. Murder and sexual immorality were particularly widespread. Husbands and wives murdered each other, and poisons were easily obtainable. Prostitution was common, and even clergy rented out lodgings to prostitutes.[10] John Phocas, visiting Acre in 1177, referred to the unhealthy miasma that hung over the city because of the constant influx of people in a crowded space.[11] This sense of discomfort is corroborated by the Andalusian traveler Ibn Jubayr in 1184, who spoke of refuse and excrement in streets that were "choked by the press of men, so that it is hard to put foot to the ground."[12]

8. *Lettres de Jacques de Vitry*, 79–97, no. 2.

9. Jacoby, "New Venetian Evidence," 240–51.

10. *Lettres de Jacques de Vitry*, 79–97 no. 2.

11. John Phocas, *Descriptio Terrae Sanctae*, IX, in *Patrologiae Cursus Completus: Series Graeca*, ed. J. P. Migne (Paris, 1857–80), 133:933.

12. *The Travels of Ibn Jubayr*, trans. R. J. C. Broadhurst (London: Jonathan Cape, 1952), 318.

Although Frankish control over most of Jerusalem was restored by treaty between 1229 and 1244, most of the religious communities that had withdrawn to Acre or Tyre in 1187 remained there rather than returning to their original locations. This made Acre a particularly crowded ecclesiastical space—ironically, perhaps, since it was not conventionally regarded as being part of the biblical Holy Land.[13] In addition to its own parish churches and the cathedral of the Holy Cross, the city hosted most of the major communities that had served shrines or holy spaces in and around Jerusalem before 1187. Denys Pringle's authoritative survey of ecclesiastical buildings lists eighty-two in total, including churches, monasteries, convents and priories, chapels of ease, and hospitals.[14] All but one of these (the church of St. Nicholas) lay within the area bounded by the city walls. The distribution of these buildings within the old city was fairly even, but in Montmusard most were located on or close to the sea front. The twenty-six religious institutions mentioned as recipients of bequests in Eudes's inventory roll are similarly distributed equally across both the old city and Montmusard, but their locations are mostly restricted to the western side of both, with the only exception being St. Mary of the Germans.

The distribution according to type of institution also reveals the variety of different churches to be found in thirteenth-century Acre. Six were houses of Holy Land monasteries or convents, most of which had withdrawn their residences to Acre after 1187. The Acre house of the convent of St. Anne, in the Pisan quarter, is first mentioned in 1168, and the nuns remained in residence until the fall of Acre in 1291.[15] St. Lazare of Bethany may refer to what was in the twelfth century a male cell of the convent at Bethany, near Jerusalem, but after the enforced abandonment of the convent in 1187, it housed the nuns. The property, located in the northwest corner of Montmusard, included houses rented to the Trinitarian order of friars, a tower, and vineyard.[16] The sisters of St. Crux de Carpita, an order associated with the Claresses, are first attested in Antioch in 1257; after the city fell in 1268, they emigrated to Cyprus. Eudes's inventory is our only source for their presence in Acre.[17] St. Mary Magdalene was originally founded before 1222 as a Cistercian nunnery; it was a daughter house of Belmont, in the county of Tripoli, and its property in Acre was leased from the Hospital of St. John.[18] The house known in the inventory roll as Notre-Dame of Tyre was the community of nuns of Great St. Mary's, the Benedictine convent in Jerusalem, who after 1187 resettled in Tyre. They were given property by Queen Isabella I of Jerusalem in 1198/1203, after

13. *Lettres de Jacques de Vitry*, 79–97, no. 2.

14. Pringle, *The Churches of the Crusader Kingdom*, 15–175.

15. Pringle, *The Churches of the Crusader Kingdom*, 70–71, no. 395.

16. Pringle, *The Churches of the Crusader Kingdom*, 120–21, no. 418.

17. Pringle, *The Churches of the Crusader Kingdom*, 45, no. 378; for the history of the foundation, see Bernard Hamilton and Andrew Jotischky, *Latin and Greek Monasticism in the Crusader States* (Cambridge: Cambridge University Press, 2020), 239–41.

18. Pringle, *The Churches of the Crusader Kingdom*, 147–48, no. 434.

which time they seem to have abandoned Tyre.[19] Finally among this group, the Premonstratensian monastery of St. Samuel, founded in the reign of Baldwin II (1118–31) at Montjoie, a few miles west of Jerusalem, owned property in Acre by 1185, to which the community withdrew after the loss of the main house in 1187.[20]

A second group of eight recipients in the inventory roll are parish churches or small hospitals unique to the Holy Land. These include a small hospital, St. Martin of the Bretons, founded in 1254 by Giles, archbishop of Tyre, a native of Saumur who had been a crusader with Louis IX, and two leper hospitals, St. Bartholomew for men, and the Lepers of Bethlehem for women.[21] St. Catherine "of the Battlefield" was founded as a priory near Gaza in 1177, to commemorate Baldwin IV's victory over Saladin on the saint's feast day. By 1232 the priory is attested as having relocated to Acre, and only two years before Eudes's arrival there a citizen of Acre left a bequest to a hospital that the priory obviously also maintained.[22]

The third group of religious institutions Eudes or his executors favored were houses of international orders in Acre. These included the priories of the major—and some minor—mendicant orders: the Jacobins (Dominicans), the Cordeliers (Franciscans), the Carmelites, and the Sack Friars. The Dominicans and Franciscans had been present in Acre since the 1230s at the earliest.[23] The Carmelites had been founded between 1205 and 1214 as a hermitage on Mount Carmel, and at the time of Eudes's visit they followed a modified Dominican ordo. Although this house continued in existence at least until the 1260s, from 1229 onward they had also established houses elsewhere in the Holy Land, and after 1241 in the West as well. Eudes may have learned about them and their spirituality from Carmelite friars settled by Louis IX in France after 1254.[24] By the late 1250s or early 1260s, the Friars of the Sack, first established in the 1240s in Provence, had a house in Acre.[25] The Friars of the Holy Trinity, established in northern France with a ministry to ransom Christians taken captive in holy war by Muslims, had been recognized as an order by Pope Innocent III in 1198. By 1210/12, they also had a priory in Acre, with an endowment consisting of considerable urban property, and by 1219 also possessed forty-three small priories in western Europe.[26] As with the other mendicants, we can assume that Eudes was already familiar with them before departing for the East.

19. Pringle, *The Churches of the Crusader Kingdom*, 142–44, no. 431; Hamilton and Jotischky, *Latin and Greek Monasticism*, 223–24.

20. Pringle, *The Churches of the Crusader Kingdom*, 148–60, no. 443.

21. Pringle, *The Churches of the Crusader Kingdom*, 129–30, no. 421.

22. Pringle, *The Churches of the Crusader Kingdom*, 73, no. 399.

23. Hamilton and Jotischky, *Latin and Greek Monasticism*, 272, 282.

24. Hamilton and Jotischky, *Latin and Greek Monasticism*, 263–71.

25. Pringle, *The Churches of the Crusader Kingdom*, 50, no. 382.

26. Pringle, *The Churches of the Crusader Kingdom*, 56–57, no. 387.

The major hospitals in Acre also benefited from Eudes's generosity. The Hospitals of St. John and St. Lazarus were primarily associated with Jerusalem but, like most other religious institutions, had withdrawn to Acre in 1187. The Hospital of the Germans was a creation of the Third Crusade, owing its origins to a field hospital established during the crusaders' siege of the city. Even before the capture of Acre in 1191 some property had been promised by King Guy and Queen Sibylla, and an early tradition pinpoints this as a garden near the gate of St. Nicholas on the east side of the city, where they built the hospital. Despite jurisdictional disputes with the Hospital of St. John, the Hospital of the Germans thrived in the thirteenth century.[27] Eudes's familiarity with the Acre hospitals to which he also left bequests is less certain. The Hospital of St. Anthony, located in the southeast corner of Montmusard, hard by the eastern wall, can be identified as a house of the rather obscure Order of St. Anthony of Vienne, a foundation of the late eleventh century whose hospital in Acre is confirmed in a charter of 1264.[28] The Hospital of the Holy Spirit, in the Pisan quarter in the south of the city, had been given to the Pisans by Richard I during the Third Crusade in 1191/92. In 1227 the hospital had a staff of a master, two priests, five brothers, and three nuns. The hospital achieved notoriety in 1214 when one of the brothers assassinated Albert of Vercelli, patriarch of Jerusalem, during a procession on the feast of the Holy Cross.[29]

Twenty out of the twenty-six institutions in the inventory roll are also mentioned in the text known as the *Pelrinages et pardouns de Acre*, which dates from 1258–64 and offers a devotional route around Acre's many churches for pilgrims, with the indulgences specific to each.[30] In some respects, Eudes's list of beneficiaries is as interesting for its omissions as for its inclusions. The houses of some of the most powerful institutions in the kingdom are not there—the Holy Sepulcher, Notre-Dame de Josaphat, and St. Mary Latin, to name only three. Although the Hospital of St. John is listed, the Templars are not. Whether these omissions reflect a particular direction of piety, which sought to privilege churches fulfilling particular kinds of ministries, or whether the beneficiaries testify to a devotional path through the urban landscape known to Eudes but now obscure to us is a matter for speculation.

27. Pringle, *The Churches of the Crusader Kingdom*, 131–36, no. 425; Marie-Luise Favreau, *Studien zur Frühgeschichte des Deutschen Ordens*, Kieler Historische Studien 21 (Stuttgart: E. Klett, 1974), 35–63, 95–161.

28. Pringle, *The Churches of the Crusader Kingdom*, 71–72, no. 396.

29. Pringle, *The Churches of the Crusader Kingdom*, 54–56, no. 386.

30. "Pelrinages et pardouns de Acre," ed. H. Michelant and G. Raynaud, *Itinéraires à Jérusalem et descriptions de la Terre Sainte redigés en français aux XIe, XIIe et XIIIe siècles* (Geneva: Imprimerie Jules-Guillaume Fick,1882), 227–36; for English translation, Denys Pringle, *Pilgrimage to Jerusalem and the Holy Land, 1187–1291*, Crusade Texts in Translation 23 (Aldershot: Routledge, 2012), 16, 229–36.

11

The Experience of Acre, ca. 1266

Jonathan Rubin

At the core of this volume is a document associated with Eudes of Nevers's death. But what about the last months of his life? What can we know about his experiences in the East? What were his main impressions from his crusading campaign? Given the scarcity of pertinent source material, it is, of course, impossible to provide definitive answers to such questions, but one might argue that the count's experiences were, to a large extent, shaped by the place in which he sojourned during these months—the city of Acre. Against this backdrop, a sketch of some of the bustling city's characteristics and the diversity of its populace at the time can offer some insights and hypotheses concerning how Eudes and his men would have related to Acre and its residents.

Eudes landed in Acre on October 20, 1265, at a time when the city and its environs would certainly have made few newcomers feel safe. In March of that year, Caesarea—a major Frankish city located about fifty kilometers south of Acre, and one that King Louis IX had spent considerable time and money supporting—had fallen to the Mamluks. Later that month the town that had sprung up just outside the great castle of *Castrum Peregrinorum* (today known as 'Atlit) was captured and destroyed by Mamluk soldiers under the command of Baybars, and the town's inhabitants most likely took shelter behind the fort's walls. Haifa, located a mere fifteen kilometers from Acre as the crow flies, seems to have fallen to the Muslims on the same day.[1] During those same weeks in March, Acre's inhabitants, fearing a Muslim raid,

1. Joshua Prawer, *Histoire du royaume latin de Jérusalem*, trans. Gérard Nahon, 2 vols. (Paris: CNRS, 1970; repr. 2007), 2:462–66.

demolished the Chapel of St. Nicholas and the mill tower at Da'uk.[2] The city in which Eudes landed, therefore, was a major stronghold in a theater of war being waged against a mighty, encroaching enemy.

During Eudes's stay in Acre, things certainly became no easier for the Franks. In June 1266, Baybars took up a position near the city before leaving to attack the castle at Safad, which fell to him on July 23, 1266, just before Eudes's death.[3] The imposing Templar fort at Safad had been constructed at great expense, and its capture by the Mamluks, followed by the execution of its defenders, must have resonated very strongly in Acre and in particular among its Templar inhabitants, with whom Eudes appears to have had close contact.[4] Surely Eudes, who traveled to the East in order to fight the Mamluks, was not surprised by events of this kind, but he may have been frustrated that he was unable to participate in them in any meaningful way.

But while such bitter fighting, with the Franks mostly on the losing end, took place around the city, Eudes and his men may have been surprised to find that Acre was hardly a city in ruins, nor even desolate. Indeed, extant sources show that it was flourishing in many ways. Despite the military challenges noted above, Acre continued to attract considerable numbers of pilgrims. With the loss of the great traditional pilgrimage sites of the Holy Land, especially in and around Jerusalem, Acre came to house its own pilgrimage route, but whenever this was possible, pilgrims also continued to use the city as a base from which to depart on journeys to more traditional sites.[5] Burchard of Mount Sion, for example, mentions that on the Feast of All Saints, 1283, he visited Mount Gilboa with many others, suggesting that this visit was part of an organized pilgrim tour.[6] He also notes in his text that the Latin-European population of Acre tended to take advantage of western pilgrims, indicating that significant numbers of such travelers continued to reach the city.[7] Riccoldo of Monte Croce, who visited Acre in 1288–89, mentions that he departed from the city to go to the Galilee with many Christians, attesting to the considerable number of pilgrims there, even in the very final years before its fall in 1291.[8]

2. Denys Pringle, *The Churches of the Crusader Kingdom of Jerusalem: A Corpus* (Cambridge: Cambridge University Press, 1993–2009), 4:11.

3. Pringle, *The Churches of the Crusader Kingdom*, 4:11; Prawer, *Histoire*, 2:473–74.

4. *TdT*, 108–11; Paul Crawford, *The "Templar of Tyre": Part III of the "Deeds of the Cypriots,"* (Aldershot: Ashgate, 2003), 50-51.

5. Fabio Romanini and Beatrice Saletti, *The Pelrinages Communes, the Pardouns de Acre and the Crisis in the Crusader Kingdom: History and Texts* (Padova: Libreriauniversitaria.it edizioni, 2012).

6. Burchard of Mount Sion, OP, *Descriptio Terrae Sanctae*, ed. and trans. John R. Bartlett (Oxford: Oxford University Press, 2019), 80: "cum aliis multis."

7. Burchard of Mount Sion, OP, *Descriptio*, 190–92.

8. Riccoldo de Monte Croce, *Pérégrination en Terre Sainte et au Proche Orient: Texte latin et traduction. Lettres sur la chute de Saint-Jean d'Acre. Traduction*, ed. and trans. René Kappler, Textes et traductions des classiques français du Moyen Âge 4 (Paris: Honoré Champion, 1997),

It is equally noteworthy that in the 1260s, despite the Mamluks' successes in restricting the Latin territories in Outremer, Acre remained economically significant, even if less so than in the years before 1250. The considerable sums of money spent to acquire land and buildings in Acre at the time serve to confirm that the city, and its port in particular, were still considered vitally important economically.[9] As late as 1288, the Venetian decision to send thirty or forty metal anchors to Acre demonstrates the city's continued commercial vitality. The anchors were presumably used to facilitate ships docking off the coast and engaging in trade, and the transport of people, goods, and animals.[10] Had the Venetians thought that Acre was no longer a profitable port, such an investment would have made no sense.

Well into the later decades of the thirteenth century, Acre remained an impressive city, or at the very least, home to many remarkable buildings and neighborhoods. Focusing, for example, on its enclosing walls, it is noteworthy that between 1251 and 1254 Louis IX rebuilt the double defensive line surrounding the city.[11] Just over a decade later, when Eudes arrived in Acre, these walls must have been very impressive. At least some quarters within the city were surely no less imposing. Such was the case, for example, with regard to the city's Templar and Hospitaller compounds, which were described by the so-called Templar of Tyre:

> It [the Templar compound] occupied a large site on the sea, like a castle; it had at its entry a tall, strong tower, and the wall was thick, twenty-eight feet wide. On each corner of the tower was a turret, and upon each turret was a gilded lion *passant*, as big as a donkey . . . and it was a most magnificent thing to see. . . . The Hospital of St. John had good quarters with towers and a very lovely palace. . . . They had another location, which was called the *Auberge*, in which was a most noble palace, very long and very lovely.[12]

Since these descriptions appear within the account of the final Muslim offensive on Acre, one must assume that the picture offered here was valid up

---

38. For more evidence on pilgrimage in the last decades of the Kingdom of Jerusalem, see Denys Pringle, *Pilgrimage to Jerusalem and the Holy Land, 1187–1291*, Crusade Texts in Translation 23 (Farnham: Ashgate, 2012), 9–10.

9. David Jacoby, "New Venetian Evidence on Crusader Acre," in *The Experience of Crusading*, vol. 2: *Defining the Crusader Kingdom*, ed. Peter Edbury and Jonathan Phillips (Cambridge: Cambridge University Press, 2003), 244, 248; Marie-Luise Favreau-Lilie, "The Teutonic Knights in Acre after the Fall of Monfort (1271): Some Reflections," in *Outremer: Studies in the History of the Crusading Kingdom of Jerusalem Presented to Joshua Prawer*, ed. Benjamin Z. Kedar, Hans E. Mayer and R. C. Smail (Jerusalem: Yad Izhak Ben-Zvi Institute, 1982), 275–76.

10. David Jacoby, "Crusader Acre in the Thirteenth Century: Urban Layout and Topography," *Studi medievali* 20 (1979): 13.

11. Adrian J. Boas, *Crusader Archaeology: The Material Culture of the Latin East* (London: Routledge, 1999), 33.

12. Crawford, *The "Templar of Tyre,"* 114–15; for the original French text, see *TdT*, 220, 222.

to the very last Mamluk assault in the spring of 1291. Such elegant edifices would certainly have impressed Eudes and the members of his retinue during their time in the East.

Additionally, there is some evidence that new construction was undertaken, or at least planned, in different quarters of the city and that buildings were repaired during these last decades of Frankish Acre. Possible evidence of one significant project is a charter granted to the Anconitans in 1257 that shows that they were planning to build a church, a communal building, and a hostel for the accommodation of their merchants.[13] Similarly, the Venetian senate decided in 1286 to ship a considerable amount of building material to Acre to renovate the *fondaco* and other public buildings in the areas under Venetian control.[14]

Eudes and his followers must have also been impressed by the variety of cultural groups whose members inhabited or visited the city. Among these were representatives of various regions in Latin Christendom, including speakers of French and Provençal as well as various Italian dialects. German speakers and English speakers were similarly represented in areas throughout the city.[15] Members of different Eastern Christian groups, such as the Greek Orthodox, Armenian, Jacobite, Coptic, Nestorian, and possibly Maronite churches, were present in the city too, as was a significant Jewish community.[16] While it is unclear whether there was a permanent Muslim community in thirteenth-century Acre, individual adherents of this faith were clearly present in the city. In other words, arriving in Acre, Eudes and his retinue would have encountered an environment bustling with people speaking different languages, holding different beliefs, of different origins, and with a variety of rationales for being there. Indeed, the turbulent events of the years preceding their arrival to Acre probably made this diversity even more pronounced as the city accommodated the influx of refugees from a multitude of cultures who had fled regions captured by the Mongols and later the Mamluks.

13. David Jacoby, "Aspects of Everyday Life in Frankish Acre," *Crusades* 4 (2005): 78; David Abulafia, "The Anconitan Privileges in the Kingdom of Jerusalem and the Levant Trade of Ancona," in *I comuni italiani nel regno crociato di Gerusalemme: Atti del Colloquio "The Italian Communes in the Crusading Kingdom of Jerusalem" (Jerusalem, May 24 – May 28, 1984)*, ed. Gabriella Airaldi and Benjamin Z. Kedar, Collana storica di fonti e studi 48 (Genoa: Università di Genova, Istituto di medievistica, 1986), 561.

14. Jacoby, "Crusader Acre," 36.

15. Jonathan Rubin, *Learning in a Crusader City: Intellectual Activity and Intercultural Exchanges in Acre, 1191–1291* (Cambridge: Cambridge University Press, 2018), 3. For a more elaborate survey of the western population of the Latin East in general, see Laura Minervini, "Le français dans l'Orient latin (XIIIe–XIVe siècles): Éléments pour la caractérisation d'une *scripta* du Levant," *Revue de linguistique romane* 74 (2010): 120–25.

16. Rubin, *Learning in a Crusader City*, 3–4, 37–45. See also Minervini, "Le français," 126–28; Pringle, *The Churches of the Crusader Kingdom*, 4:59–60 (Maronites), 42 (Armenians), 148–49 (Jacobites), 73, 78 (Greek Orthodox), 21 (Nestorian).

Although some clues remain, it is difficult to say much about the interactions of Eudes and his companions with members of these varied cultural communities. Starting with the Latins, it is worth noting, as Morreale and Lester do, that very few of Eudes's bequests were made to institutions located in the sections of Acre dominated by the Italian city-states. This may reflect some kind of tension between those originating from the Kingdom of France as opposed to those from the Italian peninsula. Such tensions may have become more acrimonious because of the damages caused by the so-called War of St. Sabas, a conflict said to have originated with a struggle concerning a strategically placed house in Acre, which was owned by the monastery of St. Sabas. Street violence between the communities escalated into a war fought mainly in Acre and Tyre. The fighting in Acre, which included the use of engines hurling heavy stones, caused much damage to the city and its residents, whether or not they were directly involved in the fighting, and one may assume that it brought about considerable resentment toward the powers involved.[17] Furthermore, one may suppose that this war left the part of the city closest to the port, where the Italian quarters were located, particularly scarred by the intense violence and destruction.[18] This may have made institutions in this area less appealing for donations.

Another sociocultural division should be taken into account when considering Eudes's experiences of Acre. As a cultural group, the Latin inhabitants of the city constituted two major groups: those who had just arrived from the West, either in order to settle there or for a short stay as pilgrims, crusaders, and merchant-visitors, and those who had spent a long period in Outremer, living as semipermanent residents, or who had been born there, some into families who had been in the Levant for several generations. Eudes's Account-Inventory certainly reflects the impact of the "Outremer Franks" on Eudes's contingent. In fact, the Account-Inventory includes a considerable number of toponyms and terms whose use was characteristic of the French of Outremer. From Eudes's perspective we see, in short, a French view of Acre communicated in a partly local French idiom and dialect.

Additional evidence for contacts between Eudes's retinue and local Franks can be gleaned from the names of two men found among the list of those to whom the count owed money, Salemon de Safforit and Lionnet de Tabarie. The word "Tabarie" could refer either to Tiberias, the ancient city on the shore of the Sea of Galilee, or to a village located not far from Acre; Safforit seems to refer to Saffuriya, a major Frankish site found near Nazareth. Extrapolating from these toponyms, we can probably identify two members of Frankish families who had long been established in the East. With regard to Lionnet,

17. For a survey of this war, see Thomas F. Madden, "The War of Towers: Venice and Genoa at War in Crusader Syria, 1256–8," in *Syria in Crusader Times: Conflict and Co-Existence*, ed. Carole Hillenbrand (Edinburgh: Edinburgh University Press, 2020), 211–24.

18. Jacoby, "Crusader Acre," 29; Pringle, *The Churches of the Crusader Kingdom*, 4:145.

one should also note that in 1247 the Franks lost control of the city of Tiberias.[19] Lionnet may therefore be an example of a Latin refugee who fled to Acre for safety. Another witness to the connections between Eudes and his men on the one hand and permanent Frankish residents of Acre on the other is Jaque Vidaut, a man whose name appears only once in the Account-Inventory, in an entry that indicates that Eudes was in possession of a horse that had belonged to Vidaut. The man whose name appears in the Account-Inventory is in all likelihood the same person as Jacques Vidal, also known as Jacobus Vitalis, a French knight and fief-holder in the Kingdom of Jerusalem, who both served as marshal of the kingdom and was renowned for his juridical expertise.[20]

It is more challenging to say anything definitive about what Eudes may have thought or felt concerning non-Latins residing in Acre or more generally in the East. One may assume, however, that—aside from a highly militant attitude toward the Muslim foe—Eudes is likely to have been at least somewhat curious about the exotic other. Evidence from John of Joinville's text supports this hypothesis, for it shows that some knights were interested in information reaching Frankish circles concerning groups with which they had only limited nonmartial contact, such as the Mamluks.[21] That Eudes would have also been interested in such matters is, of course, impossible to prove, but the presence of fabrics produced in the East—referred to in the Account-Inventory as *boqueranz*, *cameline*, or *dras de tartais*—is an indication that Eudes entertained at least some level of curiosity and interest in Eastern cultures in terms of their material products.[22]

Finally, Acre, even in its final decades as a Christian stronghold, was home to several figures who produced valuable written texts addressing a range of topics. While Eudes was first and foremost a knight rather than a man of learning, he did carry books with him. It is not unreasonable, therefore, that he would have devoted some attention to Outremer writers, or have come into contact with some of them during his sojourn. For example, at precisely the time Eudes was living in the city, the Italian jurist John of Ancona was active there, composing his *Summa Iuris Canonici* and, among other things, working for the Templars.[23] Since the Templars figure prominently in the inventory, it is possible that John and Eudes may have actually met. This possibility tends toward probability if one takes into account that the abovementioned Jaque Vidaut, who seems to have had some kind of relationship with Eudes, was also praised by John of Ancona in his work on feudal law, thereby implying that

19. Pringle, *The Churches of the Crusader Kingdom*, 2:351.

20. Rubin, *Learning in a Crusader City*, 29–30, 186 and the references there.

21. Jean de Joinville, *Vie de Saint Louis*, ed. and trans. Jacques Monfrin (Paris: Garnier, 1995), 138–41.

22. See the essay by Sharon Farmer in this volume.

23. Rubin, *Learning in a Crusader City*, 92–93, 179, 186.

the two were personally acquainted.[24] We can thus begin to imagine a circle of men, gathering or meeting on occasion, to talk about laws of inheritance, disputed legal claims, contracts, and the like, all members of an expansive Latin cultural network that spanned the Mediterranean and whose writings, opinions, and exigencies informed practice and principle. Eudes's Account-Inventory can therefore be understood in part as a product of just such a cultural matrix.

Additional possibilities for intellectual and cultural connections emerge with regard to Acre's mendicant convents. The Franciscans and Dominicans had established houses in the city, and both of these served as centers of learning. Given that both houses received bequests from Eudes, it is not impossible that Eudes or some of his followers had personal connections to individual Franciscan and Dominican friars housed there. Particularly noteworthy in this regard is William of Tripoli, a member of Acre's Dominican convent who in 1271 dedicated his *Notitia de Machometo* to Theobald Visconti, later Pope Gregory X.[25] This is an elaborate, generally well-informed, treatise on Islam, the main parts of which are devoted to the following: Muhammad and the rise of his people; the Qur'an and its compilation; and the Qur'anic teachings regarding Christian faith.[26] An analysis of this text shows that it was composed in a milieu in which other texts about Islam were written and read, and where some Latins were able to attain a high level of knowledge of Arabic and of Islamic practice and belief.[27] More than a decade before Eudes reached Acre, John of Joinville seems to have been impressed by another Dominican, Yves the Breton, who not only spoke Arabic, but also, for example, brought to Acre impressions of his interactions with the head of the Syrian Nizaris.[28] It thus seems quite possible that Eudes or members of his entourage would have been similarly appreciative of someone like William, whose knowledge of Arabic and Islamic traditions would have been evident in these environments. Similarly, Eudes and those with him must have relied upon Arabic-speaking contacts, probably including Latin friars and local men and women, to translate for them, to transact business locally, and to serve as cultural brokers to some extent.[29]

Eudes's crusade brought him to a city of paradoxes: Acre in 1266 was almost completely engulfed by the forces of a threatening and determined enemy, which seemed to be unstoppable. And yet, it remained the destination

24. Rubin, *Learning in a Crusader City*, 29–30.

25. Wilhelm von Tripolis, *Notitia de Machometo; De Statu Sarracenorum*, ed. Peter Engels, CISC Series Latina 4 (Würzburg: Echter, 1992), 66, 71.

26. Rubin, *Learning in a Crusader City*, 123–24.

27. Rubin, *Learning in a Crusader City*, 68–69, 118–29.

28. Joinville, *VSL*, 226–29.

29. For a considerable body of evidence concerning translators in the Latin East, see William Stephen Murrell Jr., "Dragomans and Crusaders: The Role of Translators and Translation in the Medieval Eastern Mediterranean, 1098–1291" (PhD diss., Vanderbilt University, 2018).

for numerous pilgrims and retained much of its beauty and status as a trading hub. It was also the home of a varied population, some elements of which Eudes probably came to know and understand well and others that must have remained a puzzle to him. This completely new cultural world is likely to have aroused, at least to some degree, Eudes's curiosity and might have led him to communicate with local men of letters. Be that as it may, the last months of Eudes's life were probably full of new, powerful experiences, only some of which were directly related to the military tasks for which he had originally sailed to Acre. What it meant to him to then die in this new and different world we can only imagine.

12

Textiles in Eudes of Nevers's Posthumous Inventory

A Meeting of East and West

Sharon Farmer

The textiles in Eudes of Nevers's posthumous inventory are indicative of the degree to which Acre served as a meeting place of eastern and western goods in the mid-thirteenth century. Luxury patterned silks, cotton or linen buckram, and soft camlets arrived there from, or via, the Mongol Empire, and luxury woolens, practical woolens, linens, and union textiles (i.e., textiles containing yarns of differing fibers, in this case, wool yarns and linen yarns) arrived from various production centers in the West, most notably northern France, the Low Countries, and northern Italy.[1] Some textiles on the market in Acre would have been produced in the Levant itself, but it is impossible to determine if any of these were among Eudes of Nevers's belongings.[2]

In nearly all cases, we need to exercise caution concerning the provenance and nature of the textiles that are named but not fully identified in Eudes's inventory. Medieval merchants, administrators, and consumers knew what

1. On shipments of western textiles to Acre and the Levant, see Patrick Chorley, "The Cloth Exports of Flanders and Northern France during the Thirteenth Century: A Luxury Trade?," *Economic History Review* 40 (1987): 349–79; and Eliyahu Ashtor, *Levant Trade in the Middle Ages* (Princeton, NJ: Princeton University Press, 1983), 4–5, 153, 155, 326.

2. For examples of Syrian silks from this period, see Sophie Desrosiers, *Soieries et autres textiles de l'Antiquité au XVIe siècle: Musée National du Moyen Âge-Thermes de Cluny-Catalogue* (Paris: Editions de la Réunion des Musées Nationaux, 2004), 284–85, nos. 152–53; also Francesco Balducci Pegalotti, *La pratica della mercatura*, ed. Allan Evans (Cambridge, MA: Medieval Academy of America, 1936), 209; and Ashtor, *Levant Trade*, 204, 323.

textile terms meant to them, but in most cases they never bothered to spell out the specific characteristics that they associated with particular textile names. Guild statutes, account books, travel narratives, merchant manuals, and literary texts can help us narrow the analysis, but terminology and technical requirements could change from one town or region to another, or from one century to another.[3] Moreover, in some cases, such as that of silk *cendal*, which I discuss below, important characteristics of textiles were never spelled out in the texts, and indeed, most consumers would not have understood those characteristics.

Additionally, ambiguity continues around naming practices related to place of production. One problem is that of extremely similar textile names that referred to textiles that were quite distinct. Some textile names associated textiles with a particular place of production, even if the place in question was extremely large, and even after other centers of production had started manufacturing the same textiles. We have the same phenomenon today with textiles such as "crêpe de Chine"—which is not always made in China. To complicate matters further, some scholarly traditions associate particular medieval textile names with particular places of origin, even when solid evidence for such connections is lacking. Nevertheless, there are strong indications that Eudes of Nevers possessed textiles from China or Central Asia, from India, and from western Europe.

Three of the textiles in the inventory—*dras de tartais*, *boqueranz* (English: buckram), and *camelot* (English: camlet)—were associated in thirteenth- and fourteenth-century European travel narratives with the Mongol Empire or with the Indian subcontinent. According to Giovanni di Pian di Carpine, the Franciscan friar who was chosen by Pope Innocent IV to lead the first European diplomatic mission to the Mongol Empire in 1245, the Mongols (or, more likely, members of the Mongol court) tended to wear tunics made of "*bucarano, purpura, vel baldachino*."[4] The first of those textiles was buckram (although we should not confuse modern buckram with the medieval textile), the second was a type of patterned silk, and the third—baudekin—was probably identical with *dras de tartais*.[5]

Dras de tartais—meaning "cloth of the Mongols"—shows up with some frequency in European inventories and account books from the thirteenth and

3. Françoise Piponnier, "À propos des textiles anciens, principalement médiévaux," *Annales: Economies, sociétés, civilisations* 22 (1967): 864–80.

4. "Tunicas vero portant de bucarano, purpura, vel baldachino," Giovanni di Pian di Carpine, *Storia dei Mongoli, edizione critica*, ed. Enrico Menestò, Italian trans. Maria Cristiana Lungarotti (Spoleto: Centro Italiano di Studi sull'Alto Medioevo, 1989), chap. 2, 233.

5. On the nature of baudekin, see "Baldachin," "The Lexis of Cloth and Clothing Project," University of Manchester, accessed December 6, 2021, http://lexissearch.arts.manchester.ac.uk/entry.aspx?id=280; and Elizabeth Coatsworth and Mark Chambers, "Baudekin," in *Brill Encyclopedia of Medieval Dress and Textiles Online*, ed. Gail Owen Crocker, Elizabeth Coatsworth, and Maria Hayward (Leiden: Brill, 2012), https://doi.org/10.1163/2213-2139_emdt_SIM_000814.

fourteenth centuries, and physical examples of textiles that have come to be identified with this name appear with relative frequency in western European church treasuries and tombs from the same period (see figures 19–20). Modern textile scholars have determined that *dras de tartais*—as well as baudekin—were extremely valuable patterned silk fabrics that were woven with a lampas weave (a luxury weave that includes both a simple background weft—usually in a taffeta weave—and a pattern weft), and employed not only silk but also gold or silver thread.[6]

In most cases in the thirteenth century these fabrics did indeed originate in the Mongol Empire, as the name suggests.[7] By the early fourteenth century, however, the picture gets more complex, because silk weavers in Lucca, Italy, figured out the lampas weave technique of Tartar brocades, so fourteenth-century western account books—such as the 1317 account of the French royal wardrobe keeper, Geoffrey of Fleury—began to refer to "Tartar cloths of Lucca." We know, in fact, that lampas-woven silk and gold brocades from Lucca could look and feel very much like Tartar cloths of gold that came from Central Asia.[8] In Eudes of Nevers's inventory, however, we can assume with relative certainty that mentions of *dras de tartais* refer to silk and metallic brocades from the Mongol Empire.

The medieval French, Italian, and English translations for Carpine's "bucaranus" were *boqueranz* (as in Eudes's inventory), *bougran* (French), *bocarrama/bucherame* (Italian), and *bukeram* (English). The modern English equivalent is "buckram," but modern *bougran*/buckram bears little resemblance to the medieval textile. Some medieval texts suggest that buckram was made with cotton; others that it was made with linen.[9] Whatever its fiber, twelfth- and thirteenth-century French literary sources associate the adjectives *rice* and *chier* with this textile, indicating that it was luxurious.[10] Carpine's description of Mongol dress also suggests that this must have been a luxury

6. Anne Wardwell, "*Panni tartarici*: Eastern Islamic Silks Woven with Gold and Silver (13th and 14th Centuries)," *Islamic Art* 3 (1988–89): 95–173; C. Y. Watt and Anne Wardwell, *When Silk Was Gold: Central Asian and Chinese Textiles* (New York: Harry N. Abrams, 1998), chap. 4.

7. Wardwell, "*Panni Tartarici*"; Watt and Wardwell, *When Silk Was Gold*, chap. 4.

8. "Tartaires de Lucques," "tartaires changeans de Luques": "Compte de draps d'or et de soie rendu par Geoffroi de Fleuri argentier du roi Philippe Le Long en 1317," in *Nouveau recueil de comptes de l'argenterie des rois de France*, ed. Louis Douët-d'Arcq (Paris: Jules Renouard, 1874), 2, 5; Anne Wardwell, "The Stylistic Development of 14th- and 15th-Century Italian Silk Designs," *Aachener Kunstblätter* 47 (1976–77): 176–226. For physical examples: Tamara Boccherini, ed., *The Prato Textile Museum* (Milan: Skira 1999), 34; Desrosiers, *Soieries et autres textiles*, cat. no. 186, pp. 48, 342–44.

9. Henry Yule, *The Travels of Marco Polo: The Complete Yule-Cordier Edition* (New York: Dover, 1993), 1: 47, citing Villani's Chronicle of Florence; Victor Gay, *Glossaire archéologique du Moyen Âge et de la Renaissance* (Paris: Librairie de la Société Bibliographique, 1887), 1:189.

10. See texts quoted by Francisque Michel, *Recherches sur les étoffes de soie, d'or et d'argent pendant le Moyen Âge* (Paris: Imprimerie de Chapelet, 1852; Typographie de Ch. Lahure, 1854), 2:29–30.

textile, since the Mongols considered it a suitable alternative to the luxurious patterned silks known as "purple" and "baudekin."

According to Marco Polo, fine buckrams were produced in Arzingan, in greater Armenia, in Abyssinia, and along the Malabar coast of the Indian subcontinent. Tana and Cambaet, in India, also exported buckrams, but, Polo claimed, "the most beautiful and refined [buckrams] in all the world, and those of the greatest value" were produced in Mutfili (Motupalli), in southeast India. Throughout the world, he continued, "there is no king or queen who wouldn't wear [the buckram of Mutfili] on account of its greatness and beauty."[11]

But not all buckram was luxurious. In Tibet, Polo claimed, the people dressed poorly, "in skins, canvas, or buckram."[12] Moreover, not all buckram was produced beyond the confines of Europe. By the thirteenth century, and perhaps even by the twelfth, cotton buckrams were being produced in Italy; in the mid-fourteenth century both Boccaccio and Pegalotti identified Cyprus as a center of buckram production.[13]

The uses of buckram varied in the medieval West and evolved over time. French records from the 1320s and 1330s indicate that it was used to make fine garments trimmed with miniver, chapel and bedroom hangings, and quilts—some of which were embroidered, as was the case with one of Count Eudes's buckram textiles.[14] Fourteenth-century accounts and literary sources also indicate that buckram was used to make quilted doublets and aketons, which military men wore as protective undergarments.[15] By the late seventeenth century, the names buckram and *bougran* had come to be attached to a textile that is associated with those names today: a form of gummed open

11. Marco Polo, *Le divisament dou monde*, chaps. 175 (direct quote), 22, 183, 185, 186, 193: Marco Polo, *Milione: Le divisament dou monde; il Milione nelle redazioni Toscana e franco-italiana*, ed. Gabriella Ronchi (Milan: Arnoldo Mondadori Editore, 1982), 325, 563, 583, 586–87, 604; Marco Polo, *The Description of the World*, trans. Sharon Kinoshita (Indianapolis: Hackett, 2016), 16, 163, 174, 176–77, 186.

12. Polo, *Le divisament*, chap. 115, ed. Ronchi, 464; trans. Kinoshita, 102.

13. Maureen Mazzaoui, *The Italian Cotton Industry in the Later Middle Ages, 1100–1600* (Cambridge: Cambridge University Press, 1981), 89–90, 93; Boccaccio, *Decameron*, Eighth Day, Novella 10, trans. J. M. Rigg (London: A. H. Bullen, 1953), 2:252; Pegalotti, *Pratica della mercatura*, 36, 108.

14. "Chronique de Valenciennes," cited by Gay, *Glossaire archéologique*, 1:188; Arras, Archives du Pas-de-Calais, Centre Mahaut d'Artois, Series A, 428, described by Jules-Marie Richard, *Inventaire-Sommaire des archives départementales antérieures à 1790, Pas-de-Calais, Archives Civiles—Série A* (Arras: Imprimerie de la Société du Pas-de-Calais, 1878–87), 1:344; "Inventaire de Clémence de Hongrois [1328]," ed. Douët-d'Arcq, *Nouveau recueil de comptes*, 74–76.

15. "Inventaire des biens de feu Raoul de Nesle Connétable de France," ed. Chrétien César Auguste Dehaisnes, in *Documents et extraits divers concernant l'histoire de l'art dans la Flandre, l'Artois et le Hainaut avant le XVe siècle* (Lille: L Quarré, Libraire et Editeur, 1886), 1:139; *Li romans de Bauduin de Sebourc, IIIe Roy de Jhérusalem: Poëme du XIVe siècle publié pour la première fois d'après les manuscrits de la Bibliothèque nationale*, ed. M. L. Roca (Valenciennes: Imprimerie de B. Henry, 1841), chant xix, lines 310–11, 2:194; cited by Michel, *Recherches*, 2:32.

weave canvas that is used to stiffen garments and book bindings. In 1838 Marie-Armand d'Avezac de Castera-Macaya, who wrote the preface to the first modern edition of Carpine's *Ystoria Mongalorum*, suggested that the etymology for *boqueranz/bougran/buckram* pointed to the town of Boukhara, in modern Uzbekistan, as the location where the textile must have first been produced. Many scholars have since subscribed to that theory—but with no solid evidence other than the resemblance of the names.[16]

Yet a third luxury textile in Eudes's inventory—camlet, or *camelot*—seems to have originated in regions of East Asia that were under Mongol rule in the thirteenth century. According to Marco Polo, the best camlets in the world were made of camels' wool and were woven in the city of Eriqaya/Ningxia (modern Zhongxing, in northwest China). He also reported that camlets were woven in Tibet.[17] In all likelihood the textiles in question were made with fur from the undercoat of the Central Asian Bactrian camel, as is the case today with high-quality camel-wool textiles. By the early fourteenth century, some camlets were identified as coming from Tripoli, and by 1333 Venetian weavers were apparently making them in Armenia. Toward the end of the fourteenth century, moreover, some camlets were identified as being produced in Reims.[18]

It is not always clear what fibers were used to make the later camlets: one English royal wardrobe account from 1328 specifically identifies a piece of camlet as being made of silk, as does the fifteenth-century posthumous inventory of the possessions of Jacques Coeur. But most sources suggest that camlet was woven with a soft, warm fiber—not only with camels' fur, but also, as suggested by later sources, with mohair, which comes from the fur of the Angora goat, which was originally from Turkey.[19]

16. M. d'Avezac, "Notice sur les anciens voyages de Tartarie en général et sur celui de Jean du Plan de Carpin en particulier," in *Relation des Mongols ou Tartares par le frère Jean du Plan de Carpin . . . première édition complete publiée d'après les manuscrits de Leyde, de Paris, et de Londres, et précédée d'une Notice sur les anciens voyages de Tartarie en général et sur celui de Jean du Plan de Carpin en particulier par M. D'Avezac* (Paris: Librairie Géographique de Arthus-Bertrand, 1838), 128. On the influence of d'Avezac's theory, see Paul Pelliot, *Notes on Marco Polo: Ouvrage posthume publié sous les auspices de l'Académie des Inscriptions et Belles-Lettres et avec le concours du Centre national de la Recherche scientifique* (Paris: Impr. Nationale, 1959), 1:111.

17. Polo, *Le divisament*, chaps. 73, 116, ed. Ronchi, 397, 465; trans. Kinoshita, 61–62, 102.

18. Camlets from Tripoli: "Compte de draps d'or et de soie rendu par Geoffroy de Fleuri," 3, 5, 6, 19. Camlet production by Venetians: document copied in the collection of Amadeo Svajer, and cited by Jacopo Filiasi, *Memorie storiche de'Veneti primi e secondi, Edizione seconda* (Padua: Presso Il Seminario, 1812), 6:59n2, and again by Victor Gay, article on "Camelot," *Glossaire archéologique*, 1:263. Camlet production in Reims: "Compte de Guillaume Brunel, argentier du roi Charles VI (1387)," ed. Douët-d'Arcq, *Nouveau recueil de comptes*, 240.

19. Silk camlet: Lisa Monnas, "Silk Cloths Purchased for the Great Wardrobe of the Kings of England, 1325–1462," *Textile History* 20 (1989): 286; "Extraits inédits de compte de la vente des biens de Jacques Coeur," ed. Pierre Clément, in *Jacques Coeur et Charles VII, ou la France au XVe siècle: Étude historique* (Paris: Librairie de Guillaumin, 1853), 217, cited by Gay, *Glossaire archéologique*, 1:263. Mohair camlet: description of goats of Cyprus by Sebastian Münster,

Some scholars have assumed that camelot and camelin were identical textiles. Camelin, however, was a type of wool cloth that was produced in various towns of northern France and the Low Countries—if not in other locations as well.[20] The thirteenth-century author John of Garland suggested that the name referred to the "camel-like" color of the cloth, but this was not always the case, since some inventories and guild statutes refer to both brown and "white" camelin.[21] In Eudes of Nevers's inventory the word *camelin* is used only as an adjective, perhaps indicating that the cloth in question—a piece of *tiretaine*—was a particular shade of brown.

Two groups of textiles in Eudes's inventory—orfreys, which were patterned woven bands with metallic threads, and tapestries—could have been created either in the West or in the East.[22] The remaining textiles—several varieties of woolen cloth, linen cloth, linen tablecloths, *tiretaine*, and *cendal*, which was a tabby-woven lightweight silk—were probably woven in western Europe. Only two of the textiles, however, were identified with a particular center of production or commercial activity: one piece of striped wool was identified in Eudes's inventory as being from Provins, which was a major center for the production of striped woolens; and one piece of linen, purchased in Troyes, could have been produced in any one of a number of centers of linen production in France and England.[23]

Eudes's woolen textiles ranged from an extremely valuable piece of wool known as "scarlet" to a less luxurious wool textile known as serge, or *saie*. "Scarlets" were heavy, fulled, woolen broadcloths that were woven with

---

Cosmographie Universelle, French trans. François de Belleforest (Paris, 1575), part 2, col. 765 (cited by Gay, *Glossaire archéologique*, 1:264); and description of the goats of Cogne (Konya), in Cilicia, Anatolia, and the camlets made with their wool by Pierre Belon, *Les observations de plusieurs singularitez et choses memorables, trouvées en Grèce, Asie, Judée, Egypte, Arabie et autres pays estranges* (Paris, 1555), bk. 2, chap. 112, 167 (cited by Gay, *Glossaire archéologique*, 1:264).

20. *Le livre des métiers d'Etienne Boileau*, ed. René de Lespinasse and François Bonnardot (Paris: Imprimerie Nationale, 1879), 96, chap. L: sections 22 and 24; "Compte de l'argenterie de Geoffroy de Fleuri," in *Comptes de l'argenterie des rois de France au XIVe siècle*, ed. Louis Douët-D'Arcq (Paris: Jules Renouard, 1851), 22.

21. Piponnier, "À propos des textiles anciens," 866–67. For white camelin: "Inventaire de Clémence de Hongrois," 71, and *Livre des métiers d'Etienne Boileau*, 96, chap. L: section 22. (refers to both brown and white camelins).

22. For examples of patterned bands with metallic thread from Paris, see Desrosiers, *Soieries et autres textiles*, 162–65, nos. 75–77; for examples from Cologne: Desrosiers, *Soieries et autres textiles*, 258–62, nos. 137–41; for an example from Central Asia, Desrosiers, *Soieries et autres textiles*, 312, no. 166. The most prestigious European centers for tapestry weaving were Paris and Arras: Sharon Farmer, "*Biffes*, *Tiretaines*, and *Aumonières*: The Role of Paris in the International Textile Markets of the Thirteenth and Fourteenth Centuries," in *Medieval Clothing and Textiles*, vol. 2, ed. Robin Netherton and Gale R. Owen-Crocker (Woodbridge: Boydell, 2006), 80. See "Inventaire des biens de feu Raoul de Nesle," 140, for a reference to a "tapis d'outremer."

23. On striped woolens from Provins, see Chorley, "The Cloth Exports of Flanders and Northern France," 363; on English and French centers of linen production, see Farmer, "*Biffes*, *Tiretaines*, and *Aumonières*," 78–81.

expensive, greased, short-stapled wool and dyed with kermes, an extremely valuable red dye made from parasitical insects that were harvested from the leaves of oak trees around the Mediterranean. Despite the name and the color of the expensive dye, however, not all "scarlets" were red in color: the one in Eudes's inventory was, in fact, identified as having a color ("*poonace*") that resembled the iridescent purple of pigeons. Serges—or *saies*—were usually woven with a warp of ungreased, long-stapled wool, known as "worsted" in English, and with a weft of "greased" short-stapled wool.[24] However, one of Eudes's *saies* is described as "black serge mantel of beaver [*saie noire de bievre*]," suggesting that beavers' fur may have been used to create the yarns for either the warp or the weft.

Two additional textiles in Eudes's inventory—a union textile known as *tiretaine* and a lightweight single-colored silk known as *cendal*—were also, in all likelihood, made in western Europe. Both were favored for summer wear. In both cases, moreover, it is difficult to come up with an appropriate modern English translation. In the mid-thirteenth century and well into the fourteenth, the Italian city of Florence was a major center for the production of *tiretaine*; and by the end of that period Paris was emerging as a center of production as well. We know that *tiretaine* was a textile made with two fibers: one for the warp—linen, cotton, or silk—and another, almost always wool, for the weft.[25] *Tiretaine* was thus a "union textile."[26] One possible English translation would be linsey-woolsey, because linsey-woolsey was, like many *tiretaines*, woven with both wool and linen yarns. But we often associate linsey-woolsey with homespun cloth from colonial North America, and that association would degrade the value and quality of many medieval *tiretaines*. Indeed, it appears to us in the inventories of kings and queens and in the account books of the highest level of the French aristocracy, and it often sold at extremely high prices. Preserving the medieval term, *tiretaine*, is most useful here.

Retaining the medieval term *cendal* also makes sense, despite the fact that fifteenth-century sources defined it as a particular type of taffeta.[27] Like taffeta, *cendal* was a silk textile that was woven with the simplest of weaves, the

24. On "scarlet" as a type of woolen cloth rather than a color, see John H. Munro, "The Medieval Scarlet and the Economics of Sartorial Splendour," in *Cloth and Clothing in Medieval Europe: Essays in Memory of E. M. Carus-Wilson*, ed. N. B. Harte and K. G. Ponting (London: Heinemann, 1983), 13–70; on the differences between "woolen cloth," "worsted," and "serge," see John H. Munro, "Medieval Woolens: Textiles, Textile Technology and Industrial Organisation, c. 800–1500," in *Cambridge History of Western Textiles*, ed. David Jenkins (Cambridge: Cambridge University Press, 2003), 1:181–227.

25. Piponnier, "À propos des textiles anciens," 873; Farmer, "*Biffes*, *Tiretaines*, and *Aumonières*," 75–78.

26. Elizabeth Coatsworth, "Tiretaine," *Brill Encyclopedia of Medieval Dress and Textiles Online*.

27. Piponnier, "À propos des textiles anciens," 871–72.

one-over one-under weave that we call tabby, linen, or indeed, taffeta weave. Before the fifteenth century *cendal* and taffeta were clearly distinguished from one another: the posthumous inventory of the French queen Clemence of Hungary, for instance, who died in 1328, included some garments that were lined with *cendal* and some that were lined with taffeta.[28]

What, then, distinguished *cendal* from taffeta, or from other forms of taffeta? First, it was a lightweight silk fabric, frequently used as the lining for summer clothing; and, second, it was always dyed in a single color. Guild statutes from Lucca indicate, moreover, that the dying of *cendal* always took place after the cloth had been woven, rather than immediately after the yarns had been created, as was always the case for patterned silks, but is often the case as well for crisp, tightly woven taffetas.[29]

Through the use of highly magnified images of the yarns that constituted medieval *cendal*, textile archeologist Sophie Desrosiers has determined that while the warp yarns of *cendal* silk were lightly twisted, the weft yarns had no discernable twist at all. The absence of any discernible twist on the weft of *cendals* provides the key to understanding why they were always woven before they were dyed: because in order to properly dye silk fiber one needs, first, to "cook" it—to run it through a hot bath treatment in order to completely remove the gummy substance called sericin that the silkworm had produced in order to hold the cocoon together. When silk yarns have no discernible twist but have not yet been woven into a textile, it is the sericin that holds the yarns together. If one were to attempt to cook untwisted yarns and dye them *before* weaving them, the filaments that constitute the yarns would simply fall away from each other and turn into a tangled mess. It is the weaving that provides stability to the untwisted yarns, so that they can then be cooked and dyed.

Most twisted silk yarns, by contrast, were—and are—cooked to remove the sericin right after they have been twisted into yarns, then they are dyed before being woven into a textile. In *cendals*, the cooking process that followed the weaving removed 25 percent of the weight of the fiber, leaving discernible spaces between the yarns. Hence, the lightweight, extremely supple nature of the fabric. Many taffetas, by contrast, are not so much "supple" as they are crisp. We know, in these cases, that the yarns are tightly twisted and that they have been cooked and dyed before being woven. Thus, these kinds of taffetas have body.

28. "Inventaire de Clémence de Hongrois," 70–71.

29. Sophie Desrosiers, "Sendal, Cendal, Zendado: A Category of Silk Cloth in the Development of the Silk Industry in Italy, 12th–15th Centuries," in *Crusading and Trading between West and East: Studies in Honour of David Jacoby*, ed. Sophia Menache, Benjamin Z. Kedar, and Michel Balard (London: Routledge, 2019), 340–50; Desrosiers, "Scrutinizing Raw Material between China and Italy: The Various Processing Sequences of *Bombyx mori* Silk," *L'atelier du Centre de recherches historiques: Review électronique du CRH* 20 (2019): https://doi.org/10.4000/acrh.10323, sections 9, 10, 28.

Taffetas come in various weights and with various kinds of yarns, and fifteenth-century sources indicate that it is indeed appropriate to label *cendal* as a type of taffeta. But if we subsume the term *cendal* into the word "taffeta" we lose the specificity of the textile. So again, my preference in dealing with this textile is to preserve the medieval name.

Eudes of Nevers's inventory is illustrative of the peculiarity of the era of the crusades, when French aristocrats in the Levant and in Europe consumed a wide variety of textiles from Europe, the Mongol Empire, and the Indian subcontinent. Before this time, by contrast, silk textiles from Byzantium had dominated much of the luxury silk textile market in the West, and Egypt had been a major center for the production of fine linens.

But centers of textile production and international textile markets changed dramatically in the intervening period. By the early thirteenth century, the Egyptian linen industry was in rapid decline, and the Byzantine silk industry would experience a similar loss of prestige due, in large part, to the fall of Byzantium to western crusaders in 1204.[30]

Almost simultaneously with the demise of the Byzantine silk industry in the early thirteenth century, the rise of the Mongol Empire led to unprecedented contacts between Central Asia and Europe. As a result, textiles and other consumer goods from Central Asia, East Asia, and the Indian subcontinent became more readily available in Europe and the Levant than ever before. Those contacts between East and West would suffer as the political unity of the Mongol Empire began to wane, especially in the second half of the fourteenth century. In the late fourteenth and fifteenth centuries, textiles from Central Asia and Asia appeared with far less frequency in Mediterranean and European markets than they had during the thirteenth century, and Italian silk and cotton textile production expanded to fill the gaps.

30. Ashtor, *Levant Trade*, 203; Angeliki Laiou and Cécile Morisson, *The Byzantine Economy* (Cambridge: Cambridge University Press, 2007), 190–91.

13

Of Gems and Drinking Cups

Richard A. Leson

On the dorsal of the Account-Inventory's Roll B, possibly with the input of the dying Eudes of Nevers, a scribe recorded those possessions of greatest personal, symbolic, and monetary value. Beneath the initial written descriptions of gems, jewelry, and reliquaries, we can almost hear the "spoken words, recollections, or negotiations" that took place as the fates of these prized objects were decided.[1] Those things of greatest value and significance were destined for family members in France, including "the count's good sapphire [that] has been sent to the lord of Bourbon." The preeminent importance of this gem is signified by its notice at the top of the roll, above and before the heading "These are the things that were given away from among the count's possessions."[2] This lord of Bourbon (see the genealogy in the appendix) was Eudes's younger brother, John, who was now heir to the comital title of Burgundy. How the sapphire reached him is unknown, but its courier, as signaled elsewhere in the Account-Inventory, might have been the knight Hugh of Augerant, one of Eudes's three executors.[3] In the initial distribution of Eudes's most precious possessions listed on Roll B, Hugh is the last of six knights to whom the count bequeathed one of his rings. We are also told that "my lord Hugh of Augerant, carries the ring that the duke [Eudes's father, Hugh IV of Burgundy] had given the count and the ring that should be [given] to the heir of Nevers," the last presumably Jean Tristan, husband of Eudes's

1. Roll B "is as close as we come to a deathbed testament or inventory and reflects Eudes's most intimate objects and spaces." See the introduction to this book.

2. Roll B Back.

3. On Hugh, see chapter 5 above.

eldest daughter, Yolande.[4] That Hugh "carries" these rings implies that it is he who will deliver them, a mission that conceivably included delivery of the sapphire. At any rate, that Hugh was entrusted with such precious objects is an indication of the high regard in which Eudes held him. That the relationship between the two men was one of trust and affection is further indicated by the fate of another prominent object in the Account-Inventory: Eudes's luxury drinking goblet, or *henap*. Multiple references to the *henap* in the Account-Inventory illustrate the scrutiny paid to the material realities of Eudes's possessions over the months-long evaluative process. They also exemplify how the "copious carrying capacity that encompassed the economic, emotional, and historical, all anchored to places, people, and moments in time," extended well beyond precious gems and rings to those more functional objects associated with the count's person and the dynamic performance of lordship.[5]

That a powerful lord like Eudes of Nevers owned one or more splendid drinking goblets is to be expected. Created for use in secular settings, *henaps* are ubiquitous in thirteenth- and fourteenth-century inventories and testaments.[6] The finest were made of gold, silver, or silver gilt, though the same term could also refer to wooden (usually maplewood) mazers embellished with precious metal fittings and enamel ornaments, and even to cups made from ivory. Eudes's great *henap* is recognized by three (possibly four) separate entries in the Account-Inventory. Together, these entries underscore the editors' observations concerning word choice and how certain descriptors suggest "valuative and affective valences that reveal even more about [an object's] meaning."[7] The first reference to the *henap* appears on the recto (or ventral) side of Roll B, where it is listed with the "things of the count of Nevers that he had the day he went from life to death" and listed among those objects placed "in the hand" of the servant Robet. The fine items that precede it in the list—enamels, gems, a cameo, rings, small golden crosses, a golden chapel set with stones and pearls, two belts made of gold, and two silver water basins—exceeded the value of the *henap* either in material or personal value or perhaps a combination of the two. It may be that the relatively lesser value assigned the cup was somehow a consequence of earlier confusion about its materials. In this first notice it is described as "1 goblet of silver set with stones and enamels, which was believed to be of gold."[8] The curious phrasing "believed to

4. Roll B Back. It is not entirely clear from this phrasing if the ring Hugh IV gave to his son (perhaps a sign of the comital dignity) and the ring intended for "the heir of Nevers" were one and the same, though this seems unlikely. Hugh IV lived until 1272, so the ring he gave to Eudes could have been returned to him (or delivered to John of Bourbon, along with the sapphire?) by Hugh of Augerant.

5. See the introduction to this book.

6. Chrétien Dehaisnes, *Histoire de l'art dans la Flandre, l'Artois et le Hainaut avant le XVe siècle*, vol. 1 (Lille: L. Danel, 1886).

7. See the introduction to this book.

8. Account-Inventory, Roll B Front.

be of gold" or a version thereof is used in every subsequent notice of the cup in the Account-Inventory. Evidently this "belief" was a defining aspect of the count's favorite drinking goblet. That it stemmed from an earlier, erroneous appraisal of the cup's base metal is indicated by the third and fullest description of the cup in the Account-Inventory, made in mid-September (Roll A, dorsal). Here for the first time the silver cup is described as silver gilt (*dargent dore*), a strong indication that at some point—although it is not clear when—a gilt veneer surface of this silver *henap* was mistaken for the vessel's base metal. The phrasing "was believed to be" raises the possibility that the true nature of the base metal was discerned only around the moment of the count's death, a reality that certainly factored into the relatively modest 25 *lb. t.* assigned the vessel shortly thereafter.[9] Nonetheless, the phrasing "was believed to have been made of gold" (or a version thereof) persists in the inventory. It is tempting to suppose that this language reflected some long-held conviction about the *henap*'s superior material, one perhaps the result of the great personal value the cup had held for its owner. Were that the case, the Account-Inventory compilers rather discreetly set the record straight.

Though Eudes's *henap* is lost, we may draw on the total "linguistic assemblages of nouns and adjectives" in the Account-Inventory to "give shape to each textual thing" and to imagine objects "as they were once made, used, and set in motion."[10] This is a useful exercise where the many types of goblets listed in the Account-Inventory are concerned. There, the term *cope* (cup) is nearly always modified by the adjective *cuvesclee* (covered), meaning a goblet with a detachable or hinged lid that could double as a serving vessel. As no *henap* is characterized as *cuvesclee*, all objects named in this way presumably lacked covers and served primarily for drinking. We may also assume that most of Eudes's *henaps* possessed a relatively wide, shallow bowl and were balanced on a stem and foot, following an ancient typology of drinking goblets (see examples in figure 16, at the top right). Such a configuration finds indirect confirmation on the back (dorsal) of Roll B in an entry for "17 silver goblets without feet [*xvii henas dargent sanz pie*]." As these are the only cups in the Account-Inventory described in this way, we may suppose that these seventeen silver *henaps* alone among Eudes's drinking goblets lacked feet, even if all the other *henaps* listed are not modified by the descriptor *a piet* so often attached to the noun *henap* in contemporary inventories and testaments. Though the majority of *henaps* to survive from the crusader period are saucer-shaped, silver or gilt-silver drinking vessels (presumably like the seventeen *sanz pie*), the *henap a piet* remained common in the mid-thirteenth century and was known in the Levant. When, for example, the dying English knight Hugh de Neville

9. As indicated by the second reference to the cup, on Roll A Front, Part 1. According to the editors' chronology, written shortly after August 7.

10. See the introduction to this book.

disposed of his possessions in Acre in 1267, he bequeathed to the Temple his "*hanap a pe*" decorated with the arms of the king of England.[11]

Because Eudes was in the Levant for a relatively short period before his death, we may reasonably assume that his *henap* was of French origin rather than an object acquired on crusade. It was set with stones (possibly gems, glass cabochons, or a combination of the two) and enamels, an aesthetic that recalls Limousin *champlevé* objects of the early thirteenth century.[12] Were the *henap* a more recent creation it might have featured *émaux de plique*, which is to say small enamel plaques or "buttons" of various shapes created with a technique similar to cloisonné.[13] These plaques, produced in Parisian workshops, could be sewn onto clothing or applied to larger metalwork objects as ornamentation. Still other possibilities for the cup's origins remain. Small, Byzantine enamel plaques or mountings adorn ancient Roman, Byzantine, and Islamic vessels in the treasury of San Marco, objects possibly looted from Constantinople in 1204.[14] And we cannot rule out the possibility that the *henap* was made in Acre, in which case its imagery or decoration might have displayed an eclectic mixture of stylistic and iconographic elements analogous to that in manuscripts attributed to that city during the crusader period, books in which the illuminations betray the influence of Western, Byzantine, and Islamic artistic traditions.[15]

Whatever its origins, the personal value of the count's great *henap* was equal to if not more than its monetary value, at least for Eudes's household knight and coexecutor Hugh of Augerant. The Account-Inventory's second reference to the cup, made shortly after the count's death, reveals that Hugh accepted "the goblet with stones that is believed to be made of gold" in lieu of 25 *lb. t.* of a total 155 *lb. t.* owed to him in salary compensation.[16] This in-kind payment pales in comparison to that made to Érard of Vallery, Hugh's more illustrious coexecutor, who accepted multiple luxury objects valued at a total of 206 *lb.* 13 *s.* 4 *d. t.*, among them the gold chapel made of stones

11. See the testament of Hugh de Neville above.

12. For example, the ciborium of Maître Alpais and its analogues. See Susan La Niece, Stefan Röhrs, and Bet Mcleod, eds., *The Heritage of "Maître Alpais": An International and Interdisciplinary Examination of Medieval Limoges Enamel and Associated Objects* (London: British Museum Press, 2010).

13. See now Giampaolo Distefano, *Esmaltis viridibus: Lo smalto de plique tra XIII e XIV secolo* (Savigliano [Cuneo]: L'Artistica editrice, 2021). I am grateful to Barbara Drake Boehm for this suggestion.

14. For an example, see Avinoam Shalem, "New Evidence for the History of the Turquoise Glass Bowl in the Treasury of San Marco," *Persica* 15 (1993–95): 91–94.

15. On painting in crusader Acre and its environs, see, inter alia, Jaroslav Folda, *Crusader Art in the Holy Land, from the Third Crusade to the Fall of Acre, 1187–1291* (Cambridge: Cambridge University Press, 2005). Indeed, the "romance of the Lands of Outremer" noted in the Account-Inventory (Roll A Front, Part 2)—probably a manuscript of Guillaume de Tyr's *Histoire d'Outremer*—might very well have been purchased in Acre. See Folda, *Crusader Art*, 357.

16. Roll A Front, Part 1.

and pearls listed above the *henap* in the initial reckonings of Eudes's possessions, an item appraised at 80 *lb. t.*[17] Regardless of its lesser monetary value, Hugh's acceptance of the cup suggests that it possessed a personal significance for him as a special reminder of his late lord. Indeed, Hugh's putative origins in the arrondissement of Nevers and his pronounced role in the transactions recorded in the Account-Inventory hint at a particularly warm relationship with Eudes, perhaps the result of many years of his service to the count. And it was Hugh, it is worth reiterating, who likely undertook the delivery of profoundly symbolic objects like "the ring that should be [given] to the heir of Nevers," an item presumably associated with the comital dignity and probably intended for the prince Jean Tristan, son of Louis IX and husband of Eudes's eldest daughter, Yolande.

What is gleaned from the Account-Inventory about the materials, configuration, and meaning of Eudes's great *henap* recalls in many ways the only extant drinking goblet with a demonstrable crusader pedigree, an engraved silver-gilt cup discovered in 1982 at Resafa, Syria (figures 27.1 and 27.2).[18] Almost certainly the Resafa cup, as it has come to be known, is an earlier creation than the count's goblet; it has been dated to circa 1200. The Resafa cup was almost certainly of northwestern European facture and, as Eudes's cup seems to have been, is a *henap a piet*. It recalls a handful of silver-gilt goblets recovered from European treasure hoards, objects thought to be of English or Scandinavian origin dated around 1200.[19] Some such objects offer general parallels for the Resafa cup's engraving technique, but the vessel's configuration, dimensions, and repoussé scaling are closest to those of a *henap* recently offered for sale by Sotheby's Paris and described—albeit without any provenance—as "French, around 1180."[20]

French origins are also probable for the Resafa cup, as indicated by the eleven authentic heraldic shields engraved in its bowl. Most of these refer to lords from the region of Picardy in northern France. The central shield is that of the lords of Coucy or that family's cadet branch, the Boves of the Amienois. By 1200 both lines could boast an impressive crusader pedigree. Raoul, lord of

17. Roll A Front, Part 2.

18. Richard A. Leson, "The Coucy, the Boves, and Heraldry's Coming of Age in the Resafa Cup," *Revue française d'héraldique et de sigillographie—Études en ligne* (March 2021): 1–28.

19. See Thilo Ulbert, *Resafa III, Der kreuzfahrerzeitliche Silberschatz aus Resafa-Sergiupolis* (Mainz am Rhein: P. von Zabern, 1990), 50–59.

20. Compare, for example, the engravings on the two cups attributed to England or Scandinavia in the recent auction catalog *Medieval Art in England* (London: Sam Fogg, 2019), 19–22 (cat. nos. 7 and 8). For the cup offered in 2011, see Sotheby's Paris, "Orfeverie Europeenne, boites en or," May 17, 2011, lot no. 250: "Coupe ronde sur pied en argent vers 1180, probablement France," https://www.sothebys.com/en/auctions/ecatalogue/2011/orfvrerie-europenne-boites-en-or-pf1102/lot.250.html. The current whereabouts of this cup are unknown (it went unsold in 2011). It may be the work of the same hand as the Resafa cup. At first glance, this cup would appear to strengthen the case for the Resafa cup's creation—and engraving—in northwestern Europe. I am grateful to Thierry de Lachaise of Sotheby's for answering questions about this object.

Coucy, and his uncle Robert of Boves died on the Third Crusade. Raoul's cousin, the redoubtable warrior Enguerrand II of Boves, died in 1225 a veteran of the Third, Fourth, and Fifth Crusades. One of these men, it seems, brought the cup to Outremer, but exactly when remains uncertain. The traditional heraldic argument for the cup's association with Raoul of Coucy and the Third Crusade is compelling but ultimately not determinative. It may be that the vessel was engraved in 1216, when Raoul's son Enguerrand III of Coucy supported the future Louis VIII in the prince's invasion of England, or even as late as 1219, in connection with Enguerrand II of Boves's foundation of the Cistercian Abbey of Le Paraclet, on the eve of his departure for the Fifth Crusade.[21] When and how the cup got to Outremer remains a mystery for now, but it never returned to France. Whether due to financial exigency, disaster, or as a gift, it became the possession of a Syrian woman, a certain Zayn al-Dār, whose name is inscribed in Arabic on the rim. She in turn gave the cup as a votive—perhaps on its own or as a part of a larger bequest—to an otherwise unknown Christian community operating in or near the Ayyubid fortress Qal'at Ja'bar on modern Lake Assad. Then, at some point, the cup traveled some fifty kilometers south to Resafa, ancient center of the cult of Saint Sergius. Why it moved from Qal'at Ja'bar to Resafa is unclear, but as Glenn Peers has insightfully observed, the votive honor initially accrued to Zayn al-Dār doubled as a result, as the cup appears to have been appropriated for Orthodox liturgical use in Resafa's so-called Basilica A.[22] The cup ended up among the basilica's liturgical furnishings, with which it was buried prior to the destruction of that city by the Mongols in 1258 or 1259.[23]

This was not the fate of the goblet "which was believed to be of gold," which probably returned to France. Eudes's *henap* and, at least initially, the Resafa cup served a similar purpose: to foster communal, knightly bonds, and to display wealth and status. Though we do not know if the enamel decorations of Eudes's *henap* included heraldic shields like those of the Resafa cup, to drink from an object of this sort was to assimilate physically those bonds in an act tantamount to a secular Eucharist. It is tempting to imagine the vessel decorated with the count's arms—bands of gold and azure blue, surrounded

21. On these possibilities, see generally Leson, "The Coucy, the Boves." A connection between the cup's creation and the 1219 foundation of Le Paraclet—perhaps as a commemoration of a collective crusade vow by Enguerrand and his followers—has yet to receive consideration. On Enguerrand II's foundation of the abbey, see Anne E. Lester, *Creating Cistercian Nuns: The Women's Religious Movement and Its Reform in Thirteenth-Century Champagne* (Ithaca, NY: Cornell University Press, 2011), 106.

22. Glenn Peers, "Translating Edges in Art of the Medieval Middle East: On the Resafa Hoard and a Painted Bottle from Lichtenstein," in *On the Edge: Time and Space. Proceedings of International Conference, 14–15 November 2014*, ed. Zaza Skhirtladze (Tbilisi: Universitetis gamomcʻemloba, 2017), esp. 15–18.

23. Word of such destruction traveled to France rapidly. It animated the imagination of Rutebeuf and became a potent theme in his poems, and in turn ignited a heightened sense of anxiety about the East that led to Eudes's crusader vow and voyage in 1265. See Rutebeuf's poems "La complainte de Coustantinoble" and "La desputizons dou croisie et dou descroizie" edited above.

by an indented red border—coupled with the heraldry of his father, brothers, in-laws, and allies.[24] No such cup survives for the Nevers family, but we know that they owned luxury objects on which heraldric decorations articulated kinship and marital ties.[25] Jean-Bernard de Vaivre, for example, showed that the Limousin enamel escutcheons on a coffret of circa 1258 now in Aachen likely referred to Hugh IV of Burgundy (Eudes's father) and the husbands and wives of his children. These included the familial arms of Mahaut of Bourbon, Eudes's wife who brought him the county of Nevers.[26]

Even if Eudes's cup lacked heraldic shields, it likely carried powerful, sentimental associations with the count, born perhaps from its role in the performance of knightly oaths of fidelity and trust. This might have been why, at the time of his lord's death, Hugh selected this particular object as partial compensation for what he was owed. Perhaps he recalled the goblet touched to the count's lips at table in the house at Acre, or proffered by Eudes to him and others including Érard of Vallery, Geoffrey of Sergines, Gaucher de Merry, Gui de Chantenai, and "*mon segnor Copin*" to foster morale and camaraderie in the hostile environment that was Acre in the summer of 1266. As ever, a scene from the famous Morgan Picture Bible—that of Joseph's reception of his brothers in Egypt—is suggestive of such experiences (Figure 16). There, Joseph and his brothers drink from golden cups and converse over a richly set table. This is an image that agrees with how the editors, drawing on an observation by Sarah McNamer, describe the Acre house as a "decidedly masculine space, in which male solidarities were reinforced through naming, gifts, and personal memories."[27] The count's great *henap*, we might imagine, was an essential element in the performance of those solidarities and the creation of those memories.

Though the ultimate fate of the *henap* is unknown, we do know that Eudes's possessions remained associated with him long after his death. Of this we may be certain from two early fourteenth-century sources. The first is a codicil to the testament of Eudes's second daughter, Marguerite of Tonnerre, the titular queen of Sicily and Jerusalem, who died without issue in 1308.[28]

24. We know Eudes's arms from the counterseal of Yolande, his eldest daughter. See Louis Douët-d'Arcq, *Collection de sceaux*, 3 vols. (Paris: H. Plon, 1863–68), no. 872 bis. For an image, see Sigilla, http://www.sigilla.org/sceau-type/yolande-bourgogne-contre-sceau-27162, accessed February 2, 2022. See also figures 13.1 and 13.2.

25. Cups with enameled heraldic decorations were probably fairly common. Beatrix of Brabant owned such a goblet at the time of her death in 1289. See Dehaisnes, *Histoire de l'art dans la Flandre*, 78: "un hanap dor que me dame li Royne de France li dena, qui est a couvercle a esmaus, a pierres et a escus de France, de Brabant et de Bourgogne."

26. Jean-Bernard de Vaivre, "Le décor héraldique de la cassette d'Aix-la-Chapelle," *Aachener Kunstblätter* 45 (1974): esp. 109–20. My thanks to Anne Lester for bringing this article to my attention.

27. See chapter 6, above.

28. Lille, AD Nord, series B 447, no. 4.621. For a transcription, Dehaisnes, *Histoire de l'art dans la Flandre*, 166.

In contrast to the Account-Inventory, Marguerite's codicil is mostly concerned with the relationships of women, though similar material and familial-social hierarchies apply. Thus, like her father, Marguerite's most valued gem was a sapphire, in this case given to her by her late husband, Charles of Anjou (d. 1285). It signified the Angevin legacy in the Regno and was therefore left to Marie of Hungary (d. 1309), wife of Marguerite's stepson, Charles II of Anjou. The next item, however, signified Marguerite's natal family and was accordingly reserved for her eldest niece, Jeanne of Flanders (ca. 1272/73–1333). The latter, the firstborn daughter of Marguerite's late sister Yolande (d. 1280), was married in 1288 to the grandson of the same lord of Coucy with whom the Resafa cup is associated. Thus, Marguerite's codicil reads, "To Jeanne, lady of Coucy, my niece, my small rubies that were my father's [*a Jehenne, dame de Couci, ma niece, mon petit rubbis qui fu monsseigneur mon pere*]."[29] Eudes must have given these rubies to Marguerite prior to his departure for Acre in 1265, perhaps as an anticipatory wedding gift. Typical clerical exegesis associated the ruby with the blood of Christ or his martyrs, though in this case that interpretation was likely enriched by the stones' special association with Eudes, his crusading self-sacrifice, and miraculous powers reputedly exercised by his former possessions (see the rubies in figure 18).[30] The latter phenomenon is reported by our second source, the Templar of Tyre (active ca. 1315–20), who wrote that physical contact with those objects Eudes had bequeathed to the poor of Outremer could heal the sick.[31] Such stories were likely known to Marguerite and informed her own charitable pursuits on behalf of the poor and infirm at her hospital of Notre-Dame-des-Fontenilles, work that probably involved the use of relics and possibly gemstones believed to possess curative properties.[32] If, half a century after his death, the possessions Eudes left to the poor of Outremer were still credited with curative powers, so might the rubies Marguerite left to her niece have been a powerful talisman that protected the wearer from sickness and harm. And perhaps, if Eudes's great *henap* still existed, its pseudo-sacramental associations were similarly augmented by a miraculous potency born of the piety and generosity of its renowned owner. As it had for Hugh of Augerant, then, the value of the cup "believed to be of gold" continued to exceed that of its materials.

29. Dehaisnes, *Histoire de l'art dans la Flandre*, 166.

30. The ruby often shared these allegorical traits with the red carbuncle. See Christel Meier, *Gemma Spiritalis: Methode und Gebrauch der Edelsteinallegorse vom frühen Christentum bis ins 18. Jahrhundert* (Munich: Wilhelm Fink, 1977), 1:147–50, esp. 150, 247, n. 12. On the affective (as opposed to the allegorical) qualities of gemstones, see now Brigitte Buettner, *The Mineral and the Visual: Precious Stones in the Medieval Secular Cultures* (University Park: Penn State University Press, 2022), 9.

31. *TdT*, para. 339; and Paul Crawford, *The "Templar of Tyre": Part III of the "Deeds of the Cypriots,"* (Aldershot: Ashgate, 2003; repr. New York: Routledge, 2016), 48. See above, chapter 7.

32. Lynn T. Courtenay, "The Hospital of Notre Dame des Fontenilles at Tonnerre: Medicine as *Misericordia*," in *The Medieval Hospital and Medical Practice*, ed. Barbara S. Bowers (Aldershot: Ashgate, 2007), 77–106.

14

The Material Culture of Devotion and Vestiture

Eudes of Nevers at Prayer

Maureen C. Miller

Can the inventory compiled after the count's death tell us anything about his beliefs? Historians seeking to explain the origins of the crusades have adduced many factors behind this European phenomenon, with religious beliefs and motives chief among them.[1] This inventory does not, of course, get us into Eudes's head or heart. It does, however, offer evidence of the place of Christian practice within the household of an elite crusader and some hints as to the count's devotions.

The inventory literally identifies a place for Christian rites: the chapel (*chapelle*). Indeed, the reference to "the chapel" reveals that upon arrival in Acre Count Eudes already had the means to outfit a space consecrated to Christian worship, but that he found that "old chapel" wanting and created the "new chapel."[2] We can only conjecture about the old chapel's inadequacies: perhaps it was too meager to accommodate the members of his entourage or too shabby for his tastes or status. Eudes spent at least 150 bezants on the decoration of his new chapel while the outfittings of the old chapel had been stored

1. Bernard McGinn, "Violence and Spirituality: The Enigma of the First Crusade," *Journal of Religion* 69 (1989): 375–79. See also the introduction to this volume, above.

2. Pringle characterizes both the old and new chapels as portable. On the differences between the two, see Denys Pringle, *The Churches of the Crusader Kingdom of Jerusalem: A Corpus* (Cambridge: Cambridge University Press, 1993–2009), 4:45–46, no. 378, and the Account-Inventory, Roll D Front.

in "boiled-leather chests." Some elements of the new chapel's decor are named. There were two "new" embroidered wall hangings, a chest, and "the tent from Château-Pèlerin." The latter suggests that the highly decorated portable liturgical spaces used by knightly elites on campaign could be redeployed within interior spaces as decor.[3] The chest was most likely used to store liturgical books and furnishings.

The chapel's liturgical furnishings, the material objects and adornments used in the celebration of Christian rites, were a mix of old and new items. The list of "old" vestments may catalog those brought from Europe and used by Eudes's household chaplain Guillaume on the journey to the Holy Land. The old chasuble, alb, amice, stole, and maniple constituted the basic priestly attire for the saying of Mass, the central Eucharistic rite of medieval Christianity. The rochet and two surplices were loose, usually linen, tunics worn over a cleric's long dark robe when saying the office or performing other non-Eucharistic rites.[4] These garments are followed in the inventory by various altar linens: cloths used to drape the altar, the square linen cloth called a "corporal" upon which the Eucharistic vessels were placed, and two "linen hand cloths" used to dry the celebrant's hands after they were washed preceding the consecration.

More precious were the vessels used on or near the altar. While it is not clear what the ivory box listed among the altar linens contained, the two "decorated pyxes" were containers, usually of silver or gold, used to store consecrated Hosts, and the monstrance, also usually an elaborately wrought holder of precious metal, was used to display the Eucharist.[5] The latter suggests that Count Eudes was attuned to the new devotions of his time: across the thirteenth century Eucharistic piety intensified, leading in 1264 to the establishment of the new universal feast devoted to the body of Christ, Corpus

3. On this tent and others, see chapter 6, note 17. Embroidery is usually described as "work," as in *opus anglicanum*, "English needlework"; these two "worked hangings" were probably described as "plain" because the embroidery did not use precious (silver or gold) thread.

4. On the development and uses of vestments, see Maureen C. Miller, *Clothing the Clergy: Virtue and Power in Medieval Europe, c. 800–1200* (Ithaca, NY: Cornell University Press, 2014), especially the glossary, 247–52, for definitions and descriptions of individual vestments with illustrative drawings.

5. Later in the inventory, on Roll D Back, as part of a list of "things that were not yet sold" from "the new chapel" were "one silver covered cup" and "one cup of gold with a cover." These very likely correspond to the "two decorated pyxes." That they are crossed out on this later list suggests that they found a buyer. Other sacred vessels appear on the back of Roll D: a golden pitcher and two silver pots, likely used in the washing of the celebrant's hands during the Mass, and two larger silver "containers" that could have been used for baptisms. On the pyx and reservation of the Eucharist as well as the monstrance and exposition of the Host, see Archdale A. King, *Eucharistic Reservation in the Western Church* (New York: Sheed and Ward, 1965), 112–20, 136–43; Miri Rubin, *Corpus Christi: The Eucharist in Late Medieval Culture* (Cambridge: Cambridge University Press, 1991), 43–48, 288–94.

Christi.[6] Prayerfully gazing upon the consecrated Host displayed in a monstrance, whether fixed on the altar or carried in a procession, became over the fourteenth and fifteenth centuries so popular and intense a devotion that ecclesiastical leaders began restricting its practice. But in 1266 when Eudes departed life in Acre, keeping a monstrance for display of the Host on the altar in his new chapel participated in a new papally sanctioned devotion just gaining ground.

The most highly decorated and precious objects in the count's chapel were listed first among the inventoried "things for the chapel." Leading off this list was the chalice, the vessel used for the wine that when consecrated became, in Christian belief, the blood of Jesus Christ. These liturgical beakers were crafted from precious metal and often decorated with filigree, gems, and enamel work: what is later listed on Roll D as a "goblet set with stones and enamels" in the new chapel may be this chalice. This sacred cup is followed in the inventory by two reliquaries, one cross shaped and holding a piece of the "True Cross" (the wooden cross upon which Jesus was crucified), and the "reliquary that the patriarch gave the count."[7] The latter could well have been what is called a "portable altar." Ecclesiastical custom and legislation required that the altar used for Mass be consecrated, and the rite of consecration included the secreting of saintly relics within it.[8] The needs of highly mobile elites, like Eudes of Nevers, led to the development of consecrated flat coffers containing relics that could be placed upon a regular table to serve as the sacred altar upon which the Eucharist was confected. Surviving medieval examples feature marble or granite slabs on top and ornately decorated—usually with carved ivory or enameled work—side panels.

These precious reliquaries were followed immediately in the inventory by two liturgical books: a missal and a breviary. The missal, an innovation of the eleventh century, brought together in one volume all the prayers, readings, and chants needed for the Mass.[9] The breviary provided the psalms, readings, and

6. Rubin, *Corpus Christi*, 164–99; on procession and exposition of the Host, see G. J. C. Snoek, *Medieval Piety from Relics to the Eucharist: A Process of Mutual Interaction* (Leiden: Brill, 1995), 260–74.

7. See Account-Inventory, Roll B Front.

8. Snoek, *Medieval Piety*, 175–97.

9. In the early Middle Ages these materials were contained in discrete volumes for different actors: the sacramentary was the celebrant's book (giving the prayers the priest spoke); evangelaries, lectionaries, or epistolaries provided the readings proclaimed by the deacon, subdeacon, or lector; and the gradual contained chanted antiphons and responses. See Josef Andreas Jungmann, *Missarum sollemnia: Eine genetische Erklärung der römischen Messe* (Vienna: Herder, 1949), 1:137–41, 273–306; in English, *The Mass of the Roman Rite: Its Origins and Development*, trans. Francis A. Brunner (New York: Benziger, 1951–55; repr. 1992), 1:103–7, 207–33; Cyrille Vogel, *Introduction aux sources de l'histoire du culte chrétien au moyen âge* (Spoleto: Centro italiano di studi sull'alto Medioevo, 1973), 87–89; in English, *Medieval Liturgy: An Introduction to the Sources*, trans. William G. Storey and Niels Krogh Rasmussen (Washington, DC: Pastoral Press, 1986), 105–6, 134.

hymns to perform what is called the divine office or the liturgy of the hours, a series of seven prayer services at fixed times across the night and day. While this devotion originated in monastic communities, it came to be enjoined on all priests as a sacred duty and practiced by devout lay persons as well. Does this mean that Count Eudes practiced this devotion? Perhaps, but not necessarily. The book was needed to allow his chaplain, Guillaume, to fulfill his duty to pray the divine office daily, and the inventory roll records it being given to him after the count's death. It is certainly possible, however, that Eudes joined his chaplain in prayer for some of the offices. The late afternoon office of Vespers, for example, attracted increasing lay participation from the thirteenth century.[10]

The count's piety is articulated most clearly, however, in the new apparel he had purchased or made for his new chapel. Here we encounter another meaning of the word "chapel [*chapel*]." Listed among the items Eudes had at the time of his death was "1 gold chapel made with stones and pearls." From the late twelfth century, it became fashionable to commission matching sets of vestments made of costly fabrics and embellishments; this is the *chapel* referenced in the inventory and valued at 80 *lb. t.* The more detailed inventory of the new chapel's contents on Roll B spells out the vestments comprising this *chapel* set: "a new chasuble of gold cloth, and tunic, and dalmatic, and 2 new liturgical cloaks all made of cloth of gold, and the altar cloths, front and back, 3 albs, 3 amices, 3 rochets, 2 surplices all new, 2 stoles and 3 new maniples." Several features of this suite of matching vestments merit comment.

First, the number and type of vestments envision Mass conducted by three clerics and other liturgies or processions by the same number. The desire for harmonious visual splendor in celebrating the Mass in the count's new chapel is evident not only in the golden vestments but also in the matching altar cloths. The set splendidly outfitted a priest (in amice, alb, stole, chasuble, maniple) assisted by a deacon (in amice, alb, stole, dalmatic, maniple) and a subdeacon (in amice, alb, tunic, maniple), all serving at a gold-draped altar. The two liturgical cloaks, or copes, could have been worn by cantors, been used in processions, or, perhaps, would have allowed the count's chaplain to concelebrate the Mass with another visiting priest.[11]

Second, the materials used represent a significant financial expenditure. Note that the estimated value of 80 *lb. t.* is twice the pay, listed at the opening of the inventory, of one of the count's knights. Cloth of gold was woven using silk core threads around which were wound strips of hammered gold. Producing such fabric required skilled labor, time, and resources. And this suite of vestments used such cloth prodigiously. The "chasuble of gold cloth" and

10. Jonathan Black, "The Divine Office and Private Devotion in the Latin West," in *The Liturgy of the Medieval Church*, ed. Thomas J. Heffernan and E. Ann Matter (Kalamazoo: Medieval Institute Publications, 2001), 45–71.

11. On copes and their uses, see Miller, *Clothing the Clergy*, 91, 185, 250.

the two "liturgical cloaks [copes] all made of cloth of gold" were constructed entirely of cloth of gold, while the other vestments (the tunic, dalmatic, albs, stoles, maniples, and altar cloths) would most likely have been trimmed with cloth of gold or gold-embroidered orphreys or bands. The summary description of the set, moreover, indicates that some, or all, of these vestments had embroidered embellishment incorporating gems and pearls.[12] The aesthetics of the Mass were important to Eudes, and to many other elites who donated *chapel* to their local churches to ensure that the Eucharist and its saving grace were honored by the best they had to offer.

Third, these golden vestments visually asserted hyperelite status. Cloth of gold garments were used in royal ceremonial: the treasurer to Philip V of France, for example, bought cloth of gold from *Tuquia* for the king's coronation.[13] In ecclesiastical inventories, cloth of gold is found only at the top of the church's hierarchy, at the level of popes, cardinals, and archbishops.[14] Eudes of Nevers's expedition certainly had the support of both Pope Clement IV and the French king, Louis IX, but note that these costly and glittering garments were not intended to clothe him. Indeed, the glimpse into the count's wardrobe provided by the inventory reveals fine, but not extravagant, attire. Although pieces of costly Tartar cloth appear on the roll, very few expensive garments are attributed to Eudes himself: one overcoat (ganache) of *cendal*; a corset, tunic, and overcoat made from an iridescent scarlet fabric, and "one old belt of gold with pearls." Like many elites, he had a taste for furs. The pelts of beavers, lynxes, and squirrels (*grosvair*, miniver) were used to line a few garments but mostly to trim them. The fabrics used in these pieces of clothing, however, were sober and relatively simple: brown *tiretaine* (a cotton-wool or wool-linen mix), black serge (wool), and camelin, an unadorned woolen cloth. Some of these were lined with *cendal*, a light silk, but in the thirteenth-century English court even "lesser clerks" received livery of camelin and *cendal*.[15]

12. For gold thread, cloth, and examples of embroidery incorporating stones and pearls, see Miller, *Clothing the Clergy*, 96, 148 (on gold vestments being melted down for their gold and used as collateral for loans), 153–58; and Gale Owen-Crocker, Elizabeth Coatsworth, Maria Hayward, eds., *Encyclopedia of Medieval Dress and Textiles of the British Isles c. 450–1450* (Leiden: Brill, 2016), s.v. cloth of gold.

13. Louis Douët-d'Arcq, ed., *Comptes de l'argenterie des rois de France au XIVe siècle publié pour la Société de l'histoire de France d'après des manuscrits originaux* (Paris: Jules Renouard, 1951), 5–73, here at 54.

14. *Regesti Clementis Papae V ex Vaticanis Archetypis Sanctissimi Domini nostri Leonis XIII Pontificis Maximi Ivssv et Mvnificentia nunc primvm editi cvra et stvdio monachorum Ordinis S. Benedicti Appendices* (Rome: Typographia Vaticana, 1892), 1:435, 440, 442–43; see also Maureen C. Miller, "A Descriptive Language of Dominion? Curial Inventories, Clothing, and Papal Monarchy c. 1300," *Textile History* 48 (2017): 176–91, and, for an archiepiscopal example, R. Barsotti, *Gli antichi inventari della cattedrale di Pisa* (Pisa: Istituto di Storia dell'Arte, Università di Pisa, 1959), 19.

15. Owen-Crocker, Coatsworth, and Hayword, *Encyclopedia of Medieval Dress and Textiles of the British Isles*, s.v. tiretaine, serge, sendal, livery (uniform).

Eudes's most opulent dress was reserved for moments of religious veneration, however.

Eudes of Nevers's costly, glittering suite or *chapel* of vestments in cloth of gold and gold embroidery studded with gems and pearls glorified the private celebration of the Eucharist and the clergy serving at the altar within his *ostel*. While elements of this golden set could have been used in processions, declaring publicly the crusader's service to Christ and his church, its design beautified and emphasized the chanting of the Mass within the count's new chapel hidden from the view of outsiders. Interior splendor for the sacrament that sustained him and his household seems prioritized in the count's inventory over outward public display of either Eudes's status or piety. That Eudes's flesh was left in Acre, while his heart entwined with gold returned to France, suggests a similar privileging of private devotion over exterior display.

15

The Crusading Households of John of Joinville and Eudes of Nevers

Caroline Smith

Over the course of the thirteenth century thousands of western European knights visited the crusader city of Acre. Some were among the many peaceful pilgrims for whom Acre was the gateway to the Holy Land. Others came ready to fight, either as participants in one of a few large-scale, papally promoted crusade campaigns or, like Eudes of Nevers, having taken a crusade vow as part of a more personal initiative.[1] Eudes was among the number of these crusaders who had sufficient wealth and status to lead a contingent of knights and to bring with him or recruit people necessary to support their military efforts and their lifestyle. We can get a deeper sense of the crusader world of Acre by examining Eudes's crusading household—the people he had with him and things they valued—as reflected in the Account-Inventory drawn up by his executors, alongside John of Joinville's *Life of Saint Louis*.[2] John had arrived in Acre in 1250 in the company of Louis IX of France, after the collapse of the king's first crusade in Egypt. He later described his own experiences as the leader of a crusading household within a text that presents itself

1. For independent crusaders in the twelfth century see Fordham University's *Independent Crusaders Mapping Project*, https://independentcrusadersproject.ace.fordham.edu/.

2. Jean de Joinville, *Vie de Saint Louis*, ed. J. Monfrin (Paris: Garnier, 1995); trans. Caroline Smith, *Joinville and Villehardouin: Chronicles of the Crusades* (Harmondsworth: Penguin, 2008). Hereafter, Joinville, *VSL*.

as a hagiography of his royal friend.[3] John's narrative of his time on crusade is unusually personal in nature and includes many details concerning his companions and their belongings; it is an ideal complement to the Account-Inventory, helping us imagine how we could fill in the outline of Eudes's household presented there.

The following comments on the people who made up Eudes's crusading household will focus on the group as a whole—the kinds of people and relationships represented—rather than the named individuals. The Account-Inventory captures a crusading household and the people associated with it at a specific moment, or series of moments, in the weeks following Eudes's death, and it shows the extent and complexity of this military and social unit.

The first thing to note about the group that accompanied Eudes in Acre is its hybrid nature. Some members appear to have had a service-based relationship with the count. They would have been long-term members of his household, and it is likely that many or all of them traveled with him from France. This subgroup included four household knights, a clerk (perhaps the person who wrote out the Account-Inventory itself), at least one chaplain (multiple chaplains are referred to later in the text, but only one is named), eight squires, and nine sergeants; these men made up the core of Eudes's knightly household. Supporting this core group were servants who were paid wages. Some of the thirty-plus people (men and women) listed as "garçons" or pages in the Account-Inventory—particularly those who were better paid and would have carried out more specialized tasks—may also have been long-term members of the count's household, while others would have been hired locally. In Acre, Eudes would also have been able to recruit the military specialists whom he paid in cash: the Account-Inventory mentions four turcopoles (light cavalrymen) and five crossbowmen.[4] Eudes's extended contingent also included knights who were not directly in his service. Thus he made payments to two knights sufficient to support their own small retinues, while Hugh of Augerant—who was one of Eudes's household knights and executors—was himself the leader of a small group of knights the count supported financially.[5]

3. The date(s) of the *Life of Saint Louis*'s composition and the nature of its author's project (hagiography, memoir, or a blend of these and perhaps other genres) have been much debated. See, for example, Monfrin's introduction to Joinville, *VSL*, lxvi–lxxvi; Caroline Smith, *Crusading in the Age of Joinville* (Farnham: Ashgate, 2006), 47–74; M. Cecilia Gaposchkin, *The Making of Saint Louis: Kingship, Sanctity and Crusade in the Later Middle Ages* (Ithaca, NY: Cornell University Press, 2008), 181–85.

4. On turcopoles and their role in crusader armies, see Yuval Harari, "The Military Role of the Frankish Turcopoles: A Reassessment," *Mediterranean Historical Review* 12 (1997): 75–116; Stephen Tibble, *The Crusader Armies, 1099–1187* (New Haven, CT: Yale University Press, 2018), 117–24. On the importance of paid fighters more generally, see Alan Forey, "Paid Troops in the Service of Military Orders during the Twelfth and Thirteenth Centuries," in *The Crusader World*, ed. Adrian Boas (London: Routledge, 2016), 84–97.

5. Monies owed and paid to Reynaud of Précigné, Robert of Juennesses, and Hugh of Augerant are mentioned in the Account-Inventory, Roll A Front, Part 2.

A similar arrangement, if on a different scale, seems to have been in place with Érard of Vallery, who appears in our sources as a partner with Eudes in his crusading enterprise.[6] But while Erard must have had his own retinue of knights, he was in part funded by monies from Eudes; the Account-Inventory lists the sum of 831 bezants owed to Erard "for his pay."[7]

There was thus a patchwork of different kinds of bonds at work in forming Eudes's extended contingent. While his household knights, squires, sergeants, and key nonmilitary personnel may have formed a familiar and stable core, other relationships were more improvised and short-term. The Account-Inventory presents a fascinating snapshot of how these complex relationships coexisted. What it cannot do is convey how the size and shape of such a contingent could change over time. Here the *Life of Saint Louis* can be helpful. The losses within Louis IX's army due to battle, disease, and captivity in Egypt were heavy. Of the nine knights John of Joinville led from their homeland of Champagne in 1248, only two were still with him when he was taken prisoner in 1250; six of them had died in (or from wounds received during) the Battle of Mansurah alone.[8]

When John arrived in Acre in 1250 he had to rebuild his household and the military unit he commanded. Through the descriptions in the *Life* we can observe him hiring servants, taking unfamiliar knights into his service, and negotiating with the king over how other knights should be supported and assigned.[9] The kinds of dangers John of Joinville and his companions were exposed to in their war of conquest in Egypt were more extreme than those that Eudes and his contingent would have anticipated when they set out to contribute to the Latin kingdom's defense, but the *Life* is a helpful counterpoint to the Account-Inventory because it reminds us that crusaders' military and social units were not permanent or static. They were all, if to varying degrees, subject to the vicissitudes of conflict, long-distance travel, and quotidian exigencies in general. This was very obviously true for Count Eudes's contingent. After his death, the people listed among his personnel would have seen their bonds of service, employment, and obligation shift, and the groups they belonged to would have been reassigned, broken apart, or dissolved completely.

The *Life of Saint Louis* also presents a useful counterpoint by allowing glimpses of the kinds of tasks some of the nonknightly members of Eudes's

6. For example, in instructions from Patriarch William of Jerusalem to the commander of the Templars in France sent after Eudes's death, edited in Gustav Servois, "Emprunts de Saint Louis en Palestine et en Afrique," *Bibliothèque de l'École des chartes* 4 (1858): 292 (Appendice).

7. See Account-Inventory, Roll A Front, Part 1.

8. Joinville, *VSL*, paras. 305, 297–98. On the knights with whom John departed from Champagne, see Jackie Lusse, "D'Étienne à Jean de Joinville: L'ascension d'une famille seigneuriale champenoise," in *Jean de Joinville: De la Champagne aux royaumes d'outre-mer*, ed. Danielle Quéruel (Langres: D. Guéniot, 1998), 28–29.

9. Joinville, *VSL*, paras. 408–10 (discussed in further detail below), 415, 440–41, 466–68.

contingent may have performed. So, for example, we know that one of John's squires brought him a fresh horse in battle, his chamberlain slept at the foot of his bed and was sent to investigate when the alarm was raised in the crusader camp, and his cellarer offered advice on what to do when facing imminent capture.[10] His priests said Mass (as you might expect) and launched solo assaults on the enemy (as you might not).[11] The richest of these examples concerns the new servant, Guillemin, whom John hired as soon as he arrived in Acre in 1250. This man made him useful by going to find coifs, combing John's hair, carving meat at table, and arranging lodgings and bathing facilities.[12] Eudes of Nevers and his knights must have had a similar range of needs, to which his "garçons" would have been attentive as well.

Unlike the Account-Inventory, the *Life of Saint Louis* does not give us a full picture of how many and what varieties of people accompanied or were employed by John of Joinville at different stages of his crusade journey. Priests, sergeants, cellarers, poultry minders, and others feature in the *Life* when they contribute to the telling of a good anecdote, but John's story of the crusade, and his household, revolved around knights.[13] The same was true of Eudes of Nevers's contingent. Nonknightly forces (such as crossbowmen and light cavalry) had proved themselves essential to the defense of the Latin Kingdom and were recruited in large numbers by the French regiment and others, but appear to have formed a relatively small part of the force Eudes maintained.[14]

The knightliness of Eudes's contingent is important when it comes to considering the things he had with him, and how they were used and valued. More in-depth studies of these objects appear elsewhere in this volume, but the fine cloth, elegant outfits, and items made of silver, gold, and precious stones that Eudes had with him were perhaps as necessary to these men as their weapons and armor as a means of carrying their status with them across the Mediterranean. As well as being useful in lieu of cash, these things could be used to display status and offer hospitality, or gifted as demonstrations of largesse. John of Joinville offers a good example of this at work in his gift of

10. Joinville, *VSL*, paras. 229, 255–56, 318–19.

11. Joinville, *VSL*, paras. 258–60, 299.

12. Joinville, *VSL*, paras. 408–11. John was disappointed when he discovered that Guillemin was an accomplished thief as well as an attentive servant: para. 417.

13. For the wide variety of people who fought, worked, and traveled with large crusade armies, but who are often not the focus of crusade narratives, see Christopher Tyerman, "Who Went on Crusades to the Holy Land?," in *The Horns of Hattin: Proceedings of the Second Conference of the Society for the Study of the Crusades and the Latin East, Jerusalem and Haifa 2–6 July 1987*, ed. Benjamin Z. Kedar (Jerusalem: Yad Izhak Ben-Zvi: Israel Exploration Society, 1992), 13–26.

14. On the importance of these nonknightly forces to the armies of the Crusader States, see Christopher J. Marshall, "The French Regiment in the Latin East," *Journal of Medieval History* 15 (1989): 304–5. Patriarch William's communication with the commander of the Templars in France in 1267 reported that monies for the defense of Acre had been spent on crossbowmen and archers; Servois, "Emprunts de Saint Louis," 292.

cloth and fur to the empress of Constantinople so she could have a dress made after the ship carrying her belongings was lost.[15] The inventory of Count Eudes's possessions confirms that men of high status had such cloth and furs to hand, ready for such an eventuality.

Valued objects and rituals of gifting also feature in the distribution of rings and other precious items to Eudes's followers.[16] It is tempting to imagine that these were physically given by the count himself from his deathbed, and in their commentary on the Account-Inventory in this volume Lester and Morreale suggest that Érard of Vallery received objects other than a ring because he was not present on the day of Eudes's death itself.[17] The objects that the count might have given in person are ones that could be worn: jewels, a cameo, and rings. These things would already have significance as mementos of Eudes, of the recipients' presence with him in the East and at his deathbed, and as symbols of the ties of friendship and obligation that bound the count to the closest members of his household and knightly colleagues. The meaning of these objects would have been further enhanced by the intimate physical act of Eudes touching the recipients as he personally gave his gifts: placing a jewel around a man's neck, pinning a cameo to his clothes, or, in the case of the rings, perhaps placing the gift not only into the recipient's hand but onto his finger.

Eudes and his companions would probably have thought of these items—fine cloth, jewelry, and other luxury goods—as necessities, but when we think of that term in relation to knights the objects that first spring to mind would usually be horses, weapons, and armor. We can get a sense of the range of equipment Eudes and his knights would have required from the Templar *Retrais* (statutes issued as additions to the rule of the order), which stipulated that every knight brother should have three or four horses, a hauberk, iron leg-coverings, a helmet, a sword, a shield, a lance, a mace, an over-tunic, shoulder guards, protective footwear, a dagger, a bread knife, and a pen knife.[18] The Account-Inventory of Eudes's executors mentions many of these items, or ones that may be equivalent, with the notable exception of the hauberk, sword, shield, and lance.[19] It is unthinkable that Eudes was on crusade in Acre without these most essential knightly items (and perhaps more than one of them in some cases—we know John of Joinville had multiple swords

15. Joinville, *VSL*, paras. 137–38.

16. On the significance of rings as tokens, including tokens bequeathed by crusaders, see Nicholas L. Paul, *To Follow in Their Footsteps: The Crusades and Family Memory in the High Middle Ages* (Ithaca, NY: Cornell University Press, 2012), 107–10.

17. See above, chapter 6.

18. Henri de Curzon, ed., *La Règle du Temple* (Paris: Librairie Renouard, 1886), 109–10.

19. The Account-Inventory mentions, for example, daggers, knives, blades, iron thigh and leg protectors, a helmet, a gambeson, coats of armor, horses (though it is unclear how many of these were suitable for use as war horses), and a small mace.

with him on crusade),[20] so what happened to them? We cannot know, but it is likely that when the Account-Inventory was begun they had already been given away or set aside for special treatment. It is important to remember that the Account-Inventory deals only with the count's possessions on the day of his death. Stephen Church has suggested that people dying of illness would normally dispose of most of their possessions before they were in extremis.[21]

For any noble, and perhaps especially for a man of elevated status like Eudes of Nevers, weapons, and swords in particular, were not just tools but important symbols of knighthood and lordship.[22] Swords could become potent dynastic treasures, as evidenced by the story of John of Warenne, who supposedly wielded a rusty and ancient sword before the court of England in 1279 as proof of the rights won by its original owner, John's ancestor, during the Norman Conquest.[23] A century later Edmond, earl of March, stipulated that his son and heir was to receive items including "our sword garnished with gold," and that these were to "remain to his next heir, and after him to his heirs forever."[24] Such weapons were probably too valuable as symbols of family status to ever have been used in battle, and if there was an equivalent sword in Eudes's family he is unlikely to have brought it with him to Acre. He might have wanted one of his sons-in-law to receive his personal sword, though. In the mid-1380s when he was departing England with the intention of going to Jerusalem, Hugh, earl of Stafford, issued a codicil to his will in which he left specific items of arms and armor to his son Thomas, including a sword given to him by a knightly colleague.[25]

Perhaps Eudes himself made gifts of his weapons and knightly equipment to friends or companions. The English lord Hugh de Neville planned to do so if he had died during the time he spent in Acre. According to his will of 1267

20. Joinville, *VSL*, para. 221.

21. Church cites the twelfth-century will of Archbishop Theobald of Bec. Stephen Church, "King John's Testament and the Last Days of His Reign," *English Historical Review* 125 (2010): 510.

22. On the ritual and symbolic significance of swords to knighthood and lordship, see Kristen Neuschel, *Living by the Sword: Weapons and Material Culture in France and Britain* (Ithaca, NY: Cornell University Press, 2020), 60–61, 72–73; Emma Mason, "The Hero's Invincible Weapon: An Aspect of Angevin Propaganda," in *The Ideals and Practices of Knighthood III: Papers from the Fourth Strawberry Hill Conference, 1988*, ed. Christopher Harper-Bill and Ruth Harvey (Woodbridge: Boydell, 1990), 123.

23. David Crouch, "The Warenne Family and Its Status in the Kingdom of England," in *Princely Rank in Late Medieval Europe: Trodden Paths and Promising Avenues*, ed. Thorsten Huthwelker, Jörg Peltzer, and Maximilian Wemhöner (Ostfildern: Jan Thorbecke Verlag, 2011), 281–82.

24. Nicholas H. Nicolas, *Testamenta Vetusta: Being Illustrations from Wills of Manners, Customs, etc. as Well as the Descents and Possessions of Many Distinguished Families, from the Reign of Henry II to the Accession of Queen Elizabeth* (London: Nichols and Son, 1826), 1:110–11.

25. Nicolas, *Testamenta Vetusta*, 119. Nicholas Paul notes that a subsequent codicil to Earl Hugh's will, issued from Rhodes, bequeathed rings (presumably ones he carried with him) to female relatives. Paul, *To Follow in Their Footsteps*, 108.

Hugh planned gifts to his knights of jeweled buckles or rings, and one of them would also receive his small sword. Another man, Hugh's squire, was to receive a horse and all the armor befitting a gentleman ("*vn gentil home*").[26] If his closest knightly companion was to get Hugh's small sword, there must have been a bigger and, possibly, more valued one too. He was not a magnate on a par with Eudes of Nevers, and his circumstances at home in England as well as his financial situation in the East were precarious.[27] His will envisaged the sale of all his possessions, including horses and arms, to continue to support his retinue for a period. Perhaps Hugh was ready for his large sword to be sold if necessary, but this would probably not have been his preferred outcome.

The first gift to a religious house in Hugh's will was to the Order of St. Thomas of Canterbury in Acre, to which he gave "my light gray palfrey and my arms, appropriate for one person." The French word *armures* could refer specifically to defensive armor, but also more generally to armor and weapons, including swords. Hugh, and possibly Count Eudes, would not have been alone if they chose to make a pious gift of weapons to one of the Latin Kingdom of Jerusalem's military or religious institutions. Such a gift could be of practical use after a knight's passing, or weapons and armor might be displayed as evidence of his presence in and dedication to the Holy Land. Many knights had bequeathed their horses and arms to a military order since they came into existence in the twelfth century.[28] In his 1241 testament, Nunó Sanç, lord of Roussillon and Cerdagne, instructed that "my horse and arms, and my own equipment and that of the horse" should be left to the Hospitaller commandery of Bajoles, near Perpignan.[29] A similar bequest may well have been made by John of Joinville's uncle before he died at the Hospitaller stronghold of Crac des Chevaliers in 1204. Decades later John retrieved his late uncle's shield from Crac during his own stay in the Latin kingdom and placed it in the chapel near his family's castle in Champagne so that, John said, his uncle's "renown should not fade."[30] This object would have had one set of meanings to the Hospitaller knights who saw it on the walls of their

26. See the will edited and translated above.

27. M. S. Giuseppi, "On the Testament of Sire Hugh de Nevill, Written at Acre, 1267," *Archaeologia* 56 (1899): 361–62.

28. Dominic Selwood, *Knights of the Cloister: Templars and Hospitallers in Central-Southern Occitania, c. 1100—c. 1300* (Woodbridge: Boydell, 1999), 176.

29. Rodrigue Treton and Robert Vinas, "Le testament de Nunó Sanç, seigneur de Roussillon et de Cerdagne (17 décembre 1241)," *e-Spania: Revue interdisciplinaire d'études hispaniques médiévales et modernes* 28 (2017), https://doi.org/10.4000/e-spania.27026; for this practice as a feature of confraternity in the Order of the Temple, see Jochen Schenk, *Templar Families: Landowning Families and the Order of the Temple in France, c. 1120–1307* (Cambridge: Cambridge University Press, 2012), 48–49.

30. "Épitaphe composée par Joinville," in Jean de Joinville, *Histoire de Saint Louis, Credo et lettre à Louis X*, ed. Natalis de Wailly, 2nd ed. (Paris: Firmin Didot, 1874), 546. Translated by Caroline Smith in *Chronicles of the Crusades*, 347.

castle, and another to members of the Joinville family and their neighbors after John reclaimed this dynastic relic. We can be confident that however Eudes disposed of his most valued knightly accoutrements he intended them to have value and meaning to whoever possessed them, and to those who saw or heard about them.

While the fate of some of Eudes's most prized possessions will remain a mystery, what happened to some of the more mundane items his executors had to dispose of is revealing. The sale of Count Eudes's remaining possessions is indicative of the priorities and concerns of individuals and institutions in Acre at this time. Some items were clearly purchased strategically, with medium- or long-term needs in mind: Geoffrey of Sergines the elder, for example, bought bulk quantities of wine, salted meats, and kitchen equipment, entirely appropriate for the captain of the French regiment, who needed to plan for a lengthy stay and a household full of mouths to feed.[31] Other selections appear more random. For example, among the detailed list of items sold off to unnamed buyers were an iron blade, two pieces of gold embroidered cloth, and a chess set, priced together as a group.[32] Perhaps this and other groupings of items reflect the particular needs or whims of individual purchasers who perused the late count's possessions as you or I might look at the items offered in a yard sale. Of course, this is pure speculation, but these purchases are a useful reminder that the Account-Inventory is not just a record of who and what was left at the end of Count Eudes of Nevers's life. It also marks a new beginning. With his death the people and things he had with him would find new usefulness, new roles, and new meanings.

31. Account-Inventory, Roll D Front.
32. Account-Inventory, Roll D Front.

16

Shared Things

Inventories of the Islamic World

Uri Zvi Shachar

Eudes of Nevers's Account-Inventory offers a rare glimpse into the life of a Frankish aristocrat who lived in the final decades of the Kingdom of Jerusalem. More than a dry list of items that were in his possession, the inventory unfolds a fascinating story about the social network to which Eudes belonged, the ties and commitments that shaped his affairs and that continued after his death. Furthermore, the inventory helps us imagine how Eudes and his contemporaries understood the way in which property (and debt, for that matter) in its many cultural forms was seen to endure over time. The potential enclosed in this document—made tangible by this volume—leads us to lament the absence of similar texts from the Kingdom of Jerusalem. The lack of such texts may be the result of contemporary archival practices or of historical circumstances of conquest and displacement. Either way, the absence of similar texts stands in contrast to the cache of documents left by the Mamluks—the successors who came to rule over the same region after 1291—that includes hundreds of inventories very much like the one that was drafted for Eudes. The estate inventories from late fourteenth-century Mamluk Jerusalem relate the stories of individuals from all walks of life, both men and women, Jews, Christians, and Muslim, wealthy and impoverished, equally concerned about the fate of their earthly possessions. This short essay introduces a number of Mamluk estate inventories from the final decade of the fourteenth century, and thus offers an additional regional, cross-cultural perspective within which to frame Eudes's text.

Jerusalem returned to Muslim hands in 1187, and save for a fifteen-year period following the Treaty of Jaffa that Frederick II negotiated (1229–44), the city remained under Muslim control until 1917. In 1250 a group of military generals effected a coup d'état that brought about the rise of the Mamluk sultanate in Cairo. While the coup successfully ended Ayyubid rule in Egypt, the first decade of the new regime was tumultuous, and the consolidation of its power northward into Syria was slow and uneven. But following his monumental triumph against Mongol forces in 'Ain Jalut, Baybars, the sixth Mamluk sultan, finally achieved political stability and ruled for seventeen years until his death in 1277.[1] During this period, Baybars launched reforms that helped build a centralized, highly sophisticated state administration for which the Mamluk sultanate became famous. Throughout the Mamluk period the military and its subsidiary institutions played a central role in the public domain. Baybars and his successors strengthened existing state offices and instituted new ones, including a *katib al-sirr* (confidential secretary) and a *sahib al-insha'* (head of chancery) among other positions.[2] In the second half of the thirteenth century, as part of the effort to legitimize the new regime, both Mamluk sultans and local rulers made major investments in public institutions. The architectural and institutional ingenuity that characterized the early Mamluk period effectively changed the urban fabric of cities like Cairo, Damascus, and Jerusalem, such that many Mamluk buildings still stand to this day. These decades saw the creation and rebuilding of shrines, madrasas, hostels, mosques, Sufi lodges, public fountains, and baths.[3] The Mamluks were renowned for erecting or renovating city walls and gates and refurbishing urban fortresses during their rule.

But the investment in two public institutions in particular left the most noticeable mark on the character of cities in the region during this period, namely, investment in charitable funds (*waqf*) and in the *shar'i* religious court. Both, of course, were not invented in this period, but came to play a decisive role in the urban landscape thanks to major state investments and the consistent policies of the central state government. Through these institutions the sultans looked to solidify the supremacy of the religious establishment over civil society and to outsource the responsibility over those who needed institutional care into the hands of nongovernmental Islamic organizations. The choice to invest in these institutions was not an obvious one, seeing as both found legitimacy and authority not in the political establishment that appointed them but in contemporary spiritual leadership and in the Islamic intellectual-religious

1. Robert Irwin, *The Middle East in the Middle Ages: The Early Mamluk Sultanate* (Carbondale: Southern Illinois University Press, 1985), 39.

2. Irwin, *The Middle East in the Middle Ages*, 40; Donald Little, "Jerusalem under the Ayyubids and Mamluks: 1187–1516," in *Jerusalem in History: 3000 BC to the Present Day*, ed. K. J. Asali (London: Kegan John, 1997), 177–99.

3. Nimrod Luz, *The Mamluk City in the Middle East: History, Culture, and the Urban Landscape* (Cambridge: Cambridge University Press, 2014), 47–68; Zayde Antrim, "Jerusalem in the Ayyubid and Mamluk Period," in *Routledge Handbook on Jerusalem*, ed. Souleiman Mourad, Naomi Koltun-Fromm, and Bedross der Matossian (New York: Routledge, 2019), 102–9.

tradition.[4] Yet by supporting these institutions financially and publicly, Mamluk rulers styled themselves as the patrons of Islamic religiosity and in so doing relegated matters that have weighty religious-legalistic bearing—such as the care for the poor and sick—to the purview of nongovernmental bodies.[5]

How these hybrid (administrative-religious) offices worked is much disputed among historians. The jurisdiction of the religious court vis-à-vis the state tribunals seems to have varied from one place to another and could differ over time in the same city. It is the fourteenth-century Mamluk *qadi* court that concerns us here. The *qadi* was not just a judge who ruled in religious disputes (such as divorce, etc.), but also a state administrator who had financial responsibilities. The qadi, for example, often settled disputes between neighbors in questions of building permits where a plaintiff claimed that their property was breached or compromised. What is more, the *shar'i* court supervised the activity of pious endowments, which in their turn were charged with the education and well-being of the young, sick, and needy in the city. This important institution, the *waqf*, was the main avenue for urban philanthropic activity. Like the *shar'i* court, the *waqf* too functioned in an indistinct space at the intersection between the private and public domains. Through private donation and regular state funding, the *waqf* administered provisions for beneficent activities and support of various civil causes.[6] As a result, in many ways, the *shar'i* court and the *waqf* regulated and shaped urban space and society in Mamluk Syria.[7]

In 1974 a large number of documents, over nine hundred in total, mostly written on paper, were discovered in the Islamic Museum in Jerusalem. The museum resides in a building on the Holy Mount (Haram al-Sharif) that was in existence and in continuous use since the Middle Ages. A tempting assumption, therefore, was that the collection somehow pertains to an institution that used to operate from the same, or a nearby, location, perhaps the court of the *qadi* itself. However, as the documents were discovered in a storage hatch and their provenance is unknown, scholars were unable to determine conclusively the purpose and the institutional context in which the documents were created

4. Yehoshua Frenkel, "Is There an Islamic Space? Urban and Social Issues as Reflected in the *Qadi* Courts of Egypt and Syria: 13th–16th Centuries," in *Towns and Material Culture in the Medieval Middle East*, ed. Yaacov Lev (Leiden: Brill, 2002), 103–17.

5. Luz, *The Mamluk City*, 110.

6. Carl Petry, "*Waqf* as an Instrument of Investment in the Mamluk Sultanate: Security vs. Profit?," in *Slave Elites in the Middle East and Africa: A Comparative Study*, ed. John Philips and Miura Toru (London: Kegan Paul International, 2000), 99–116; George Maqdisi, *The Rise of the Colleges: Institutions of Learning in Islam and the West* (Edinburgh: Edinburgh University Press, 1981), 35–74; Muḥammad Amīn, *Al-Awqāf Wa-ăl-ḥayāt Al-Iğtimā'iyya Fī Miṣr 648–923 H. 1250–1517 M.: Dirāsa Tārīḫiyya Wa-ṯaqāfiyya* (al-Qāhira: Dār an-Nahḍa al-'Arabiyya, 1980).

7. Yaakov Lev, "The *Cadi* and the Urban Society: The Case Study of Medieval Egypt, 9th–12th Centuries," in Lev, *Towns and Material Culture*, 89–90; Luz, *The Mamluk City*, 121, 139; Petry, "*Waqf* as an Instrument of Investment," 99–100.

and preserved.[8] A team of historians from McGill University documented the find and created a meticulous catalogue that Donald Little published in 1984.[9]

The documents span a time period of 250 years, but the vast majority pertain to the final decade of the fourteenth century. Similarly, the collection contains a range of document types: petitions, reports, records of public sales, acknowledgement deeds, court hearings, marriage and divorce contracts, and the like.[10] By far the largest group, about half of the entire collection, is estate inventories drawn up for individuals, both deceased and elderly, from all walks of life. Most of the documents mention the Shafi'i Qadi of Jerusalem, Sharf al-Dīn al-Ḥazrajī, who died in 1395, which led scholars to assume that the collection is associated with the *shar'i* court in Jerusalem during the period of his office.[11]

The inventories offer a detailed view of the possessions of various inhabitants of fourteenth-century Jerusalem. In this way, they provide a striking parallel to Eudes's inventory from the earlier period. The purpose of the inventories was both to record the earthly possessions of a person dead or alive (including debts and loans) and to establish their legal heir(s). Unlike a will, the inventory does not necessarily inscribe a decision about how to divide items or wealth among heirs, but rather it lists and enumerates property. The Haram documents include both inventories that pertain to living people who turn to the service of the court proactively and those of deceased persons, whose possessions sometimes are no more than what is found on or with the dead body. For example, in June 1393, the body of a man was found inside the al-Aqsa Mosque. Seeing as the unidentified person was in possession of only two rags and three old wooden boards ("*thalāthah alwāḥ khashaba 'utuq*"), the expense of his burial was determined to be covered by the pious endowment.

8. On the resemblance of the Haram al-Sharif cache to the Cairo Geniza, see Marc Cohen, "Geniza for Islamicists, Islamic Geniza, and the 'New Cairo Geniza,'" *Harvard Middle Eastern and Islamic Review* 7 (2006): 137.

9. Donald Little, *A Catalogue of the Islamic Documents from al-Ḥaram aš-Šarīf in Jerusalem* (Beirut: Orient-Institut der Deutschen Morgenländischen Gesellschaft, 1984).

10. Christian Müller, "Écrire pour établir la preuve orale en Islam: La pratique d'un tribunal à Jérusalem au XIVe siècle," in *Les outils de la pensée Étude historique et comparative des "textes,"* ed. Yusuke Nakamura (Paris: Éditions de la Maison des sciences de l'homme, 2014), 63–97.

11. Lutfi and Little suggest that the cache was the court archive, the purpose of which was to preserve the records of the various litigants and stakeholders in protection of the public interest; see Huda Lufti, *Al-Quds al Mamlūkiyya: A History of Mamluk Jerusalem Based on the Haram Documents* (Berlin: Klaus Schwarz Verlag, 1985), 11–13; and Little, *Catalogue of the Islamic Documents*, 11–22. Christian Müller, in contrast, thinks the cache was a dossier that was compiled as part of an attempt to level corruption charges against the *qadi*. Müller notes that the documents lack physical uniformity and were not preserved in chronological (or any other) order. Furthermore, the fact that the *qadi* is mentioned, even if sometimes marginally, in the vast majority of documents suggests that someone may have selected them for a reason from a larger pool of court transactions; see Christian Müller, "The Ḥaram al-Šarīf Collection of Arabic Legal Documents in Jerusalem: A Mamlūk Court Archive," *Al-Qanṭara* 32 (2011): 435–59.

In contrast, the documentation of the property belonging to a wealthier deceased woman is far more complex. In August of the same year, the court recorded the possessions of a certain Fatima bint Zayn al-Din, whose family apparently came from Damascus. That Fatima was relatively affluent can be seen from the wide variety of garments she had owned: a white linen chemise, a white Ba'albaki tunic (or upper garment, *qaba'*, from Ba'albek, Lebanon),[12] a wrapping (or robe, *shamlah*) embroidered with blue silk and gold threads,[13] a loincloth (*'izār*), a Venetian chemise, three old Alexandrian silk underpants, two old kerchiefs, and a Yemenite quilt (or blanket, *liḥāf*).[14] Clearly Fatima had a taste for luxurious products of various kinds hailing from renowned centers of textile production—Ba'albek, Venice, and Alexandria. It is worth noting, however, that this wardrobe is the only property that is attributed to Fatima and that at the time of the inspection both her husband and brother were absent (the former in Ramla and the latter in Damascus); as a result her sister-in-law was the one who oversaw the inventory process.

In November 1393 a certain Nafisa b. Ali b. Jami turned to the court in order to make a deposition pertaining to her possessions. The document created from this process yielded one of the richest and most detailed inventories found among the Haram records. Estate inventories, like other documents found in this collection, are formulaic in that scribes tended to follow a highly rigid structure: beginning with an invocation of God ("the best of all judges") and the prophet, there is then the date and a phrase that states the type of form—usually, in our case, indicating that an inventory was recorded. The document next introduces the owner of the surveyed property by name, and then marks the legal ramifications of the statement by addressing their physical condition, specifically whether alive or dead, elderly or young, and the like. Here the text states that the subject of the inventory, Nafisa, "was in sound mind and in possession of her mental faculties but sick in body."[15] Her imminent death, in other words, created the need for the document.[16] Like in the previous examples, Nafisa owned a sizeable collection of clothes, including chemises, tunics, undergarments, cloaks, overcoats, turbans, and veils of various manufacture. She also possessed abundant housewares including a number of carpets (both a small and a large Rumi/Byzantine mat, *bisāṭ*; and

12. Ba'albak was associated with the production of luxurious cotton products; see Robert Serjeant, *Islamic Textiles: Material for a History up to the Mongol Conquest* (Beirut: Libr. du Liban, 1976), 7.

13. Bethany Walker, "Rethinking Mamluk Textiles," *Mamluk Studies Review* 4 (2000): 177; Louise Mackie, "Toward an Understanding of Mamluk Silk: National and International Considerations," *Muqaranas* 2 (1984): 127–46.

14. Franz Rosenthal, "A Note on the Mandīl," in *Four Essays on Art and Literature in Islam* (Leiden: Brill, 1971), 63–99.

15. Lufti, *Al-Quds al Mamlūkiyya*, 58 (Arabic), 54 (English).

16. Christian Müller, *Der Kadi und seine Zeugen: Studie der mamlukischen Haram-Dokumente aus Jerusalem* (Wiesbaden: Harrassowitz Verlag 2014), 312, 351.

a cotton prayer rug, *sajjadah*); one white-blue *Qudsi* (from Jerusalem) towel and another large *Shami* (Syrian) towel; copper bowls; trays, plates, and cases all made of brass; chests, shelves with some Ba'albaki glassware on them, and a number of chairs.

Like Eudes's inventory, Nafisa's also closed with a section detailing her financial obligations and the possession of coinage. Here we learn that a number of individuals, all living in villages not far from Jerusalem, owed Nafisa money: Ali b. Yusuf owes her 350 silver *dinars*, a certain Sidiqi from Qusur owes her 28 *dinars*, and a certain Amir from Urtas has an outstanding debt of 44 *dinars*. Furthermore, we learn that Nafisa owned a vineyard (lit. grape vine plants, *ghirās karm*) in Dayr Abu Thawr, which is also in close proximity to Jerusalem, as well as trees or plants of unspecified type in the same place.[17] In the immediate context of these items the document states that Nafisa owned a "young Muslim black female slave named Mubaraka." If the decision to place these items together is not arbitrary, it is possible that Nafisa was in the business of growing and distributing produce (grapes and other fruits) in and around Jerusalem. She is said to have owned an apartment in Jerusalem, which could have been a storefront or a warehouse. Mubaraka could have worked in this firm, and a number of individuals, or more likely vendors, in the region are shown to have incurred some debt. A possible indication that Nafisa was indeed a wealthy merchant is the fact that she bore a golden ring (with an unspecified stone, *faṣṣ*) on her right hand and a necklace with precious stones (*'aqīq*—could be onyx, agate, jacinth, or ruby). Be that as it may, unlike most other inventories, Nafisa does leave instructions regarding her property to be carried out after her death. She asks that one hundred *dirhams* go to her granddaughter (the daughter of Nafisa's daughter), Fatima, who was nine years old at the time the document was signed. Additionally, she bequeaths the same amount, one hundred *dirhams*, "for the honorable complete recitation [of the Quran] and for charity," and asks that her husband oversees the disbursement of the money.[18]

The inventory of another relatively affluent individual gives yet more insight into the objects and possessions that animated the eastern Mediterranean and the world of Outremer. This inventory was drafted in October 1393 for a certain Muhammad b. Muhammad b. 'Umar, who we are told was "weak," meaning that like Nafisa he was probably in poor health and/or elderly. The statement furthermore identifies Muhammad as a copyist ("nāsikh").[19] As in

17. For a discussion of this place, based in large part on Mujir al-Din, see Amikam Elad, *Medieval Jerusalem and Islamic Worship: Holy Places, Ceremonies, Pilgrimage* (Leiden: Brill, 1999) 171–72.

18. For the one hundred *dirhams* to Fatima and the Quran recitation, see Lufti, *Al-Quds al Mamlūkiyya*, 56 (English), 59 (Arabic).

19. Little transcribed this word as *nāsij*, meaning "weaver"; see *Catalogue of the Islamic Documents*, 130 (entry no. 494). The only difference between the two options is whether the diacritic goes above or under the last letter, making it a kha or jim, respectively. In Muhammad

the previous cases, the inventory begins by listing the clothes Muhammad was wearing and those that were in his possession. These include chemises, turbans, cloaks, overcoats made of fur, linen, silk, or cotton. Significantly, some of the items listed in Muhammad's home could very well be associated with his profession. This section begins by stating that he owns twelve bound books (or codex volumes). The items that are listed subsequently could have served as his working space: a bench covered with a blue garment, a towel made of velvet, an old leather placement map, and a quilt embroidered with black and green threads. Additionally, he had a striped cloak made of silk and an apron. The inventory then states that Muhammad possessed three additional bound books and lists a number of items that, I propose, could have been used for the production of ink: one desk with a blue cotton tabletop, a copper tray and wooden bowl, a copper cauldron, a copper pan, an iron ladle, a sack with almonds inside, another sack with stones, pebbles, and combustion/lighting material, one leather bag with egg shells, two glass jars and a kettle, another sack with copper and lead inside. Muhammad may have used this equipment to mix, boil, and filter the substances from which he produced ink for his own needs as a copyist.[20] The inventory ends with a brief notice regarding sums of money that Muhammad owed and that were owed to him.

The inventories found in the Haram collection speak to the lives and livelihoods of people living in Jerusalem at the end of the fourteenth century. The court and the pious endowments associated with it served people from all walks of life—both poor and wealthy, free and enslaved—holding a variety of occupations (weavers, merchants, etc.) and coming from various backgrounds. As could be expected in a collection that was overseen by a *shar'i* court, the majority of individuals mentioned in the documents—as either the subjects of inventories, witnesses, or related stakeholders (spouses, heirs, debtors etc.)—were Muslim, to judge by their names. But a number of Jews and Christians (as well as Sufis) can be found as well.[21] Between the lines of dry inventory lists, these documents are able to relate the stories of ordinary people living in late medieval Jerusalem, evoking details of their lives in ways unlike any other narrative or documentary source from the period could.

'Isa Salihiyya's edition the reading is *nāsikh*. While it is true that throughout the collection many weavers are mentioned, in this particular document a copyist is more likely, seeing as Muhammad was in possession of several bound volumes or books, something quite rare in this context; see Muḥammad ʿĪsā Ṣāliḥiyya, *Min waṯāʾiq al-Ḥaram al-Qudsī al-Šarīf al-mamlūkiyya* (Kuwait: Ḥawlīyāt Kulliyat ad-dāb, 1985), 10.

20. On ink in medieval Near Eastern codices, see Adam Gacek, *Arabic Manuscripts: A Vademecum for Readers* (Leiden: Brill, 2009), 132–33; Ibrahim Chabbouh, *Le Manuscrit* (Tunis: Alīf, 1989), 66; François Dérouche et al., *Islamic Codicology: An Introduction to the Study of Manuscripts in Arabic Script*, trans. Deke Dusinberre and David Radzinowicz (London: al-Furqan Islamic Heritage Foundation, 2005), 111–15.

21. Specifically on Jews in this cache, see Donald Little, "Haram Documents Related to the Jews of Late Fourteenth-Century Jerusalem," *Journal of Semitic Studies* 30 (1985): 227–64.

Appendix: Genealogy of Eudes of Nevers

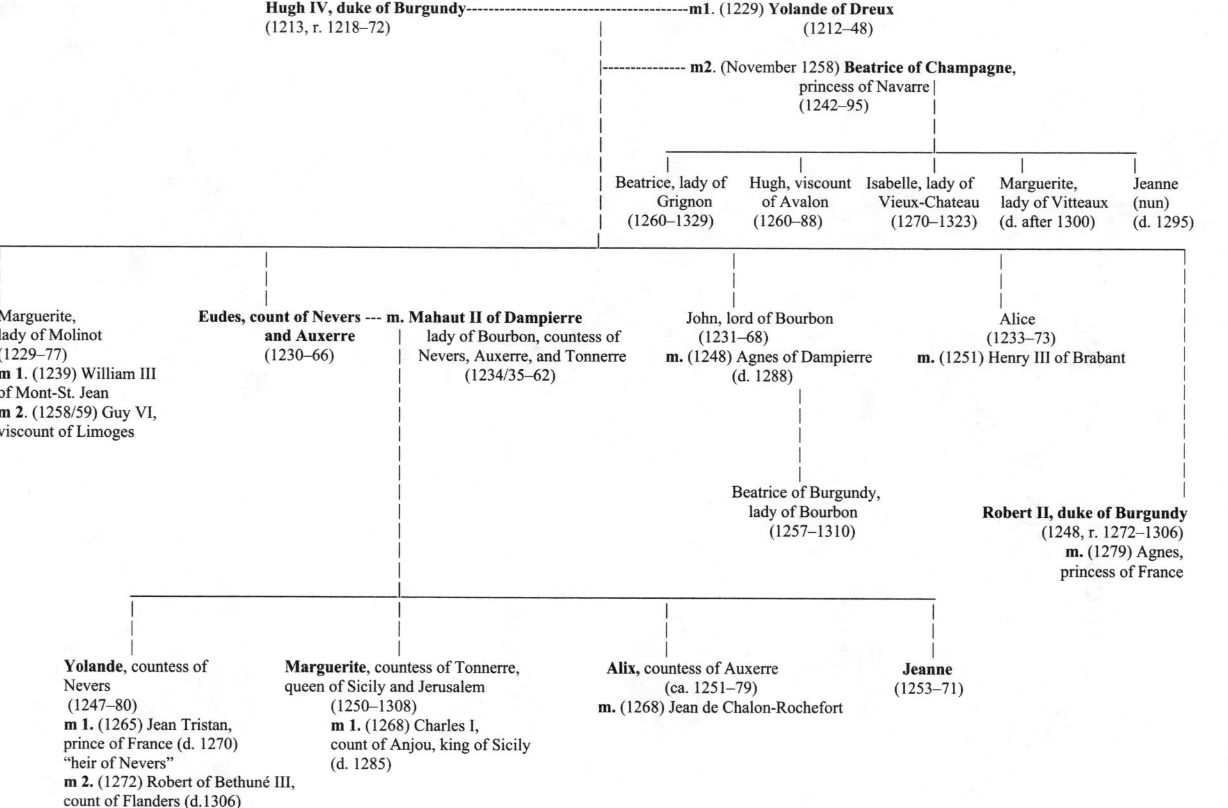

The genealogy of the counts of Nevers with Eudes of Nevers at the center and showing his parents, wife, siblings, and four daughters with their births, deaths, and reigns listed. Constructed from Ernest Petit, *Histoire des ducs de Bourgogne de la race Capétienne* (Dijon: Darantiere, 1885–1905), vol. 3; and Jean Richard, *Les ducs de Bourgogne et de la formation du duché, du XIe au XIVe siècle* (Dijon: Bernigaud et Privat, 1954). We thank Richard Leson for consulting on some of the details above.

Glossary

Sources Consulted

CHL	Alan V. Murray, *The Crusades to the Holy Land* (Santa Barbara: ABC-CLIO, 2015).
EMD	Gale Owen-Crocker, Elizabeth Coatsworth, and Maria Hayward, eds., *Encyclopedia of Medieval Dress and Textiles* (Leiden: Brill, 2012).
MN	Kathryn L. Reyerson and Debra A. Salata, eds., *Medieval Notaries and Their Acts: The 1327–1328 Register of Jean Holanie* (Kalamazoo: Medieval Institute Publications, 2004).

Absalon: Absalom in the biblical tradition, the third son of King David.

Acre: Economic and political capital city of the Kingdom of Jerusalem from the late twelfth century (after 1187) and headquarters of the western Christian forces in the Latin East until 1291; now known as Akko, located in modern-day Israel.

alb: Long, white liturgical undergarment worn by those who served at the altar (*EMD*).

amice: Liturgical vestment, usually made of linen, placed around the neck to protect other vestments from becoming soiled (*EMD*); see essay by Maureen Miller.

Antioch: Frankish state in northern Syria, established in the late eleventh century during the First Crusade. It was under western Christian control until 1268 (*CHL*).

Apulia: Region of the southwestern Italian peninsula, with a capital in Bari; part of the kingdom of Sicily. In the late 1260s, Apulia came under the rule of the Naples-based Angevin Empire. See **Sicily.**

assises: Court of law, often presided over by noblemen in service to their lord.

Asturias: Kingdom in northern Spain known as a battleground between Christian and Muslim forces for control over the Iberian Peninsula; part of the medieval pilgrimage route to Santiago de Compostela.

Ayoul: Eponymous hero of the lesser-known thirteenth-century French *chanson de geste* entitled *Aiol.*

Baybars(July 19, 1223 – July 1, 1277): Powerful and respected **Mamluk** general who led the first wave of Muslim victories to dismantle the remaining Frankish holdings in Syria and Palestine, taking **Antioch** in 1268. His successors would take Tripoli in 1289 and **Acre** in 1291.

bezant: The most valuable form of gold coinage that circulated commonly in the Islamic states and throughout **Outremer**.
Bohemond: Leader of the First Crusade who then took rulership of the Principality of **Antioch** in 1098 (*CHL*, 40).
Boukhara cloth: Also known as buckram, a luxurious cloth made of cotton or linen; see essay by Sharon Farmer.
bourgeois: Inhabitants of a bourg, or village.
breviary: Liturgical book containing the text of the church service for each day, most often read aloud by a member of the clergy; see essay by Maureen Miller.
bursar: Member of Eudes's household responsible for issuing pay to other members in the count's employ.
butt: Unit of measurement for wine, corresponding to 126 gallons.
Caesarea: City located on the coast of modern-day Israel, captured by western crusaders during the First Crusade but retaken by the **Mamluk** sultanate in 1265.
camlet: Textile typically made from camel fur, often sourced from Central Asia.
carole (to dance the): Popular dance in France and England between 1100 and 1400, performed by all levels of society in secular and ecclesiastical settings often following a feast or celebration.
cendal: A kind of cloth that may have been either silk or very fine linen; by the thirteenth and fourteenth centuries it referred to silk (*EMD*).
chansonnier: Song book or collection of poems.
chapel: Portable set of items to celebrate the Mass; see essay by Maureen Miller; in other instances, the location in a church where an altar might be found and where the Mass could be performed.
Charlemagne: King of the Franks from 771 CE, declared emperor of the Romans by Pope Leo III on Christmas, 800; figure of ecclesiastical legends relating to the liberation of holy sites from Muslims in the East and in Spain; central figure of the Old French epic tradition known for battles against non-Christians, as in the *Song of Roland*.
Château Pèlerin: Crusader castle in modern-day Israel, also known as 'Atlit Castle.
chasuble: Liturgical vestment worn over the **alb** and the **stole** that covers the wearer's arms (*EMD*).
Cîteaux: First Cistercian monastery founded in 1098 in northern Burgundy, head of the Cistercian order, site of the necropolis of the dukes of Burgundy.
complaint: Translation of the French word *complainte*, a poetic form that either mourns the loss of a person or place, or functions as a criticism about a set of circumstances.
conclave: Private meeting, often of high-level church or political leaders.
Constantinople: Capital city of the Byzantine Empire, conquered by western Christian crusaders during the Fourth Crusade (1204).
corporal: Cloth upon which the consecrated body and blood of Christ were placed during the celebration of the Eucharist (*EMD*).
Corsica: Large Mediterranean island off the coast of southern France between Marseille and Rome whose rulership was often contested throughout the thirteenth century.
courtoisie, courtois: Terms denoting a code of ethics and behaviors relating to medieval aristocratic court life, defined against the *vilainie* of agricultural life; involves ideas of nobility, refinement, good manners, and aristocratic obligation.

Crete: Large island in the Aegean Sea that came under Latin domination after the Fourth Crusade in 1204; it eventually came under Venetian rule, and remained so for several centuries thereafter.

cross (to take the): To take a vow to go on crusade.

cuirass: Two-piece armor consisting of a breastplate and a backplate.

Cumans: Nomadic Turks whose origins lay in the Eurasian steppe; in the thirteenth century they were forced westward by Mongol conquests.

Cyprus: Island territory conquered in 1191 by Richard the Lionheart that remained under Latin control until the late fifteenth century (*CHL*).

dalmatic: Full-length, wide-sleeved overgarment used by the clergy when celebrating the liturgy; see essay by Maureen Miller.

de reaus: Of the realm, meaning a unit of currency that circulated in the Kingdom of Jerusalem; may be related to *réaux* (*regales*), which are royal, gold coins that circulated in southern France (*MN*).

Dominicans: Religious order founded in the early thirteenth century (ca. 1210) by Saint Dominic that has preaching as its primary mission. The Dominicans were criticized by Rutebeuf as hypocrites. Also called **Jacobins**.

doublet: Close-fitting, padded garment with a round neck and fitted sleeves (*EMD*).

ell: Unit of measure for cloth, corresponding to about a yard (36 inches) in length (*EMD*).

escheat: Return of land to one's feudal lord upon the death of the landowner if there is no direct inheritor.

feast of the Holy Cross: Traditionally held on September 14.

feast of Saint Leu: Traditionally held on September 1.

feast of Saint Lawrence: Traditionally held on August 9.

feast of Saint Michael: Traditionally held on September 29.

feast of Saint Remy: Traditionally held on October 7.

Franciscans: Religious order founded in the early thirteenth century (1209) around Saint Francis of Assisi and dedicated to a life of poverty. Like the **Dominicans** the Franciscans were criticized by Rutebeuf as hypocrites. Also called the Minors or Friars Minor.

frontal: Liturgical cloth that covers the front of the altar (*EMD*); see essay by Maureen Miller.

gambeson: Over-jacket for armor made of padded, quilted material (*EMD*).

ganache: Thick cape or overdress that covered the body, often made of wool, could be lined with **vair** or other material.

gentillesse: Term that suggests aristocratic birth, generosity, and kindness; the life of a ***prudhomme*** was often described in terms of his *gentillesse*.

Godfrey of Bouillon: One of the leaders of the First Crusade, and the first ruler of the Kingdom of Jerusalem that was established in 1099 (*CHL*).

grosvair: The gray and white belly fur of a northern European squirrel, used as trim or lining for expensive garments (*EMD*); see also **miniver**.

henap: Goblet, cup, or footed cup; see essay by Richard Leson.

Holy Sepulcher: The church believed to be built over the sites where Jesus Christ was crucified and buried; securing dominion over this space was a motivating rationale for crusading efforts from the West.

The Hospital: Military order, also known as the Hospitallers, whose mission was to provide aid and care for Christian pilgrims to the Holy Land; located in Jerusalem at the Hospital of St. John.

Jacobins: In France the first **Dominican** convent was located on the rue St.-Jacques in Paris, and therefore they came to be called Jacobins.

Jaffa: Ancient port city in modern-day Israel and a part of the County of Jaffa, a larger territory established by western Christians after the First Crusade that included the city and surrounding areas, with boundaries that shifted over time.

***lais*:** A word with multiple meanings; in Rutebeuf's poem relating to a will or testament, also spelled *legs*, as in legacy, what one leaves to inheritors.

lament: See **complaint.**

lynx: Fur of a wild cat, ranging in color from gold to dark brown and often spotted (*EMD*).

Mamluk: Initially referred to slave mercenaries of Turkic descent from the Eurasian steppes; rebelled against Ayyubid rule in 1258 and came to rule a unified Muslim territory that stretched from Egypt to northern Syria from 1258 to 1517. In 1291 the Mamluks effectively expelled the crusaders from **Outremer**.

maniple: Ornamental, nonfunctional handkerchief worn on the left forearm by members of the clergy (*EMD*); see essay by Maureen Miller.

mark: Unit of currency and of account in silver, often referring to the English pound, which was of slightly higher value than the French pound.

Matins: In the Christian liturgy, the service that takes place in the dark hours of the early morning.

miniver*:** The white belly fur of a northern European squirrel, used as trimming for luxurious garments; gros miniver or ***grosvair includes both gray- and white-colored fur, while miniver is only white in color (*EMD*).

Minors: See **Franciscans.**

missal: Liturgical book containing all the texts used during the Mass for the year; see essay by Maureen Miller.

***mon segnor*:** My lord, a term that referred to a person of elevated social status, of the knightly rank or higher. The term *messire* was used similarly to denote respect and elite status.

monstrance: Receptacle with a transparent window used to display the Eucharist or other consecrated object in an ecclesiastical setting.

The Morea: Crusader settlement, also known as the Principality of Achaea, established in the years after the Fourth Crusade in the northern part of the region of southern Greece now called the Peloponnese.

Naime of Bavaria: Figure of Old French epic (*chanson de geste*) and of Italian romance epic; wise and trusted advisor to **Charlemagne** of the older generation; fails to perceive Ganelon's treachery in the *Song of Roland.*

Ogier: Figure of Old French epic and later of Scandinavian legend; part of **Charlemagne**'s close circle in the cycle of poems related to the king; later a central figure of the cycle of the rebel barons.

orphrey: Detailed and decorative embroidered band, used on liturgical vestments or aristocratic robes.

Outremer: This term, which means "overseas" or "beyond the sea," refers to a configuration of eastern Mediterranean territories with ever-changing boundaries where western Christians exerted political control following their conquest of these territories during the First Crusade. Also called the Holy Land (by Christians), the Levant, the Latin East, or the Crusader States, among other terms.

pagan: Derogatory and inaccurate term used to describe a person who was of neither Christian nor Jewish faith. In the context of the 1260s, this refers to persons of the Muslim faith or other eastern communities, such as the Mongols.

palfrey: Horse used for riding, as opposed to a war horse.

***passage*:** The trip to the Holy Land, taken from the West, or return trip from the East.

patriarchs: Title used for the heads of the Eastern churches; the bishop of Jerusalem is referred to as the patriarch, meaning "father" in Greek.

phylactery: Small metalwork or glass container for carrying small relics, fragments of the True Cross, as well as oil, balm, or water; term is used in both secular and scared contexts.

Poitiers: City located in what is now the west-central part of France; was the main city within the duchy of Aquitaine and one of the principle cities in the county of Toulouse. After 1249, Alphonse of Poitiers (1220–71), brother of King Louis IX, became the Count of Toulouse and is often referred to as the Count of Poitiers.

prebendery: Member of the clergy who receives a prebend, or stipend, from the church.

prelate: Exalted member of the church hierarchy, such as a bishop or archbishop.

Promised Land: At various times, another term for the Holy Land, modern-day Palestine, or for heaven.

***prudhomme*:** Term combining *prode* or *preux*, as in "prowess," with *homme* to denote a wise, brave, and prudent man; associated with good counsel; by the turn of the fourteenth century it also described members of judicial councils charged with litigation involving artisans.

pyx: In the Christian tradition, a box or other container to carry the consecrated Host.

***quarroble*:** Unit of eastern currency, smaller than a **bezant**.

regiment: Military unit of soldiers, often of knights and their retainers, or those in their **retinue** including squires, pages, and servants. Typical medieval regiments were of twenty, thirty, or fifty knights. The regiment of knights that the French king Louis IX established in **Acre** in 1254 was made up of approximately one hundred men. The company of knights in Prince Edward's force in 1271 may have had as many as two hundred men.

reliquary: Container, box, or vase use to hold and often transport holy objects such as wood of the True Cross, bones and bone fragments of saints, oil, water, dust, cloth, stones from holy places, and other materials that are venerated as relics. Reliquaries can take many forms and be decorated or simple boxes, or reused vases or cases.

retinue: Followers of a lord or knight, those within the household including other knights, **vavassors**, squires, pages, and servants; a closer household unit and group of followers, often sharing the same livery; the number of men in a retinue surrounding a single knight or lord depended on his resources.

rochet: White overgarment worn by members of the clergy for non-Eucharistic occasions; see essay by Maureen Miller.

Roland: Figure of Old French epic, nephew of **Charlemagne**, leader of his uncle's armies in Spain in the fight against King Marsile in the *Song of Roland*, dies as a result of the treachery of Ganelon.

***s. lb t./l. t.*:** Abbreviation for units of currency that correspond to *sous tournois* and *pounds/livres tournois* referring to denominations from the city of Tours, located in the Kingdom of France.

Saint Peter of Rome: First pope of the Roman Catholic Church.

Saracens: Term commonly used by western Europeans in the Middle Ages to refer to Muslims; it is derogatory, based on a myth that Muslims lied about their ancestry, claiming descent from Abraham and his wife Sara when they were (according to the myth) descendants of the offspring of Abraham's relationship with his slave, Hagar.

Sepulcher: See **Holy Sepulcher.**

serge: Type of woolen fabric, often used to make soft furniture and overcoats and outer garments (*EMD*).

serpent's tongue: Spiky-leafed plant most likely of the *Ophioglossum* family, commonly used in poultices to relieve soreness and inflammation; or implement used for testing food.

Sicily: From the late 1260s until the fifteenth century, Sicily was ruled by the Angevins, a dynasty whose rulers originated in the county of Anjou, within the Kingdom of France. The Angevin dynasty is named for Charles of Anjou, the brother of Louis IX (also known as Saint Louis). In the late 1270s, Charles of Anjou purchased the title of king of Jerusalem.

***sous*:** Monetary denomination used in the Kingdom of France.

sterling: Currency valuation originating in England but used internationally during the medieval period.

stole: Narrow strip of cloth worn by members of the clergy during the liturgy (*EMD*).

sultan: The most senior rank of secular ruler in the Muslim world. In the 1260s the crusader Kingdom of Jerusalem suffered heavy losses to the **Mamluk** sultans of Egypt.

surplice: Simple sleeved garment worn by clergymen, made of linen (*EMD*); see essay by Maureen Miller.

Tancred: Hero of the First Crusade who took the title of prince of Galilee and regent of the Principality of **Antioch.**

Tartars: Generalizing and pejorative term commonly used by western Europeans in the Middle Ages to refer to the Mongols.

The Temple: Military order also known as the Templars; location in Jerusalem associated with the Temple of David.

***tiretaine*:** Mixed-blend cloth, in which two types of materials, such as wool and silk, or wool and linen, are woven together in one fabric; see essay by Sharon Farmer.

***tireteinne cameline*:** Camelin **tiretaine,** a linen-wool blend cloth; see essay by Sharon Farmer.

tourneyers: Young knights, noblemen, and warriors who participate in tournaments and competitions to test their skills for battle.

***tournois*:** Coming from the city of Tours, located in the Kingdom of France.

tunic: Loosely fitting garment, often made from a single piece of cloth and lacking shoulder sleeves.

turcopole: Mercenary, a man hired to fight by force of arms.

vair: Squirrel fur used to line or trim garments; see **miniver** and **grosvair.**

vavassor: Lord who had his own retainers, but who owed allegiance to his own lord; ranked lower than a baron.

Bibliography

Manuscripts and Archival Material

Belgium

Brussels, Bibliothèque royale de Belgique, MS 9411–9426

England

Kew, National Archives
MS DL 25/177 (1267)
MS DL 25/1317
MS DL 34/1/2
MS E 36/274

France

Arras, Archives départementales du Pas-de-Calais, Centre Mahaut d'Artois, Series A, 428
Lille, Archives départementales du Nord, series B 447, no. 4.621.
Paris, Archives nationales, series J 821, no. 1, Rolls A–D: *The Account Inventory of Eudes of Nevers*
Paris, Bibliothèque nationale de France
Collection de Picardie, MS 331
MS Dupuy 98
MS français 837
MS français 1622
MS français 1635 (https://gallica.bnf.fr/ark:/12148/btv1b9058335d)
MS français 1977
MS français 4329
MS français 4508

United States

New York, Morgan Library, MS M 638 (https://www.themorgan.org/collection/Crusader-Bible)

Primary Sources

Baudouin de Sebourg. *Li romans de Bauduin de Sebourc, IIIe Roy de Jhérusalem: Poëme du XIVe siècle publié pour la première fois d'après les manuscrits de la Bibliothèque Nationale.* Edited by M. L. Roca. 2 vols. Valenciennes: Imprimerie de B. Henry, 1841.

Belon, Pierre. *Les observations de plusieurs singularitez et choses memorables, trouvées en Grèce, Asie, Judée, Egypte, Arabie et autres pays estranges.* Paris, 1555.

Bird, Jessalynn, Edward Peters, and James M. Powell, eds. *Crusade and Christendom: Annotated Documents in Translation from Innocent III to the Fall of Acre, 1187–1291.* Philadelphia: University of Pennsylvania Press, 2013.

Boccaccio. *Decameron.* Translated by J. M. Rigg. 2 vols. London: A. H. Bullen, 1953.

Boileau, Etienne. *Le livre des métiers d'Etienne Boileau.* Edited by René de Lespinasse and François Bonnardot. Paris: Imprimerie Nationale, 1879.

Burchard of Mount Sion, OP. *Descriptio Terrae Sanctae.* Edited and translated by John R. Bartlett. Oxford: Oxford University Press, 2019.

Calendar of Inquisitions Miscellaneous (Chancery). Prepared by the Deputy Keeper of the Records. 8 vols. London: His Majesty's Stationery Office, 1916.

Chazaud, A.-M. "Inventaire et comptes de la succession d'Eudes, comte de Nevers (Acre 1266)." *Mémoires de la Société nationales des Antiquaires de France*, 4th series, 2 (1871): 164–206.

Crawford, Paul. *The "Templar of Tyre": Part III of the "Deeds of the Cypriots."* Aldershot: Ashgate, 2003.

de Curzon, Henri, ed. *La Règle du Temple.* Paris: Librairie Renouard, 1886.

Douët-d'Arcq, Louis, ed. *Comptes de l'argenterie des rois de France au XIVe siècle publié pour la Société de l'histoire de France d'après des manuscrits originaux.* Paris: Jules Renouard, 1951.

Douët-d'Arcq, Louis, ed. *Nouveau recueil de comptes de l'argenterie des rois de France.* Paris: Jules Renouard, 1874.

Filangieri, Richardo, et al., eds. *I registri della Cancelleria angioina.* 50 vols. Naples: L'Accademia, 1951–2006.

Geoffrey of Villehardouin. *La conquete de Constantinople.* Edited and translated by Edmond Faral. 2 vols. Paris: Les Belles Lettres, 1938–39; 2nd ed. 1961.

Giovanni di Pian di Carpine. *Storia dei Mongoli, edizione critica.* Edited by Enrico Menestò, Italian translation by Maria Cristiana Lungarotti. Spoleto: Centro Italiano di Studi sull'Alto Medioevo, 1989.

Guiraud, Jean, ed. *Les registres d'Urbain IV (1261–1264): Recueil des bulles de ce pape publiées ou analysées d'après les manuscrits originaux du Vatican.* 4 vols. Paris: Thorin et Fils, 1901–58.

Haskett, Timothy S., and Sarah B. White, eds. *The Wills of Medieval England, 1066–1300.* Toronto, forthcoming.

Hey, David, Lisa Liddy, and David Luscombe, eds. *A Monastic Community in Local Society: The Beauchief Abbey Cartulary.* Cambridge: Cambridge University Press, 2012.

Huillard-Breholles, J.-L.-A., and A. Lecoy de La Marche, eds. *Titres de la maison ducale de Bourbon.* 2 vols. Paris: H. Plon, 1867–74.

Ibn Jubayr. *The Travels of Ibn Jubayr.* Translated by R. J. C. Broadhurst. London: Jonathan Cape, 1952.

"Inquisitions Post Mortem, Edward I, File 63." In *Calendar of Inquisitions Post Mortem*, vol. 3: *Edward I*, edited by J. E. E. S. Sharp and A. E. Stamp. London: His Majesty's Stationery Office, 1912. *British History Online*, http://www.british-history.ac.uk/inquis-post-mortem/vol3/pp30-54.

"Inquisitions Post Mortem, Edward II, File 20." In *Calendar of Inquisitions Post Mortem*, vol. 5: *Edward II*, edited by J. E. E. S. Sharp and A. E. Stamp. London: His Majesty's Stationery Office, 1908. *British History Online*, http://www.british-history.ac.uk/inquis-post-mortem/vol5/.

Jacques de Vitry. *Lettres de Jacques de Vitry*. Edited by R. B. C. Huygens. Leiden: E. J. Brill, 1960.

Jakemés. *Le roman du Castelain de Couci et de la Dame de Fayel par Jakemes*. Edited by John E. Matzke and Maurice Delbouille. Paris: SATF, 1936.

Jean de Joinville. *Histoire de Saint Louis, Credo et lettre à Louis X*. Edited by Natalis de Wailly. 2nd ed. Paris: Firmin Didot, 1874.

Jean de Joinville. *Vie de Saint Louis*. Edited by J. Monfrin. Paris: Garnier, 1995.

John Phocas, Descriptio Terrae Sanctae, IX. In *Patrologiae Cursus Completus: Series Graeca*, edited by J. P. Migne. Paris: J. P. Migne, 1857–80.

Lalou, Elisabeth, ed. *Les comptes sur tablettes de cire de la chambre aux deniers de Philippe III le Hardi et Philippe IV le Bel (1282–1309)*. Paris: Boccard, 1994.

Le livre au roi. Edited by Myriam Greilsammer. Paris: Académie des Inscriptions et Belles-Lettres, 1995.

Longnon, Auguste. *Rôles des fiefs du comté de Champagne sous le règne de Thibaud le Chansonnier, 1249–1252*. Paris: Henri Menu, 1877.

Malicote, Sandra C., and A. Richard Hartman, ed. and trans. *Aiol: A Chanson de Geste, Modern Edition and First English Translation*. New York: Italica Press, 2014.

Marie de France. *Laustic*. Translated by Judy Shoaf. University of Florida, 1991. https://people.clas.ufl.edu/jshoaf/files/laustic.pdf.

Martene, Edmund, and Ursini Durand, *Veterum Scriptorum et Monumentorum Historicorum, Dogmaticorum, Moralium Amplissima Collectio*. 9 vols. Paris: Montalant, 1724–33.

Martino da Canale. *Les estoires de Venise: Cronaca veneziana in lingua francese ale origini al 1275*. Edited by Alberto Limentani. Florence: L. S. Olschki, 1972.

Minervini, Laura, ed. and trans. *Cronaca del Templare di Tiro (1243–1314): La caduta degli Stati Croniati nel racconto di un testimone oculare*. Naples: Liguroi, 2000.

Münster, Sebastian. *Cosmographie universelle de tout le monde*. Vol. 1. Translated into French by François de Belleforest. Paris, 1575.

"Pelrinages et pardouns de Acre." In *Itinéraires à Jérusalem et descriptions de la Terre Sainte redigés en français aux XIe, XIIe et XIIIe siècles*, edited by H. Michelant and G. Raynaud. Geneva: Imprimerie Jules-Guillaume Fick, 1882.

Polo, Marco. *The Description of the World*. Translated by Sharon Kinoshita. Indianapolis: Hackett, 2016.

Polo, Marco. *Milione: Le divisament dou Monde; il Milione nelle redazioni Toscana e franco-italiana*. Edited by Gabriella Ronchi. Milan: Arnoldo Mondadori Editore, 1982.

Quantin, Maximilien. *Recueil de pièces pour faire suite au cartulaire général de l'Yonne*. Paris: Durand et Pédone-Lauriel, 1878.

Regesti Clementis Papae V ex Vaticanis Archetypis Sanctissimi Domini nostri Leonis XIII Pontificis Maximi Ivssv et Mvnificentia nunc primvm editi cvra et stvdio monachorum Ordinis S. Benedicti Appendices. Rome: Typographia Vaticana, 1892.

Riant, Paul-Édouard, ed. "Déposition de Charles d'Anjou pour la canonisation de Saint Louis." In *Notices et documents publiés pour la Société de l'histoire de France à l'occasion du cinquantième anniversaire de sa fondation*, 155–76. Paris: Librairie Renouard, 1884.

Riccoldo of Monte Croce. *Pérégrination en Terre Sainte et au Proche Orient: Texte latin et traduction. Lettres sur la chute de Saint-Jean d'Acre. Traduction*. Edited and translated by René Kappler. Textes et traductions des classiques français du Moyen Âge 4. Paris: Honoré Champion, 1997.

Robert de Clari. *La conquête de Constantinople: Édition bilingue, Publication, traduction, présentation et notes*. Edited and translated by Jean Dufournet. Paris: Honoré Champion, 2004.

Röhricht, Reinhold, ed. *Regesta*. http://crusades-regesta.com/about.

Röhricht, Reinhold, ed. *Regesta Regni Hierosolymitani (MXCVII–MCCXCI)*. Oeniponti: Libraria Academica Wageriana, 1893.

Rutebeuf. *Rutebeuf: Oeuvres complètes*. Edited and translated by Michel Zink. Paris: Classiques Garnier, 2001.

Rutebeuf. *Oeuvres complètes de Rutebeuf*. Edited by Julia Bastin and Edmond Faral. 4th ed. Vol. 1. Paris: Picard, 1977.

Rutebeuf. *Oeuvres complètes de Rutebeuf, Trouvère de XIIIe siècle: Recueillies et mises au jour pour la première fois*. Edited by Archille Jubinal. 2 vols. Paris: É. Pannier, 1839.

Rutebeuf. *Onze poèmes de Rutebeuf concernant la croisade*. Edited by Julia Bastin and Edmond Faral. Paris: Libraire Orientaliste Paul Geuthner, 1946.

Rymer, Thomas, ed. "Testimentum Domini Edwardi primogeniti Regis conditum apud Acres." In *Foedera*, vol. 1. London: J. Tonson, 1726.

Smith, Caroline, trans. *Joinville and Villehardouin: Chronicles of the Crusades*. Harmondsworth: Penguin, 2008.

Teulet, Alexandre, et al., eds. *Layettes du Trésor des chartes*. 5 vols. Paris: H. Plon, 1863–1909.

Treton, Rodrigue, and Robert Vinas. "Le testament de Nunó Sanç, seigneur de Roussillon et de Cerdagne (17 décembre 1241)." *e-Spania: Revue interdisciplinaire d'études hispaniques médiévales et modernes* 28 (2017), https://doi.org/10.4000/e-spania.27026.

Wilhelm von Tripolis. *Notitia de Machometo; De Statu Sarracenorum*. Edited by Peter Engels. CISC Series Latina 4. Würzburg: Echter, 1992.

Secondary Sources

Abulafia, David. "The Anconitan Privileges in the Kingdom of Jerusalem and the Levant Trade of Ancona." In *I comuni italiani nel regno crociato di Gerusalemme: Atti del Colloquio "The Italian Communes in the Crusading Kingdom of Jerusalem" (Jerusalem, May 24 – May 28, 1984)*, edited by Gabriella Airaldi and Benjamin Z. Kedar, Collana storica di fonti e studi 48, 523–70. Genoa: Università di Genova, Istituto di medievistica, 1986.

Aladjidi, Priscille. *Le roi père des pauvres, France XIIIe–XVe siècle*. Rennes: Presses Universitaires de Rennes, 2008.

Amīn, Muḥammad. *Al-Awqāf Wa-ăl-ḥayāt Al-Iğtimāʿiyya Fī Miṣr 648–923 H. 1250–1517 M.: Dirāsa Tārīḫiyya Wa-ṯaqāfiyya*. al-Qāhira: Dār an-Nahḍa al-ʿArabiyya, 1980.

Anderlini, Tina. "The Shirt Attributed to St. Louis." In *Medieval Clothing and Textiles*, vol. 11, edited by Robin Netherton, Gale R. Owen-Crocker, and Monic L. Wright, 49–78. Woodbridge: Boyell, 2015.

Angotti, Claire, Pierre Chastang, Vincent Debiais, and Laura Kendrick, eds. *Le pouvoir des listes au moyen âge: Écritures de la liste*. Paris: Éditions de la Sorbonne, 2019.

Antrim, Zayde. "Jerusalem in the Ayyubid and Mamluk Period." In *Routledge Handbook on Jerusalem*, edited by Souleiman Mourad, Naomi Koltun-Fromm, and Bedross der Matossian, 102–9. New York: Routledge, 2019.

Appadurai, Arjun, ed. *The Social Life of Things: Commodities in Cultural Perspective*. Cambridge: Cambridge University Press, 1986.

Ashtor, Eliyahu. *Levant Trade in the Middle Ages*. Princeton, NJ: Princeton University Press, 1983.

Aslanov, Cyril. "Crusaders' Old French." In *Research on Old French: The State of the Art*, edited by Deborah L. Arteaga, 207–20. Dordrecht: Springer Netherlands, 2012.

Aslanov, Cyril. *Le français au Levant, jadis et naguère: À la recherche d'une langue perdue*. Paris: Champion, 2006.

Aslanov, Cyril. "Languages in Contact in the Latin East: Acre and Cyprus." *Crusades* 1 (2002): 155–81.

Auffroy, Henri. *Evolution du testament en France des origines au XIIIe siècle*. Paris: A. Rousseau, 1899.

Auslander, Leora. "Beyond Words." *American Historical Association* 110 (2005): 1015–45.

Auslander, Leora. "Deploying Material Culture to Write the History of Gender and Sexuality: The Example of Clothing and Textiles." In "Making Gender with Things," special issue, *Clio*, no. 40 (2014): 157–78.

"Baldachin." "The Lexis of Cloth and Clothing Project," University of Manchester, http://lexissearch.arts.manchester.ac.uk/entry.aspx?id=280. Accessed December 6, 2021.

Bale, Anthony. "Reading and Writing in Outremer." In *The Cambridge Companion to the Literature of the Crusades*, edited by Anthony Bale, 85–101. Cambridge: Cambridge University Press, 2018.

Barber, Malcolm. "The Order of Saint Lazarus and the Crusades." *Catholic Historical Review* 80 (1994): 439–56.

Barsotti, R. *Gli antichi inventari della cattedrale di Pisa*. Pisa: Istituto di Storia dell'Arte, Università di Pisa, 1959.

Barthélemy, Dominique. "L'affaire Enguerran de Coucy (1259)." In *Affaires, scandales et grandes causes: De Socrate à Pinochet*, edited by Nicolas Offenstadt and Stéphane Van Damme, 59–77. Paris: Stock, 2007.

Baudin, Arnaud. *Les sceaux des comtes de Champagne et de leur entourage (fin XIe – début XIVe siècle)*. Paris: Éditions Dominique Guéniot, 2012.

Beam, Amanda. "'At the Apex of Chivalry': Sir Ingram de Umfraville and the Anglo-Scottish Wars." In *England and Scotland at War, c.1296–c.1513*, edited by Andy King and David Simpkin, 53–76. Leiden: Brill, 2012.

Beaudry, Mary Carolyn, ed. *Documentary Archaeology in the New World*. Cambridge: Cambridge University Press, 1988.

Bildhauer, Bettina. *Medieval Things: Agency, Materiality, and Narratives of Objects in Medieval German Literature and Beyond*. Columbus: The Ohio State University Press, 2020.

Black, Jonathan. "The Divine Office and Private Devotion in the Latin West." In *The Liturgy of the Medieval Church*, edited by Thomas J. Heffernan and E. Ann Matter, 45–71. Kalamazoo: Medieval Institute Publications, 2001.

Boas, Adrian J. *Crusader Archaeology: The Material Culture of the Latin East*. London: Routledge, 1999.

Boccherini Tamara, ed. *The Prato Textile Museum*. Milan: Skira, 1999.

Borrelli de Serres, Léon. "Compte d'une mission de prédication pour secours à la Terre Sainte (1265)." *Mémoires de la société de l'histoire de Paris et de l'Ile-de-France* 30 (1903): 243–80.

Bouchard, Constance Brittain. "Three Counties, One Lineage, and Eight Heiresses: Nevers, Auxerre, and Tonnerre, Eleventh to the Thirteenth Centuries." *Medieval Prosopography* 31 (2016): 25–46.

Branner, Robert. "The Painted Medallions in the Sainte-Chapelle in Paris." *Transactions of the American Philosophical Society* 58 (1968): 1–42

Bronstein, Judith. *The Hospitallers in the Holy Land: Financing the Latin East, 1187–1274*. Woodbridge: Boydell, 2005.

Brown, Bill. *Other Things*. Chicago: University of Chicago Press, 2015.

Brown, Bill. "Thing Theory." *Critical Inquiry* 28 (2001): 1–23.

Brown, Elizabeth A. R. "Authority, the Family, and the Dead in Late Medieval France." *French Historical Studies* 16 (1990): 803–32.

Brun, Laurent. "Le cycle des Lorrains." *ARLIMA: Archives de littérature du moyen âge*. Last updated December 12, 2023. https://www.arlima.net/ad/cycle_des_lorrains.html.

Buc, Philippe. *Holy War, Martyrdom, and Terror: Christianity, Violence, and the West*. Philadelphia: University of Pennsylvania Press, 2015.

Buettner, Brigitte. *The Mineral and the Visual: Precious Stones in Medieval Secular Culture*. University Park: Pennsylvania State University Press, 2022.

Buettner, Brigitte. "Le système des objets dans le testament de Blanche de Navarre." *Clio*, no. 19 (2004), https://doi.org/10.4000/clio.644.

Büntgen, Ulf, and Nicola Di Cosmo. "Climatic and Environmental Aspects of the Mongol Withdrawal from Hungary in 1242 CE." *Scientific Reports* 6, no. 1 (2016): 1–9.

Burgtorf, Jochen. *The Central Convent of Hospitallers and Templars: History, Organization, and Personnel (1099/1230–1310)*. Leiden: Brill, 2008.

Burns, E. Jane. *Sea of Silk: A Textile Geography of Women's Work in Medieval French Literature*. Philadelphia: University of Pennsylvania Press, 2006.

Cassidy-Welch, Megan. *War and Memory at the Time of the Fifth Crusade*. University Park: Pennsylvania State University Press, 2019.

Cerrini, Simonetta. "La tradition manuscrite de la règle du Temple." In *Autour de la première croisade: Actes du colloque de la Society for the Study of the Crusades and the Latin East (Clermont-Ferrand, 22–25 juin 1995)*, edited by Michel Balard, 203–19. Paris: Publications de la Sorbonne, 1996.

Chabbouh, Ibrahim. *Le Manuscrit*. Tunis: Alīf, 1989.

Chorley, Patrick. "The Cloth Exports of Flanders and Northern France during the Thirteenth Century: A Luxury Trade?" *Economic History Review* 40 (1987): 349–79.

Church, Stephen. "King John's Testament and the Last Days of His Reign." *English Historical Review* 125 (2010), 505–28.

Claverie, Pierre-Vincent, ed. "De l'entourage royal à l'entourage pontifical: L'example méconnu de l'archevêque Gilles de Tyr (d. 1266)." In *À l'ombre du pouvoir: Les entourages princiers au moyen âge*, edited by Alain Marchandisse and Jean-Louis Kupper, 57–76. Geneva: Droz, 2003.

Claverie, Pierre-Vincent, ed. "Un nouvel éclairage sur le financement de la première croisade de saint Louis." *Mélanges de l'École française de Rome: Moyen Âge* 113 (2001): 621–35.

Claverie, Pierre-Vincent, ed. *L'ordre du Temple dans l'Orient des croisades*. Brussels: De Boeck, 2014.

Claverie, Pierre-Vincent, ed. *L'ordre du Temple en Terre Sainte et à Chypre au XIIIe siècle*. 3 vols. Nicosia: Centre de Recherche Scientifique, 2005.

Clément, Pierre, ed. *Jacques Coeur et Charles VII, ou la France au XVe siècle: Étude historique*. Paris: Librairie de Guillaumin, 1853.

Coatsworth, Elizabeth. "Tiretaine." In *Brill Encyclopedia of Medieval Dress and Textiles Online*, edited by Gail Owen Crocker, Elizabeth Coatsworth, and Maria Hayward. Leiden: Brill, 2012. https://referenceworks.brill.com/display/entries/EMDO/COM-641.

Coatsworth, Elizabeth, and Mark Chambers. "Baudekin." In *Brill Encyclopedia of Medieval Dress and Textiles Online*, edited by Gail Owen Crocker, Elizabeth Coatsworth, and Maria Hayward. Leiden: Brill, 2012. https://doi.org/10.1163/2213-2139_emdt_SIM_000814.

Cohen, Anne-Lise. "Exploration of Sounds in Rutebeuf's Poetry." *French Review* 40 (1967): 658–67.

Cohen, Deborah. *Household Gods: The British and Their Possessions*. New Haven, CT: Yale University Press, 2006.

Cohen, Marc. "Geniza for Islamicists, Islamic Geniza, and the 'New Cairo Geniza.'" *Harvard Middle Eastern and Islamic Review* 7 (2006): 129–45.

Cole, Andrew. "The Call of Things: A Critique of Object-Oriented Ontologies." *minnesota review* 80 (2013): 106–17.

Constable, Giles. "The Historiography of the Crusades." In *The Crusades from the Perspective of Byzantium and the Muslim World*, edited by Angeliki E. Laiou and Roy Parviz Mottahedeh, 1–22. Washington, DC: Dumbarton Oaks, 2001.

Cook, B. J. "The Bezant in Angevin England." *Numismatic Chronicle* 159 (1999): 255–75.

Courtenay, Lynn T. "The Hospital of Notre Dame des Fontenilles at Tonnerre: Medicine as *Misericordia*." In *The Medieval Hospital and Medieval Practice*, edited by Barbara S. Bowers, 77–106. Aldershot: Ashgate, 2007.

Crouch, David. *The Chivalric Turn: Conduct and Hegemony in Europe before 1300*. Oxford: Oxford University Press, 2019.

Crouch, David. "The Warenne Family and Its Status in the Kingdom of England." In *Princely Rank in Late Medieval Europe: Trodden Paths and Promising Avenues*, edited by Thorsten Huthwelker, Jörg Peltzer, and Maximilian Wemhöner, 281–308. Ostfildern: Jan Thorbecke Verlag, 2011.

Cutler, Anthony. "Everywhere and Nowhere: The Invisible Muslim and Christian Self-Fashioning in the Culture of Outremer." In *France and the Holy Land: Frankish Culture at the End of the Crusades*, edited by Daniel H. Weiss and Lisa Mahoney, 253–81. Baltimore: Johns Hopkins University Press, 2004.

d'Arbois de Jubainville, Henri. *Histoire des ducs et des comtes de Champagne*. 6 vols. Paris: Durand, 1865.

d'Avezac, M. "Notice sur les anciens voyages de Tartarie en général et sur celui de Jean du Plan de Carpin en particulier." In *Relation des Mongols ou Tartares par le frère*

Jean du Plan de Carpin . . . première édition complete publiée d'après les manuscrits de Leyde, de Paris, et de Londres, et précédée d'une Notice sur les anciens voyages de Tartarie en général et sur celui de Jean du Plan de Carpin en particulier par M. D'Avezac, 3–206. Paris: Librairie Géographique de Arthus-Bertrand, 1838.

Davis, R. H. C. *The Medieval Warhorse: Origin, Development and Redevelopment*. London: Thames & Hudson, 1989.

de Flamare, H. "La charte de depart pour La Terre-Sainte de Gaucher de Châtillon." *Bulletin de la Société Nivernaise* 13 (1886–89): 174–82.

de Rapin de Thoyras, Paul. *The History of England*. Translated by N. Tindal. 2nd ed. London: Printed for James John and Paul Knapton, 1732–47.

de Vaivre, Jean-Bernard. "Le décor héraldique de la cassette d'Aix-la-Chapelle." *Aachener Kunstblätter* 45 (1974): 97–124.

Dehaisnes, Chrétien. *Histoire de l'art dans la Flandre, l'Artois et le Hainaut avant le XVe siècle*. Lille: L. Danel, 1886.

Delisle, Léopold. *Mémoire sur les opérations financières des Templiers*. Paris: Impr. Nationale, 1889.

Delobette, Laurence. "'Faites ceci en mémoire de moi': Calices et testaments du diocèse de Besançon XIIIe–XVe siècles." In *Le miracle de Faverney (1608) l'eucharistie: Environnement et temps de l'histoire*, edited by Corinne Marchal and Manuel Tramaux, 95–125. Besançon: Press Universitaires de Franche-Comté, 2010.

Demurger, Alain. "Pour trois mille livres de dette: Geoffroy de Sergines et le Temple." In *La presence latine en orient au moyen âge*, edited by Ghislain Brunel, Marie-Adélaïde Nielen, and Marie-Paule Arnauld, 67–76. Paris: C.H.A.N./Champion, 2000.

Derolez, Albert. *The Paleography of Gothic Manuscript Books from the Twelfth to the Early Sixteenth Century*. Cambridge: Cambridge University Press, 2003.

Dérouche, François, et al. *Islamic Codicology: An Introduction to the Study of Manuscripts in Arabic Script*. Translated by Deke Dusinberre and David Radzinowicz. London: al-Furqan Islamic Heritage Foundation, 2005.

Desrosiers, Sophie. "Scrutinizing Raw Material Between China and Italy: The Various Processing Sequences of *Bombyx mori* Silk." *L'atelier du Centre de recherches historiques: Review électronique du CRH* 20 (2019): https://doi.org/10.4000/acrh.10323.

Desrosiers, Sophie. "Sendal, Cendal, Zendado: A Category of Silk Cloth in the Development of the Silk Industry in Italy, 12th–15th Centuries." In *Crusading and Trading Between West and East: Studies in Honour of David Jacoby*, edited by Sophia Menache, Benjamin Kedar, and Michel Balard, 340–50. London: Routledge, 2019.

Desrosiers, Sophie. *Soieries et autres textiles de l'Antiquité au XVIe siècle: Musée National du Moyen Âge-Thermes de Cluny-Catalogue*. Paris: Editions de la Réunion des Musées Nationaux, 2004.

DeVries, Kelly. *Medieval Military Technology*. 2nd ed. Toronto: University of Toronto Press, 2012.

Dictionnaire du Moyen Français, version 2023 (DMF 2023). ATILF - CNRS & Université de Lorraine. http://www.atilf.fr/dmf.

Distefano, Giampaolo. *Esmaltis viridibus: Lo smalto de plique tra XIII e XIV secolo*. Savigliano (Cuneo): L'Artistica editrice, 2021.

Doudet, Estelle. "Rhétorique en mouvement: Rutebeuf, prêcheur et polémiste de la Croisade." *Méthode! Revue de littératures* 9 (2006): 11–17.

Douët-d'Arcq, Louis. *Collection de sceaux*. 3 vols. Paris: H. Plon, 1863–68.

Downes, Stephanie, Sally Holloway, and Sarah Randles, eds. *Feeling Things: Objects and Emotions through History*. Oxford: Oxford University Press, 2018.

Dufournet, Jean. *L'univers de Rutebeuf*. Orléans: Paradigme, 2005.

Dunbabin, Jean. *Charles I of Anjou*. London: Longman, 1998.

Dunbabin, Jean. *The French in the Kingdom of Sicily, 1266–1305*. Cambridge: Cambridge University Press, 2005.

Dunbabin, Jean. "The Household and Entourage of Charles I, King of the Regno, 1266–85." *Historical Research* 77 (2004): 313–36.

DuPlessis, Robert S. *The Material Atlantic: Clothing, Commerce, and Colonization in the Atlantic World, 1650–1800*. Cambridge: Cambridge University Press, 2016.

Edbury, Peter. "Ernoul, *Eracles*, and the Collapse of the Kingdom of Jerusalem." In *The French of Outremer: Communities and Communications in the Crusading Mediterranean*, edited by Laura K. Morreale and Nicholas L. Paul, 44–67. New York: Fordham University Press, 2018.

Elad, Amikam. *Medieval Jerusalem and Islamic Worship: Holy Places, Ceremonies, Pilgrimage*. Leiden: Brill, 1999.

Ertl, Thomas, and Barbara Karl, eds. *Inventories of Textiles—Textiles in Inventories: Studies on Late Medieval and Early Modern Material Culture*. Göttingen: Vandenhoeck & Ruprecht, 2017.

Evergates, Theodore. *Feudal Society in the Bailliage of Troyes under the Counts of Champagne, 1152–1284*. Baltimore: Johns Hopkins University Press, 1975.

Evergates, Theodore. *Geoffroy of Villehardouin, Marshal of Champagne: His Life and Memoirs of the Fourth Crusade*. Ithaca, NY: Cornell University Press, 2023.

Farmer, Sharon. "Aristocratic Power and the 'Natural' Landscape: The Garden Park at Hesdin, ca. 1291–1302." *Speculum* 88 (2013): 644–80.

Farmer, Sharon. "*Biffes*, *Tiretaines*, and *Aumonières*: The Role of Paris in the International Textile Markets of the Thirteenth and Fourteenth Centuries." In *Medieval Clothing and Textiles*, vol. 2, edited by Robin Netherton and Gale R. Owen-Crocker, 73–89. Woodbridge: Boydell, 2006.

Farmer, Sharon. "Global and Gendered Perspectives on the Production of a Parisian Alms Purse, c. 1340." *Journal of Medieval Worlds* 1 (2019): 45–85.

Farmer, Sharon. *The Silk Industries of Medieval Paris: Artisanal Migration, Technological Innovation, and Gendered Experience*. Philadelphia: University of Pennsylvania Press, 2017.

Favreau, Marie-Luise. *Studien zur Frühgeschichte des Deutschen Ordens*. Kieler Historische Studien 21. Stuttgart: E. Klett, 1974.

Favreau-Lilie, Marie-Luise. "The Teutonic Knights in Acre after the Fall of Monfort (1271): Some Reflections." In *Outremer: Studies in the History of the Crusading Kingdom of Jerusalem Presented to Joshua Prawer*, edited by Benjamin Z. Kedar, Hans E. Mayer, and R. C. Smail, 272–84. Jerusalem: Yad Izhak Ben-Zvi Institute, 1982.

Filiasi, Jacopo. *Memorie storiche de'Veneti primi e secondi. Edizione seconda*. Padua: Presso Il Seminario, 1812.

Folda, Jaroslav. *Crusader Art in the Holy Land, from the Third Crusade to the Fall of Acre, 1187–1291*. Cambridge: Cambridge University Press, 2005.

Forey, Alan. "*Milites ad terminum* in the Military Orders during the Twelfth and Thirteenth Centuries." In *The Military Orders*, vol. 4: *On Land and By Sea*, edited by Judi Upton-Ward, 23–30. London: Routledge, 2016.

Forey, Alan. "The Office of Master *deça mer* in Military Orders." In *The Templars and Their Sources*, edited by Karl Borchardt, Karoline Döring, Philippe Josserand, and Helen Nicholson, 125–32. London: Routledge, 2017.

Forey, Alan. "Paid Troops in the Service of Military Orders during the Twelfth and Thirteenth Centuries." In *The Crusader World*, edited by Adrian Boas, 84–97. London: Routledge, 2016.

French, Katherine L. *Household Goods and Good Households in Late Medieval London: Consumption and Domesticity after the Plague*. Philadelphia: University of Pennsylvania Press, 2021.

Frenkel, Yehoshua. "Is There an Islamic Space? Urban and Social Issues as Reflected in the *Qadi* Courts of Egypt and Syria: 13th–16th Centuries." In *Towns and Material Culture in the Medieval Middle East*, edited by Yaacov Lev, 103–17. Leiden: Brill, 2002.

Fritz, Jean-Marie. "La clepsydre et l'oxymore: Variations sur la 'chantepleure.' " *Romania* 134 (2016): 346–401.

Gacek, Adam. *Arabic Manuscripts: A Vademecum for Readers*. Leiden: Brill, 2009.

Galvez, Marisa. *The Subject of Crusade: Lyric, Romance, and Materials, 1150 to 1500*. Chicago: University of Chicago Press, 2020.

Gaposchkin, M. Cecilia. *Invisible Weapons: Liturgy and the Making of Crusade Ideology*. Ithaca, NY: Cornell University Press, 2017.

Gaposchkin, M. Cecilia. *The Making of Saint Louis: Kingship, Sanctity and Crusade in the Later Middle Ages*. Ithaca, NY: Cornell University Press, 2008.

Gay, Victor. *Glossaire archéologique du Moyen Âge et de la Renaissance*. Paris: Librairie de la Société Bibliographique, 1887.

Georges, Patrice. "L'exérès du cœur dans l'embaumement medieval occidental." In "Il cuore / The Heart," special issue, *Micrologus: Natura, Scienze e Società Medievali* 11 (2003): 279–86.

Gertwagen, Ruth. "The Crusader Port of Acre: Layout and Maintenance." In *Autour de la première croisade: Actes du colloque de la Society for the Study of the Crusades and the Latin East (Clermont-Ferrand, 22–25 juin 1995)*, edited by Michel Balard, 553–82. Paris: Publications de la Sorbonne,1996.

Gilbert, Jane, Simon Gaunt, and William Burgwinkle. "History, Time, and Empire: The *Histoire ancienne* in the Latin Kingdom of Jerusalem." In *Medieval French Literary Culture Abroad*. Oxford Scholarship Online, 2020. doi: 10.1093/oso/9780198832454.003.0005.

Giuseppi, M. S. "On the Testament of Sir Hugh de Nevill, Written at Acre, 1267." *Archaeologia* 56 (1899): 351–70.

Gorra, Michael. *The Saddest Words: William Faulkner's Civil War*. New York: Liverlight, 2020.

Gouwens, Kenneth. "Emasculation as Empowerment: Lessons of Beaver Lore for Two Italian Humanists." *European Review of History: Revue européenne d'histoire* 22 (2015): 536–62.

Graham-Goering, Erika. *Princely Power in Late Medieval France: Jeanne de Penthièvre and the War for Brittany*. Cambridge: Cambridge University Press, 2020.

Haines, John. "Aristocratic Patronage and the Cosmopolitan Vernacular Songbook: The *Chansonnier du Roi (M-trouv.)* and the French Mediterranean." In *Musical Culture in the World of Adam de la Halle*, edited by Jennifer Saltstein, 95–120. Leiden: Brill, 2019.

Halbouni, Ranya. "The Treasured Testicles of the Medieval Beaver." *The Iris* (blog), Getty, May 7, 2018. https://blogs.getty.edu/iris/the-treasured-testicles-of-the-medieval-beaver/.

Ham, Edward Billings. *Rutebeuf and Louis IX*. Chapel Hill: University of North Carolina Press, 1962.

Ham, Edward Billings. "Rutebeuf—Pauper and Polemist." *Romance Philology* 11 (1958): 226–39.

Hamilton, Bernard, and Andrew Jotischky. *Latin and Greek Monasticism in the Crusader States*. Cambridge: Cambridge University Press, 2020.

Handyside, Philip. "*L'Estoires d'Eracles* in Outremer." In *The French of Outremer: Communities and Communications in the Crusading Mediterranean*, edited by Laura K. Morreale and Nicholas L. Paul, 68–85. New York: Fordham University Press, 2018.

Harari, Yuval. "The Military Role of the Frankish Turcopoles: A Reassessment." *Mediterranean Historical Review* 12 (1997): 75–116.

Hélary, Xavier. *L'armée du roi de France: La guerre de Saint Louis à Philippe le Bel*. Paris: Perrin, 2012.

Hélary, Xavier. *L'ascension et la chute de Pierre de La Broce, chambellan du roi († 1278): Étude sur le pouvoir royal au temps de Saint Louis et de Philippe III (v. 1250–v.1280)*. Paris: Honoré Champion, 2021.

Hélary, Xavier. *La dernière croisade Saint Louis à Tunis (1270)*. Paris: Perrin, 2016.

Hélary, Xavier. "La mort de Pierre, comte d'Alençon (1283), fils de Saint Louis, dans la mémoire capétienne." *Revue d'histoire de l'église de France* 94 (2008): 5–22.

Hélary, Xavier. "Les rois de France et la Terre Sainte de la Croisade de Tunis à la chute d'Acre (1270–1291)." *Annuaire-Bulletin de la Société de l'histoire de France* 118 (2005): 21–104.

Hélary, Xavier, Jean-François Nieus, Alain Provost, and Marc Suttor, eds. *Les archives princières, XIIe–XVe siècles*. Arras: Artois Presses Université, 2106.

Heller, Sarah-Grace. "Revisiting the Inventories of Artois: Fashion, Status, and Taste at the Court of Mahaut, ca. 1307–1310." In *Inventories of Textiles—Textiles in Inventories: Studies on Late Medieval and Early Modern Material Culture*, edited by Thomas Ertl and Barbara Karl, 71–87. Vienna: Vienna University Press, 2017.

Hermand, Xavier, Jean-François Nieus, and Étienne Renard, eds. *Décrire, inventorier, enregistrer entre Seine et Rhin au Moyen Âge*. Mémoires et documents de l'école des chartes 92. Paris: École des chartes, 2012.

Hodder, Ian. *Entangled: An Archaeology of the Relationships between Humans and Things*. Malden, MA: Wiley-Blackwell, 2012.

Holsinger, Bruce. *On Parchment: Animals, Archives and the Making of Culture from Herodotus to the Digital Age*. New Haven, CT: Yale University Press, 2022.

Housley, Norman. *The Italian Crusades: The Papal-Angevin Alliance and the Crusades against Christian Lay Powers, 1254–1343*. Oxford: Clarendon Press, 1982.

Independent Crusaders Mapping Project. Fordham University. https://research.library.fordham.edu/ddp_archivingdossier/5/.

Irwin, Robert. *The Middle East in the Middle Ages: The Early Mamluk Sultanate*. Carbondale: Southern Illinois University Press, 1985.

Jackson, Peter. "The Crisis in the Holy Land in 1260." *English Historical Review* 95 (1980): 481–513.

Jackson, Peter. *The Mongols and the West: 1221–1410*. 2nd ed. London: Routledge, 2018.

Jacoby, David. "Aspects of Everyday Life in Frankish Acre." *Crusades* 4 (2005): 73–105.

Jacoby, David. "Camlet Manufacture, Trade in Cyprus and the Economy of Famagusta from the Thirteenth to the Late Fifteenth Century." In *Medieval and Renaissance Famagusta: Studies in Architecture, Art and History,* edited by Michael J. K. Walsh, Peter W. Edbury, and Nicholas S. H. Coureas, 45–72. Farnham: Ashgate, 2012.

Jacoby, David. "Crusader Acre in the Thirteenth Century: Urban Layout and Topography." *Studi medievali* 20 (1979): 1–45.

Jacoby, David. "L'évolution urbaine et la fonction méditerranéenne d'Acre à l'époque des croisades." In *Citta portuali del Mediterraneo, storia e archeologia: Atti del Convegno Internazionale di Genova 1985*, edited by Ennio Poleggi, 95–109. Geneva: Sagep, 1989.

Jacoby, David. "Montmusard, Suburb of Crusader Acre: The First Stage of Its Development." In *Outremer: Studies in the History of the Crusading Kingdom of Jerusalem Presented to Joshua Prawer*, edited by Benjamin Z. Kedar, Hans E. Mayer, and R. C. Smail, 205–17. Jerusalem: Yad Izhak Ben-Zvi Institute, 1982.

Jacoby, David. "New Venetian Evidence on Crusader Acre." In *The Experience of Crusading*, vol. 2: *Defining the Crusader Kingdom*, edited by Peter Edbury and Jonathan Phillips, 240–56. Cambridge: Cambridge University Press, 2003.

Jones, Claire Taylor. "Relics and the Anxiety of Exposure in Konrad von Würzburg's *Herzmaere*." *Journal of English and Germanic Philology* 116 (2017): 286–309.

Jordan, William Chester. *The Apple of His Eye: Converts from Islam in the Reign of Louis IX*. Princeton, NJ: Princeton University Press, 2019.

Jordan, William Chester. "*Etiam Reges*, Even Kings." *Speculum* 90 (2015): 613–34.

Jordan, William Chester. *Louis IX and the Challenge of the Crusade*. Princeton, NJ: Princeton University Press, 1979.

Jordan, William Chester. "Rituals of War: Departure for Crusade in Thirteenth-Century France." In *The Book of Kings: Art, War, and the Morgan Library's Medieval Picture Bible*, edited by William Noel and Daniel Weiss, 99–105. London: Third Millennium, 2002.

Jungmann, Josef Andreas. *The Mass of the Roman Rite: Its Origins and Development*. Translated by Francis A. Brunner. 2 vols. New York: Benziger, 1951–55; repr. 1992.

Jungmann, Josef Andreas. *Missarum sollemnia: Eine genetische Erklärung der römischen Messe*. 2 vols. Vienna: Herder, 1949.

Kay, Sarah. *Animal Skins and the Reading Self in Medieval Latin and French Bestiaries*. Chicago: University of Chicago Press, 2017.

Kedar, Benjamin Z. *Cultures of the Medieval Kingdom of Jerusalem: Frontier Inventiveness in the Age of the Crusades*. Ithaca, NY: Cornell University Press, 2025.

Khanmohamadi, Shirin A. *In Light of Another's Word: European Ethnography in the Middle Ages*. Philadelphia: University of Pennsylvania Press, 2013.

King, Archdale A. *Eucharistic Reservation in the Western Church*. New York: Sheed and Ward, 1965.

Kinoshita, Sharon. *Medieval Boundaries: Rethinking Difference in Old French Literature*. Philadelphia: University of Pennsylvania Press, 2006.

Knowles, C. H. "The Resettlement of England after the Barons' War, 1264–67." *Transactions of the Royal Historical Society* 32 (1982): 28–29.

Lachaud, Frédérique. "Documents financiers et histoire de la culture matérielle: Les textiles dans les comptes des hôtels royaux et nobiliaires (France et Angleterre, XXIe–XVe siècle)." *Bibliotheque de l'École des chartes* 164 (2006): 71–96.

Lachaud, Frédérique. "Liveries of Robes in England, ca. 1200–1330." *English Historical Review* 111 (1996): 279–98.

Lachaud, Frédérique. "Les tentes et l'activité militaire: Les guerres d'Edouard Ier Plantagenet (1272–1307)." *Mélanges d l'école française de Rome: Moyen-Âge* 111 (1999): 443–61.

Laiou, Angeliki, and Cécile Morisson. *The Byzantine Economy*. Cambridge: Cambridge University Press, 2007.

Lambourn, Elizabeth A. *Abraham's Luggage: A Social Life of Things in the Medieval Indian Ocean*. Cambridge: Cambridge University Press, 2018.

Langlois, Charles-Victor, and Charles Kohler. "Lettres inédites concernant les croisades (1275–1307)." *Bibliothèque de l'Ecole des chartes* 52, no. 1 (1891): 46–63.

La Niece, Susan, Stefan Röhrs, and Bet McLeod, eds. *The Heritage of "Maître Alpais": An International and Interdisciplinary Examination of Medieval Limoges Enamel and Associated Objects*. London: British Museum Press, 2010.

Latour, Bruno. *Reassembling the Social: An Introduction to Actor-Network Theory*. Oxford: Oxford University Press, 2005.

Latowsky, Anne. "Charlemagne, Godfrey of Bouillon, and Louis IX." In *The Cambridge Companion to the Literature of the Crusades*, edited by Anthony Bale, 200–214. Cambridge: Cambridge University Press, 2018.

Le Maistre, L. "Marguerite de Bourgogne, reine de Naples, de Sicile et de Jérusalem, Comtesse de Tonnerre." *Annuaire historique du département de l'Yonne* 31 (1867): 43–109.

Leson, Richard A. "The Coucy, the Boves, and Heraldry's Coming of Age in the Resafa Cup." *Revue française d'héraldique et de sigillographie—Études en ligne* (March 2021): 1–28.

Lespinasse, Réne de. *Le Nivernais et les comtes de Nevers*. 3 vols. Paris: Honoré Champion, 1909–14.

Lester, Anne E. *Creating Cistercian Nuns: The Women's Religious Movement and Its Reform in Thirteenth-Century Champagne*. Ithaca, NY: Cornell University Press, 2011.

Lester, Anne E. "Crusading as a Religious Movement: Families, Community, and Lordship in a Vernacular Frame." In *Between Orders and Heresy: Rethinking Medieval Religious Movements*, edited by Jennifer Kolpacoff Deane and Anne E. Lester, 127–69. Toronto: University of Toronto Press, 2021.

Lester, Anne E. "Intimacy and Abundance: Textile Relics, the Veronica, and Christian Devotion in the Aftermath of the Fourth Crusade." In "Material Religion in the Crusading World," edited by William Purkis, special issue, *Material Religion* 14 (2018): 533–44.

Lester, Anne E. "Possession, Production and Power: Reading Objects in the Material Field." *Medieval Feminist Forum* 56 (2020): 204–20.

Lester, Anne E. "Remembrance of Things Past: Memory and Material Objects in the Time of the Crusades, 1095–1291." In *Remembering Crusades and Crusading*, edited by Megan Cassidy-Welch, 73–94. London: Routledge, 2017.

Lester, Anne E. "What Remains: Women, Relics and Remembrance in the Aftermath of the Fourth Crusade." *Journal of Medieval History* 40 (2014): 311–28.

Lester, Anne E., and Katherine C. Little, eds. "Medieval Materiality." Special issue, *English Language Notes* 53 (2015).

Lev, Efraim. "Healing with Animals in the Levant from the 10th to the 18th Century." *Journal of Ethnobiology and Ethnomedicine* 2 (2006), https://doi.org/10.1186/1746-4269-2-11.

Lev, Yaakov. "The *Cadi* and the Urban Society: The Case Study of Medieval Egypt, 9th–12th Centuries." In *Towns and Material Culture in the Medieval Middle East*, edited by Yaacov Lev, 89–102. Leiden: Brill, 2002.

Lillich, Meredith Parsons. *The Queen of Sicily and Gothic Sainted Glass in Mussy and Tonnerre*. Philadelphia: American Philosophical Society, 1998.

Little, Donald. *A Catalogue of the Islamic Documents from al-Ḥaram aš-Šarīf in Jerusalem*. Beirut: Orient-Institut der Deutschen Morgenländischen Gesellschaft, 1984.

Little, Donald. "Haram Documents Related to the Jews of Late Fourteenth Century Jerusalem." *Journal of Semitic Studies* 30 (1985): 227–64.

Little, Donald. "Jerusalem under the Ayyubids and Mamluks: 1187–1516." In *Jerusalem in History: 3000 BC to the Present Day*, edited by K. J. Asali, 177–99. London: Kegan John, 1997.

Little, Katherine C. "The Politics of Lists." *Exemplaria* 31 (2019): 117–28.

Lo, Melissa. "Recasting the *Castor*: From *The Book of Beasts* to Albertus Magnus's *On Animals*." *Thresholds* 35 (2009): 92–95.

Lower, Michael. *The Barons' Crusade: A Call to Arms and Its Consequences*. Philadelphia: University of Pennsylvania Press, 2005.

Lower, Michael. "Conversion and St Louis's Last Crusade." *Journal of Ecclesiastical History* 58 (2007): 211–31.

Lower, Michael. "Louis IX, Charles of Anjou, and the Tunis Crusade of 1270." In *Crusades: Medieval Worlds in Conflict*, edited by Thomas Madden, James Naus, and Vincent Ryan, 173–93. Farnham: Ashgate, 2009.

Lower, Michael. *The Tunis Crusade of 1270: A Mediterranean History*. Oxford: Oxford University Press, 2018.

Lufti, Huda. *Al-Quds al Mamlūkiyya: A History of Mamluk Jerusalem Based on the Haram Documents*. Berlin: Klaus Schwarz Verlag, 1985.

Lusse, Jackie. "D'Étienne à Jean de Joinville: L'ascension d'une famille seigneuriale champenoise." In *Jean de Joinville: De la Champagne aux royaumes d'outre-mer*, edited by Danielle Quéruel, 7–47. Langres: D. Guéniot, 1998.

Luyster, Amanda R., ed., *Bringing the Holy Land Home: The Crusades, Chertsey Abbey, and the Reconstruction of a Medieval Masterpiece*. Turnhout: Brepols/Harvey Miller, 2023.

Luyster, Amanda R. "Reassembling Textile Networks: Treasuries and Re-collecting Practices in Thirteenth-Century England." *Speculum* 96 (2021): 1039–78.

Luz, Nimrod. *The Mamluk City in the Middle East: History, Culture, and the Urban Landscape*. Cambridge: Cambridge University Press, 2014.

Mackie, Louise. "Toward an Understanding of Mamluk Silk: National and International Considerations." *Muqaranas* 2 (1984): 127–46.

Madden, Thomas F. "The War of Towers: Venice and Genoa at War in Crusader Syria, 1256–8." In *Syria in Crusader Times: Conflict and Co-Existence*, edited by Carole Hillenbrand, 211–24. Edinburgh: Edinburgh University Press, 2020.

Maines, Clark. *The Western Portal of Saint-Loup-de-Naud*. New York: Garland, 1979.

"Maison d'Angerant." Terres et Seigneurs en Donziais, July 4, 2021. http://www.terres-et-seigneurs-en-donziais.fr/wp-content/uploads/2021/07/dAngerant.pdf.

Maqdisi, George. *The Rise of the Colleges: Institutions of Learning in Islam and the West*. Edinburgh: Edinburgh University Press, 1981.

"Marguerite de Bourgogne (morte en 1277)." Wikipédia. Last modified April 14, 2024. https://fr.wikipedia.org/wiki/Marguerite_de_Bourgogne_(morte_en_1277).

Marshall, Christopher J. "The French Regiment in the Latin East, 1254–91." *Journal of Medieval History* 15 (1989): 301–7.

Marshall, Christopher J. *Warfare in the Latin East, 1192–1291*. Cambridge: Cambridge University Press, 1992.

Mason, Emma. "The Hero's Invincible Weapon: An Aspect of Angevin Propaganda." In *The Ideals and Practices of Knighthood III: Papers from the Fourth Strawberry Hill Conference, 1988*, edited by Christopher Harper-Bill and Ruth Harvey, 121–37. Woodbridge: Boydell, 1990.

Mazzaoui, Maureen. *The Italian Cotton Industry in the Later Middle Ages, 1100–1600*. Cambridge: Cambridge University Press, 1981.

McGinn, Bernard. "Violence and Spirituality: The Enigma of the First Crusade." *Journal of Religion* 69 (1989): 375–79.

Medieval Art in England. London: Sam Fogg, 2019.

Meier, Christel. *Gemma Spiritalis: Methode und Gebrauch der Edelsteinallegorse vom frühen Christentum bis ins 18. Jahrhundert*. 2 vols. Munich: Wilhelm Fink, 1977.

Merceron, Jacques E. "Rutebeuf, marchand de croisades et le système de la comptabilité spirituelle: Le dit et le non-dit." *Romania* 131 (2013): 382–408.

Metcalf, David Michael. "Burgundian Money in the Latin East." *Israel Numismatic Journal* 5 (1981): 73–82.

Metcalf, David Michael. *Coinage of the Crusades and the Latin East in the Ashmolean Museum, Oxford*. 2nd ed. London: Royal Numismatic Society and Society for the Study of the Crusades and the Latin East, 1995.

Metcalf, David Michael. "The Templars as Bankers and Monetary Transfers between West and East in the Twelfth Century." In *Coinage in the Latin East: The Fourth Oxford Symposium on Coinage and Monetary History*, edited by Peter Edbury and D. M. Metcalf, 2nd ed., 1–17. Oxford: Ashmolean Museum, 1995.

Metcalf, David Michael, Robert Kool, and Ariel Berman. "Coins from the Excavations of 'Atlit' (Pilgrims' Castle and Its Faubourg)." *'Atiqot* 37 (1999): 89–164.

Michel, Francisque. *Recherches sur les étoffes de soie, d'or et d'argent pendant le Moyen Âge*. 2 vols. Paris: Imprimerie de Chapelet, 1852; Typographie de Ch. Lahure, 1854.

Miles, Tiya. *All That She Carried: The Journey of Ashley's Sack, a Black Family Keepsake*. New York: Random House, 2021.

Miller, Daniel. *Stuff*. Cambridge, MA: Polity, 2010.

Miller, Maureen C. *Clothing the Clergy: Virtue and Power in Medieval Europe, c. 800–1200*. Ithaca, NY: Cornell University Press, 2014.

Miller, Maureen C. "A Descriptive Language of Dominion? Curial Inventories, Clothing, and Papal Monarchy c. 1300." *Textile History* 48 (2017): 176–91.

Minervini, Laura. "Le français dans l'Orient latin (XIIIe–XIVe siècles): Élements pour la characterisation d'une *scripta* du Levant." *Revue de linguistique romane* 74 (2010): 121–98.

Minervini, Laura. "What We Do and Do Not Know about Outremer French." In *The French of Outremer: Communities and Communications in the Crusading Mediterranean*, edited by Laura K. Morreale and Nicholas L. Paul, 15–29. New York: Fordham University Press, 2018.

Monnas, Lisa. *Merchants, Princes and Painters: Silk Fabrics in Italian and Northern Paintings, 1300–1500*. New Haven, CT: Yale University Press, 2009.

Monnas, Lisa. *Renaissance Velvets*. London: V&A Publications, 2012.

Monnas, Lisa. "Silk Cloths Purchased for the Great Wardrobe of the Kings of England, 1325–1462." *Textile History* 20 (1989): 283–307.

Moon, Sung-Wook. "Engagement difficile: Les poèmes de croisade de Rutebeuf." *Loxias* 54 (2016): 1–23.

Morato, Nicola, and Dirk Schoenaers, eds. *Medieval Francophone Literary Culture Outside France*. Turnhout: Brepols, 2019.

Morreale, Laura K. "French-Language Documents Produced by the Hospitallers, 1231–1310." *Journal of Medieval History* 40 (2014): 439–57.

Morreale, Laura K. *Pilgrims and Writing in Crusader Acre*. Accessed December 21, 2020. https://scalar.lauramorreale.com/pilgrims-and-writing-in-crusader-acre/index.

Morreale, Laura K., and Nicholas L. Paul, eds. *The French of Outremer: Communities and Communications in the Crusading Mediterranean*. New York: Fordham University Press, 2018.

Müller, Christian. "Écrire pour établir la preuve orale en Islam: La pratique d'un tribunal à Jérusalem au XIVe siècle." In *Les outils de la pensée étude historique et comparative des "textes,"* edited by Yusuke Nakamura and Akiro Saito, 63–97. Paris: Éditions de la Maison des sciences de l'homme, 2014.

Müller, Christian. "The Ḥaram al-Šarīf Collection of Arabic Legal Documents in Jerusalem: A Mamlūk Court Archive." *Al-Qanṭara* 32 (2011): 435–59.

Müller, Christian. *Der Kadi und seine Zeugen: Studie der mamlukischen Haram-Dokumente aus Jerusalem*. Wiesbaden: Harrassowitz Verlag, 2014.

Munro, John H. "The Medieval Scarlet and the Economics of Sartorial Splendour." In *Cloth and Clothing in Medieval Europe: Essays in Memory of E. M. Carus-Wilson*, edited by N. B. Harte and K. G. Ponting, 13–70. London: Heinemann, 1983.

Munro, John H. "Medieval Woolens: Textiles, Textile Technology and Industrial Organisation, c. 800–1500." In *The Cambridge History of Western Textiles*, edited by David Jenkins, 1:181–227. Cambridge: Cambridge University Press, 2003.

Murat, Philippe. "La croisade en Nivernais: Transfert de propriété et lutte d'influence." In *Le concile de Clermont de 1095 et l'appel à la croisade: Actes du Colloque Universitaire International de Clermont-Ferrand (23–25 juin 1995)*, Publications de l'École française de Rome 236, 295–312. Rome: École Français de Rome, 1997.

Murray, Alan V. *The Crusades to the Holy Land*. Santa Barbara: ABC-CLIO, 2015.

Murrell, William Stephen, Jr. "Dragomans and Crusaders: The Role of Translators and Translation in the Medieval Eastern Mediterranean, 1098–1291." PhD diss., Vanderbilt University, 2018.

Neuschel, Kristen. *Living by the Sword: Weapons and Material Culture in France and Britain*. Ithaca, NY: Cornell University Press, 2020.

Newman, Barbara. *Medieval Crossover: Reading the Secular against the Sacred*. Notre Dame, IN: University of Notre Dame Press, 2013.

Nichols, Stephen G. "Introduction: Philology in a Manuscript Culture." *Speculum* 65 (1990): 1–10.

Nichols, Stephen G. "What Is a Manuscript Culture? Technologies of the Manuscript Matrix." In *The Medieval Manuscript Book: Cultural Approaches*, edited by Michael Johnston and Michael Van Dussen, 34–59. Cambridge: Cambridge University Press, 2017.

Nichols, Stephen G. "Why Material Philology." *Zeitschrift für deutsche Philologie* 116 (1997): 10–30.

Nichols, Stephen G., Joachim Küpper, and Andreas Kablitz, eds. *Spectral Sea: Mediterranean Palimpsests in European Culture*. New York: Peter Lang, 2017.

Nicolas, Nicholas H. *Testamenta Vetusta: Being Illustrations from Wills of Manners, Customs, etc. as Well as the Descents and Possessions of Many Distinguished Families, from the Reign of Henry II to the Accession of Queen Elizabeth*. 2 vols. London: Nichols and Son, 1826.

Noble, Pierre. "Écrire dans le Royaume franc: La *scripta* de deux manuscrits copies à Acre au XIIIe siècle." In *Variations linguistiques: Koinés, dialectes, français régionaux*, edited by Pierre Noble, 33–52. Besançon: Presses universitaires de Franche-Comté, 2003.

Nuti, Giovanni. "William II of Agen (Guillaume d'Agen)." In *Dizionario Biografico degli Italiani*, edited by Alberto M. Ghisalberti, vol. 47. Rome: Instituto della Enciclopedia italiana, 1997.

Otaka, Yorio. "La valeur monétaire exprimée dans les oeuvres épiques." In *L'épopée romane: Actes du XVe Congrès international Rencesvals tenu à Poitiers du 21 au 27 août 2000*, 969–78. Poitiers: Centre d'études supérieures de civilization médiévale, 2002.

Owen-Crocker, Gale, Elizabeth Coatsworth, and Maria Hayword, eds. *Encyclopedia of Medieval Dress and Textiles*. Leiden: Brill 2012.

Owen-Crocker, Gale, Elizabeth Coatsworth, and Maria Hayword, eds. *Encyclopedia of Medieval Dress and Textiles of the British Isles c. 450–1450*. Leiden: Brill, 2016.

Park, Danielle E. A. *Papal Protection and the Crusader: Flanders, Champagne, and the Kingdom of France, 1095–1222*. Woodbridge: Boydell, 2018.

Park, Katherine. *Secrets of Women: Gender, Generation, and the Origins of Human Dissection*. New York: Zone, 2006,

Paterson, Linda. *Singing the Crusades: French and Occitan Lyric Reponses to the Crusading Movements, 1137–1336*. Woodbridge: D. S. Brewer, 2018.

Paul, Nicholas L. "In Search of the Marshal's Lost Crusade: The Persistence of Memory, the Problems of History and the Painful Birth of Crusading Romance." *Journal of Medieval History* 40 (2014): 292–310.

Paul, Nicholas L. "Possession: Sacred Crusading Treasure in the Material Vernacular." In "Material Religion in the Crusading World," edited by William Purkis, special issue, *Material Religion* 14 (2018): 520–32.

Paul, Nicholas L. *To Follow in Their Footsteps: The Crusades and Family Memory in the High Middle Ages*. Ithaca, NY: Cornell University Press, 2012.

Paviot, Jacques. "England and the Mongols (c. 1260–1330)." *Journal of the Royal Asiatic Society* 10 (2000): 305–18.

Peers, Glenn. "Translating Edges in Art of the Medieval Middle East: On the Resafa Hoard and a Painted Bottle from Lichtenstein." In *On the Edge: Time and Space. Proceedings of International Conference, 14–15 November 2014*, edited by Zaza Skhirtladze, 9–36. Tbilisi: Universitetis gamomcʿemloba, 2017.

Pegalotti, Francesco Balducci. *La pratica della mercatura*. Edited by Allan Evans. Cambridge, MA: Medieval Academy of America, 1936.

Pelliot, Paul. *Notes on Marco Polo: Ouvrage Posthum. Publié sous les auspices de l'Académie des Inscriptions et Belles-Lettres et avec le concours du Centre Nationale de la Recherche Scientifique*. 3 vols. Paris: Impr. Nationale, 1959.

Peraino, Judith A. "Taking *Notae* on King and Cleric: Thibaut, Adam, and the Medieval Readers of the *Chansonnier de Noailles (T-trouv.)*." In *Musical Culture in the World of Adam de la Halle*, edited by Jennifer Saltstein, 121–52. Leiden: Brill, 2019.

Petit, Ernst. *Histoire des ducs de Bourgogne de la race capétienne*. 9 vols. Dijon: Darantière, 1885–1905.

Petry, Carl. "*Waqf* as an Instrument of Investment in the Mamluk Sultanate: Security vs. Profit?" In *Slave Elites in the Middle East and Africa: A Comparative Study*, edited by John Philips and Miura Toru, 99–116. London: Kegan Paul International, 2000.

Piponnier, Françoise. "À propos des textiles anciens, principalement médiévaux." *Annales: Économies, sociétés, civilisations* 22 (1967): 864–80.

Piponnier, Françoise. "Archéologie et histoire." In *Le Moyen Âge aujourd'hui: Actes de la Rencontre de Cerisy-la-Salle, juillet 1991*, edited by Guy Lobrichon and Jacques Le Goff, 83–100. Paris: Le Léopard d'Or, 1998.

Piponnier, Françoise. "Linge de corps et linge de maison au Moyen Âge d'après les inventaires bourguignons." *Ethnologie française* 16 (1986): 239–48.

Plancher, Urbain. *Histoire générale et particulière du duché de Bourgogne*. 4 vols. Dijon: A. de Fay, 1739–81.

Prawer, Joshua. *Histoire du royaume latin de Jérusalem*. Translated by Gérard Nahon. 2 vols. Paris: CNRS, 1970; repr. 2007.

Prestwich, Michael. *Edward I*. London: Guild, 1988.

Prestwich, Michael. *The Three Edwards*. London: Routledge, 1980.

Pringle, Denys. *The Churches of the Crusader Kingdom of Jerusalem: A Corpus*. 4 vols. Cambridge: Cambridge University Press, 1993–2009.

Pringle, Denys. "The Order of St Thomas of Canterbury in Acre." In *The Military Orders*, vol. 5: *Politics and Power*, edited by Peter W. Edbury, 75–82. London: Routledge, 2012.

Pringle, Denys. *Pilgrimage to Jerusalem and the Holy Land, 1187–1291*. Crusade Texts in Translation 23. Farnham: Ashgate, 2012.

Purkis, William J. *Crusading Spirituality in the Holy Land and Iberia, c.1095–c.1187*. Woodbridge: Boydell, 2008.

Purkis, William J. "Introduction: Material Religion in the Crusading World." In "Material Religion in the Crusading World," edited by William Purkis, special issue, *Material Religion* 14 (2018): 433–37.

Purkis, William J., et al. "Bearers of the Cross: Material Religion in the Crusading World, 1095–c.1300." Arts and Humanities Research Council–funded project, 2015–2017. https://www.bearersofthecross.org.uk/project/.

Purvis, J. S., ed. *The Chartulary of the Augustinian Priory of St John the Evangelist of the Park of Healaugh*. Cambridge: Cambridge University Press, 1936.

Rawcliffe, Carole. "A Marginal Occupation? The Medieval Laundress and Her Work." *Gender and History* 21 (2009): 147–69.

Regalado, Nancy Freeman. *Poetic Patterns in Rutebeuf: A Study in Noncourtly Poetic Modes of the Thirteenth Century*. New Haven, CT: Yale University Press, 1970.

Renault, Edmond. "Les tombes de l'eglise de l'hôpital des Fonteneilles à Tonnerre." *Annuaire historique et statistique du départment de l'Yonne 50e année*. 2e série, v. 25 (1886): 193–251.

Reyerson, Kathryn L., and Debra A. Salata, eds. *Medieval Notaries and Their Acts: The 1327–1328 Register of Jean Holanie*. Kalamazoo: Medieval Institute Publications, 2004.

Richard, Jean. "La croisade de 1270, premier 'passage général'?" *Comptes rendus des séances de l'Académie des Inscriptions et Belles-Lettres* 133 (1989): 510–23.

Richard, Jean. *Les ducs de Bourgogne et de la formation du duché, du XIe au XIVe siècle*. Dijon: Bernigaud et Privat, 1954.

Richard, Jean. *Saint Louis: Roi d'une France féodale, soutien de la Terre sainte*. Paris: Fayard, 1983.

Richard, Jules-Marie. *Inventaire-sommaire des archives départementales antérieures à 1790, Pas-de-Calais, Archives Civiles—Série A.* 2 vols. Arras: Imprimerie de la Société du Pas-de-Calais, 1878–87.

Riley-Smith, Jonathan. "The Crown of France and Acre, 1254–1291." In *France and the Holy Land: Frankish Culture at the End of the Crusades*, edited by Daniel H. Weiss and Lisa Mahoney, 45–62. Baltimore: Johns Hopkins University Press, 2004.

Riley-Smith, Jonathan. "The Death and Burial of Latin Christian Pilgrims to Jerusalem and Acre, 1099–1291." *Crusades* 7 (2008): 165–79.

Riley-Smith, Jonathan. *The Feudal Monarchy and the Kingdom of Jerusalem*. London: Macmillan, 1973.

Riley-Smith, Jonathan. *The First Crusade and the Idea of Crusading*. Philadelphia: University of Pennsylvania Press, 1986.

Riley-Smith, Jonathan. "Towards an Understanding of the Fourth Crusade as an Institution." In *Urbs Capta: The Fourth Crusade and its Consequences / La IVe Croisade et ses consequences*, edited by Angeliki Laiou, 71–87. Paris: Lethielleux, 2005.

Riley-Smith, Jonathan. *What Were the Crusades?* 4th ed. New York: Palgrave, 2009.

Röhricht, Reinhold. "Études sur les derniers temps du royaume de Jérusalem: Croisade d'Edouard d'Angleterre." *Archives de l'Orient Latin* 1 (1881): 617–32.

Romanini, Fabio, and Beatrice Saletti. *The* Pelrinages Communes, *the* Pardouns de Acre *and the Crisis in the Crusader Kingdom: History and Texts*. Padova: Libreriauniversitaria.it edizioni, 2012.

Rosenthal, Franz. *Four Essays on Art and Literature in Islam*. Leiden: Brill, 1971.

Rousset, Paul. "Rutebeuf, poète de la croisade." *Zeitschrift für schweizerische Kirchengeschichte* 60 (1966): 103–11.

Rubin, Jonathan. *Learning in a Crusader City: Intellectual Activity and Intercultural Exchanges in Acre, 1191–1291*. Cambridge: Cambridge University Press, 2018.

Rubin, Jonathan. "Multilingualism and the Attitude toward French in the Latin Kingdom of Jerusalem." In *Multilingualism and History*, edited by Aneta Pavlenko, 123–37. Cambridge: Cambridge University Press, 2023.

Rubin, Miri. *Corpus Christi: The Eucharist in Late Medieval Culture*. Cambridge: Cambridge University Press, 1991.

Runciman, Steven. *The Sicilian Vespers: A History of the Mediterranean World in the Late Thirteenth Century*. Cambridge: Cambridge University Press, 1992.

Rustow, Marina. *The Lost Archive: Traces of a Caliphate in a Cairo Synagogue*. Princeton, NJ: Princeton University Press, 2020.

Ṣāliḥiyya, Muḥammad ʿĪsā. *Min waṯāʾiq al-Ḥaram al-Qudsī al-Šarīf al-mamlūkiyya*. Kuwait: Ḥawlīyāt Kulliyat ad-dāb, 1985.

Sassier, Yves. "Conflit de succession entre heritieres et sentence du parlement royal au XIIIe siècle: La partition du grande comté de Nevers-Auxerre-Tonnerre (Toussaint 1273)." In *Inheritance, Law and Religions in the Ancient and Medieval Worlds*, edited by Béatrice Caseau and Sabine R. Huebner, 67–74. Paris: ACHAByz, 2014.

Sayous, A. "Les mandats de saint Louis sur son trésor et le movement international des capitaux pendant la septième croisade (1248–1254)." *Revue historique* 167 (1931): 254–304.

Schenk, Jochen. "Forms of Lay Association with the Order of the Temple." *Journal of Medieval History* 34 (2008): 79–103.

Schenk, Jochen. *Templar Families: Landowning Families and the Order of the Temple in France, c. 1120–1307*. Cambridge: Cambridge University Press, 2012.

Schlumberger, Gustave. *Numismatiques de l'Orient latin*. Paris: Leroux, 1878.

Schmitz-Esser, Romedio. *The Corpse in the Middle Ages: Embalming, Cremating, and the Cultural Construction of the Dead Body*. Translated by Albrecht Classen and Carolin Radtke. Turnhout: Brepols/Harvey Miller, 2020.

Schmitz-Esser, Romedio. *Der Leichnam in Mittelalter: Einbalsamierung, Verbrennung, und die kulturelle Konstrukion des toten Körpers*. Mittelalter-Forschugen 48. Ostfindern: Thorbecke, 2014.

Selwood, Dominic. *Knights of the Cloister: Templars and Hospitallers in Central-Southern Occitania, c. 1100–c. 1300*. Woodbridge: Boydell, 1999.

Serjeant, Robert. *Islamic Textiles: Material for a History up to the Mongol Conquest*. Beirut: Libr. du Liban, 1976.

Serper, Arié. "Le roi Saint Louis et le poète Rutebeuf." *Romance Notes* 9 (1967): 134–40.

Servois, Gustav. "Emprunts de Saint Louis en Palestine et en Afrique." *Bibliothèque de l'École des chartes* 4 (1858): 113–31, 283–93. Reprinted, Paris: Firmin Didot, 1858.

Shachar, Uri Zvi. *A Pious Belligerence: Dialogical Warfare and the Rhetoric of Righteousness in the Crusading Near East*. Philadelphia: University of Pennsylvania Press, 2021.

Shalem, Avinoam. "New Evidence for the History of the Turquoise Glass Bowl in the Treasury of San Marco." *Persica* 15 (1993–95): 91–94.

Shawcross, Teresa. *The Chronicle of Morea: Historiography in Crusader Greece*. Oxford: Oxford University Press, 2009.

Sheehan, Michael M. "A List of Thirteenth-Century English Wills." In *Marriage, Family, and Law in Medieval Europe*, edited by James K. Farge, 8–15. Toronto: University of Toronto Press, 1997.

Sheehan, Michael M. *The Will in Medieval England, from the Conversion of the Anglo-Saxons to the End of the Thirteenth Century*. Toronto: Pontifical Institute of Mediaeval Studies, 1963.

Siberry, Elizabeth. "The Crusading Counts of Nevers." *Nottingham Medieval Studies* 34 (1990): 64–70.

Smail, Daniel Lord. "A Fur Corset as Daily Wear." DALME, May 1, 2021. http://dalme.org/features/fur-corset/.

Smail, Daniel Lord. *Legal Plunder: Households and Debt Collection in Late Medieval Europe*. Cambridge, MA: Harvard University Press, 2016.

Smail, Daniel Lord, et al., eds. "Methodology." DALME: The Documentary Archaeology of Late Medieval Europe. https://dalme.org/project/methodology/.

Smith, Caroline. *Crusading in the Age of Joinville*. Farnham: Ashgate, 2006.

Snoek, G. J. C. *Medieval Piety from Relics to the Eucharist: A Process of Mutual Interaction*. Leiden: Brill, 1995.

Solterer, Helen. "Dismembering, Remembering the Châtelain de Coucy." *Romance Philology* 46 (1992): 103–24.

Spiegel, Gabrielle M. "The Limits of Empiricism: The Utility of Theory in Historical Thought and Writing." *Medieval History Journal* 22 (2019): 1–22.

Spiegel, Gabrielle M. *Romancing the Past: The Rise of Vernacular Prose Historiography in Thirteenth-Century France*. Berkeley: University of California Press, 1993.

Spufford, Peter. *Handbook of Medieval Exchange*. London: Royal Historical Society/Boydell and Brewer, 1986.

Stahl, Alan M. "The Circulation of European Coinage in the Crusader States." In *The Meeting of Two Worlds: Cultural Exchange between East and West during the Period of the Crusades*, edited by Vladimir P. Goss and Christin V. Bornstein, Studies in Medieval Culture 21, 85–102. Kalamazoo: Medieval Institute Publications, 1986.

Stahl, Alan M. "The *Denier* Outremer." In *The French of Outremer: Communities and Communications in the Crusading Mediterranean*, edited by Laura K. Morreale and Nicholas L. Paul, 30–43. New York: Fordham University Press, 2018.

Strayer, Joseph R. *The Administration of Normandy under Saint Louis*. Cambridge, MA: Medieval Academy of America, 1932.

Strayer, Joseph R. "The Crusade against Aragon." *Speculum* 28 (1953): 102–13.

Strayer, Joseph R. "The Crusades of Louis IX." In Strayer, *Medieval Statecraft and the Perspectives of History*, 159–92. Princeton, NJ: Princeton University Press, 1971.

Strayer, Joseph R. *Medieval Statecraft and the Perspectives of History*. Princeton, NJ: Princeton University Press, 1971.

Stuckey, Jace, ed. *The Eastern Mediterranean Frontier of Latin Christendom*. Farnham: Ashgate, 2014.

Sweeney, James Ross. "'Spurred on by the Fear of Death': Refugees and Displaced Populations during the Mongol Invasion of Hungary." In *Nomadic Diplomacy, Destruction and Religion from the Pacific to the Adriatic: Papers Prepared for the Central and Inner Asian Seminar, University of Toronto, 1992–93*, edited by Michael Gervers and Wayne Schlepp, 34–62. Toronto: Joint Centre for Asia Pacific Studies, 1994.

Symes, Carol. "Knowledge and Transmission: Media and Memory." In *A Cultural History of Theater in the Middle Ages*, edited by Jody Enders, A Cultural History of Theater 2, 199–211. London: Bloomsbury, 2017.

Symes, Carol. "The Medieval Archive and the History of Theater: Assessing the Written and Unwritten Evidence for Premodern Performance." *Theater Survey* 52 (2011): 29–58.

Tibble, Stephen. *The Crusader Armies, 1099–1187*. New Haven, CT: Yale University Press, 2018.

Trotter, D. A. *Medieval French Literature and the Crusades (1100–1300)*. Geneva: Droz, 1987.

Tyerman, Christopher. *How to Plan a Crusade: Reason and Religious War in the High Middle Ages*. London: Alan Lane, 2015.

Tyerman, Christopher. "Who Went on Crusades to the Holy Land?" In *The Horns of Hattin: Proceedings of the Second Conference of the Society for the Study of the Crusades and the Latin East, Jerusalem and Haifa 2–6 July 1987*, ed. Benjamin Z. Kedar, 13–26. Jerusalem: Yad Izhak Ben-Zvi: Israel Exploration Society, 1992.

Ulbert, Thilo. *Resafa III, Der kreuzfahrerzeitliche Silberschatz aus Resafa-Sergiupolis*. Mainz am Rhein: P. von Zabern, 1990.

Ulrich, Laurel Thatcher, et al. *Tangible Things: Making History through Objects*. Oxford: Oxford University Press, 2015.

Vale, Malcolm. *The Princely Court: Medieval Courts and Culture in North-West Europe*. Oxford: Oxford University Press, 2001.

Van Tricht, Filip. *The Latin "Renovatio" of Byzantium: The Empire of Constantinople (1204–1228)*. Leiden: Brill, 2011.

Vincent, Nicholas. "An Inventory of Gifts to King Henry III, 1234–5." In *The Growth of Royal Government under Henry III*, edited by David Crook and Louise J. Wilkinson, 121–48. Woodbridge: Boydell and Brewer, 2015.

Vogel, Cyrille. *Introduction aux sources de l'histoire du culte chrétien au Moyen Âge.* Spoleto: Centro italiano di studi sull'alto Medioevo, 1973.
Vogel, Cyrille. *Medieval Liturgy: An Introduction to the Sources.* Translated by William G. Storey and Niels Krogh Rasmussen. Washington, DC: Pastoral Press, 1986.
Walker, Bethany. "Rethinking Mamluk Textiles." *Mamluk Studies Review* 4 (2000): 167–217.
Ward-Perkins, Bryan, and Robert Wiśniewski, eds. "The Cult of Saints in Late Antiquity Database." http://csla.history.ox.ac.uk/
Wardwell, Anne. "*Panni tartarici*: Eastern Islamic Silks Woven with Gold and Silver (13th and 14th Centuries)." *Islamic Art* 3 (1988–89): 95–173.
Wardwell, Anne. "The Stylistic Development of 14th- and 15th-Century Italian Silk Designs." *Aachener Kunstblätter* 47 (1976–77): 176–226.
Warren, Michelle R. *Creole Medievalism: Colonial France and Joesph Bédier's Middle Ages.* Minneapolis: University of Minnesota Press, 2011.
Watt, C. Y., and Anne Wardwell, *When Silk Was Gold: Central Asian and Chinese Textiles.* New York: Harry N. Abrams, 1998.
Whitaker, Cord J. *Black Metaphors: How Modern Racism Emerged from Medieval Race-Thinking.* Philadelphia: University of Pennsylvania Press, 2019.
Wild, Benjamin Linley. "A Gift Inventory from the Reign of Henry III." *English Historical Review* 125 (2010): 529–69.
Wilson, Katherine Anne. "The Household Inventory as Urban 'Theatre' in Late Medieval Burgundy." *Social History* 40 (2015): 335–59.
Woolgar, C. M. *The Great Household in Late Medieval England.* New Haven, CT: Yale University Press, 1999.
Young, Charles R. *The Making of the Neville Family in England, 1066–1400.* Woodbridge: Boydell and Brewer, 1996.
Yule, Henry. *The Travels of Marco Polo: The Complete Yule-Cordier Edition.* New York: Dover, 1993.
Zammit-Maempel, George. "Fossil Sharks' Teeth: A Medieval Safeguard against Poisoning." *Melita Historica* 6 (1975): 391–410.
Zink, Michel. "Poète sacré, poète maudit." *Recherches et Rencontres* 1 (1990): 233–47.
Zink, Michel. "Si je t'oublie, Constantinople . . ." *Médiévales*, no. 12 (1987): 43–46.

Index

Maps and tables are indicated by *m* and *t* following page numbers. The insert figures are indicated by "insert" and their figure number.

Account-Inventory: Chazaud as editor of, 6n5, 14, 16–17, 92; chronology of, 16–22, 20*t*; currencies used in, 21, 23, 62, 62n22, 69; form and function of, 13–16, *insert* 1–7; French language used for, 3, 15, 15n35, 66–71, 70n20, 85; knightly narrative style in, 70–71; lack of scholarly attention given to, 6; literary qualities of, 12–13; as living document, 8, 62, 62n21; materiality approach to, 9–13, 9nn14–15, 17n41; memorial and emotive qualities of, 12, 12nn27–28; Outremer provenance of, 66–71, 91; rolls in order of size, 25, 25*f*, *insert* 1; transcription and translation conventions, 17n40, 23–24; visibility of Acre within, 63–69, 65*m*, 91–92. *See also* Roll A; Roll B; Roll C; Roll D

Acre: building projects in, 201; charitable landscape of, 64n3; cultural diversity in, 198, 201–3; economic significance of, 191, 192, 200; fall of (1291), 5, 119, 195, 199; fortifications of, 192, 194, 200; as gateway to Holy Land, 229; graphic practices in, 66–67, 66n9, 67n12; hospitals in, 64, 195–97; housing in, 192–93; intellectual exchange in, 203–4; knights stationed in, 60, 60n13, 81, 126n56; landscape and topography of, 191–97, 193n7; money for defense of, 232n14; painting in, 218n15; paradoxes in, 204–5; pilgrimage routes through, 199; religious institutions of, 64–66, 65*m*, 195–96, 204; Rutebeuf's "The Complaint of Acre," *insert* 32; seneschal of, 60, 60n16; *stipendarii* in, 60, 60n13, 81; Templar and Hospitaller compounds in, 180nn17–18, 193, 200; textiles in, 206, 206n1; translators in, 204, 204n29; visibility within Account-Inventory, 63–69, 65*m*, 91–92; War of St. Sabas in, 194, 202, 202n17; western-oriented institutions in, 67, 67n10

Agnes of Dampierre (sister-in-law of Eudes), 77

Albert of Vercelli, 197

Alphonse of Poitiers, 135, 141, 147

Andrew (saint), 151n114

annominatio (rhetorical device), 115, 174n158

Aragon, crusade of (1285), 26n5

Arnaut, William, 87

'Atlit Castle. *See* Château Pèlerin

Ayyubid dynasty, 220, 238

Baldwin II (king of Jerusalem), 58, 58n4, 59n7, 77–78, 196

Baldwin IV (king of Jerusalem), 196

baptism, 98, 98n32, 224n5

Barons' Crusade (1239), 57, 58n3, 85

Bastin, Julia, 114–15, 123n42, 138n85, 158n127, 170nn146–47

battles. *See specific names of battles*

Baume, Hugh de la, 87, 87n68, 107

Baybars (Mamluk sultan), 46n72, 58, 82, 156, 191, 194, 198–99, 238

Beam, Amanda, 182n33

Beatrice of Champagne (stepmother of Eudes), 21, 21n9

beavers, 43n63, 94, 94n12, 98–99, 212, 227, *insert* 22

Bek, Anthony, 185, 187

Benedictines, 195–96

bequests: charitable, 61, 178, 222, 242; clothing, 18, 180n16, 181nn19–20, 181nn22–27; delivery of, 44n69, 84, 104, 215–16, 216n4, 219; on dorsal of Roll B and Roll C, 18, 101–5, 103*f*; to hospitals, 18, 64, 103, 180–81, 181nn19–20, 196, 197;

bequests (*continued*)
knightly equipment, 235; public performance of, 101; to religious houses, 64, 195–96, 204, 235; rings, 18, 71, 102–4, 182, 215–16, 219, 233–35, 233n16, 234n25
Béraud, Thomas, 30–31n24, 89n77, 188
Bese, Jehan de, 88
bestiaries, 94, *insert* 22
Boccaccio, Giovanni, 209
Boron, Robert de, *insert* 15, *insert* 26
Bougre, Robert le, 134n73
Brabant, Beatrix de, 221n25
Brabant, Henri de, 88
Broce, Pierre de la, 79n21
Brothers of the Penitence of Jesus Christ (Friars of the Sack), 181n24, 196
Brown, Bill, 12n26
buckram (*boqueranz*), 41n54, 66, 203, 206–10
Burchard of Mount Sion, 199
Burnell, Robert, 187
Byzantium. *See* Constantinople

Cairo Geniza, 97n28, 240n8
camelin, 40n52, 43n65, 66, 99, 203, 211, 211n21, 227–28
cameos, 92, 102–3, 216, 233
camlet (*camelot*), 43n65, 93, 206–7, 210–11, 210–11nn18–19
Canale, Martino da, 124n48
Carmelites, 46n72, 181, 181n23, 196
Carpine, Giovanni di Pian di, 207–10
cendal silk, 41n56, 43–44n67, 207, 211–14, 227–28
Champenois knights, 26n2, 75, 99n36
Chananians, 140n89
chansons de geste, 36–37n38, 71, 130n59
Chantenai, Gui de, 26n5, 86–88, 102, 221
Chantenai, Hervé de, 86–88, 102
"La Chantepleure" (poem), 134n73
chapels: in Acre, 98n31, 195, 199; for crusading households, 7, 223–28; decor for, 209, 216, 218, 223–24, 224n3; Érard of Vallery and, 80, 82, 93n5; liturgical furnishings for, 97–98, 224–28, 224n5, 225n9; portable, 82, 97, 97–98n29, 223n2, 224, 225
chaplains, 85–86, 98, 103, 178, 224, 226, 230
Charles of Anjou: campaigns in Italy, 59, 156; Érard of Vallery and, 77, 83, 141; Hohenstaufen heirs and, 75, 135; marriage of, 61, 72, 83, 222; Princedom of Achaea and, 59n7
Charles II of Anjou, 222
Château Pèlerin (Israel), 66, 69, 82, 82n38, 95, 95n17, 193, 198
Chaworth, Payn de, 185, 187
Chazaud, A.-M., 6n5, 14–17, 15n35, 32–33n33, 41n57, 92, 102nn48–49
chessboards, 107, 236, *insert* 30
Chiara of Montefalco, 108n10
chivalry (*chevalerie*), 8, 71, 74, 120, 128, 132n67, 141
Christianity and Christians: baptism, 98, 98n32, 224n5; chaplains and, 85–86, 224, 226, 230; conversion to Christianity, 98, 98n32; criticisms by Rutebeuf, 154n120; devotions, 62, 85, 94n12, 98, 109, 119, 197, 223–28; estate inventories of, 237; Eucharist, 98, 220, 224–25, 224n5, 227–28; Haram al-Sharif documents and, 243; Mass, 82, 85, 97–98, 98n31, 224–28, 224n5, 232; in Outremer, 5, 8; priests, 85, 97, 119, 192, 197, 224, 226, 232; vestments, 18, 98, 98n30, 100, 101n45, 224–28, 224n4, 227n12. *See also* chapels; crusades
Church, Stephen, 234, 234n21
Cistercians, 36n37, 89, 91, 133n70, 195, 220
Cîteaux monastery (Burgundy), 36n37, 89, 91, 91n1, 109, 109n12, 141
Claresses, 195, 195n17
Clemence (queen of Hungary), 213
Clement IV (pope), 58, 59, 88, 135, 227
clerks, 62, 69, 84–86, 178, 182, 192, 227–28, 230
Clifford, Roger de, 185, 187
clothing: appraisal of value, 18, 99–100; bequeathed, 18, 180n16, 181nn19–20, 181nn22–27; embroidered, 241; of Eudes of Nevers, 98–99, 227–28; of Franciscans, 124n49, 133n70; fur used for, 29n17, 40–41n53, 98–99, 227, 233, 243, *insert* 15, *insert* 21; houppelandes, 43n64, 99, 99n39; of Louis IX, 99, 99n36; as portable stores of wealth, 99. *See also* textiles; vestments
Coeur, Jacques, 210
coffrets, 40n48, 221, *insert* 25
complaintes (laments), 71, 74, 120. *See also* Rutebeuf
conduit (poetic genre), 155n123
Constantinople: fall to crusaders (1204), 128, 214; fall to Greeks (1261), 59n7, 119, 128; gifts to empress of, 232–33; Latin Empire of, 3; objects looted from, 218; recovery of, 77; Rutebeuf's "The Complaint of Constantinople," 128–34; textile production in, 214
copes (liturgical cloaks), 226–27, 226n11
Copin, 86, 88, 102, 221
copyists, 242–43, 243n19
Cordeliers. *See* Franciscans
courtly conduct, 8, 120, 121n39
courtoisie, 71, 120, 121n39, 123, 123n44, 125, 147
crossbowmen, 86, 87n62, 230, 232, 232n14
crusade poems. *See* Rutebeuf
Crusader States. *See* Outremer

crusades: Andrew as patron saint of, 151n114; Barons' (1239), 57, 58n3, 85; Fifth (1217–21), 57, 220; First (1095–99), 3, 7, 118, 139n86, 140n88; Fourth (1202–4), 3–4, 86n59, 220; independent, 59, 59n8, 229, 229n1; Louis IX and, 57–60, 58n3, 59n7, 76–78, 119, 122, 147, 156, 196, 229, 231; religious motivations for, 7, 7n10, 223; renewed call for, 58, 58n6; in romance texts, 8n13; Third (1189–92), 57, 91n1, 180n16, 197, 220; Tunis (1270), 59, 72, 78, 115, 118–20, 147, 147n104, 156. *See also* knights
crusade vows, 58, 135, 141, 143n97, 147, 151n116, 156, 177, 220n21, 220n23, 229
crusading households: chapels for, 7, 223–28; as masculine spaces, 97, 221; material standards of living for, 193; members of, 7, 86–90, 218, 229–33, 232n13; possessions in, 7–8, 232–36
cups. *See* drinking cups
currencies, 33–34n35, 53n80, 62, 62n22, 66, 69, *insert* 8–12
currency changers, 29n16, 32n31

DALME (Documentary Archaeology of Late Medieval Europe) database, 6n5, 24, 62n21
d'Artier, Jean, 83
d'Avezac de Castera-Macaya, Marie-Armand, 210, 210n16
Demurger, Alain, 82n40
Desrosiers, Sophie, 213
devotions, 62, 85, 94n12, 98, 109, 119, 197, 223–28
Diepe, Henri de, 88
Dijon, Jehan de, 95, 95n15
al-Dīn al-Ḥazrajī (judge), 240
dit (poetic genre), 148n106
documentary archaeology, 11, 11n23, 91–105
Documentary Archaeology of Late Medieval Europe (DALME) database, 6n5, 24, 62n21
Dominicans, 132n66, 133n70, 135, 181, 181n25, 196, 204
dress. *See* clothing
drinking cups: ancient typology of, 217, *insert* 16; of Eudes, 84, 93, 107–8, 216–22; heraldic decorations on, 221, 221n25; liturgical, 97, 224n5, 225; Resafa cup, 219–20, 219–20nn20–21, 222, *insert* 27
Dufournet, Jean, 118–19n33

Edmond (earl of March), 234
Edward I (king of England), 61n20, 79, 167n139, 176, 184–88
Edward II (king of England), 185
Egypt: Ayyubid rule in, 238; Cairo Geniza, 97n28, 240n8; crusades in, 229, 231; Louis IX's treaty with Muslims in, 131n64; Mamluk rule in, 119, 238; textile production in, 214
Eleanor of Castile, 184, 187–88
embalming practices, 61, 89, 108–9, 108n10, 141
embroidery: clothing and, 241; gold for, 36n37, 227, 228, 236; quilts and, 209, 243; vestments and, 227, 227n12, 228; wall hangings and, 224, 224n3
Enguerrand II of Boves, 220, 220n21
Enguerrand III of Coucy, 133n68, 220
Enguerrand IV of Coucy, 145n102
enslaved persons, 242, 243
Érard of Nanteuil, 59, 59n11, 75
Érard of Vallery: at Battle of Tagliacozzo, 77, 77n12; bequests made to, 79–80, 93n5, 102–3; as Champenois knight, 75; as constable of Champagne, 77–78, 77n13, 78nn15–16; death of, 141n91; drinking cup and, 221; Eudes's possessions purchased by, 104, 107; as executor for Eudes, 16, 61, 74, 141; family background, 75–77; French language used by, 15, 68n15; in-kind payment made to, 218–19; Louis IX and, 75–78; marriage and children, 78–79; as partner in Eudes's crusade, 59, 75, 231; Philip III and, 75n4, 79; poetic portrait by Rutebeuf, 74, 80; seal of, 79n26, *insert* 14; tokens of Eudes received by, 233; transfer of funds and loans by, 60, 61n18, 77; will of, 78, 79, 79n26
escrin (box for relics), 36n37, 89, 108–9, *insert* 24
estate inventories, 237, 240–43
Étienne le Clerc, 84–85, 86n59, 103
Eucharist, 98, 220, 224–25, 224n5, 227–28
Eudes III of Burgundy (grandfather of Eudes), 57
Eudes of Nevers: Acre as experienced by, 198–205; books of, 79–80, 80n28; chapel of, 80, 82, 97–98, 98n31, 223–28, 223n2, 224n5; clothing of, 98–99, 227–28; coat of arms, 220–21, 221n24; crusade vow taken by, 220n23, 229; crusading household of, 86–90, 97, 193, 223–24, 229–36; death of (1266), 3, 16–18, 61, 104, 175; French language used by, 16, 16n37; genealogy of, 21n49, 57–58, 57n1, 246; heart embalming and burial at Cîteaux, 36n37, 89, 91, 91n1, 108–9, 109nn12–13, 141; as independent crusader, 59, 229; interest in Eastern cultures, 203; knightly equipment of, 233–36; miracles reported at tomb of, 101; poetic portrait by Rutebeuf, 74, 80; Rutebeuf's "The Lament for Count Eudes of Nevers," 39n46, 80, 106, 141–46, *insert* 31; seals of, *insert* 13. *See also* Account-Inventory
Eustache of Conflans, 77n13

Faral, Edmond, 114–15, 123n42, 138n85, 158n127, 170nn146–47
Farmer, Sharon, 206
Fieschi, Opizzo, 42n61
Fifth Crusade (1217–21), 57, 220
First Crusade (1095–99), 3, 7, 118, 139n86, 140n88
Folda, Jaroslav, 14, 80n28, 92
folk taxonomies, 11
Fontainebleau, forest of, 154n121
Fourth Crusade (1202–4), 3–4, 86n59, 220
Franciscans: bequests made to, 181, 181n26, 196, 204; Clement IV's exhortation to, 135; clothing of, 124n49, 133n70; headquarters in Montmusard, 64; Urban IV's commission to, 128
Frederick II (Holy Roman emperor), 237
French language: Account-Inventory and, 3, 15, 15n35, 66–71, 70n20, 85; documentary writing style in, 70–71, 70n20; Eudes's use of, 16, 16n37; geographical studies of, 16n38; knightly narrative style in, 70–71; Outremer French, 5, 66–71, 85n55; Rutebeuf's use of, 15n35, 85, 85n55; vernacular tradition, 70n20; wills written in, 176
Friars of the Holy Trinity, 196
Friars of the Sack (Brothers of the Penitence of Jesus Christ), 181n24, 196

Galvez, Marisa, 109n13
garçons. *See* pages
garments. *See* clothing
Gaucher of Châtillon, 101n45
Gautier of Châtillon, 76n7
gems, 71, 104n55, 215–16, 218, 222, 222n30, 225, 227–28, *insert* 17–18
Genart, Adam, 76
gentillesse, 8, 120, 143, 168
Geoffrey of Fleury, 208
Geoffrey of Sergines (the elder): bequests made to, 102; conversion and baptism overseen by, 98n32; death of, 83, 83n41, 122; debts of, 82, 83; drinking cup and, 221; Eudes's possessions purchased by, 87, 107, 236; French language used by, 15; John of Joinville on, 60n14, 81; letter asking for funds, 140n90; Louis IX and, 60, 81; poetic portrait by Rutebeuf, 74, 81; portable altar of, 97–98n29; Rutebeuf's "The Lament for My Lord Geoffrey of Sergines," 81, 115, 122–27; Templar of Tyre on, 81n31, 82, 83n41
Geoffrey of Sergines (the younger): death of, 83; as executor for Eudes, 16, 61, 74, 75, 82; French language used by, 15; transfer of funds and loans by, 60, 61n18
gifts: as demonstration of status, 232–33; of knightly equipment, 234–35; male solidarities reinforced through, 221; for weddings, 222. *See also* bequests
Giles (archbishop of Tyre), 196
Gilles of Sergines, 83
Giuseppi, M. S., 177, 180n15
Givri, Huguenin, 88
goblets. *See* drinking cups
Godfrey of Bouillon, 117, 118, 139n86, 140n88
Grandson, Otto de, 184n39, 187
Gregory X (pope), 83, 204
Guillaume le Chapelain, 85, 85n53, 98, 224, 226
Guy (king of Jerusalem), 197
Guy of Châtillon, 145n102
Guy IV of Forez, 61n20, 85, 103n54
Guy VI of Limoges, 89n73

Ham, Edward Billings, 169n144
Haram al-Sharif documents, 239–43, 240n8, 240n11, 243n21
heart, embalming and burial of, 36n37, 61, 89, 91, 91n1, 108–9, 109nn12–13, 141, 228
henaps. *See* drinking cups
Henry III (king of England), 15, 15n34, 79, 177
Henry of Rosnay, 77
Homede, 87
horses, 42n60, 87, 96, 232–33, 233n19, 235, *insert* 21. *See also* war horses
Hospitallers: Acre compound, 180n18, 193, 200; bequests made to, 18, 103, 180, 235; debts owed to, 31n27, 90, 90n79; grand master of, 185; jurisdictional disputes with, 197; written texts produced by, 67, 68
Hospital of Saint Brigid, 181, 181n21
Hospital of St. Anthony, 197
Hospital of St. John. *See* Hospitallers
Hospital of the Brothers and/or Sisters of Bethlehem, 180, 180–81n19
Hospital of the Germans, 197
Hospital of the Holy Spirit, 197
houppelandes, 43n64, 99, 99n39
Hugh (earl of Stafford), 234, 234n25
Hugh III of Burgundy (great-grandfather of Eudes), 57, 91n1
Hugh IV of Burgundy (father of Eudes), 21n9, 57–58, 58nn3–4, 135, 141, 215, 216n4, 221
Hugh de Neville, 61n20, 176–83, 217–18, 234–35
Hugh of Augerant: bequests made to, 102, 104, 215; delivery of Eudes's bequests, 44n69, 84, 104, 215–16, 216n4, 219; drinking cup accepted by, 84, 218–19, 221; as executor for Eudes, 16, 61, 74, 82, 84, 215, 218, 230; French language used by, 15; lands given to, 26n6, 84; payments made to, 230, 230n5
Hugh of Châtillon, 122, 145n102
Hugh of Conflans, 77n13, 78n15
Humbert of Romans, 115
hunting, 154n121, *insert* 22

Ibn Jubayr, 194
independent crusaders, 59, 59n8, 229, 229n1
ink production, 243, 243n20
Innocent III (pope), 196
Innocent IV (pope), 207
Isabella I (queen of Jerusalem), 195–96
Islam and Muslims: in Acre, 201; conversion to, 131n62, 131n64; Haifa conquered by, 198; Haram al-Sharif documents and, 243; intellectual-religious tradition in, 238–39; Jerusalem controlled by, 237; Louis IX's treaty with, 131n64; in Outremer, 5, 8; Qur'an and, 204, 242; Rutebeuf on, 116; *shar'i* courts, 238–40, 243; Sufis, 238, 243; Sunnis, 140n89; William of Tripoli's treatise on, 204
Islamic Museum (Jerusalem), 239

Jack the Palmer, 182, 182n31
Jacobins. *See* Dominicans
Jacoby, David, 80n28
Jaffa, Treaty of (1229), 237
Jami, Nafisa b. Ali b., 241–42
Jean de Sergines, 83–84
Jeanne of Constantinople, 130n59
Jeanne of Flanders, 222
Jeanne of France (countess of Champagne, queen of Navarre), 83
Jean of Châtillon, 76, 76n7
Jean of Vallery, 75–76nn5–7, 75–77
Jean Tristan (prince of France): bequests made to, 84, 102, 104, 115; crusades and, 91n1, 147, 156; heart separated from body, 109; marriage to Yolande of Nevers, 61, 72, 141, 144n99, 216, 219
Jehan le Porer, 87
Jerusalem, Kingdom of: built environment of cities in, 192–93; charitable landscape of, 64n3; Haram al-Sharif documents from, 239–43, 240n8, 240n11, 243n21; Mamluk rule in, 237, 238; Muslim control of, 237; pilgrimage sites in, 199, 200n8; political frontiers of, 191. *See also* Acre
jeu-parti (poetic genre), 160n134
jewelry: brooches, *insert* 18, *insert* 21; cameos, 92, 102–3, 216, 233; necklaces, 104n55, 242; rings, 18, 71, 102–4, 182, 215–16, 219, 233–35, 233n16, 234n25, *insert* 17
Jews, 5, 8, 137, 201, 237, 243, 243n21
John of Ancona, 203–4
John of Bourbon (brother of Eudes), 84, 102, 103, 215, 216n4
John of Brittany, 187
John of Châtillon, 145n102
John of Garland, 211
John of Ibelin, 81
John of Joinville: on chapel tent sent to Mongols, 95n18; crusading household of, 229–36, 232n12; on food provisions for armies, 96nn21–22; on Geoffrey of Sergines (the elder), 60n14, 81; gifts to empress of Constantinople, 232–33; injury and recovery of, 64; on Jean of Vallery, 75–76, 75–76n5; knightly equipment of, 233–36; knights led by, 96n22, 231, 231n8; *Life of Saint Louis*, 8, 75, 81, 229–32, 230n3; on Yves the Breton, 204
John of Montmirail, 40n48, *insert* 25
John of Saint-Maxentius, 28n13
John of Warenne, 234
Jordan, William Chester, 96n21, 98n32
Jotischky, Andrew, 191
Jubinal, Achille, 134n73, 148n105

Khwarazmians, 140n89
Kingdom of Jerusalem. *See* Jerusalem, Kingdom of
knights: Champenois, 26n2, 75, 99n36; chivalry and, 8, 71, 74, 120, 128, 141; in crusading households, 7, 86–88, 90, 218, 229–33; in cultural imaginary, 70n21, 71, 103; equipment used by, 233–36, 233n19; Eudes's possessions purchased by, 107; interest in Eastern cultures, 203; maintenance of, 60, 60n15, 86n60, 88n70; oaths of fidelity and trust taken by, 221; payment of, 35n36, 37n41, 86–87, 86–87nn60–62; stationed in Acre, 60, 60n13, 81, 126n56; Teutonic, 47n74, 67, 68, 83n41, 95. *See also* crusades; horses; Hospitallers; swords; Templars

lais (instructions), 25–26n1, 61, 175
Lambourn, Elizabeth, 97n28
Le Paraclet Abbey (France), 220, 220n21
Leson, Richard A., 215
Lespinasse, Réne de, 6n7, 92
Levant: drinking cups in, 217; Eudes's short period in, 218; Latin inhabitants of, 202; local vocabulary in, 66, 68–69; textiles in, 206, 206n1, 214
Le Veaul, Hermenin, 88
light cavalrymen (turcopoles), 66, 86, 230, 230n4, 232
Little, Donald, 240, 240n11, 242n19
Louis VIII (king of France), 220
Louis IX (king of France): Caesarea supported by, 198; closure of royal court to entertainers, 114; clothing of, 99, 99n36; crusades and, 57–60, 58n3, 59n7, 76–78, 119, 122, 147, 156, 196, 229, 231; cult of martyrs' crowns established by, 126–27n56; death of, 104, 147; Eudes's expedition supported by, 227; fortifications

Louis IX (king of France) (*continued*) of Acre rebuilt by, 192, 200; Geoffrey of Sergines (the elder) and, 60, 81; heart separated from body, 109; Joinville and, 229–31; payment of knights by, 87n62; Templars as bank of deposit for, 67, 68n15; treaty with Muslims in Egypt, 131n64
Lower, Michael, 77n12, 156
Lufti, Huda, 240n11

Mahaut II of Bourbon (wife of Eudes), 57, 76, 221
Mamluks: Caesarea conquered by, 82, 198; campaigns against crusader castles and towns, 58; in Egypt, 119, 238; fall of Acre to (1291), 5; Haram al-Sharif documents and, 239–43, 240n8, 240n11, 243n21; refugees from regions captured by, 191, 201; *shar'i* courts and, 238–40, 243; in Syria, 119, 238, 239; Templar fort captured by, 199; waqf (charitable system) of, 238–39
Mansurah, Battle of (1250), 76, 76n5, 231
Marguerite of Burgundy (sister of Eudes), 27n10, 89, 89n73
Marguerite of Tonnerre (daughter of Eudes), 61, 72, 83, 83n46, 105, 221–22
Marie of Hungary, 222
Martin (saint), *insert* 21
Mass, 82, 85, 97–98, 98n31, 224–28, 224n5, 232
materiality, 9–13, 9nn14–15, 17n41
material philology, 10–11
Matins, 134n74
McNamer, Sarah, 221
Menant, Odet de, 88
Merry, Gaucher de, 26n2, 86, 86n59, 88, 102, 221
Merry, Geoffrey de, 86n59
Michael VIII Palaeologus (Byzantine emperor), 58, 128
Middleham Jewel, 104n55
Miller, Maureen C., 223
Minors. *See* Franciscans
Mongols: chapel tent sent to, 95n18; emergence of, 58, 214; Mamluk defeat of, 238; perceived fear of the sea, 133n72; refugees from regions captured by, 201; Resafa conquered by, 220; textile production in, 206–9, 214; threat of European expansion, 133n71
Mont-Cornet, Hugh de, 87, 87n68, 107
Morgan Picture Bible, 95n18, 221, *insert* 16
Morreale, Laura, 11
Müller, Christian, 240n11
Munchensy, Ralph de, 181, 181–82n28
Muslims. *See* Islam and Muslims
Mussy, Jehan de, 88
Al-Mustansir (emir of Tunis), 156

Naime (counselor of Charlemagne), 133n69
necklaces, 104n55, 242
Nemours, Marguerite de, 79, 79n21
Nichols, Stephen G., 10–11

Order of St. Lazarus, 46n70, 181, 181n20
Order of St. Thomas of Canterbury, 180, 180n16, 235
Order of the Holy Trinity, 181, 181n22
orfreys, 211, 211n22
Outremer: Account-Inventory and, 66–71, 91; boundaries of, 3–5, 4*m*; cultural diversity in, 5, 8; currencies used in, 33–34n35, 69; French language used in, 5, 66–71, 85n55; housing in, 192–93; knightly culture of, 70n21, 71, 103; material, 9–13, 96n18, 109; nonknightly forces in armies of, 232n14; religious houses in, 64n5; Rutebeuf's "The Complaint of Outremer," 118, 135–40; Rutebeuf's "The New Complaint of Outremer," 81, 117, 118, 164–74. *See also* Acre; Jerusalem, Kingdom of

pages (garçons), 27n9, 60n15, 78, 86, 88, 93–94, 230, 232
Paul (saint), 118, 160n132, 164
Paul, Nicholas, 234n25
Peers, Glenn, 220
Pegalotti, Francesco Balducci, 209
Petit, Ernst, 86n59, 92
Philip III (king of France), 26n2, 75n4, 79, 79n26, 83, 141, 147, 156, 164, 167n139
Philip Augustus (king of France), 130n59
Phocas, John, 194
Pierre of Alençon, 98n33, 147, 156
pilgrimages, 159n130, 199, 200n8
Pizorrno, Gabe, 11
Polo, Marco, 209, 210
priests, 85, 97, 119, 192, 197, 224, 226, 232
Pringle, Denys, 64, 64n1, 181n21, 195, 223n2
prudhomme, 8, 118–19n33, 118–27, 121n39, 142, 149–50, 168–69, 173, 187
pyxes, 98, 224, 224n5, *insert* 29

quilts, 93, 209, 241, 243
Qur'an, 204, 242

Ralph of Ecclesall, 182, 182n30
Raoul of Coucy, 219–20
Regalado, Nancy Freeman, 116
relics, 40n48, 71, 80, 97, 97n29, 99n37, 101, 103, 104, 109, 222
religious houses: Benedictines, 195–96; bequests made to, 64, 195–96, 204, 235; Carmelites, 46n72, 181, 181n23, 196; Cistercians, 36n37, 89, 91, 133n70, 195,

220; Claresses, 195, 195n17; Dominicans, 133n70, 135, 181, 181n25, 196, 204; Friars of the Holy Trinity, 196; Friars of the Sack, 181n24, 196. *See also* Franciscans
reliquaries, 36n37, 97, 104, 215, 225, *insert* 28
Resafa cup, 219–20, 219–20nn20–21, 222, *insert* 27
Revel, Hugh, 188
Reynaud of Précigné, 86–87, 230n5
Riccoldo of Monte Croce, 199
Richard, Jean, 59
Richard I (king of England), 197
Riley-Smith, Jonathan, 6nn6–7, 7, 33n34, 80n28, 86–87, 92
Robert of Artois, 76n5, 147
Robert II of Béthune, 164
Robert of Birdsall, 182, 182n29
Robert of Boves, 220
Robert II of Burgundy (brother of Eudes), 91n1, 109n12
Robert of Clari, 70n20
Robert of Flanders, 26n6, 72, 84
Robert of Juennesses, 33n34, 86–87, 102, 230n5
Röhricht, Reinhold, 6
Roland (nephew of Charlemagne), 117, 137n82
Roll A: chronology of, 19, 20*t*; debts owed and paid on, 82, 230n5; description of, 13, 25, 25*f*, *insert* 1, *insert* 3–6; drinking cups and, 217, 217n9; function as feudal register, 72; stitching on, 29, 29–30n19, 38; translation and transcription, 25–39
Roll B: bequests listed on dorsal side of, 18, 101–5; chronology of, 17–20, 20*t*; commemorative function of, 73; as deathbed testament or inventory, 18, 215n1; description of, 13, 17–18, 25, 25*f*, *insert* 1, *insert* 3, *insert* 7; items absent from, 97, 98; items recorded on, 92–99, 215–17, 226; knightly narrative style in, 71; spatial recording of possessions on, 96–97; translation and transcription, 39–44; visibility of Acre within, 91–92
Roll C: appraisal of items on, 99–100; bequests listed on dorsal side of, 18, 101–5, 103*f*; chronology of, 18–20; commemorative function of, 73, 100–101; description of, 13–14, 18, 25, 25*f*, *insert* 1–3; knightly narrative style in, 71; place-names recorded on, 64; translation and transcription, 45–48; visibility of Acre within, 91–92
Roll D: chronology of, 18–19, 20*t*; commemorative function of, 73; description of, 14, 18–19, 25, 25*f*, *insert* 1, *insert* 3; liturgical furnishings and, 224n5, 225; on sale of Eudes's possessions, 99n37, 106–8; translation and transcription, 48–53
Rubin, Jonathan, 198
Rutebeuf: background of, 114; "The Complaint of Acre," *insert* 32; "The Complaint of Constantinople," 128–34; "The Complaint of Outremer," 118, 135–40; contemporary observations through poetry of, 74–75; "The Disputation between the Crusader and the Noncrusader," 156–63; French language used by, 15n35, 85, 85n55; "The Lament for Count Eudes of Nevers," 39n46, 80, 106, 141–46, *insert* 31; "The Lament for My Lord Geoffrey of Sergines," 81, 115, 122–27; "The New Complaint of Outremer," 81, 117, 118, 164–74; "The Poem of the Route to Tunis," 118, 147–55; poetic persona of, 113–14; as propagandist, 113, 114, 117–18; on religious life, 123n47; as social critic, 117, 119, 154n120, 164, 171n150; terminology considerations, 120–21; themes in poetry of, 116–17, 220n23; transcription and translation of works, 115–16, 119n34, 123n42
Rymer, Thomas, 184

Safforit, Salemon de, 87, 87n65, 202
St. Denis church (Montmusard), 181, 181n27
St. Giles church (Montmusard), 183, 183n34
St. Nicholas cemetery (Acre), 89, 101, 101n46, 108, 109n12, 180, 180n14
Saladin (Ayyubid sultan), 120, 191, 196
Salihiyya, Muhammad 'Isa, 242n19
Sanç, Nunó, 235
Saumur, Gilles de, 28n13, 89n73, 196
sergeants, 7, 17, 19, 88, 230–32
Sergius (saint), 220
serpent's tongues, 94–95, *insert* 23
servants, 7, 37n41, 61, 85, 86, 88–89, 91, 93–94, 178, 230–32, 232n12
serventois (poetic genre), 150n112
Shachar, Uri Zvi, 237
shar'i courts, 238–40, 243
Sibylla (queen of Jerusalem), 197
Sissy, Étienne de, 30n21, 88
Sissy, Perriau de, 88
Smail, Daniel Lord, 11, 96, 97n23
Smith, Caroline, 229
Souilly, Hugh de, 85n53
squires, 60n15, 78, 86, 88, 230–32
status, 27nn8–9, 83, 193, 205, 220, 223, 227–29, 232–34
stipendarii in Acre, 60, 60n13, 81
Sufis, 238, 243
swords, 14, 95, 95n15, 97, 182, 233–35, 234n22

Syria: French commitment to, 59; Mamluk rule in, 119, 238, 239; Mongol destruction in, 220; textile production in, 206n2

Tabarie, Lionnet de, 87, 87n65, 202–3
Tagliacozzo, Battle of (1268), 77, 77n12
Tancred, 117, 118, 140n88
Tartar cloth (*dras de tartais*): baudekin and, 207–9, 207n5; clothing made with, 227, *insert* 19; of eastern provenance, 21, 41n54, 66; of Eudes, 93, 93n5, 94, 108; lampas weave technique, 208, *insert* 20; as material product of the East, 203; woven with gold thread, 36n37
Templar of Tyre, 81n31, 82–83, 83n41, 101, 105, 110, 200, 222
Templars: Acre compound, 180n17, 193, 200; as bank of deposit for Louis IX, 67, 68n15; bequests made to, 180, 218; communication with William of Jerusalem, 231n6, 232n14; debts owed to, 18, 19, 82, 83, 90; Eudes's possessions purchased by, 31n25, 93, 99n37, 107–8; grand master of, 30n24, 89, 89n77, 185; *Rule* and *Retrais*, 68, 68n16, 233; Safad fort held by, 199; written texts produced by, 67, 68
tents, 80, 82n38, 95, 95nn17–18, 108, 224, 224n3, *insert* 26
Teutonic Knights, 47n74, 67, 68, 83n41, 95
textiles: altar cloths, 224, 226, 227; buckram, 41n54, 66, 203, 206–10; camelin, 40n52, 43n65, 66, 99, 203, 211, 211n21, 227–28; camlet, 43n65, 93, 206–7, 210–11, 210–11nn18–19; *cendal* silk, 41n56, 43–44n67, 207, 211–14, 227–28; meanings of Eastern cloth, 21–22, 21n50, 94n11; orfreys, 211, 211n22; production centers, 21n9, 206–14, 211n23, 241, 241n12; reuse of, 100, 100n42; terminology and technical requirements, 207; *tiretaine*, 40n52, 98, 98n35, 211, 212, 227; *toile* linen cloth, 40n49; weavers and, 208, 210, 242–43n19; woolen, 43n63, 206, 211–12, 211–12nn23–24, 227. *See also* clothing; Tartar cloth
textual stratigraphy, 12
Thibaut IV of Champagne, 76, 80n28
Thibaut V of Champagne and Navarre, 21n9, 77–78, 78n15, 109, 147, 150n113
Third Crusade (1189–92), 57, 91n1, 180n16, 197, 220
Thoyras, Rapin de, 184
Tibetot, Robert, 185, 187
tiretaine, 40n52, 98, 98n35, 211, 212, 227
toile linen cloth, 40n49
Tor, William de la, 87
treaties. *See specific names of treaties*
Tunis crusade (1270), 59, 72, 78, 115, 118–20, 147, 147n104, 156
turcopoles. *See* light cavalrymen

'Umar, Muhammad b. Muhammad b., 242–43, 242–43n19
Umfraville, Ingram de, 182, 182–83n33
Urban IV (pope), 82, 88, 97–98n29, 128

Vaivre, Jean-Bernard de, 221
Valence, William de, 187
vestments, 18, 98, 98n30, 100, 101n45, 224–28, 224n4, 227n12
Vidaut, Jaque (Jacques Vidal), 87, 87n66, 96, 203
Villehardouin, Geoffrey de, 70n20
Viterbo, Treaty of (1267), 59n7
Vitry, Jacques de, 193–94

waqf (charitable system), 238–39
wardrobe. *See* clothing
war horses, 78, 95, 107, 178, 182, 203, 232, 233n19
War of St. Sabas (1258–61), 194, 202, 202n17
weavers, 208, 210, 242–43n19
West-Kappel, Battle of (1253), 76
Wilbrand of Oldenbourg, 192
William II of Agen, 42n61, 97n29
William of Beaujeu, 164
William of Jerusalem, 231n6, 232n14
William of Nangis, 81
William of Tripoli, 204
William of Tyre, 80n28
wills: authenticity of, 176; Edward I (England), 61n20, 176, 184–88; Érard of Vallery, 78, 79, 79n26; format required for, 176; French language for recording of, 176; Hugh (earl of Stafford), 234, 234n25; Hugh de Neville, 61n20, 176–83, 234–35; Robert II of Burgundy, 91n1, 109n12. *See also* Account-Inventory; bequests
woolen textiles, 43n63, 206, 211–12, 211–12nn23–24, 227

Yolande of Dreux (mother of Eudes), 21n49, 57
Yolande of Nevers (daughter of Eudes): children of, 222; counterseal of, 221n24; marriage to Jean Tristan, 61, 72, 141, 144n99, 216, 219; marriage to Robert of Flanders, 26n6, 84
Yves the Breton, 204

Zayn al-Dār, 220
Zayn al-Din, Fatima bint, 241
Zink, Michel, 116n17, 118, 118n29, 123n42, 145n102, 159n129, 169n144